MW01284315

Indigenous Spiritualities at Work

Transforming the Spirit of Enterprise

A volume in
Advances in Workplace Spirituality: Theory Research and Application
Louis W. Fry, *Series Editor*

Indigenous Spiritualities at Work

Transforming the Spirit of Enterprise

edited by

Chellie Spiller
University of Auckland

Rachel Wolfgramm
University of Auckland

INFORMATION AGE PUBLISHING, INC.
Charlotte, NC • www.infoagepub.com

Library of Congress Cataloging-in-Publication Data

A CIP record for this book is available from the Library of Congress
http://www.loc.gov

ISBN: 978-1-68123-155-6 (Paperback)
       978-1-68123-156-3 (Hardcover)
       978-1-68123-157-0 (ebook)

CONTENTS

PART II

BELONGING AND RELATIONALITY

PART III

IDENTITIES

PART IV

TRANSFORMATIONS

SERIES EDITOR'S INTRODUCTION

A major change is taking place in the personal and professional lives of many organizational leaders and their employees as they aspire to integrate their spirituality and religion with their work. Many argue that the reason behind this change is that society is seeking spiritual solutions to better respond to tumultuous social, business, geopolitical changes. The result has been a remarkable explosion of scholarship that provides the opportunity for more specialized interest areas, including the role of spirituality and religion in shaping organizations: structures, decision making, management style, mission and strategy, organizational culture, human resource management, finance and accounting, marketing and sales—in short: all aspects of leading, managing, and organizing resources and people. As evidenced by the growing influence of the *Journal of Management, Spirituality and Religion* and the success of the Management, Spirituality, and Religion Special Interest Group of the *Academy of Management*, a field with a broad focus on workplace spirituality is gathering momentum.

This book series, *Advances in Workplace Spirituality: Theory, Research, and Application*, focuses on the study of the relationship and relevance of spirituality and/or religion to organizational life. Its vision is to draw from a diverse range of scholarly areas to become a pivotal source for integrative theory, research and application on workplace spirituality. The purpose of the series is to (1) provide scholars with a meaningful collection of books in key areas and create a forum for the field, (2) support a growing trend toward paradigm integration and assimilation through the interdisciplinary

Indigenous Spiritualities at Work, pages ix–x
Copyright © 2015 by Information Age Publishing
All rights of reproduction in any form reserved.

nature of this series, and (3) draw from a wide variety of disciplines for integrative thinking on workplace spirituality with the broad goal of adding to the value of workplace spirituality theory, research, and its application. The series aims to serve as a meeting forum and help cross-fertilization in these communities. Our sole criterion is academic rigor and scientific merit.

The latest edited book of this series, *Indigenous Spiritualities at Work: Transforming the Spirit of Enterprise,* is a seminal work in the truest sense of the word. The term "Indigenous" is a generalized reference to the thousands of small scale societies who have distinct languages, kinship systems, mythologies, ancestral memories, and homelands. These different societies comprise more than 370 million people throughout the planet today. Central to Indigenous traditions is an awareness of the integral and whole relationship of spiritual and material life. Therefore ritual practices and the cosmological ideas which undergird society are inseparable from daily life including business activities.

The fundamental questions Indigenous wisdom traditions seek to answer in business include: How do Indigenous ways of being and doing balance wealth creation and well-being? How do Indigenous peoples define success? How is Indigenous Spiritualities manifested in the workplace? How have Indigenous tribes and their institutions, in an ever changing world dominated by a colonial mindset and hegemony, been able to reinvent, change, adapt, and transform throughout the ages and how can they continue to do so? In seeking to answer these questions this book proposes dimensions of Indigenous spiritualties that bridge the chasm between scholarly work and practice. In doing so this work has potential for enriching our experience of organizational life and putting into proper perspective the necessity for balance between human well-being, our collective responsibility for co-creating a conscious, sustainable world that works for everyone, and the requirement for performance excellence to make this possible.

—**Louis W. (Jody) Fry**
Series Editor

PREFACE

Chellie Spiller and Rachel Wolfgramm

Naku te rourou nau te rourou ka ora ai te iwi
With your basket and my basket the people will live

Are you intrigued by ancient wisdom traditions? Do you ever wonder if they have any relevance in today's world? How do Indigenous ways of being and doing balance wealth creation and well-being? How might Indigenous peoples define success? What are Indigenous spiritualities? How is spirituality manifested in Indigenous organizations today?

These questions have intrigued us for many years. As a consequence, we invited scholars from around the world to contribute to a ground-breaking book, *Indigenous Spiritualities at Work: Transforming the Spirit of Business Enterprise,* to explore these questions from different worldviews. A key focus of this book is how Indigenous spiritual approaches revitalize identities and relationships within the workplace. However, the notion of workplace is not narrow, as it includes communities of engagement and practice in ecologies of creativity and enterprise in the broadest sense. This enables Indigenous spiritualties at work to be explored from diverse perspectives, disciplines, cultures, and sectors.

The contributions build bridges between scholarly work and practice. They include empirical studies of spirituality, mindfulness, presence, and authenticity. A diverse range of research methodologies, impact studies, and examples of development programs are offered alongside artistic works, photographic essays, stories, and poetry.

Indigenous Spiritualities at Work, pages xi–xix
Copyright © 2015 by Information Age Publishing

These unique contributions from across Indigenous worlds evoke a valuable view of the potential for a more humanistic and ecological view of life. In particular, the authentic voices of authors in this book enrich our understandings, offer points of enlightenment, and amplify spiritual traditions of Indigenous peoples in a way that honors traditions of the past, present, and future.

THE GENESIS OF THIS BOOK

Chellie

As I sit here and think about the genesis of this book, an image of my Nana Wikitoria Atkinson's kitchen in my mind's eye keeps calling for my attention. So I am going with that image as a starting place. Her kitchen was the hub of the home. I am a child sitting at the table watching Nana move between the kitchen bench and the stove preparing our *kai*, our food. She would usually be whistling, or singing, old-time songs or hymns. I can imagine her beaten-up aluminium pot with a wobbly lid belching steam on the front left element of the stove. Inside the pot, two fish eyes stare up as a fat-lipped smile dissolves into the soup made of native *pūhā* (prickly sowthistle) greens and doughboys (flour dumplings). The rear right element belongs to the whistling kettle that bubbles, sputters, squawks, then screams. A tatty flannel is tidily folded and rests on the handle to quickly lift the kettle to pour a cup of Choysa tea. Food scraps and tea bags go into a plastic bread bag hanging from the cupboard door knob. Week after week, year after year, small mounds of scraps have been put on the compost heap in the back yard.

The cupboards of the kitchen are daffodil yellow with mission brown trim, and the floor is rippled green linoleum. The cupboard doors are mostly ajar or stuck. The drawers are hideaways for stained silver forks with wonky prongs and mottled knives that bluntly refuse to do their job. In the middle of the table is a white crockery swan that glides across Nana's chequered yellow plastic tablecloth. Its hollow back is crammed with letters, cards, bills, junk mail and prescriptions. Pink plastic roses fading to beige are crammed in a small vase with tussock from the last visit to her tribal home, Iwitea—a small village just out of Wairoa on the East Coast of New Zealand's North Island. I found a note of hers once. She had been writing her memoirs:

> We were never short of a variety of kai [food] in abundance. There was always plenty of meat, eels dried, split grilled and dried and hung up and plenty of dried carps, wild ducks sealed down in dripping. Varieties of potatoes, kumara [sweet potato] in well prepared pits, and beef and mutton preserved in beef dripping. Fermented corn preserved in ashes and then in water—"kaanga

wai." These were kept in running water until fermented. We had a Pataka [storehouse] where the potatoes and pumpkins and kamokamo [squash] and kaanga [corn] for the hens and ducks and pigs were also kept.

This simple scene in the kitchen and in my Nana's writing speaks to a spiritual reservoir of plenitude, of ancestral lines, of love, caring, abundance, and thriftiness. It is scenes like this, the many and multifaceted spiritual homes to which we belong, that have given rise to this book.

As I was starting out as an academic, going to my first Academy of Management annual conference, my mentors Pare Keiha and Edwina Pio encouraged me to go and find my "international niche." I walked into the room where I was to give a presentation at a management, spirituality, and religion (MSR) stream. Richard Peregoy was the first to greet me—he gave me a big welcome hug. Then Judi Neale, Jerry Biberman, Jody Fry, Jim Chapple, and many others embraced me. I started my presentation with a short karakia (prayer) and finished with a waiata (song) in Māori. No one thought this odd, and the room was shining. I went to the MSR retreat after the conference and we shared a very precious time together. I had found much more than a "niche" at MSR, I had found a spiritual home. And, like my Nana's home, it is simple, warm, caring, and full of people who show their love.

When Jody Fry at the Academy of Management in San Antonio asked me to curate this book I was thrilled—and happier still when Rachel, whose office is just two doors down from mine, agreed to be a co-editor. Jody has been a wonderful guide on this journey and has encouraged a "pace of grace" as Rachel and I, and our wonderful authors, have collectively brought this book into being.

Rachel

I have always been captivated by questions like: Why are we here, what is our purpose, are we made by design or did we evolve from matter, where do we go after we die? Is death the end or the beginning of a new life journey? Did god(s) create us or did we create god(s), and if so, why? How do we live our lives and take care of our environment to ensure we leave a healthy legacy for future generations? These philosophical questions are often muted by the demands of daily living, yet they persist for many and remain a puzzle throughout most of our lives.

In my postgraduate studies, I became interested in organization cultures, an interest stimulated by mentors Mānuka Hēnare, Ella Henry, and Judith Pringle. I studied this area extensively and found that studies on Indigenous organizations were scarce, particularly in management, leadership, and organization literature. However, at a Governing First Nations conference in Waikato, New Zealand in 2000, I had the privilege of meeting Professor Stephen Cornell, co-founder with economist Professor Joseph P. Kalt, of the Harvard Project on American Indian Economic Development. Seeing the investment being made into research highlighting native ways of doing and being in Native development empowered my own decision to pursue research in the area. In 2005, I met Professor Gregory Cajete at an international sustainability conference at the University of Hawaii. Gregory's thoughts about my work at the time were a source of encouragement as I was by then a great fan of his work on Native Science. I was also honored to meet Rose von Thater Braan, who became a mentor to me. Through Rose, we were able to host a workshop with her, Peter Senge, and Māori leaders on Indigenous Knowledge Systems and Transformation. This led to new insights into understanding Indigenous spiritualities at work.

However, while working full-time as an educator, researcher, and consultant, reviews for my doctoral dissertation found literature at the time on Indigenous culture originated from social anthropology, with only a cursory glance given to Indigenous ontologies in organization studies. Yet Indigenous tribes and institutions are the oldest and in many cases the largest forms of social technology known to humankind. They are never static, and they seem able to reinvent, change, adapt, and transform themselves throughout the ages while holding certain things constant. This compelled me to investigate further sources of resilience and transformation in social organization. I completed my doctoral dissertation on the dynamic interactions between the spiritual and secular in Indigenous organizations, situating the theoretical contribution in the field of organizational culture. Given that I had only a superficial understanding of my own Indigenous spiritualities, Māori organization was the focus of my research.

I was therefore delighted when Chellie invited me to co-edit this book on Indigenous spiritualities at work, as it offered an opportunity to be part of a worldwide community of scholars interested in pursuing and sharing insights in this fascinating area.

ABOUT THIS BOOK

The purpose of this book is twofold. First, for everyone interested in creating wealth and well-being, the works in this book collectively contribute fresh ways of thinking about some fundamental ways in which we can work together to transform "business as usual" practices in organizations. Rather than being places we want to escape from, transforming social spaces to enable healthy, wealthy, and wise individuals and organizations to thrive and flourish is a timely endeavour.

Second, this book advances the field of spirituality at work by offering compelling views of Indigenous spiritualities at work. The collective works contribute Indigenous-based theoretical and empirical grounding to this burgeoning field.

This is particularly so as many of the authors are experienced practitioners in Indigenous development, and others are scholars and educators. This important blend of experience and expertise leads to generating an influential range of expressions in a riveting way. However, their voices differ as they convey a range of perspectives on how people and organizations experience Indigenous spiritualities.

Importantly, what is also unique about this book is that the authors have collectively developed a position that argues that a critical part of the answer to the questions and challenges of 21st-century enterprise is captured in dynamic wisdom offered by Indigenous perspectives of wealth creation and multidimensional well-being.

WHO IS THIS BOOK FOR?

This book has broad appeal, as many of the authors are actively involved in governance, management, and leadership roles in Indigenous development. Therefore, executives, managers, and leaders, as well as those undertaking executive education, will benefit from the practice-based examples and cases developed by the authors. In addition, managers and leaders who are stakeholders in Indigenous development or who are involved in executive education will find that this book offers refreshing perspectives on wealth and well-being.

While Indigenous development now represents a multibillion dollar global enterprise, a diverse range of outcomes is expected to be achieved in Indigenous development. This focus on pluralistic outcomes that advance the social, economic, spiritual, and cultural well-being of peoples is in fact attuned to the needs of 21st-century enterprise. Indigenous organizations have a "head and heart start" in terms of leadership in complex organizations and therefore insights offered by the authors in this book are highly relevant to executives worldwide.

In addition, many of the authors are educators, and chapters are written in such a way as to appeal to researchers across disciplinary fields. Researchers will find interest in the different methodologies articulated by the authors, such as the role of Indigenous storytelling and narrative as heuristic devices. Indigenous and non-Indigenous undergraduate and graduate students who are studying Indigenous development or who are interested in advances in management, leadership, and organization research will also benefit from the fresh insights this book has to offer. The book will therefore act as a great supplement to critical learning in mainstream material in a number of faculties such as science, education, business, theology, and health as it cogently offers students and faculty a different dimension to material more commonly found in mainstream education.

In their own ways, the authors are wise and compassionate leaders, bringing a great variety of perspectives and experience to the book. Therefore, this book will also appeal to all those interested in the dynamics of spiritualities, or those who are on their own unique journeys of transformation. The authentic voices of authors enrich understandings, offer enlightenment, and amplify spiritual traditions of Indigenous peoples in a way that honors traditions of the past, present, and future.

THE STRUCTURE OF THE BOOK

A unique feature of this book on Indigenous spiritualities at work is the inclusion of touchstones. These touchstones add a distinctive dimension, in particular inviting readers to pause and enter into a space of native consciousness. They are powerful and highly engaging.

They also provide a point of entry into each section of the book, as this collection of different types of chapters is clustered around key meta-themes, as follows:

1. Wisdom and native praxis
2. Belonging and relationality
3. Identities
4. Transformations

While we have structured the book around these themes, it is important to note that authors often touch on all of these themes in their chapters.

Part I: Wisdom and Native Praxis

This section begins with a touchstone by wisdom leader and founder of the Native Science Academy, Rose von Thater Braan. Rose's touchstone invites readers to enter into a space of Indigenous consciousness.

Joe Gladstone's chapter follows with an exploration into Native American spirituality of the Southwest and northern plains. He introduces us to the concept of multidimensional transplanar wisdom, the source of which comes from the past, present, and future. Gladstone draws upon Native storytelling approaches and the dynamic multidirectional medicine wheel to highlight the animated world in which we live and our roles and responsibilities.

Xuezhu Bai and Nicholas Morris delve into the philosophy of Taoism, which has guided China for thousands of years and continues to underpin the survival and prosperity of Chinese society. They explore how the Yin-Yang and Five Virtues system can serve as an effective guide in modern workplaces.

Ella Henry's evocative chapter concludes this section. She explores the relationship between physical spaces and metaphysical well-being within the context of Māori knowledge and spirituality, as a form of practical wisdom. As a Māori academic, she adopts an autoethnographic approach to take us into learning spaces.

Part II: Belonging and Relationality

A touchstone by Hiroshi Takeda opens this section. Drawing upon multi-layered Japanese philosophic traditions of Zen, Shinto, Confucianism, and Buddhism, he invites us to consider the many dimensions of these interacting philosophies and how they can inspire ethical workplaces.

Mānuka Hēnare follows with a chapter that explores the cosmic religious worldview and belief systems of Māori, notably his tribal group from Te Tai Tokerau in the northernmost parts of Aotearoa, New Zealand's North Island. He examines the meaning of vitalism and cosmos and presents a spiral of ethics that reflects the Māori reverence of life.

Mariaelena Huambachano, from an Andean vantage point, discusses how the guiding sustainable philosophy of the Andean civilization for thousands of years, the Sumak Kawsay philosophy, can be located in business through respect and practice of the Ayni principle. This principle encourages a humanistic and spiritual expression of "collective common good" to achieve what the Andean communities regard as "good living" and in business supports notions of "value creation."

Jane Riddiford, in an autoethnographic mode, discovers how the notion of being Indigenous to the cosmos can be a generative foundation for participative and ethical leadership. She investigates the creative tensions and seismic shifts that can occur when we orient to a bigger, cosmic picture of who we are and draws inspiration from Indigenous traditions in her quest.

In the final chapter of this section, Rica Viljoen and Loraine Laubscher bring a creative lens to their study of African consciousness through the color purple. They explain how the human, sacred, physical, and external present domains can return us to the wisdom of the cradle of mankind.

Part III: Identities

Edwina Pio's touchstone invites us to consider the original inhabitants of India, the Adivasis. Drawing upon the insights of individuals who have worked with Adivasis for decades, she highlights the Adivasis' spirituality of co-existence and presents seven guiding life-affirming energies that offer a pedagogy of hope.

Dennis Foley then offers us a critical account of how Aboriginal Australian businesses are being corralled by culturally inappropriate definitions of what constitutes an Aboriginal business. Drawing on his own life experience, as well as his extensive studies of Aboriginal business, Dennis delivers a powerful piece that speaks to the heart of spiritual distress when identity is stripped away by dominant forces that impose their external concepts upon peoples.

Dara Kelly and Patrick Kelly draw upon their experiences as Canadian First Nations Stó:lō Coast Salish people. They explore the economic philosophy of gifting in Stl'e'áleq, or "potlatch" traditions and the devastation of an economic way of life, and identity, through laws that banned the potlatch. They also show a pathway of hope through a case study that highlights how relationships between business and Stó:lō Coast Salish can be strengthened through Stl'e'áleq.

In the final chapter in this section, Tania Wolfgramm calls our attention to how tools of evaluation oppress Indigenous peoples and dismiss their own value systems and ways of evaluating. She highlights how evaluation mechanisms such as testing, examination, assessment, benchmarking, grading, analysis, ranking, and rating are linked with power and control. Tania offers a creative, culturally embedded system of evaluation for Polynesian peoples through her HAKAMANA and FALE LOTU models.

Part IV: Transformations

An evocative touchstone by master carver and artist Wikuki Kingi invites us to accompany him on his journey to the sacred land of Raiatea, the site of Whare Hape, an ancient "Whare Wānanga," a university of higher learning for Pacific navigators based in the centre of Tahiti. Wikuki asks us to consider that, "Whare Hape represents all that was and perhaps can be again, a large part of what could be an important part of our collective survival on our life boat 'planet earth.'"

I find myself looking longer and listening more intently—like a newborn baby as it emerges from the womb, its eyes' pupils dilated to their maximum to take in every facet of information. I feel like a child such as this and in doing so I realize that I am seeing these images and sounds through my father and grandfather's eyes—bringing their Wairua (spirit) back with us in the kahukura (red feathers that adorn our toki). We imagine and dream and relive their emotions back along those whakapapa lines.

In the first chapter of this section, Rachel Wolfgramm and Cheryl Rowles Waetford focus on how god narratives are actively interpreted and animated by elders and native scientists in a Māori ecology of creativity. They show how these narratives, as cultural and spiritual resources, provide spiritual leadership and cultural continuity; enhance spiritual efficacy; and increase motivation, citizenship, and productivity in organization life.

Greg Cajete, Native American Tewa, then illuminates possibilities for us when we undertake the transformational "process for learning about life and the nature of the 'spirit that moves us,' with the ultimate goal of becoming fully knowledgeable about this spirit." His chapter offers rich insights into interrelationships and how we find our sacred place in this world.

Amber Nicholson, Chellie Spiller, and Mānuka Hēnare offer a chapter on creating destinies. They argue that when the energies and wills of people in an organization are sufficiently aligned and people cohere around a clear intention, the enterprise gains powerful impetus towards its common-good purpose. Their notion of collective will binds business to a wider panoply of relationship that endows will to help a business become "in sync" with its purpose and create multidimensional well-being.

The final chapter in this book, by Chellie Spiller and Rachel Wolfgramm, offers a comprehensive discussion on some of the key themes identified rippling through this diverse collection of works. In order to capture these themes, we developed a model entitled "Star Spiral Dynamics." This model highlights seven enfolded dimensions of Indigenous spiritualities at work: being, belonging, remembering, reciprocating, healing, transforming, and integrating. We highlight the importance of integrative praxis to a Native consciousness of Being.

We welcome you to the works in this book, prepared with care and with blessings.

ACKNOWLEDGMENTS

We would like to acknowledge and thank the 20 authors who responded to our invitation to contribute chapters and touchstones to this ground-breaking book. We acknowledge you as leaders in your communities, knowing that each of you dedicates yourself to advancing the interests of Indigenous peoples around the world. We also acknowledge you as agents of transformation in the academic communities in which you actively participate and to which you contribute as scholars and teachers. Your interest in building and contributing to this community is deeply valued and we are humbled by the unique range of Indigenous voices that converge within this volume. We feel privileged to be able to play a role in amplifying the individual and collective expressions herein, and we appreciate that without your participation and willingness to spend precious time and energy dedicated to this project, this book would not exist. Your contributions are a testament to the collective will we hold to make a difference in the world, and we appreciate the personal and professional sacrifices that you have all made in the process.

Our special gratitude goes to Professor Jody Fry, the series editor of Advances in Workplace Spirituality: Theory, Research and Application. Without Jody's interest, encouragement and invitation, this book would not exist. We sincerely hope this book makes a contribution to the field of spirituality at work.

Our appreciation also goes to colleagues in the Department of Management and International Business, University of Auckland Business School, for their support. In particular we thank Manuka Hēnare and Carla Houkamau, with whom we have shared many lively conversations. We are privileged to work with them. We are deeply indebted to our mentors Ella Henry,

Indigenous Spiritualities at Work, pages xxi–xxii
Copyright © 2015 by Information Age Publishing
All rights of reproduction in any form reserved.

Pare Keiha, Judith Pringle, Edwina Pio, and Donna Ladkin for being so inspiring and encouraging. We also thank Professor Rod McNaughton and the MIB research committee for financial support, and special thanks to our extraordinary copy editor John Moriarty for his professional services.

Finally, we are deeply indebted to our loved ones for their endless support. Chellie: I would like to thank my husband Rodger for his incredible support of the work I do in the world, and for being my spiritual companion. To Monica and Tony (parents); Vince (brother) and Sarah, Tessa, Abbey, Cammie; Ariana (sister) and Bryson, Olivia, Millie, Ruben; Chris (brother) and Jeanette, Harrison and Katie—thanks for always being enthusiastic and interested in what I am up to and for keeping me grounded. Honoring each other by sharing what we love about each other is a family ritual that sustains me. To my wider whānau and friends, journeying with you all is a great blessing.

Rachel: I would like to thank my best friend and partner Jim Rolfe and my wonderful sons Isaac and Ashlin for all the fun distractions; you make everything worthwhile. To my dad David especially, whom I will also love and respect: I miss you every day dad. To my mother Georgina for her support, insight and her faith: it is inspiring to me. Andrew and Janine; Benny and Rach; Celia and Rick; Helen and Jean-Pierre; Mike and Kim; Ruth and Dave; Tania and Wikuki; Brooke, Whits, Janni, Darcy and Vinnie especially, all my beautiful nieces and nephews around the world, you all inspire me in different ways. Arohanui to all my whānau and friends for your amazing support and for reminding me what Home really is.

PART I

WISDOM AND NATIVE PRAXIS

CHAPTER 1

THOUGHTS ON A WORLD IN WHICH INDIGENOUS CONSCIOUSNESS IS REALITY . . .

Rose von Thater Braan-Imai (Tuscarora/Cherokee)

The following is a revised version of an essay written for the Primacy of Consciousness Project for the John E. Mack Institute, Cambridge, MA.

There is a dual challenge in writing about consciousness in English
The challenges are the writing and the English
For I must attempt to translate into a noun-based language
a world learned, known, experienced and described orally
in process-based languages
To write about consciousness is an experience a friend described
as like talking about talking
Having accepted the invitation it will now require
the knowledge of everyone I know to help me keep my word
It is fortunate that in the Native world,
knowledge belongs to the people as a collective
It is our legacy and is gathered, shared and contributed for the good of all

Indigenous Spiritualities at Work, pages 3–19
Copyright © 2015 by Information Age Publishing
All rights of reproduction in any form reserved.

So I begin these writings with thanks and gratitude
to all my relations
for their knowledge, wisdom and generosity

What follows is a collage, a spiral of thoughts that though related
are not set in a linear progression
This form more closely models my way of perceiving
It reflects notions of relationship and interdependence
I invite you to walk the circle of these thoughts with me
in the hope it will make visible my view of consciousness
An additional note to the reader:
Though these words come to you in written form,
they are presented following an oral tradition
The thoughts and words are meant to be heard,
they follow the breath
after that perhaps they may meet up with the usual rules
of grammar punctuation and tense
You will notice the words are formatted to represent a spiral
This is because by standing at different places on a spiral
you gain different views of whatever you are observing

The universe to which I belong is conscious, animate, and interactive
Time is movement
An unending shifting of patterns
that appear and disappear in multiple layers of rhythms
Concepts of a linear and finite time
are superimposed over an innate experience of time
Space is a chaotic flux that is constantly transforming
From this view of the world, "relationship" best describes
the core of consciousness
In this universe, it is relationship to place that lies at the heart of learning, and
this is where we discover the pleasures, obligations, kindnesses,
and duties of self in community
In an exploration of relationship and interdependence
we can immerse our sensibilities, integrate wordless knowing,
and, within the spontaneous patterns of time,
create and share our expressions of what we have come to know
and how we have come to know it

The voices of consciousness are heard through our senses
Through feeling, they become images, then words
In a purely material perception of reality,
one that suppresses or dismisses feeling
it is a simple step to isolate or limit meaning from thought,
choice from action
and to feed spiraling levels of excess and conflict that deny the spirit

Human thought and creativity isolated from feeling
forms a society with limited proscribed channels for its expressions of culture and
values, and sustains a distorted collective consciousness
A reality recognizing only the material
is bereft of balance
and therefore malnourished
Such malnourishment fosters ever-growing loops of addiction

To live in relationship with an interactive universe, a conscious world,
is to live a practice of the art of listening
It is in the internal world where we find the connection
to the creation and to that which creates
That internal place of connection
is the place of hearing and understanding and the place from which to listen
It is not possible to have a good relationship
without permitting the intimacy of hearing what is being spoken
in whatever languages are used
What is heard and how it is heard
when confined to the intellect delivers too narrow an understanding
to allow full comprehension

Through nourishing the internal connection to the creation
the voices of that which creates
comes to meet the senses
and using the physical world as teacher
can be heard, understood and interacted with
Through these interactions one is formed as a person of community
It is the same as the way water forms the land, or the wind forms the feather, bringing intelligence, meaning, shape, and function
The English words "person" and "community" infer separate worlds,
an inference unique to the Eurocentric paradigm
and it is in English, a language of dividing and holding in place
where fragmentation is born
Inversely, this noun language
also fuels the desire for connection and wholeness
It is a frightening, dangerous and lonely journey
when feeling and meaning are discarded or left by the side of the path

Developing oneself, in good relationship with life
is the first responsibility of a person of community
It is through our contributions that the dance of relationship is learned
Living as kin, in an animate reality, opens understandings and realizations
about the place of humans in the creation
The place of humans is not elevated, it is equal
Humans have their duties to the creation, as do the plants, the stones,
and all other forms of life

The concepts of hierarchy and "other-ness" are
intellectual/social constructs that have been devised
to create and further material reality
and a particular quality of consciousness

The primary relationship from which we learn about the creation of life
is the relationship between the male and female principles
as they engage one another in nature
If I speak about the Sun as an embodiment of the male principle
and the Earth as an embodiment of the female principle
then it is easy to see how the meeting of these two forces
and the quality of their meeting determines that which emerges
from their coming together
The warmth of the sun attracted to the dark fecundity of a receptive Earth travels
to her and in their meeting activates her capacity to give life
Learning the qualities of the female and male principles
as they express throughout the natural world brings us to the essence
of these principles and the opportunity to rediscover meanings, boundaries and
purposes that are alive in these energies
The core of a conscious world rests in dancing the balance
that brings these two principles into harmony over and over and over again
By appreciating, sustaining, restoring and renewing these principles
we attract a creative relationship between the living universe and the person, the
couple, the family, the community, and the society
Living in an awareness that we are of the Earth rather than on the Earth brings us
to recognize and respect our interdependence

Learning the essence and expressions of these two principles
is a life-long journey
We must understand both, of course, since both male and female live inside us
I first explore the consciousness of the feminine,
its interplay and expressions is one of my duties as a woman
In a matriarchal society, such as the Haudenosaunee,
also known as the Iroquois Confederacy,
one of the primary expressions of the feminine principle
is to animate, model, guide, and influence ethical social conduct
This is done in many ways; one of them is the preservation
of culture and traditions which promote harmony among the people
and serve and defend life

This confederacy has continued unbroken since its founding
on the Great Law of Peace in about 1000 AD, ending war among the Mohawk,
Onondaga, Oneida, Seneca, Cayuga and later the Tuscarora tribes
To the present day it is the responsibility of the Clan Mothers
to choose the candidate for the fifty coequal chiefs
that make up the Grand Council of the confederacy

as well as the presiding moderator, (Tadodaho) who presides over them
(Arden & Hall, 1990)

The female principle with its ability to attract
is intended to harmonize, influence, and provide structure
to the potent force of the male principle;
why else would it have such an intense ability to attract?
The strength of the feminine capacity for vision, intuition, and the realms
of emotion provide guidance and protection to our societies
as well as inspiration and innovation
It is difficult to write about these matters in a culture
where the word "feminine" is heard as a challenge
And in an environment where the feminine
has been fragmented, commoditized, politicized, pathologized, and marginalized
Nevertheless, in a world that is awake,
distortions fall away and deeper, richer, and wiser understandings
of the feminine and masculine return to view
Essential meanings and purpose are once again respected
as gifts, skills, and capacities and known as sacred components for the nurturance,
flowering and continuance of life

When something is innately equal,
struggling to prove that it is so
creates a dynamic that is dependent on the oppression
against which one is struggling
The need to be heard, to be visible and respected as a valued part of life
is a basic need and originates in what is called by some
the Great Mystery or that which creates or in some versions of the I Ching,
the Creative
Authenticity and a sense of validity emerge from the internal world
to be reflected in the external world
In a society that is unbalanced and dominated by a single worldview,
the act of "proving" is rooted in an assumption that only what is defined
as rational within that worldview can be real
But if you look to the natural order, you see that what manifests
remains invisible until it is birthed from the internal into a temporal reality
From an internal place of learning, proof of equity
is the embodiment and expression of principles congruent
with the natural laws of harmony and balance,
attraction and complementarity
Expressions of equality generated from an internal knowing exist within cycles of
reflection, discernment, and sharing
that strengthen and broaden the capacity to experience interdependence
These expressions can enhance the ability to generate
harmony, perseverance, respect, humor, and humility

When feminine and masculine principles are out of balance there is oppression
Not oppression just of the feminine,
but oppression of the masculine as well
because you cannot oppress one without distorting both
Oppression does not discriminate. It oppresses all
Its invisible and pervasive force constricts the heart,
suppresses the spirit, and censors expression
When the focus of our attention lives in stillness
and animates balance and renewal,
there is an endless breadth of possibilities
that nourish heart, spirit and creativity
There is coherence in a process that encourages the sharing of diverse
understandings that add to the body of knowledge and support life
The profound aspects of the feminine and masculine principles
are sensible in a conscious world
All is interconnected and the wheel of movement, process and performance
continues its spin, coming together and moving apart, emerging and
disappearing in the chaos of flux

I envision a conscious world evolving through the healing and restoration
of the masculine and feminine to their place of symmetry and cohesion
And because they are inextricably joined
I see this accomplished through the restoration of the feminine
to its place of respect
It is a task in which many people are deeply engaged,
this recovery and revitalization
of the essential powers of the feminine and masculine principles
The dominance and distortion of male power has abused men
and the spirits of men, warping their creative drive
It has brought loneliness to men, to women, and to our children
And it has brought grief and suffering to the Earth
Men and women who have nurtured their knowledge
of the female and male principles
project an understanding of the sacredness of life
and a deep commitment to the visible inclusion
of the profoundly feminine into mundane life
With courage these ones look into the face of violence and the brutalities that
have resulted from dominance and control
They act to learn what must be known about the mutations and their terrors
It is said that we carry our wounds as medicine for the healing
These ones use their consciousness to hold the stillness while they stand, speak
and act with reverence for life
and for the compelling need for a humility that is consistent
with our limited view as humans
These ones monitor their ambitions,
master their desires, and examine their weaknesses to find the way

to wisdom and compassion
These ones explore their mistakes, recognizing them as learning,
and use their knowledge to devise inclusive strategies,
demonstrate productive collaborations
and construct questions to draw out deeper answers that have the potential to
move all to health and renewal

In a conscious world,
we are introduced from infancy to our duties and responsibilities
to the creation
We understand the critical necessity for strengthening
the best parts of our nature and to cultivate our creativity as a contribution for the
good of all
The taking of life, whether it is plant, animal, element, or human
requires the restoration of balance through performance of ceremony, reconciliation, and embodied acts of conscious responsibility
Acquisitiveness and force are not symbols of strength or leadership
but clear signals of a weakness of spirit and character

If you look at an internalized, embodied understanding of consciousness there is
a shift from a hierarchical perception,
as in levels of consciousness,
to the perception of a geography of consciousness
An ecology of interdependent relationships
Living pragmatically within a world that is conscious
calls for a different understanding of time
Here, time reveals itself as essence not *of* the essence
and that *as essence* it is innately creative
This is a fundamental understanding
Living with time as the creative power in action
cultivates the ability to distinguish different patterns,
harmonies and rhythms
and invigorates perception and perseverance
It builds courage
because the sisters of illusion, confusion, and delusion
are encountered in waiting
Waiting well means waiting happily in the core of stillness
while living fully in the assault of distractions that suffuse society
Waiting is not a peripheral ability, but central to a way of being
that links us to time as movement and the worlds
of Earth, Water, Air and Skies, of the visible and the invisible,
of sound and silence
Within waiting lives the potential for fulfillment
Waiting well combines with listening well
to breed a way of seeing that cultivates thoughts and actions
that harmonize with place, life, and the Mystery

With our desires come the rush of ambition
Ambition, unmediated, fears time
and feeds the demand for solutions that appear absolute
and that soothe our anxieties with fantasies of control

Waiting is a part of movement
To prevent waiting from becoming paralysis entails trust,
a knowledge of self and of the languages consciousness uses
In waiting we surrender to following the processes that are in play,
looking to see where beauty will make itself visible
attracting our attention to the knowledge it contains
The heart recognizes pure beauty uncommoditized,
as harmonized expressions of the consciousness of the creation,
the perceiver and perceived

Waiting is not passive
There is a lot to do while waiting
Mastering balance and spontaneity, polishing discernment,
perceiving movement and patterns, fostering humor,
deepening appreciation and flexibility and practicing kindness
The fulfillment of vision rests in the preparation
and in learning the patterns of time
The longer one ignores the consequences of impatience,
the greater the distance grows between vision and fulfillment
The reward for impatience is time

In the world I describe, time is not a commodity
To mechanize time and attempt to contain it within a singular framework
is an undertaking with implications and consequences
that have revealed themselves as destructive and dangerous
Time is movement and movement is constant and chaotic
Discerning the myriad movements of time
and its overlapping layers of diverse rhythms
is one of the great pleasures of consciousness
Within the human body, just as in the natural world,
there are many different times and rhythms
It is useful to agree on a type of time for certain purposes,
just as nouns are useful in naming
However, imagining that an intellectual agreement
can fully describe time in its entirety,
especially when that description does not match what we observe
and experience within ourselves,
is comparable to wearing your shoes on the wrong feet
It is a strange, disorienting experience
The effect of living with an artificial definition of time
imposed over natural time works like an addictive drug

causing people to function and believe in a social reality
separate from the movement of the creation
If the theory of linear time were accepted as a tool for measuring movement, an
intellectual construct
devised for certain practical purposes like a chair is made for sitting,
and if that understanding of time was commonly practiced
within the acceptance of many different perceptions of time,
then time, in the wider society,
would no longer wear the mask of adversary and commodity
It would not have the ill effects
that have resulted from the singular perception of time as linear
The belief in linear time
and its imposition has distorted, mechanized, and limited life
And, in so doing, it separates humans from that on which they depend,
the heartbeat of the mother Earth to whom we belong
and to whom we owe
kindnesses, as well as duties and obligations

It is profoundly intimate to listen,
to listen to the sunlight, or to someone, or to yourself
Automatically your breathing blends with what you are listening to (or for) and
your listening becomes an opening to feeling
Listening is skill, art, and capaciousness
The skill comes in distinguishing, refining, clarifying, and tuning
to that which resonates inside you
When you think about communication in terms of different consciousnesses,
listening is more important than speaking
and speaking is exposed as the least refined of the means of communication
It is said that at one time the animals, the stones, the many forms of life
and humans all spoke the same language
Humans became arrogant so the animals and the other forms of life
stopped speaking in order to aid humans in their learning of many things—
among them, listening

Tumult and stimulation fill the material world,
and it can appear that choice and selectivity are the answers to overwhelm,
yet selectivity can carry its own consequences
and isolation is an extreme
that leads away from the human need for connection
In a world with constant stimulation,
where a cacophony of voices, sounds, and languages immerse,
discernment is high art
but what or who to listen to is a lesser question
Where to listen from is of greater importance
Knowing where to listen from provides a compass through the flux
to find the pathway to clarity or resonant answers

Vision emerges from stillness and stillness precedes clarity
Clarity must guide action in an interrelated, interdependent world
If it is true for you, as it is posited by many,
that the external world
is the reflection of the internal world,
then our listening choices
determine which parts of our nature we value and wish to nourish
If illness and disease are understood as imbalances in a living system,
then the task is to restore balance
Balance by its nature can be renewed,
and from this we see that there exists a medicine for each ill
Yet medicine, if isolated from the fullness of its song,
can catalyze further imbalance or become poison
The practice of deconstructing medicine plants
to a mathematical formula of components
fractures the unity of the natural structure, and what is lost
is the medicine's song
It is the song emerging and invoking harmony
that can transform poison into medicine
The alchemy of that transformation
is learned through listening, observing and feeling
In perceiving the song being sung
(using the sensing capacities of the entire body,
we gain access to the knowledge sent by organs, skin, blood, hair, etc.),
we experience a transformative process
Through our attention we honor the medicine plant, creature, or element
as well as the harmony that has created it

There is alchemy
in the resolve to maintain humility, patience, and integrity
as we wait for the medicine
This is not the world of simple dualism,
straight paths from "a" to "b"
and the false hope of absolutes;
it is the world of process and performance
of knowledge and exploration, paradox and insight
It is an understanding that the quality of our consciousness
is a critical factor in medicine and healing
Healing and renewal are veiled in the deepest realms of the Great Mystery,
and it is only with its participation that healing and insight occur

Humor and good character mature with listening,
and inner vision improves with time
Humility is the doorway to listening and respect opens the door
Hearing is a full body sport
I notice where in my body I hear someone or something or silence

When I am with an accomplished listener
I know my name will be safe in moving across their lips
Dancing the flux of paradox breeds lightness and virtuosity
Listening makes great dancers

Human consciousness relates in the most intimate of ways
to the consciousness of the Earth
The Earth's consciousness is made visible through her beauty
It is the mystery of that beauty and the longing to reflect and know it
that teaches us

There is intimacy in the transmission of knowledge
Listening and learning are intimate
It is a falling in love
When a learning is for you, you are attracted
You fall in love and your attention travels over and over
to the paths that lead to that which attracts you,
discovering and exploring aspects, pitfalls, anomalies, practices,
possibilities
Listening opens the senses
When the teacher you are learning from is the Earth,
a heightened awareness develops
The intellect becomes a fine and useful tool for integration
like a softly leaded pencil moving smoothly, guided by many intelligences
to write your song, make your medicine, offer your knowledge

The manner
in which knowledge is transmitted has far-reaching consequences
In the Native paradigm the forms, the processes by which education is gained, its
uses and refinement cannot be separated from place and relationship
Sense of place equals land, family, community, and traditions
Learning is not bounded by a physical structure
or confined to a designated set of people,
nor is it restricted to interactions with humans or linear definitions of time
The transmission of knowledge
is not confined to words;
it comes through our dreams, ceremonies, songs, visions
In the Native paradigm, knowledge is catalogued in holistic symbols
that embody principles and experiences
These symbols
describe the unity between people, animals, plants, air, water, sky, etc.
They describe the ecology of relationship
and the principles, ceremonies and ways for living in a sustainable community
This knowledge
has become highly valued and sought after in a modern world
that faces the consequences of excess

However, a consciousness that diminishes feeling, creates excess, and caters
to acquisitiveness, a consciousness that separates knowledge from service,
cannot fully perceive the Earth's intelligence
In the Native paradigm,
the gateway and safe passage to deeper realms of perception,
comprehension and ultimately to wisdom rest in traditional values
Indigenous knowledge cannot be learned through writings and photographs, nor
can it be bought or sold by an individual
This knowledge of process and performance requires sharing
It requires humility, discipline, perseverance and patience,
each a quality that takes copious amounts of time to develop
The tempo of the passage to learning,
the enhancement of perception,
and the ability to transmit and share knowledge
are inextricably linked to the development and refinement of character
Indigenous knowledge lives in the unity
of the people, the land, and that which created all
There is a coherence in a conscious world to which we must be attuned
Distinguishing that coherence and aligning your life to it is a governing principle
of animating consciousness

The United Nations designated 1996 The Year of Indigenous Peoples
That July an International Summer Institute was convened
at the University of Saskatchewan in Saskatoon, Canada
The attendees represented Indigenous people from around the globe
From lands that colonizers called Australia, New Zealand,
South America, Europe, and North America
Among them were artists, traditional knowledge holders,
allies of Indigenous people
and a generation of mature post-colonial Indigenous scholars

The Summer Institute met to share perspectives
and gain a holistic view of colonization
They came together to map and diagnose colonization,
to evolve and share processes and strategies to heal the colonized
and to imagine and invoke a new society
"Through sharing, feeling, listening and analyzing we engaged
in a critique of the trauma of colonization . . .
We came to understand that it is the systemic nature of colonization
that creates cognitive imperialism, our cognitive prisons" (Battiste, 1996)

In Western science and in traditional educational institutions,
students are taught in a Eurocentric educational model
What is taught has been drawn from a limited sample,
projected as universal
and normed on this limited sample of experience and ways of knowing

This excludes the majority of women, diverse cultures and Indigenous people
Children enter school with open minds and a sense of discovery,
and the longer their education, the narrower their view becomes
By the time they reach the doctoral level
their knowledge of a fragment of a specific subject
will have grown and deepened,
but their perspective of knowledge itself has become narrow
I remember being in school and realizing that what was being presented
did not reflect or honor my innate understandings
It was then that I turned to look out the window at my true teacher
and never again took as whole
the fragments presented in the Eurocentric educational system
Many have had experiences of pure intelligence
Its purity gives nourishment that bathes and feeds the entire being
and passes itself through the mind, the body and the spirit
to express itself in thought, action, and creativity that is marked by a congruence
with and devotion to life

The systemic nature of cognitive imperialism remains, for the most part,
invisible and inviolate
As human consciousness evolves, an educational model
that divides and oppresses grows in its destructive force
For instance, medical training, which focuses on localized treatment
of specific symptoms and ignores the matrix in which an imbalance occurs,
devises medical interventions that often cause deeper imbalance
By dividing and isolating, Western medicine has
unwittingly separated itself from its own healing songs
in the same way that by imposing a singular system of thought,
Eurocentric education has isolated itself from traditional knowledge,
the learning inherent in community, and the wisdom contained in feeling

I recently heard an Ojibway man speak of teaching his children about wild rice
He took them out to the waters where the wild rice grows so
they could hear the sound the rice made when it touched the canoe
It is a good example of a transmission of knowledge
that includes process, performance, community, and timelessness
It is a teaching method that brings the learners
into the presence of pure intelligence

To think about the need for cognitive pluralism
as if it were a matter of social justice is to minimize it
Valuing cognitive pluralism is not an act of social justice;
it is recognizing and valuing consciousness
The validity of cognitive pluralism is beyond the artificial constructs
of a social system
Cognitive pluralism is consistent with the natural order

that we see expressed throughout the creation
Part of the human journey is learning the geography, voices, and languages
of consciousness
The imposition of a series of assumptions, as practiced in colonialism
and its pervasive, incessant demands for assimilation
are an assault on the human spirit, on our learning spirit(s)
and on consciousness itself

A transformed and transformative educational system
will reflect, embody, and teach skills and capacities
that realize the centrality of consciousness
and the benefits of diversity in learning, thought, and expression
As long as a colonizers' consciousness remains invisible
to both the colonizers and the colonized,
the methods and possibilities for change that are brought forward
remain within the systems of thought and consciousness
that produced the disease,
and as Mi'kmaq educator Marie Battiste says,
"you cannot be the doctor if you are the disease"

To attempt to separate knowledge and power from service and meaning
is a known path to failure of purpose and the wounding of the spirit
Ultimately
the achievements, lacking integrity at their core,
cannot be sustained and eventually reflect in the external world
an internal weakness of character
In a reality where the material is held as primary and time linear,
human accomplishments beguile and seduce
Fortunately, transformation is a constant and false steps a part of learning
In a reality experienced as transformative and interdependent,
our embodiment of learning and its expressions into daily life
carry the potential for improving the quality of our relationships
and ultimately the quality of our communities, societies, and institutions

Taking what is known
and valuing it outside the context of relationship
further limits our already limited view
Knowledge is only potential, when disconnected from meaning
and its relational context and from the realms of the invisible,
it is seen to generate excesses that destroy balance and harmony
Unlimited excess that occurs in the human body is called cancer
When excess occurs in the natural world,
inevitably there is a reorientation, adaptation, and change
to support the restoration of balance using time as a vehicle
Excess starves the spirit and the being
It triggers desires and hungers that cannot be sated or slowed

by the material
In a conscious society,
it is understood that the value is in the quality of the question,
the constancy of attention,
the clarity of discernment, the fullness of observation,
the capaciousness of listening and the generosity of spirit
The power of the invisible is dismissed only by the foolish
and actions taken whether they are innocent or contrived
that ignore the power of the invisible generate consequences
These consequences are known as fate

Leadership is the responsibility of each person
We must be able to lead ourselves away
from that which feeds the lesser parts of our nature,
toward that which nourishes and strengthens the good
What is "good"?
In this notion of kinship and interdependence "good" holds a meaning
of being in harmony with the natural order,
of causing creativity to continue itself, of preserving cultural integrity
while mirroring the diversity of the natural world
"Good" is something that sustains the whole
Among the leadership qualities that generate and strengthen the good
are kindness, generosity, humor, humility, compassion, and truthfulness
These words sound so "soft"
How could such gentle-sounding qualities lead a people to nurturance and
safety in a terrorist world?

Terror has always been available in the world
In prehistory it was found as it is now in the unknown, the unexpected
And so it seemed that a powerful leader was one who controlled
and dominated threatening forces
This view slanders the unknown as threatening, cruel, unfeeling
And with the practice of control and domination,
century after century terror never left
It was magic that went underground
Terror stayed above ground and became a tool of power
A tool like a chainsaw or a jet engine in its harshness
deadened the senses, stimulated fear, and refocused resolve
to the narrowest corridors of survival and supremacy
If you deny the power of ethical conduct to disperse fear,
you deny the power of the Creative to expand the ways
in which the invisible resolves the impossible
By denying the importance of the internal world,
by trading the knowledge of the deeper realms of perception
for trinkets large and small,
one ends up with an illusion of safety that rests on foundations so flimsy

that they threaten to shake to pieces at the very thought of loss or change
It is a poor trade

Through learning the principles that govern the manner in which life moves
from the primordial to the temporal,
we find our opportunity to collaborate with and contribute to life
Learning these principles requires the cultivation of those soft-sounding qualities
because they compel a person to build courage, humility, resolve,
a strong, flexible mind,
and an unwavering dependence on the Great Mystery
This is the power of the gentle

To return power to that which creates it is in alignment with life
This is seen clearly in the circle of relationship
between Mother Earth and Father Sky
It is seen in the life of water as cloud, mist, rain, river, and ocean,
the warmth of the sun or the cold wind quickening its transformations
It is seen in the life of a tree, its nourishment rising from the Earth
to activate the seed, feed the bud, blossom, fruit, then return to ground
Each transformation alive,
performing an act of beauty, power, and continuance

It has been said so often that it has become a cliché that power corrupts
But the Earth has immeasurable power
Consider the way a volcano builds an island
It is Earth's human children
who attempt to actively hold power over one another
How does this happen?
Blackfoot scholar, Leroy Little Bear
once posed these questions:
What is it in the nature of a consciousness
that causes it to impose itself on others?
And what is it in the nature of a consciousness
that would allow itself to be imposed upon?
One hundred people sat together and reflected on those questions
for 10 days
The answers provided both a map and a revisioning
of Indigenous voice and vision

My observation is that energy that is defined as "power"
will distort and corrupt if the intention is to gather it and hold on to it
In the natural world, energy is movement, and it returns to its source
in a constant cycle
There is pure intelligence in that cycle
In that movement there is room for the Mystery to serve the good
The movement of the Mystery lies beyond usual human perception

Great thinkers, women and men of knowledge who spend their lives
hoping to glimpse the Unknowable, if they succeed,
unfailingly express awe, humility, and gratitude
At the heart of ritual and ceremony
is a need to express gratitude to the Unknowable,
to acknowledge our helplessness and the infinite love
that has allowed us to continue our learning

I offer you these thoughts with respect
and the wish that they will bring beauty, strength, and a smile to your heart

All my relations

Rose v. T. Braan-Imai

REFERENCE

Arden, H., & Hall, S. (1990). *Wisdomkeepers: Meetings with Native American spiritual elders.* Hillsboro, OR: Beyond Words.

Battiste, M. (1986). *You cannot be the doctor if you are the disease: Tenets of systematic colonialism in Canadian language education.* Unpublished manuscript., INEP, University of Sakatchewan.

Battiste, M. (1996). *Cultural restoration of oppressed indigenous peoples.* Program presented at the International Summer Institute, "Cultural Restoration of Oppressed Indigenous Peoples," Saskatoon, Saskatchewan.

Battiste, M. (2011). Introduction: Unfolding the lessons of colonization. In, M. Battiste (Ed.) *Reclaiming Indigenous Voice and Vision.* (p. xvii). UBC Press: Vancouver, British Columbia.

Leroy Little Bear (1996). Relationship of aboriginal people to the land and the aboriginal perspective on aboriginal title. In For seven generations: an informational legacy of the royal commission on aboriginal peoples. ed. Royal Commission on Aboriginal Peoples, CD-Rom (Ottawa: Canada Communications Group, 1996), cited in Royal Commission on Aboriginal Peoples, Treaty Making in the spirit of Co-existence: An alternative to Extinguishment (Ottawa: Canada Communications Group, 1994).

CHAPTER 2

NATIVE AMERICAN TRANSPLANAR WISDOM

Joseph Scott Gladstone

ABSTRACT

In this chapter I share an understanding of Native spirituality and describe it as an active awareness of an animate tangible and intangible world beyond oneself and an extrasensory connectedness with that world. In our connectedness, we are equal with this world and thus we can never dominate it. When we have such a spiritual connection with the world, we understand and appreciate our responsibility to it. We gain this connected appreciation via transplanar wisdom, the source of which comes from our past, present, and future that approaches from multiple directions and can be understood through stories.

INTRODUCTION

Indigenous Spiritualities contribute to vitalizing relationships within the workplace, community, and the natural environment—ecology. This chapter introduces Native American spirituality, specifically that of American Indian tribes in the western United States. Since a discussion on Native spirituality

Indigenous Spiritualities at Work, pages 21–32
21

can be very broad, I will focus on it as a source for wisdom and this wisdom's usefulness for appreciating community and ecological relationships.

A Caveat on Reading Native Thought

For those accustomed to communicating within a Native mindset, it naturally makes sense to lay out the supporting arguments for a thesis prior to stating that thesis. This mode of thought is opposite to Western communication, where an author's thesis statement is stated at the beginning and supporting arguments follow. I thus apologize in advance for loquaciousness in this chapter introduction, but this being a text in Native and Indigenous thought, I embrace the spirit of decolonized writing (Smith, 2012) and take the liberty to follow Indigenous convention and frame my thinking before I state my thesis. This normal convention among Native people is an example of nonlinear thought. Among Natives, it is a courtesy to help the listener understand the context of a story via front matter presented before the story's thesis. So, unlike Western, linear-oriented writing, you will not find my thesis statement within the first two paragraphs of this chapter. Entering into nonlinear conversations does require patience for those unaccustomed to it. However, if you take the time to work through the framing process you will soon find my thesis; before I present my thesis, I must add an additional caveat for readers new to Native studies.

A Note on Using the Word Native

Hereinafter I will use the word *Native* to represent the Indigenous North American people of pre-Columbian heritage. The Native philosopher Gerald Vizenor (1994) inspires my use of this single word choice over the more common vernacular *Native American* or *American Indian.* This best represents what Boje (2001) describes as the living story that describes experiences shared by the modern North American Indigenous people. Throughout this chapter I will use Native to identify ideas and things that belong to or are connected to the descendants of the Indigenous people of North America, since the word connotes a stronger feeling of Indigenous thought and values that are separate from non-Native Western ideals. Although I will make an effort to use Native exclusively to reference Indigenous North American people and their way of thinking, at times I will use Native American, American Indian, and *Indian Country* when such descriptions are commonly used in the vernacular and when necessary to fit these terms into the context of my story.

SPIRITUALITY

Spirituality Defined

There is diversity in defining spirituality in organizations. First and foremost, spirituality is not religion (Deloria, 1994; Foucault, Gros, Ewald, & Fontana, 2005; Marques, Dhiman, & King, 2007; Mitroff, 2003; Mitroff & Denton, 1999). In contrast to spirituality, religion emphasizes constraining dogma and formal structure (Bruce, 2000; Mitroff, 2003). An empirical study on workplace spirituality found every informant defining spirituality as a total integration of a whole person and that person's total connection with everything in the universe, and this connection did not require facilitation via organized religion (Mitroff, 2003; Mitroff & Denton, 1999).

In her discussion tying spirituality with organization processes, Kostera embraces Anthony de Mello's summary that spirituality is "awareness, awareness, awareness" (Kostera, 2005, p. 56). Although parsimoniously eloquent, de Mello's definition does need some expansion. Mitroff (2003) defines spirituality as "not only the intense feeling of being totally integrated as a whole person, but also the feeling of being totally connected with everything else in the universe" (p. 377). Vine Deloria, Jr., brings us into a Native understanding of spirituality, as "two paths [leading people] to make sense of their world: empirical observation of the physical world and the continuing but sporadic intrusion of higher powers in their lives, manifested in unusual events and dreams" (Deloria, 2006, p. xxiv).

In this chapter, I define spirituality as an active awareness of an animate tangible and intangible world beyond oneself, and an extrasensory connectedness with it. This definition is expressed in Native spirituality.

Native Spirituality

North American Native people exist from coast to coast, and because this geographic area is very broad there is some variation in Native spirituality. In this chapter I will concentrate on those in the U.S. southwest and northern plains, the home of most of the following Native American philosophers: Vine Deloria, Jr.; Viola Cordova; Donald Fixico; Gregory Cajeta; and Gerald Vizenor.

The Dakota philosopher Vine Deloria, Jr., helps us better understand relatedness. According to him, the idea of relatedness for Natives is not understood within separate and distinct compartments; rather, relatedness is a physical and metaphysical connection to everything temporal, spatial, and material (Deloria, Deloria, Foehner, & Scinta, 1999). Time, space and matter are not distinct and separate, an idea often tied to Einstein (1920/1995). By seeing everything as related, Native philosophy encourages patient observation as a process for understanding the real world. Through senses tuned to see relatedness in everything, Natives sense purpose in everything, a "science of wholeness" (Deloria, Deloria, Foehner, & Scinta, 1999, p. 40), which I interpret as a pragmatic view (Peirce, 1878).

Deloria points out that Native spirituality is built on a framework of relatedness. The Native universe is living (Deloria, Deloria, Foehner, & Scinta, 1999); there is no separation between organic life and inorganic matter: All matter is living and must be respected in the same way that we respect familial relations. Vi Cordova (2007) describes the same philosophy among Natives.

Viola Cordova, Jicarilla Apache, helps us understand our place and our relationship with the world. She writes that Native people know their place in the world and respect boundaries in their relationship with it (2007, p. ix). Native spirituality embraces complex connections between humans, the Earth, all others inhabiting it, and a broader complex cosmos. Native spirituality is driven by complex cosmological forces connecting people with their universe (2007). Humans are equal to, not superior to, the universe. The universe includes all things, animate and inanimate. All things possess both spirit and intelligence. Such intelligence is revealed in Napi and the Rock:

> Napi had been walking for a long time and he was tired, so he sought a place where he could rest. Not too far in the distance he saw a rock and decided it would be a good place to sit and rest. When he arrived at the rock, he asked, "Oki, Brother. I'm tired. Can I rest on you?"
>
> The rock, of course, agreed and Napi spread his robe on the rock and sat. After he had rested, Napi thanked the rock and offered him his robe in return for allowing him to rest on him.
>
> Not too long after Napi walked on from the rock, the weather changed. It became cold and windy and soon rain fell. Napi ran back to the rock and asked for his robe back; but the rock refused, saying that Napi had given it to him as a gift. Napi became mad and took the robe back.
>
> As he was walking away from the rock, his old robe wrapped around him, Napi heard a rumbling sound behind him. He turned and saw that it was the rock rolling toward him. Napi ran to avoid being run over by the rock. After being chased for a while Napi called out to nearby birds to save him. The birds dove at the rock, breaking it into pieces and saving Napi.[1]

In this story, the rock establishes a relationship of trust with Napi. Sadly, that trust is broken, much to the rock's detriment. I will share with you a modern story about another relationship where rock again must trust a person.

Yvonne Chouinard, the founder of Patagonia, Inc., at one time had a successful business manufacturing pitons, steel spikes once used in technical rock wall climbing that climbers hammered into rock crevices and used as anchor points for climbing rope:

By 1970 Chouinard Equipment had become the largest supplier of climbing hardware in the United States. It had also started down the path to becoming an environmental villain. The popularity of climbing, though growing steadily, remained concentrated on the same well-trained routes.... The repeated hammering of hard steel pitons... was severely disfiguring the rock. After an ascent of the Nose route on El Capitan, which had been pristine a few summers earlier, I came home disgusted with the degradation I had seen. Frost and I decided we would phase out the piton business.... Pitons were the mainstay of our business, but we were destroying the very rocks we loved. (Chouinard, 2005, p. 31)

Chouinard, like Napi, recognizes the spirit within rock, something that others may see as inanimate. Unlike Napi, he chose to not fail the trust that the rock had in him. Rather than destroying the rock, Chouinard sacrificed some personal comfort, his business income, in order to sustain the environment's trust in him.

But the cosmic ecological connection described by Cordova and illustrated by Chouinard does not mean that we are required to live Spartan lives, as demonstrated by Cordova's desire to live comfortably, taking no vows of poverty (Hogan, 2007), and by the success of Chouinard's clothing business.

Our cosmic relationship with the universe is not just spatial, it is also temporal, a relationship described by Donald Fixico, whom I will next discuss.

The Miccosuki philosopher, Donald Fixico, agrees with others that Native spiritual thought is nonlinear, but we should also think about linearity as more than space; we must include time (Fixico, 2003). With the exception of Barad (2007) and Einstein (1920/1995), this is seen as an intangible reality in Western philosophy, yet it is accepted as physically real in Native spirituality. Another Native philosopher, Ted Jojola, points out that this reality is expressed with every prayer to the four directions, acknowledging direct connection with space as a physical reality (Jojola, 2004).

The Santa Clara Pueblo philosopher Gregory Cajete pushes Native spirituality as grounding Native science. Cajete describes Native science as an earth-based phenomenological practice objectively explaining the world through knowledge gained via a lived subjective experience (Cajete, 2004). Phenomenology precedes categorized facts and applied scientific principles (Cajete, 2004). This is a pragmatic view because it "has value and meaning only in reference to [a] primordial and open realm" (Abram, as referenced in Cajete, 2004, p. 45).

Native science brings together the philosophic and spiritual traditions described above. It is grounded in human experience and culturally distinct and relevant knowledge (Cajete, 2000, 2004). Native science explains a way for people to interact with their world spiritually, a way quite unlike Western science, which seeks how to classify and control the world (Cajete, 2000, 2004). This mindset of control and manipulation extends beyond physical science, but through trickster stories we are able to break from such mindsets. Gerald Vizenor describes trickster stories as imaginative acts that free people's minds while simultaneously forcing self-awareness on them (Vizenor, 1998).

Vizenor, an Anishinaabe (Chippewa) storyteller and philosopher, coined three concepts relevant to Native spirituality: *survivance, sovenance,* and *transmotion* (Vizenor, 1998). Survivance is an active presence within a Native reality. Sovenance connects survivance with a conscious awareness of the past and to our spiritual selves, such as through Native trickster stories. Transmotion is a "reciprocal use of nature" (p. 15), a conscious act of practicing life as a Native aware of his or her place in the universe (Vizenor, 1998).

Native Spirituality as Native Praxis

My work with Native American spirituality began with my inquiry that investigated an assumption that Native American entrepreneurs risk alienating their traditional tribal values and collective consciousness in exchange for entering what is perceived as a nontraditional activity (Frantz, 1999; Garsombke & Garsombke, 2000; Gladstone, 2012; Miller, 2008; Stewart & Schwartz, 2007). I found that historical evidence, on the contrary, reveals that trading activities—private business practices—by individual Natives are a traditional activity practiced over time, and that modern day Native "traders" interviewed in my study embraced a Native trading spirit (Gladstone, 2012).

American Indian entrepreneurs participating in my study revealed that what people learn and discover during their life experience is useful for business planning and even working with competitors. As one informant described it, being a Native businessperson requires a capacity to speak on a spiritual plane (Gladstone, 2012). Those interviewed in the study described drawing upon wisdom from multiple sources and multiple directions. The stories that they shared appear similar to Vizenor's transmotion awareness.

However, transmotion awareness describes only a sense of existing within a spiritual world. I subscribe to the pragmatist maxim that knowledge needs to be useful. Peirce writes that we need to consider the effects that theories have toward the "practical bearings [that exist within] the object of our conception" (Peirce, 1878, p. 294). What we conceive as these effects, then, is the whole of our conception of the object (Peirce, 1878). How we understand what an object is to be is how we understand what an object is. The pragmatic maxim is also implied within Native American philosophy (Lokensgard, 2003; Pratt, 2002). Transplanar wisdom (Gladstone, 2014) helps us understand what the object that we call spirituality is to be.

TRANSPLANAR WISDOM

I earlier defined spirituality as an active awareness of an animate tangible and intangible world beyond oneself and an extrasensory connectedness with it. Transplanar wisdom facilitates this awareness.

Relationships within Indian Country are important for individuals' understanding about their place within a community. But in the Native sense, *place* means much more than simply occupying a physical, static, in-the-moment geographic location. Place is dynamic, extending beyond a geographic position on a map. It is not possible to walk up to a directory in a transplanar mall and see an arrow pointing to a specific spot and saying, "You are here." To say that you are in one specific location denies your acceptance that you can be somewhere else simultaneously. De Mello & Stroud (1990) said that spirituality is awareness, an idea supported by several Native philosophers (Cajete, 2000, 2004; Cordova 2007; Deloria, Jr. 2006; Fixicp, 2003). This awareness includes the animate and supposedly inanimate.

David Boje's recent work in storytelling theory reaches into the quantum world (Boje & Gladstone, 2011). In quantum storytelling, stories are deconstructed into narratives (Boje, 2001), existing as strings. These narrative strings exist as quantum spirals, rising up from their source and allowing one point of a narrative string to reach directly across to another (Boje, 2012). This quantum storytelling approach helps us understand the individual influences that exist within organization discourse upon which organization storytelling occurs.

Native transplanar wisdom is applicable the same way and is applicable to understanding Native organizations. However, rather than being a uniplanar spiral, narrative strings approach us from multiple angles. By being conscious of these narrative strings approaching us from multiple angles, we become aware of and appreciate a tangible and intangible world beyond our self and have an extrasensory connectedness with it. The tangible is the world that we can see, touch, and feel with our physical senses, about which we can read and hear and observe stories. The intangible are the stories that we accept as real, stories from our present, our written past, our past oral tradition, although they weren't personally lived by us, and our futures. Awareness of these transplanar stories influences our wisdom. This wisdom is quite dynamic: I will illustrate this via the *dynamic medicine wheel.*

THE DYNAMIC MEDICINE WHEEL

The Native American medicine wheel is often used in the Native wellness movement, a holistic integrative approach for understanding, diagnosing, and

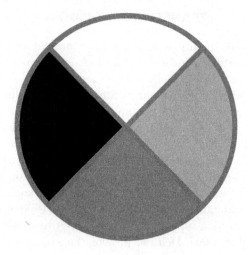

Figure 2.1   Native American medicine wheel (Gladstone, 2014).

managing an individual's physical and temporal place within a larger complex transplanar world. In wellness, the medicine wheel is commonly depicted as a circle separated into four equal parts, each section representing an aspect of wellness (Figure 2.1), most often wellness being a composition of physical, mental, emotional, and spiritual components. The medicine wheel as a metaphor is not limited only to wellness; Cowan (1995) has demonstrated its applicability to organization studies. Cowan and I agree that in addition to the four components listed above, there exists a social component. I therefore briefly integrate the mental and emotional aspects of wellness and insert social wellness into the vacated quadrant of the model.

Unfortunately the wellness movement illustrates the medicine wheel as a static two-dimensional image (Figure 2.1). This two-dimensional representation limits the medicine wheel to four quadrants and does not reflect dynamic influences of transplanar wisdom. Transplanar wisdom is fluid and dynamic and is best represented by a spinning wheel (Figure 2.2).

At this point, however, the weakness of a single-plane wheel remains, limited to representing four directions. This model also does not fit with a Native American blessing event, called a *smudge* in some tribes. During a smudge you will see the celebrant acknowledge not only the four cardinal directions—east, south, west, and north—but also above and below plus the center of all these directions. When taking in these multiple directions and connecting each point together simultaneously, the medicine wheel takes on the illusion of a moving sphere (Figure 2.3).

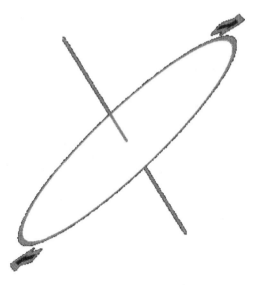

Figure 2.2   Dynamic medicine wheel (Gladstone, 2014).

Figure 2.3   Dynamic multiplanar medicine wheel (Gladstone, 2014).

Transplanar Wisdom as a Pragmatic Ideal for Spirituality

The pragmatist maxim is helpful for seeing place as a way for understanding what is, but place is only one aspect of this understanding. People and societies are not static; they move continuously in both place and time. This movement creates experience. We gain experience by interacting with the world. This interaction is not passive. Because we experience an active world, we are able, over time, to make inferences about it (Hookway, 2010). Native American oral traditions, such as Napi and other trickster stories, are a process for people to listen to experiences from which they can make their own inferences about the world around them. Integrating an appreciation for the spiritual aspects of transplanar wisdom may be useful for discovering what contributes to these inferences.

SUMMARY

In this chapter I shared an understanding of Native spirituality and described it as a conscious awareness of a world much greater than us, one that we can both see and feel with physical senses and with senses beyond our bodies. Because everything in this world is animate, we are equal with it, and since we are equals with this world, we can never dominate it. When we have such a spiritual connection with the world, we understand and appreciate our responsibility to it. We gain this extrasensory appreciation via transplanar wisdom, the source of which comes from our past, present, and future that approach from multiple directions and can be understood through stories.

As with all story, this chapter does not end after these words conclude. Rather, I expect it to continue as an inspiration into further inquiry into organization research, especially in spirituality, ethics, and cultural values as strategic resources for management. Work in the latter is a natural extension of Muller's (2000) work exploring community values and strengths for designing management education suitable for tribal business (Verbos, Kennedy, & Gladstone, 2011) and public administration.

NOTE

1. Adapted from Bullchild (1985) and Grinnell (1962).

REFERENCES

Barad, K. (2007). *Meeting the universe halfway: Quantum physics and the entanglement of matter and meaning.* Durham, NC: Duke University Press.

Boje, D. M. (2001). *Narrative methods for organizational and communication research.* London, England: Sage.

Boje, D. M. (2012). *Quantum spirals for organization consulting.* Unpublished manuscript, revised August 1, 2012. Retrieved from http://business.nmsu.edu/~dboje/448/QUANTUM%20SPIRALS%20for%20Business%20Consulting%20a%20book%20by%20David%20M%20Boje%20July%209%202012.pdf

Boje, D. M., & Gladstone, J. (2011). Academic storytelling consultancy supporting a local arts scene: An agential realist and socioeconomic approach to management perspective. In S. M. Adams & A. Zanzi (Eds.), *Preparing better consultants: The role of academia* (pp. 165–183). Charlotte, NC: Information Age.

Bruce, W. M. (2000). Public administrator attitudes about spirituality: an exploratory study. *American Review of Public Administration, 30*(4), 460–472.

Bullchild, P. (1985). *The sun came down: The history of the world as my Blackfeet elders told it.* San Francisco, CA: Harper & Row.

Cajete, G. (2000). *Native science: Natural laws of interdependence.* Santa Fe, NM: Clear Light.

Cajete, G. (2004). Philosophy of Native science. In A. Waters (Ed.), *American Indian thought: Philosophical essays* (pp. 45–57). Malden, MA: Blackwell.

Chouinard, Y. (2005). *Let my people go surfing: The education of a reluctant businessman.* New York, NY: Penguin Press.

Cordova, V. F. (2007). *How it is: The Native American philosophy of V. F. Cordova* (K. D. Moore, K. Peters, T. Jojola, & A. Lacy, Eds.). Tucson: University of Arizona Press.

Cowan, D. A. (1995). Rhythms of learning: Patterns that bridge individuals and organizations. *Journal of Management Inquiry, 4*(3), 222–246.

Deloria Jr., V., Deloria, B., Foehner, K., & Scinta, S. (Eds.). (1999). *Spirit & reason: The Vine Deloria, Jr. reader.* Golden, CO: Fulcrum.

Deloria Jr., V. (1994). *God is red: A Native view of religion.* Golden, CO: Fulcrum.

Deloria Jr., V. (2006). *The world we used to live in: Remembering the powers of the medicine men.* Golden, CO: Fulcrum.

de Mello, A., & Stroud, J. F. (1992). *Awareness: a de Mello spirituality conference in his own words.* New York, NY: Image Books/Doubleday.

Einstein, A. (1995). *Relativity* (R. W. Lawson, trans.). Amherst, NY: Prometheus Books. (Original work published in 1920)

Fixico, D. L. (2003). *The American Indian mind in a linear world: American Indian studies and traditional knowledge.* New York, NY: Routledge.

Foucault, M., Gros, F., Ewald, F., & Fontana, A. (2005). *The hermeneutics of the subject: Lectures at the Collège de France, 1981–1982.* New York, NY: Palgrave-Macmillan.

Frantz, K. (1999). *Indian reservations in the United States.* Chicago, IL: University of Chicago Press.

Garsombke, D. J., & Garsombke, T. W. (2000). Non-traditional vs. traditional entrepreneurs: Emergence of a Native American comparative profile of characteristics and barriers. *Academy of Entrepreneurship Journal, 6*(1), 93–100.

Gladstone, J. S. (2012). *Old man and coyote barter: An inquiry into the spirit of a Native American philosophy of business.* Thesis (PhD)–Business Administration, Order No. 3537767, New Mexico State University. ProQuest Dissertations and Theses, 284 pages.

Gladstone, J. S. (in press). Transplanar wisdom: the quantum spirit of Native American storytelling. In D. Boje & T. H. Wakefield (Eds.), *Being Quantum: Ontological storytelling in the age of antenarrative.* Newcastle upon Tyne, United Kingdom: Cambridge Scholars Publishing.

Grinnell, G. B. (1962). *Blackfoot Lodge Tales: The story of a prairie people.* Lincoln, NE: University of Nebraska Press.

Hogan, L. (2007). Foreword. In K. D. Moore, K. Peters, T. Jojola, & A. Lacy (Eds.), *How it is: The Native American philosophy of V. F. Cordova* (pp. vii–xii). Tucson: University of Arizona Press.

Hookway, C. (2010). *Pragmatism.* Stanford Encyclopedia of Philosophy. Retrieved from http://plato.stanford.edu/archives/spr2010/entries/pragmatism/

Jojola, T. (2004). Notes on identity, time, space and place. In A. Waters (Ed.), *American Indian thought: Philosophical essays* (pp. 87–96). Malden, MA: Blackwell.

Kostera, M. (2005). When spaces meet: Images of spirituality and organizing. *Tamara Journal Of Critical Postmodern Organization Science, 3*(3), 56–66.

Lokensgard, K. (2003). Native American pragmatism. *Journal of Critical Research Theory, 4*(3), 66–74.

Marques, J., Dhiman, S., & King, R. (2007). *Spirituality in the workplace: What it is, why it matters, how to make it work for you.* Fawnskin, CA: Personhood Press.

Miller, R. J. (2008). American Indian entrepreneurs: Unique challenges, unlimited potential. *Arizona State Law Journal. 40*(4), 1297–1342.

Mitroff, I. I. (2003). Do not promote religion under the guise of spirituality. *Organization, 10*(2), 375–382.

Mitroff, I. I., & Denton E. A. (1999). *A spiritual audit of corporate America: A hard look at spirituality, religion and values in the workplace.* San Francisco, CA: Jossey-Bass.

Muller, H. (2000). It takes a community to create an American Indian business and management course. *Journal of Management Education, 24*(2), 183–212.

Peirce, C. S. (1878). How to make our ideas clear. *Popular Science Monthly, 12*(17), 286–302.

Pratt, S. L. (2002). *Native pragmatism: Rethinking the roots of American philosophy.* Bloomington: Indiana University Press.

Smith, L.T. (2012). Decolonizing methodologies: Research and indigenous peoples (2nd Ed.). London, UK: Zed Books.

Stewart, D., & Schwartz, R. G. (2007). Native American business strategy: A survey of northwest US firms. *International Journal of Business Performance Management, 9*(3), 259–277.

Verbos, A. K., Kennedy, D. M., & Gladstone, J. S. (2011). "Coyote was walking": Management education in Indian Time. *Journal of Management Education, 35*(1), 51–65.

Vizenor, G. R. (1994). *Manifest manners: Postindian warriors of survivance.* Middletown, CT: Wesleyan University Press.

Vizenor, G. (1998). *Fugitive poses.* Lincoln: University of Nebraska Press.

CHAPTER 3

TAOISM

Chinese Cultural DNA and Its Implications for Business Strategy

Xuezhu Bai and Nicholas Morris

BACKGROUND

Arnold Toynbee, one of the 20th century's most illustrious historians, in *A Study of History*, concluded that the breakdown of civilizations is caused by large "loss of mental and moral balance" in the values and conduct of their leaders and constituents (Toynbee, 1947, p. 337). This was true of the fall of the Roman Empire, and some of the same features may be seen in the lack of ethical standards that led up to the Global Financial Crisis. Enduring and sustainable civilizations must adhere to an underlying ethical base that encapsulates the spiritual and moral principles of the Indigenous populations of which they are comprised. In the most successful civilizations, these principles are reflected in a guiding philosophy. A key example is Taoism, which has guided China for thousands of years and has underpinned its recent successes (Bai & Morris, 2015).

Other chapters of this book show how spiritual leadership can create commitment and productivity: how the Agni system from South America

Indigenous Spiritualities at Work, pages 33–50

embodies the spirit of reciprocity to strengthen the collective will, and how the Māori culture of reciprocal exchange, and its references to *wa* (time) and *ka* (fire), provide a method of defining cultural interactions. All of these have echoes in the symbolic structures that form the essence of Taoism.

Literature reveals that the persistence of Chinese civilization for thousands of years may be attributed to the moral strengths embedded in its philosophical foundations by both Taoism and Confucianism (Marinoff, 2009). Taoism is believed, in particular, to contribute to the fundamental value system in Confucianism that is at the core of Chinese civilization (Bai, 2012). Taoism and Confucianism were concerned primarily with inculcating and transmitting moral virtues of leaders in governing so as to keep social order and stability and to maintain harmony between diversified interest groups (Tang, Zhang, & Fang, 2001). The same virtues can be extended to the management of businesses, both locally and globally.

We argue in this chapter that the value system shared by both Taoism and Confucianism, namely the Yin-Yang and Five Virtues Theory, can be regarded as the "DNA" of Chinese civilization. Indeed, the ancient philosophical wisdom embodied in Yin-Yang and Five Virtues today serves as an effective guide for maintaining the survival and prosperity of Chinese society, permitting successful adaptation to changing circumstances, and even providing guidance in climates of adversity. China used this value system to govern a large population effectively and to maintain the continuation of a large "central kingdom" for thousands of years (Bai, 2012; Liu, 2006; Zhang, 1992). So it is worthwhile to explore the logic and rationale of the value system shared by both Taoism and Confucianism that contributed to the miracle of unbroken Chinese civilization. How did the Chinese ancient philosophy manage to provide effective mechanisms for its rulers to maintain balance during periods of instability so it could thrive in times of opportunity? In what follows we therefore undertake an in-depth analysis of the value system or the "cultural DNA" embedded in Chinese civilization and seek to test its relevance and value in the strategy-making process in today's business world.

THE TAO-ORIENTED CONFUCIAN VALUE SYSTEM, THE CHINESE CULTURAL DNA

Taoism (Tao) is well accepted as the Indigenous philosophy of Chinese civilization and provides a framework of core values for the development of a mature Confucianism (Bai & Roberts, 2011). Although embracing various different disciplines in China, "Tao" is generally translated as "the universal way" or "the absolute truth" in philosophical studies. Taoism developed the Yin-Yang and five element theory, a universally accepted model of the universe that provided a rational and sophisticated theory to explain the complicated phenomena existing in the universe and mankind. This was subsequently accepted by Confucianism, which further developed it into a more comprehensive Confucian five-virtue theory from around 200 BC. The Confucian five-virtue theory was developed and promoted by many great Confucian masters at different times and became the core value system in the Confucianism that played its role as the dominant ideology in China before Communist China was established in 1949 (Bai, 2012).

In this chapter, we describe this five-virtue theory as the Tao-oriented Confucian value system, due to the fact that it was evolved originally from Taoism. Its philosophy of moral virtues, codified as rules or principles for human society has been regarded as one of the wisest revelations for mankind (Liu, 2006; Shan, 1993). The Tao-oriented Confucian Value System has been utilized for thousands of years in China for selecting and cultivating capable leaders and guiding their behaviours in their daily administration (Bai, 2012; Liu, 2006; Zhang, 1992).

The following framework is a model of the Yin-Yang and five element theory of Taoism, initially used to explain the basic movement and the relationship of the five major energies (wood, fire, earth, metal, and water) in the universe (Xie, 1989; Yu & Yu, 2005). However, at a later stage it was used and developed by Confucianism to describe how the five virtues (benevolence, propriety, faithfulness, justice, and wisdom in parallel to the five energies) should be cultivated and applied in society through a series of Taoist and Confucian meditation exercises such as tai chi, qigong, and other Taoist and Confucian religious rituals, following the rules of Tao in the universe. We describe the combined system as the "Tao-oriented Model of the Universe and Mankind" (Figure 3.1).

The above diagram provides an abstract framework demonstrating the evolution and movement of the universe. It postulates that the fundamental energy "Chi," making up everything in the universe, originates from nothing (the void) and eventually returns to nothing. The Chi or energy combines two opposite forces—Yin (the black part, passive force) and Yang (the white part, proactive force), which depend on each other for existence. Within each force there is a seed of its opposite force to enable it to grow into its opposite, which reveals that everything in the universe runs and evolves in a cyclic manner.

The framework highlights the truth that everything combines two opposite forces and emphasizes the co-existence of opposite forces in the universe (Bai, 2012; Shan, 1993). Some universal rules of every existence in the universe are generalized by Taoism as follows:

- Self-existence: Tao is self-existent, born before the universe.
- The unity of heaven and mankind: "Mankind follows the rule of the Earth, the Earth follows the rules of Heaven or the Universe, the

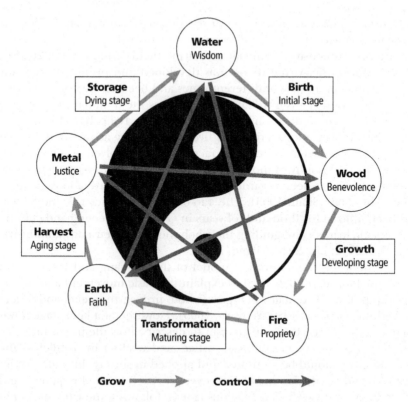

Figure 3.1 Tao-Oriented Model of the Universe and Mankind

Heaven or the Universe follows the rule of Tao, and Tao follows its own nature" (Lao Tzu, 2006).

- Dialectics of the Opposite Forces: "Tao exists as the movement of Yin and Yang", "Every existence combines Yin and Yang" (Liu, 2006, pp. 422–423). Everything combines two opposite forces (Yin and Yang), which co-exist in the universe.
- Golden mean principle: No extremist views should be called Tao.
- Interdependence of the opposite forces: "Yin depends on Yang's existence and vice versa" (Liu, 2006, p. 438).
- Interchangeability of the opposite forces: "Termination of Yin follows by the beginning of Yang, and vice versa" (Liu, 2006, p. 441).
- Infiniteness: Tao is not limited with boundaries either internally or externally.
- Eternal changing: "Changing is the universal law" (Liu, 2006, p. 449). Everything is in the process of eternal changes, in a cyclic manner for upward or downward evolution.

In addition, the Tao-oriented Confucian value system explains that Yin and Yang are parents of everything in the universe, and they give birth to the five most fundamental energies, or the so-called "five elements": wood, fire, earth, metal, and water, which exist in all living matter. According to Taoism, the rule of Yin and Yang is the fundamental law for everything in the universe, and the five-energy rule provides more subtle rules for all existing matter in the universe (Bai, 2008). Figure 3.1 demonstrates a dynamic cycle where Wood energy gives birth to Fire energy, Fire to Earth, Earth to Metal, and Metal to Water, which then returns to Wood. Nevertheless, each energy controls its opposite and keeps a good balance of other elements functioning in the universe. The Tao-oriented Confucian Value System describes the universe as made up of the five fundamental energies, and human beings too are microcosms of the universe that follow the operating rules of the five energies (Liu, 2006). Table 3.1 describes some basic functions and virtues of the five major energies in the universe.

The principles of the Tao-oriented value system have been applied to nearly all aspects of Chinese ancient disciplines. Since everything that is out of Tao thus follows the law of Yin and Yang and its associated five-element theories, it has provided the guideline for Chinese politics, military, arts and agricultural practices (Feng, 2004; Tang et al., 2001). For example, *The Art of War* by Sun Tzu, Chinese traditional medicine, Chinese martial arts, Mao Zedong's military strategy, and even most recently Deng Xiaoping's

TABLE 3.1   Content of Tao-Oriented Confucian Model of Five-Elements and Associated Rules

Name	Wood	Fire	Earth	Metal	Water
Stage	Infancy	Youth	Maturity	Declining	Dying
Feature	Yang	Yang	Neutral	Yin	Yin
Function	Growing	Developing	Transforming	Harvesting (Restricting)	Storing (Inertia)
Virtues	**Benevolence**	**Propriety**	**Faithfulness**	**Justice**	**Wisdom**
Nature	Yang— positive, dynamic and masculine	Yang (greater in degree)— positive, dynamic and masculine	Neutral— balanced	Yin— passive, static and feminine	Yin (greater in degree)— passive, static and feminine
Growing pattern	Grow into Fire	Grow into Earth	Grow into Metal	Grow into Water	Grow into Wood
Controlling pattern	Control Earth	Control Metal	Control Water	Control Wood	Control Fire

economic policy of reforming and opening up are all brilliant applications guided by Taoist principles (Bai, 2008; Jin, 2005).

IMPLICATIONS FOR BUSINESS STRATEGY MAKING

The Tao-oriented Confucian value system as a philosophy emphasizes a holistic perspective in its exploration of the origin and rules of the universe and mankind and includes both a macro and a micro approach that provide dialectic investigation of all the subjects covered. For modern business, although we have made significant progress in the application of Sun Tzu's strategy of war and some principles of Confucianism in marketing and business competition, there has so far been no systematic application of the ancient Tao-oriented Confucian value system in organizational operation and business strategy making. Since the organizational environment system and social-economic environment system are systems existing in human society, according to Taoism they should without exception follow the rules and principles designated by the Tao-oriented Confucian value system. Hence we seek to apply the Tao-oriented Confucian value system to modern business strategy-making processes and to test its reliability and validity.

To test whether the Tao-oriented Confucian value system is relevant to modern business, it is crucial to know if phenomena like Yin-Yang forces and the five-element factors exist in modern organizations. The presence of such factors in an organization is the key to applying the Tao-oriented Confucian value system to the process of business strategy making. From a deliberate study of economic and business textbooks (Bass, 1990; Hitt, Ireland, & Hoskisson, 2008; Johnson & Scholes, 2008), we know that things, events, or situations that occur inside or outside an organization that affect the way a business operates are called "driving forces." It is generally agreed that there are two kinds of driving forces: internal driving forces and external driving forces, which can be regarded as Yin and Yang forces that directly impact an organization.

At the micro level of an organization, internal driving forces refer to those that occur inside the business and are generally under the control of the enterprise. For example, micro factors in an organization could consist of machinery and equipment, technological capacity, organizational culture, management systems, financial management, and employee morale.

Following the principles of Taoism, we can simplify and categorize internal factors into five major internal forces that are divided into Yin, Yang, and neutral categories:

Technology: technological capacity, machinery and equipment, and productivity

Finance: financial situation and its management
System: management system, organizational structure, regulations, and rules
Culture: organizational values, mission, customs, group norms, and others
People: leaders, employees and their scale, quality, and morale
Yang: technology (wood, growing force), finance (fire, development force)
Yin: system (metal, restricting force), culture (water, inertia force)
Neutral: people (earth, transforming force)

To make such a division, we have relied on a number of features of Taoism: first of all, according to Taoism, an enterprise should contain two major contradictory and dialectic forces—Yang (dynamic and proactive) and Yin (static and passive). In an enterprise, technology and finance are usually the dynamic and driving force for development, which fall into categories of wood and fire. In contrast to technology and finance, system and culture are the restricting and regulating forces for an enterprise, which are therefore categorized into the static and passive metal and water. For instance, once system and culture are formed, they would exert some inertia on the development of the enterprise. They are in effect the organizational stabilizers and often act as hindrances to enterprise transformation. As for people, they are fundamentals for an enterprise in terms of transforming and impacting the other four factors in the enterprise, which therefore can be categorized into the neutral and transforming force of Earth.

The interrelationship of technology, finance, system, culture, and people is also consistent with functions of the Taoist model. For instance, their growing relationship in the system follows the Five-Force Growing Pattern: Technological factors push forward productivity of an enterprise, which subsequently increases financial flow, financial performance improves quality and morale of people, people serve as the fundamentals for creating the organizational system, the system enhances the uniqueness of organizational culture, and unique organizational culture would further provide an environment for introducing new technology to the enterprise. The following diagram shows more clearly their growing relationship:

Technology → Finance → People → System → Culture →
New Technology

The restricting relationship between them, unsurprisingly, also follows that of the Five-Force Restricting Pattern: System regulates and restricts the application of technology (including equipment and machinery), finance decides how a system works (such as management structure and its associated regulations), technology restricts the scale and quality of people, people decide the mode of organizational culture, and organizational culture

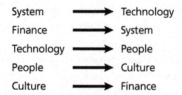

Figure 3.2 Restricting relationships.

guides the financial pattern in an enterprise. The relationship between them is shown in Figure 3.2.

As the Tao-oriented Confucian value system always emphasizes self-awareness of one's own situation before making a strategy, to make business strategy, it is necessary for leaders to be fully aware of the internal context of their enterprises first, then follow the principles of virtues to implement various strategies. From this sense, we have designed an internal strategy-making model (Figure 3.3) based on Tao-oriented Confucian Value principles to guide leaders to predict and make the right strategies.

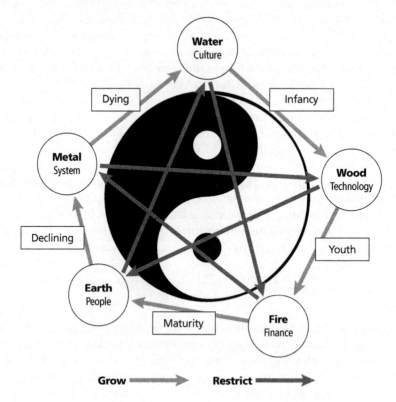

Figure 3.3 Tao-oriented Confucian model of inter-environment analysis.

According to this model, although all five forces are important to an enterprise and must be taken into consideration for strategic decisions, each force plays a decisive role at a particular stage. For example, technology is decisive in the infant stage of an enterprise, finance in its youth stage, people in its maturing stage, system in its declining stage, and culture in its dying stage. Therefore, different strategies should be applied in organizations at different stages for better operation and development of the organization. As a result, in an infant organization, technology-leading strategies should be applied. Similarly, capital-leading strategies should be deployed in young and fast-developing organizations, human resources-leading strategies for in stable and maturing organizations, system re-engineering strategies in rigidly bureaucratic and declining organizations, and culture-transforming strategies in dying organizations.

As each stage requires different virtues to guide the strategy, leaders in an infant organization are advised to follow the principle of benevolence to encourage technological innovation and tolerate the mistakes of innovative and creative talents. Only in this way can an infant organization improve its technological level and accumulate sufficient innovative people to enter the next stage. Similarly, leaders in the fast-developing stage need to follow the principle of propriety to implement a capital-leading strategy. Such leaders should not be afraid of making bold investments to enable fast expansion; however, they should also be warned not to overuse the strength of the organization, for example by establishing too many subcompanies or borrowing too much from banks to finance ambitious expansion plans; otherwise the organization may collapse. Leaders in a stable and maturing organization should be faithful and loyal to the organization in the implementation of a human resources-leading strategy, and they are also required to be honest to all people in the organization. Only in this way would they be able to attract the best people and make them contribute to the development of the organization. In a rigidly bureaucratic and declining organization, it is vital for leaders to use their powers to re-engineer the systems in the organization, guided by justice and fairness. They should not tolerate wrongdoing in the organization; they should dare to abolish outdated regulations and systems and to streamline the workforce so as to revitalize the organization. Leaders in a dying organization are required to follow the principle of wisdom to change the decayed culture of the organization. They should be able to provide an inspiring vision and values so as to encourage people to make changes in the organization. Without successfully changing the decaying and dying culture, the leaders would not be able to lead the dying organization into a new cycle.

Table 3.2 gives a summary of the internal strategy making of an organization at different stages, following the principles of Taoism.

TABLE 3.2 Content of Tao-Oriented Confucian Model of Internal Strategy Making

Stage	Infancy	Youth	Maturity	Declining	Dying
Function	Growing	Developing	Transforming	Restricting	Inertia
Five forces	Technology (Wood)	Finance (Fire)	People (Earth)	System (Metal)	Culture (Water)
Virtues	Benevolence	Propriety	Faithfulness	Justice	Wisdom
Strategy	Technology leading	Capital leading	Human resources leading	System reengineering	Culture transforming
Description	Technological capacity, machinery and equipment, and productivity	Financial activities associated with productivity	Leaders, employees and their scale, quality, and morale	Management system, organizational structure, regulations and rules	Organizational values, mission, customs, group norms, and others
Methods	1. build up Wood (self) 2. build up Water (mother) to accelerate Wood (child) to grow 3. restrict Metal (ruler) to provide a relax environment for Wood(subject)	1. build up Fire (self) 2. build up Wood (mother) to accelerate Fire (child) to grow 3. restrict Water (ruler) to provide a dynamic environment for Fire (subject)	1. build up Earth (self) 2. build up Wood (Mother) to control Earth (child) to prevent enter the declining stage 3. build up Water (subject) to counter-balance Earth(ruler)	1. reduce Metal (Mother) to prevent declining tendency 2. build up Wood (subject) to counter-balance Metal 3. build up Fire(Ruler) to control Metal	1. reduce Metal (mother) to slow down dying process 2. build up Water (self) to make ready for a new birth to Wood 3. build up Earth (ruler) to stop dying tendency 4. build up Fire(subject) to counter balance Water 5. build up Wood(child) to enable a new beginning

At the macro level of an organization, understanding the external environment enables leaders to know better the macro context for their business strategy and what necessary approaches should be utilized to better implement their strategy. We can use a similar approach, guided by an analysis of the textbooks of economics and business (Hitt et al., 2008; Johnson & Scholes, 2008), to find the five driving forces in the external environment of an organization. We can find various environmental factors defined in different ways in the literature in a number of macro-environmental analysis tools, such as SLEPT analysis (Social, Legal, Economic, Political, and Technological); STEPE analysis (Social, Technical, Economic, Political, and Ecological); PESTLE analysis (Political, Economic, Social, Technological, Legal and Environmental); PESTLIED analysis (Political, Economic, Social, Technological, Legal, International, Environmental, Demographic); STEEPLE analysis (Social/Demographic, Technological, Economic, Environmental, Political, Legal, and Ethical); and many others. Following the principles of Taoism, we can then summarize the major five forces in the external environment as follows:

> **Yang:** technological (wood, growing force), economic (fire, development force)
>
> **Yin:** political/legal (metal, restricting force), sociocultural (water, inertia force)
>
> **Neutral:** demographic/environmental (earth, transforming force)

The five environmental forces (or factors) are in fact the positivist outcome from the macro-environmental analysis in the business textbooks. To make such a division for the five essential environment factors, we draw on the following evidence: First, according to the theory of political economy, the economic activities of human society contain two major contradictory and dialectic forces—the productivity (dynamic Yang) and the productive relationship (passive Yin). In this relationship, productivity is the prime driver of the development of human society, or in other terms, of economic and technical forces, which are the tangible form of productivity and the driving force for human society. Technological and economic forces are positive, dynamic, and proactive, attributes that fall into the categories of wood and fire. In addition, in contrast to economic and technological forces, political, legal, and sociocultural forces are restricting and regulating forces for economic performance and technological application. They are therefore categorized into the passive and static metal and water. For instance, once the political, legal, and sociocultural entities are formed, they exert inertia on productivity and society. They are in effect social stabilizers and often act as hindrances to economic and social transformation. Demographic and environmental forces can be categorized as the neutral force of Earth.

Not only technological, economic, political/legal, sociocultural, demographic/environmental factors demonstrate the attributes of Yin-Yang and five forces, but the inter-relationship between them is also consistent with functions of the Tao-oriented Confucian model. To be more accurate, their growing relationship within the system follows the five-force growing pattern: technological factors push forward economic growth, and economic development improves the quality of demography and environment, demographic and environmental factors provide the fundamentals for political/legal realities, and political/legal forces lead the direction of social and cultural activities. Figure 3.4 shows more clearly their growing relationship.

The restricting relationship between them, unsurprisingly, also follows that of the five-force restricting pattern: political/legal factors regulate the application of science and technology (including military technology), and economic context decides the state of political/legal activities; while technological force lays boundaries for the scale and quality of demography and environment, and demographic and environment factors decide the sociocultural mode and its development trend; finally, sociocultural factors restricts the selection of economic development patterns. The relationship between them is described Figure 3.5.

To better understand the external environment of an organization and to better implement strategy, a dynamic analytical model of the macro-environment based on the Tao-oriented Confucian value system can be established for external analysis in business (Figure 3.6). This model provides an overview of the different macro-environmental factors and also shows a clear picture of the relationships of each component in the real-world situation and the relevant virtues needed for each phase.

By consulting the literature of existing economic and management textbooks (Bass, 1990; Hitt et al., 2008; Johnson & Scholes, 2008), with reference to Taoist principles in relation to macro-environmental factors, we

Figure 3.4

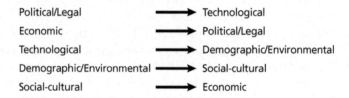

Figure 3.5   Five-force restricting pattern.

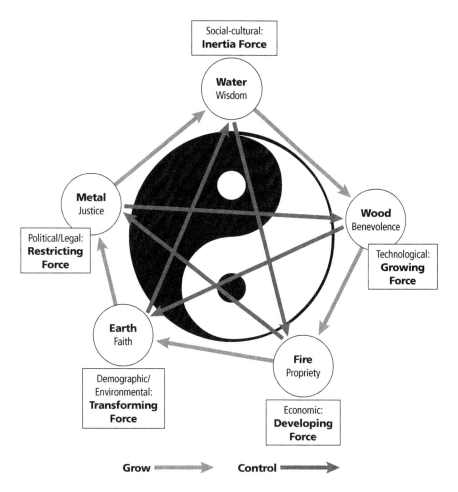

Figure 3.6 Tao-oriented Confucian model of macro-environment analysis.

categorize relevant content for the Tao-oriented Confucian Model of Macro-Environment Analysis in Table 3.3.

The strength of this model is that it combines existing findings in major management textbooks and explains the dynamic situation that exists in the real business world. In general, the cycle of a macro system of an economy following the natural cycle of a revolutionary technology or productive instrument—for example, the steam engine was the major revolutionary technology or productive instrument in the era of the industrial economy, while the computer is that of the contemporary era of the IT and knowledge economy. Table 3.4 describes the four eras of human society to date, which clearly shows that the introduction of iron tools, steam engines, and computer technology brought about a new cycle of human economy and society.

TABLE 3.3   Content in Tao-oriented Confucian Model of Macro-Environment Analysis

Period	Infancy	Youth	Maturity	Declining	Dying
Five Energy	Wood	Fire	Earth	Metal	Water
Environmental Force	Technological	Economic	Demographic/Environmental	Political/Legal	Social-cultural
Virtues	Benevolence	Propriety	Faithfulness	Justice	Wisdom
Function	Growing	Developing	Transforming	Restricting	Inertia
Content	New, innovative and revolutionary technology, materials, skills and methods coming up and start to change the development pattern in the economy. These productive factors are driving force for economy and society.	Active and dynamic state appears in domestic and international economic activities, and industries and economy demonstrate positive development trend. The economic factors contribute to development power.	Stable and maturing state appears in demography, education, health, labor market, welfare environment, and other relevant factors. The demographic and environmental factors make up the transforming force for economic and social achievements.	Policies, regulations, legislative and administrative systems are getting more rigid and over-complicated. These political and legal factors contribute to the restricting power of economy and society.	Economic recession and political corruption result in an unstable society. Social and cultural factors such as customs, historical values, religion, education, and others play an increasing role in society. These social-cultural factors provide inertia force to prevent rapid changes in society; however, new thoughts are cropping up at this time.
Characteristics of the Period	Active technological innovation in economy and society with open and tolerant political environment	Rapid economic development with positive and liberal political environment	Stable and mature society and economy with solidity political environment	Economic immobility and social monotony with a rigid and conservative political environment	Economic recession, crisis and social decay with a corrupt and irresponsible political environment. Time for new thoughts cropping up

TABLE 3.4   Four Economic Eras of Human Economy (Bai, 2012, p. 58)

Era / Features	Primary Economy	Agricultural Economy	Industrial Economy	Knowledge Economy
Revolutionary Technology	Stone tools and other primary tools	Iron tools and other metal tools	Steam engine	Computer
Society Form	Primary	Agricultural	Industrial	IT
Social Unit	Tribes	Extended families	Families	Families and individuals
Habitation	Natural or man-made simple shelters	Villages	Townships	Villages and townships
Major Wealth	Fruits and game	Grains and tamed animals	Resources and products	Knowledge
Wealth-making qualifications	Luck and instinct	Land and climate	Capital and labor	Website and brainpower
Factors for success	Agility and practice	Strength and experience	Resources, equipment, and mobilization	Creativity for knowledge
Productive feature	Mobility and randomicity	Seasonal changes	Fixed wage system and clear division of labor	Continuous study and exposure to information

The models of business strategy-making based on the Tao-oriented Confucian value system highlight the changes of contexts and relevant virtues for implementing strategies. Thus, they require relevant traits and behaviours of leaders to fit the changing circumstances. Leaders should adopt appropriate virtues and behaviours to fit in with the relevant business environment. Therefore, selecting the right personnel to be leaders will also strengthen the Tao-oriented Confucian models. Table 3.5 describes the best leaders and theories at the different organizational stages of development.

The above application of the Tao-oriented Confucian value system in the business strategy-making process has been largely consistent with practices and realities of daily operation in the business world. However, Tao-oriented Confucian models of business strategy making are more comprehensive and systematic than the existing tools of business strategy making. In addition, the Tao-oriented Confucian value system emphasizes virtues in the process of strategy making and implementation. In ancient China, a leader was required to be a saint with complete virtues and competence (Bai & Roberts, 2011), based on an analysis of the organization's situation by following the rule of Tao. As a result, Confucianism believes that a successful leader needs to continuously improve his or her virtues and competencies so as to meet all challenges in the rapidly changing world. However, as in the real-world situation,

TABLE 3.5 Tao-Oriented Confucian Model of Traits of Successful Leaders and Adaptive Leadership Theories

Name	Wood	Fire	Earth	Metal	Water
Relationship between leaders and followers	Proactive and relatively strong	Proactive and very strong	Match proactive or passive	Passive and relatively strong	Passive and very strong
Traits of Leaders	Benevolence	Propriety	Faithfulness	Justice	Wisdom
Traits of successful leaders	Compassionate, easy-going, caring, listening to others, tolerance of mistakes	Doing things or treating followers appropriately, deciding or convincing by demonstrating good balance in actions and behaviours	Consistency of behaviors, faithful to words and acts, loyal to vision and mission, democratic way of doing things	Strong responsibility, doing things by law and regulations, justice on reward and punishment	Visionary, far-sighted, super-cognitive capability
Leadership style	Power of Embracing	Power of Convincing	Power of Cohesion	Power of Accountability	Power to inspire
Best theories	Charismatic	Traits/behavioral	Transformational/ Transitional or Transactional or Laissez Faire	Behavioral (Managerial)	Visional
Organizational stage	Infancy	Youth	Maturity	Declining	Dying

it is difficult to find a saint with complete virtues and competencies: Human beings usually have shortcomings in their traits or competencies. Therefore, the Tao-oriented Confucian model suggests that to ensure the success of an organization, a satisfactory leadership team consisting of different kinds of leaders balanced in traits and competences is a more practical option.

CONCLUSION

From the above discussion of how the Tao-oriented Confucian value system may be applied to the business strategy-making process, it is clear that the philosophy of Tao-oriented Confucianism highlights virtue-dominating approaches in the process of leaders making and implementing strategies. In addition, by following the dialectical nature of the major driving forces in an organization, the Tao-oriented Confucian models of strategy making reveal the subtle and dynamic relationships of depending, conflicting, and transforming in all the forces and therefore requires leaders to follow the changes and make the most appropriate strategy at different organizational stages to enable business success. It is thus not surprising that many scholars attribute the persistence of Chinese civilization for thousands of years to the value system shared by both Taoism and Confucianism, and both the moral strengths and the strategic wisdom embedded in them have enabled the Chinese to maintain harmony with diversity and tolerate conflicting forces in the historical evolution of Chinese civilization. The Tao-oriented Confucian value system was the greatest philosophy for ancient rulers to govern a vast country by naturally assimilating and changing different races and religions in Chinese history. Similarly, we believe that this philosophy should be able to benefit today's business world in the organizational strategy-making process.

In investigating the relevance and validity of the Tao-oriented Confucian value system in business strategy making, in this chapter we have utilized both the holistic approach of Taoism and approaches from the research outcomes of Western positivism. From the above discussion, we argue that the Tao-oriented Confucian value system is a philosophy that is able to integrate conflicting and confronting factors, and even competing theories, into one dynamic model. We believe that through a combination of the holistic Tao-oriented Confucian approach and the more analytic Western positivist approach, we can develop a more complete theory that may reflect the real business world.

REFERENCES

Bai, X. (2008). The thinking system of Taoism and leadership studies. *Theoretical Investigation, 1,* 142–146.

Bai, X. (2012). *Taoism for kings: Tao-oriented strategic leadership*, Shanghai: Far-East Publishing Corporation.

Bai, X., & Morris, N. (2015). China, economic Taoism and development: Different paradigms, different outcomes?, In Toohey, L, Picker, C., & Greenacre, J. (Eds.), *China in the new international economic order: New directions and changing paradigms* (pp. 211–224). Cambridge, UK: Cambridge University Press.

Bai, X., & Roberts, W. (2011). Taoism and its model of traits of successful leaders, *Journal of Management Development, 30*(7/8), 724–739.

Bass, B. M. (1990). Bass and Stogdill's handbook of leadership (2nd ed.). New York, NY: Free Press.

Feng, Y. L. (2004). *The new edition of Chinese philosophy.* Beijing: The People's Press.

Hitt, M. A., Ireland, R. D., & Hoskisson, R. E. (2008). Strategic management: Competitiveness and globalization (8th ed.). Independence, KY: South-Western, Thomson Learning

Jin, W. K. (2005). On the comprehensive studies and holistic approaches of Taoism. *Theoretical Investigation, 3.*

Johnson, G., & Scholes, K. (2008). *Exploring corporate strategy* (8th ed.). London, England: Pearson Education Limited.

Lao Tzu. (2006). *Tao Te Ching, Chen Zhong's version.* Changchun, China: Culture and History Press of Jilin.

Liu, C. L. (2006). *Chinese image science—Yiching, Taoism, military, and medicine.* Beijing, China: Press of Social Science Literature

Marinoff, L. (2009). Landmarks in human progress: Reflections on the 5th Global China Business Meeting. Retrieved from http://www.loumarinoff.com/Global%20China%20Business%20Meeting%20report%20LM%20final.pdf

Shan, Q. (1993). *Figures of Yiching in Zhou dynasty.* Shanxi, China: People's Education Press.

Tang, Y. J., Zhang, Y. N., & Fang, M. (2001). *Confucianism* (A grand exposition of Chinese culture series). Peking, China: Peking University Press.

Toynbee, A. (1947). *A study of history* (Vol. 1: Abridgement of Volumes I–VI, 337). Oxford, UK: Oxford University Press.

Xie, S. L. (1989). *Heaven, mankind and images: An introduction to the history of yin yang and five elements theory.* Jinan, Shandong, China: Shandong Literature and Arts Press.

Yu, X. X., & Yu, Y. (2005). *The theories and practices of feng shui.* Beijing, China: Guangming Daily Press.

Zhang, K. Z. (1992). *The history of Chinese thinking.* Taipei, Taiwan: The Water Buffalo.

CHAPTER 4

TE WHARE AKO

Architecture Speaks to Heart, Mind, and Spirit

Ella Henry

INTRODUCTION

This chapter explores the relationship between physical spaces and meta-physical well-being, within the context of Māori knowledge and spirituality, as a form of practical wisdom. It presents a personal narrative, a form of autoethnography (Learmonth & Humphreys, 2012), about the impacts of specific physical spaces, *te whare ako*, on my journey as a Māori student and academic in tertiary institutions. This narrative is couched within a discussion of the "practical wisdom" literature, and in particular, the literature from Indigenous sources.

Māori are the Indigenous people of Aotearoa, New Zealand. A *whare wānanga* is an institution of higher learning, a set of buildings, and also a process for in-depth acquisition of arcane knowledge (that is, a building, *whare*, in which the community, *wānanga*, engage in higher learning and debate), which is most commonly associated with tertiary institutions. However, the term *whare ako* is utilized in this chapter to discuss educational

Indigenous Spiritualities at Work, pages 51–67
Copyright © 2015 by Information Age Publishing
51

marae (see Glossary for full translation), which form the basis of the narrative presented below. In traditional Māori society, the *marae* was the centre of the community, and it continues to be an important institution in contemporary society. Simmons and Voyle cite Ngata and Pomare (1992) when they note:

> The term *marae* refers to much more than a physical complex of buildings: It also embraces a human and spiritual dimension and has come to symbolise the essence of Maori health aspirations. . . . It is where a person has *turanga-waewae* (a place to stand), a sense of belonging or identity and where Maori values, cultural and health practices are reaffirmed. (Simmons & Voyle, 2003, p. 41)

Māori use the same verb, *ako*, for learning and teaching because of the symbiotic aspect of the two actions. The *whare* is a building, often glossed as a house. In Māori communities, a *whare* is frequently named for an ancestor, location, or event. *Te whare ako*, the concept of houses of learning and teaching, evolves out of the notion that teaching and learning occur in spaces and places that resonate with teachers and learners. The physical and metaphysical nature of those spaces and places speaks to *manawa* (heart), *hinengaro* (mind), and *wairua* (spirit).

MĀORI WISDOM

Spiller, Pio, Erakovic, and Henare (2011) focus on traditional Māori culture and values as the basis for analysing Māori knowledge and wisdom in the management context. They emphasize the "relational approach" of Māori culture and society: that is, a social system predicated on understanding the profound and intimate relationship between individuals, communities, and their physical and metaphysical environment. They draw on Māori values and note, "we present a wisdom position through an ethic of *kaitiakitanga* or stewardship," (2011, p. 223). They go on to state that "wisdom theorists seek to assist organizations to address increasing complexity, fragmentation, and uncertainty, which are accompanied by the call for more sustainable, equitable, and values-oriented organizations" (p. 224).

These Māori scholars draw together philosophy, culture, and business when they write, "Humans exist in a web of reciprocal relationships with many stakeholders apart from shareholders. A relational wisdom paradigm, using an integrated model to explain that wisdom, is constituted not only from what people in organisations think, but also how they relate and respond in practice" (Spiller et al., 2011, p. 224). This "ethic of stewardship" highlights the relationship between person and environment, which in ancient Māori society was encapsulated in the genealogical (*whakapapa*) connections that linked the individual to their place of origin. On this point, they write,

> According to a Māori perspective, well-being embraces a wide variety of rela-tionships as the business organization seeks to uplift and empower the *mana* [prestige, authority and spiritual power] of others—it is an ethic of power and the common good which is threaded into a fabric of existence.... Thus, wise organizations, according to a Māori world view, construct community with their customers, employees, and local people (communities), and, in doing so, deepen the connection with each other and with the place. They achieve this through the process of sharing common ground upon which an affinity and respect can grow" (Spiller et al., 2011, p. 226)

They also refer to *Mātauranga*, traditional Māori knowledge, which

> is about developing the creative powers of the mind, and of expanding hori-zons, and reaching beyond the limitations of circumstance and adversity. Our definition of wisdom involves the enlightened weaving of knowledge, exper-tise, and authority to nurture and unfold the life-force to achieve well being. We posit that acquiring wisdom is an unfolding nonlinear journey. (Spiller et al., 2011, p. 226)

Thus, Spiller and colleagues provide a theoretical and philosophical framework for incorporating traditional Māori values and beliefs into a management context. Earlier, one of the co-authors of that paper (Hena-re, 1998), argued that the fundamental ethics of traditional Māori society are derived from core beliefs that emphasize connection with the spiritual realm, the sacredness and vitality of all things, and the significance of reci-procity in human relations (cited in Henry & Pene, 2001). Henare states,

> Māori religion is not found in a set of sacred books or dogma, the culture is the religion. History points to Māori people and their religion being con-stantly open to evaluation and questioning in order to seek that which is *tika,* the right way. Maintaining *tika* is the means whereby ethics and values can be identified. (1998, p. 3)

Thus, spirituality is an expression of doing things the right way. In Māori that is glossed in a word derived from *tika*, as *tikanga*, the set of traditional cultural practices. For the purposes of this paper, the theoretical and philo-sophical framework proposed by Spiller et al., woven around an ethic of *kaitiakitanga* (stewardship), will be extended to include the ethic of *wairua-tanga* (spirituality).

On this point, Ka'ai and Higgins (2004), writing on Māori spirituality, refer to notions of *tapu* (sacred), *noa* (unrestricted, free from tapu), and *mana* (spiritual power) as primary, holistic Māori cultural concepts, which

TABLE 4.1   Whare Tapa Whā Model

	Taha Wairua	Taha Hinengaro	Taha Tinana	Taha Whānau
Focus	Spiritual	Mental	Physical	Extended family
Key aspects	The capacity for faith and wider communion	The capacity to communicate, think and feel	The capacity for physical growth and development	The capacity to belong, to care and to share
Themes	Health is related to unseen and unspoken energies	Mind and body are inseparable	Good physical health is necessary for optimal development	Individuals are part of a wider social system

Source: Durie, 1998

collectively form a spiritualistic worldview. This worldview links every living thing to the *atua* (ancestors, spiritual beings) through *whakapapa* (genealogy), connecting *taha wairua* (the spiritual, metaphysical dimension) and *taha kikokiko* (the physical dimension). Durie (1998) contributes to this analysis, having developed a framework for understanding and contributing to Māori health, through *Whare Tapa Whā*. The Whare Tapa Whā model (Table 4.1) identifies four dimensions of wellbeing, using the walls of a house as the metaphor for good health.

This model of Māori knowledge and wisdom is deeply rooted in a holistic view of the human being as an incorporation of physical, spiritual, and social dimensions, with a practical component embedded in ritual practice, all of which contribute to individual and community wellbeing and sustainability.

Practical Wisdom

The "practical wisdom" literature covers a diverse range of thinking. It incorporates analyses and understandings of intrinsic human qualities such as "wisdom" and "goodness," topics usually reserved for philosophy and theology. However, the "practical" component of wisdom suggests a less esoteric focus on the nature of wisdom and how it might be passed on.

According to Hamlin, Wynn, and Bloom (2007) and Wynn (2008), through their studies of infants and the foundations of moral cognition, "goodness" and "fairness" may be innate, and identifiable even in babies. Curnow (2008), focusing on the teaching and understanding of wisdom in Europe, states, "[T]he fifteenth and sixteenth centuries... marks the end of wisdom as a commonly shared cultural ideal and aspiration. After the

Renaissance, knowledge rather than wisdom would come to occupy the central stage in Western intellectual life" (p. 12). He goes on to acknowledge that "the philosophy of Descartes ushered in a new age of philosophical scepticism. Knowledge became, not only a philosophical problem in its own right, but also the pre-eminent one" (p. 14).

For Park and Peterson (2008), "Wisdom has long occupied the attention of psychologists, philosophers, educators, and theologians concerned with the good life and how to lead it" (p. 58). They have attempted to "unpack" wisdom, identifying its component parts and how those parts might best be taught. Their paper identifies strengths of character and ways of measuring them, using the VIA (Values in Action) Classification of Character Strengths (Table 4.2).

Park and Peterson go on to outline a comprehensive range of factors that enhance and encourage these character strengths, which can contribute to an education strategy (Table 4.3).

From another perspective, Berthrong (2008) provides an overview of the teachings of the Chinese philosopher Zhu, writing, "wisdom leads us to authentic humane virtue.... It is a vision of wisdom that leads to humane flourishing for all human beings and indeed the whole cosmos" (p. 109). Kemmis (2010) discusses wisdom by focusing on praxis and defines it from two perspectives, Aristotelian and Marxist. Therefore, it is either "action that is morally committed, and oriented and informed by traditions" (Aristotelian) (Kemmis, 2010, p. 9) or "understood as history-making action"

TABLE 4.2 Classification of Character Strengths

Character Strengths	Characteristics
Wisdom & Knowledge	Cognitive strengths that entail the acquisition and use of knowledge through creativity, curiosity, love of learning, open-mindedness, and wise counsel
Courage	Emotional strengths that involve the exercise of will to accomplish goals in the face of opposition, through authenticity, bravery, persistence, and zest for life
Humanity	The interpersonal strengths that involve tending and befriending others through kindness, love, and social intelligence
Justice	Civic strengths that underlie healthy community life, fostered by fairness, leadership, and teamwork
Temperance	Strengths that protect against excess, underpinned by forgiveness, modesty, prudence, and self-regulation
Transcendence	Strengths that forge connections to the larger universe and provide meaning through appreciation of beauty and excellence, gratitude, hope, humour and spirituality

Source: Park & Peterson, 2008, p. 62

TABLE 4.3   Encouraging Spirituality

Enabling Factors	Parental socialization
	Family cohesion
	Crisis (sometimes)
Societal Institutions	Formal religion
	Volunteer work
Deliberate Interventions	Conversion
	Faith-based initiatives
	Contact with nature

Source: Park & Peterson, 2008, p. 68

(Marxist) (Kemmis, 2010, 0 9). For Kemmis, "the principal objective for social science with a phronetic approach is to carry out analyses and interpretations of the status of values and interests in society aimed at social commentary and social action, *i.e.,* praxis" (2010, p. 15), whether it is "morally committed action" or "history-making action."

In another paper, Kemmis (2012) notes,

> Phronēsis cannot be understood outside of its relationship with praxis. Praxis is today understood in two broad ways. In the Anglo-American tradition, praxis is generally understood as 'right conduct', whereas in much of Europe it is understood as social action with moral and political consequences, that is, as 'socially consequential history-making action'. For the ancient Greeks, however, phronēsis was the disposition toward wisdom and prudence that orients praxis. (p. 149)

He provides a summary of these different perspectives and their concomitant dispositions and actions (see Table 4.4).

Kemmis concludes this discussion by stating,

> It thus might be that we are making a mistake when we hope to or try to teach phronēsis *directly.* If I am right, phronēsis can only be learned indirectly, as a result of committing ourselves, with others, to praxis and acting in praxis. Praxis teaches us when our actions are directed toward forming a better world for each and for all, and when it thus forms us because we pay attention to what happens to ourselves, to others, and to the world around us as a consequence of our actions. (2012, p. 159)

Further research on Phronēsis, or 'practical wisdom', includes the lyrical writing of Higgs (2012), who draws on Aristotle to tell the story of the three intellectual virtues:

> Episteme, a youth of some stature brought the virtue of independent knowledge. He loved science with a passion and applauded truths that were uni-

TABLE 4.4   Four Perspectives on Dispositions and Actions

	Theoretical perspective	Technical perspective	Practical perspective	Critical-emancipatory perspective
Aim	The attainment of knowledge or truth	The production of something	Wise and prudent judgment, acting rightly in the world	Overcoming irrationality, injustice, suffering, felt dissatisfactions
Disposition	Epistemē	Technē	Phronēsis	Critical
	The disposition to seek the truth for its own sake	The disposition to act in a true and reasoned way according to the rules of a craft	The moral disposition to act wisely, truly and justly; with both goals and means always open to review	The disposition toward emancipation from irrationality, injustice, suffering, felt dissatisfactions
Action	Theoria	Poiēsis	Praxis	Emancipatory
	Contemplation, involving theoretical reasoning about the nature of things	"Making" action, involving means–ends or instrumental reasoning to achieve a known objective	"Doing" action, involving practical reasoning about what is wise, right, and proper to do in a given situation	Collective critical reflection and action to overcome irrationality, injustice, suffering, harm, unproductiveness, or unsustainability

Source: Kemmis, 2012, p. 149

versal, invariable, and independent of context. Techne was the practical one. Her desire was to create and to learn how things worked and how to make things that suited the current task and goal. Her favourite answer was "it depends." Phronēsis was the quiet achiever. She often pondered over whether her planned actions would be wise and proper as well as practical. She was fascinated by two ideas praxis—a tantalising blend of reflective, right, and transformative practice and poiesis—developing technique through artistry and creativity. (p. 73)

In the prelude to her paper, Higgs writes of the student Novitius, who wanted to be wise like her master Veteratoris. Novitius stated, "I want someday to be wise like you, to make what I do make a positive difference to people's lives, so I need to accept the challenge of Phronēsis, to bring reflection, ethics, and practicality to my journey of becoming a good and wise practitioner" (Higgs, 2012, p. 74).

Finlay also contributes to this discussion, with a paper on praxis and reflexivity (Finlay, 2002). She notes that, "Reflexivity in qualitative research…has a long history. It has moved from introspection towards critical realist and subjective accounts and more recently towards highlighting the socio-political, post-modern context through deconstructing the research encounter" (2002, pp. 209–210). Further, Finlay states,

> [R]esearch is co-constituted, a joint product of the participants, researcher and their relationship.... We no longer seek to eradicate the researcher's presence—instead subjectivity in research is transformed from a problem to an opportunity.... In short, researchers no longer question the need for re-flexivity: the question is how to do it. (2002, p. 212)

She concludes, "Reflexivity as social critique offers the opportunity to utilize experiential accounts while situating these within a strong theoretical framework about the social construction of power" (Finlay, 2002, p. 222).

Prusak (2013) underpins his analysis by acknowledging the transition in management research from a focus on data, information and more recently knowledge, to a "clear resurgence with respect to a focus on wisdom" (Prusak, 2013, p. 312). He posits the reason for the resurgence as being "the failure of abundant, easy to find and use information and even knowledge to ensure moral, equitable, virtuous, positive and healthy organizations.... What is missing is often spoken of as 'values' or 'ideals', but can easily be understood as a form of wisdom" (Prusak, 2013, p. 312).

For McKenna, Rooney, and Kenworthy, "Wisdom was not a word that appeared in management, organisation, or leadership books until quite recently. In fact, it wasn't even taken seriously in psychology until the 1980s. Now, wisdom seems to be taken more seriously across both disciplines and domains" (2013, p. 306). McKenna and colleagues go on to note that the "wisdom in management" research has also embraced non-Western and nontraditional perspectives, but they noted there is a dearth of research on Indigenous forms of wisdom, though they do cite Māori (Spiller et al., 2011) and Australian Aboriginal (Sveiby & Skuthorpe, 2006) contributions to this field of inquiry.

In summary, this necessarily brief review of some of the practical wisdom literature complements the Māori worldview, and the consequent discussion in the the Māori academy about the importance of spirituality, as a set of cultural practices (tikanga) that draw together physical and metaphysical realms. *Wairuatanga*, the expression of spirituality, like *kaitiakitanga*, the expression of stewardship, are *tikanga* that embody social practices that enhance individual and collective wellbeing, and can be seen as a form of social action. They are also, in and of themselves, sources of knowledge and wisdom. That is, knowledge about how and why to do things in a specific manner, but also practical vehicles for the intergenerational transfer of wisdom about "doing things right" and "doing the right things" (Drucker, 2003). It is in this milieu that I present my "personal experience narrative" (Clandinin & Connelly, 1994).

PERSONAL NARRATIVE EXPERIENCE

I will begin, as Māori frequently do, at the beginning. I was born in Kaitaia in 1954, descendant of three of the six tribes of the Far North. My parents brought me to the city when I was six. We were part of the urban migration, fueled by what Dame Joan Metge called the "fantasy contagion" (King, 2003, p. 473), an idea that spread around the North like wildfire, that we were moving to a better life. We lived in West Auckland, where I found out for the first time that we were poor compared to our Pākeha neighbours. At fifteen I was kicked out of school for being a general miscreant, and for the next ten years I traveled extensively. Upon my return to New Zealand, at the age of thirty, I found myself pregnant and abandoned. A friend suggested I do some study, so I enrolled at Auckland Girls' Grammar as an adult student to do School Certificate English. My teacher there encouraged me to enroll in the New Start program at Auckland University, and it truly was a "new start." In February of 1986, with a babe-in-arms, I started a journey that has defined my life ever since. I expected at every turn to be exposed as a "dummy," an interloper. Instead, I discovered the true history of my country and my people, through the newly opened Māori studies department. In 1988, Waipapa Marae opened, and I found a new home: physically, intellectually, and spiritually.

The University of Auckland, *Te Whare Wānanga o Tamaki Makaurau,* is often represented by sandstone spires and cloisters, the clock tower at its helm, peering elegantly over Albert Park to Auckland's commercial and

Figure 4.1   Waipapa, University of Auckland.

business center. The School of Māori Studies and Waipapa Marae were far-flung outposts, at the bottom of the hill, when they opened in the late 1980s, in the shadow of human sciences and history. However, the University of Auckland was the first university in the city to acknowledge the unique and distinctive character of Māori knowledge and history by allowing the Māori studies department to become a stand-alone school, distinct from its origins in anthropology. Further, in February 1988, Waipapa Marae was opened to great fanfare. Named after the *Māori Pā*, which was once located on the foreshore below the current Marae, it is a magnificent example of traditional and contemporary carving and weaving styles. Pakariki Harrison was appointed the *Tōhunga Whakairo* (master carver). His wife Hinemoa, a weaving expert, helped design and weave the *Tukutuku* and *Kōwhaiwhai* panels that grace the walls between the carvings (Tane-nui-a-Rangi, 1988).

I was present for the opening of the *Marae*, but not during the earlier protests to secure one, which involved years of submissions to the university and culminated in 1984 in the occupation of the Registry building and the garage of then Vice Chancellor, Colin Maiden, to highlight the aspirations of Māori staff and students (Morrison, 1999). From its opening, I was one of the Māori students, a significant minority on campus, who used the *Marae* and Māori studies department as our second home, and for whom the lecturers and staff were our benevolent aunts and uncles. For over fifteen years the *Marae* was as far removed as possible from the epicenter of the university—that is, until the Owen Glenn Building, home of the Business School, moved that epicenter slightly and reframed the *Marae* as a gateway, albeit at the back door, to the new precinct surrounding the Business School.

In 1992 I began to tutor in the School of Management at the then Auckland Institute of Technology. I taught there for two years, getting to know the Māori staff and community, though from a distance, as most of the business faculty were physically removed from the Māori studies complex, and I felt somewhat isolated from that community. Then, in 1996, I took up a lectureship in management, in the commerce faculty at Auckland University, where I spent the next five years. Being outside of the Māori studies fraternity, I was less involved with the *Marae* but was always welcomed at *Hui* (community meetings) and *Pōwhiri* (formal welcomes), and I utilized the venue for any events I was organizing. It remained a spiritual home in the urban landscape, despite the fact that I was also closely associated with my tribal *Marae* in the Far North.

In 2001, Sir John Turei, the *Kaumātua* (chief elder) of UNITEC Institute of Technology, encouraged me to apply for the position as Head of Puukenga, the Māori School of Education, which up until the opening of their *Marae* in 2009 had provided a physical and spiritual center for Māori programs, staff, and students from across the campus. I was fortunate to be part of the original planning group for the *Marae* at Unitec, *Te Whare*

Wānanga o Wairaka. The institution is located on the slopes of *Owairaka* (Mount Albert), in an idyllic garden, upon land that once housed an institution, first opened in 1865, variously named the Whau Lunatic Asylum, the Auckland Lunatic Asylum, Auckland Mental Hospital, Oakley Hospital, and Carrington Psychiatric Hospital. Those names alone speak volumes about our changing perceptions of mental health. Interestingly, the *Whau* is the name of a local river that traverses the portage between the Waitemata and Manukau Harbours and along which the *Tainui waka* (canoe) traveled upon its arrival in Aotearoa many hundreds of years ago.

At the center of the campus is the magnificent *Marae, Te Noho Kotahitanga,* named for the compact signed between UNITEC and *Tangata Whenua* (literally meaning "people of the land," and in this case the tribes of the Auckland region) in 2001. It is nestled beside *Te Puna o Wairaka,* the stream

Figure 4.2   Te Noho Kotahitanga, UNITEC Institute of Technology.

that emerges from *Owairaka* Mountain. The *Whare Hui* (meeting house) is named *Te Ngākau Mahaki*, literally meaning the "peaceful heart." The master carver, Lionel Grant, brought together a team of carvers and weavers from around the country, to create a *whare* that incorporates traditional architectural forms (the building is held up by the carvings lashed together), with striking contemporary innovations such as three-dimensional woven panels. Plans were developed in 2002, while I was the head of Puukenga, but the first foundations were not laid until 2007, and the *Whare Hui* opened in March 2009. The *Whare Kai* (dining hall) was opened in 2012.

I left UNITEC at the end of 2003 and spent the next five years doing other things, working for my Iwi back in the North and a bit of television work until they cancelled my TV show in 2007. At that time, an old friend and colleague offered me part-time work in Te Ara Poutama, the faculty of Māori development, at the now renamed Auckland University of Technology. When I first came to AIT in 1992, it comprised an eclectic assortment of spaces reflecting its long and varied heritage. On my return in 2008, AUT, founded in 2000, had been transformed to possess a futuristic environment. *Te Wānanga Aronui o Tamaki Makaurau* draws its Māori name from the *Kete Aronui*, one of the three baskets of knowledge given to humanity by *Tane-nui-a-Rangi*, one of the *atua*, children of *Papatuanuku* (earth mother) and *Ranginui* (sky father). The *Kete Aronui* contains knowledge of peace and the arts and crafts that can benefit the earth and all living things.

The AUT *Marae, Ngā Wai o Horotiu*, was opened in 1997. It is named for the stream, *Waihorotiu*, that once coursed down the gully now known as Queen Street. It stands proudly at the apex of the campus. As with other *Marae*, the *kaitiaki* (custodians) are staff and students. The *Whare Hui* is

Figure 4.3   Ngā Wai o Horotiu, Auckland University of Technology.

named *Te Purengi*, representing the ropes that hold the mast of a *waka* in place, keeping it strong and sturdy on its long journey. The *Whare Kai* is named *Te Kaipara*, for the West Coast harbor, which has traditionally provided food and shelter to the *tangata whenua* of the land on which this *Marae* is built, *Ngāti Whātua*.

Each of these names, individually and taken in combination, tells a story about the land and the buildings, the history of the places and spaces, as well as the philosophy and values of those who bestowed those names. That story speaks to Māori who enter this place; it acknowledges and thereby gives *mana* to local *Iwi* and their history. It affirms the role of the university, to care for the physical and metaphysical environment, to bring people together and thereby strengthen the *waka* that is the institution, and to provide pathways for teaching and learning. It is a story that resonates intellectually, emotionally, and spiritually.

CONCLUSION

These urban, pan-tribal, educational *Marae*, situated as they are within broader houses of learning (*whare whānanga*), are the foundations, the touchstones, of experiences for many Māori in tertiary institutions. They are the *whare ako*, the places where learners and teachers, students and scholars, interact and merge in a holistic, overarching relationship of shared and practical wisdom. Though these *Marae* have different origin stories, reflecting different genealogies and aspirations, they all serve similar needs. They are places where I have learned to work collectively and cohesively in a variety of important ways: as a *ringawera* (preparing and serving food), a *kaikāranga* (calling a welcome to visitors), a *kaiwaiata* (singing my support for a speaker), a *kaiwhakahaere* (organizer), making the transition from subordinate to leadership roles in a safe and nurturing environment. They are meeting places for Māori and others; they welcome visitors from near and far; they resonate for all New Zealanders as places and spaces that speak to the hearts, minds and spirits of all those who choose to enter and learn more about the Māori world, which sits alongside mainstream New Zealand society. They have given me refuge and helped to shape my life over the last 25 years.

On these *Marae*, the ethic of *wairuatanga* overlays the practical skills we acquire as members of a vibrant community, which enables us to inculcate and share the values of our ancestors. The buildings are the physical manifestation of practical wisdom. They are also places and spaces where ancient knowledge and wisdom are shared. While *Marae* are primarily physical spaces, they are also the wellsprings out of which Māori culture and practice flow and which nurture the university environment more generally. These *Marae* resonate for Māori, and increasingly non-Māori, about the important and relevant place that Māori culture and people hold in these institutions. That discourse empowers present and future generations of Māori to enter and succeed in tertiary education, which in turn contributes to the empowerment and enlightenment of the Māori communities, tribal and urban, from which we have sprung. Importantly, Māori culture and practice is not limited to Māori alone. Like all strong and healthy cultures, the physical and spiritual spaces embodied in and around *Marae* have developed and adapted to and for wider notions of whānau and community.

GLOSSARY

Ako	To learn, study, teach, advise
Aotearoa	The land of the long white cloud, the Māori name for New Zealand
Atua	Ancestor, deity, ghost
Hapū	A kinship group, a collective of whānau, a subtribe
Hinengaro	Mind, thought, intellect
Hui	Meeting, formal gathering, community decision-making
Iwi	Extended kinship group, collective of hapū, a tribe
Kaikāranga	Karanga, the woman's call of welcome at the welcome ritual; "kai" is a prefix added to verbs to express action
Kaitiaki	Guardian, steward
Kaitiakitanga	Guardianship
Kaiwaiata	Waiata, a song, kaiwaiata, a singer, who sings after and to support a kaikōrero, speaker of oratory
Kaiwhakahaere	Manager, organizer
Kaumātua	Chiefly elder, male or female, community leader
Kete Aronui	Basket of knowledge of peace, the arts, crafts that benefit the Earth
Mahaki	Humble, peaceful
Mana	Prestige, influence, status, spiritual power
Mana	Authority, prestige, power, inherited status
Manawa	The heart of a person
Māori	Natural, normal, the name for the Indigenous people of New Zealand
Marae	The courtyard of a community center for formal welcomes, usually comprising one or more buildings, meeting house, dining hall, and ablutions

Mātauranga	Education, knowledge, wisdom
Ngākau	Heart, seat of affection
Noa	Absence of prohibitions
Pōwhiri	Ritual welcome
Ringawera	Means "hot hands," for those who serve guests in the Whare Kai
Taha Kikokiko	The physical
Taha Wairua	The spiritual dimension
Tamaki Makaurau	Tamaki, an ancestress, pursued by throngs who wanted to be her Lover, is the name for the Auckland city isthmus
Tangata Whenua	People of the land, tribes
Tapu	Sacredness, prohibition, under protection of atua (see below)
Te	The (definite article)
Tika	To be correct and true
Tikanga	Correct procedure, custom, and ritual
Wairua	Spirit, soul
Wairuatanga	Spirituality
Waka	The canoe, and origin of tribal identity in Aotearoa
Wānanga	To meet and discuss, tribal knowledge and lore, tertiary institution
Whakapapa	Genealogy, lineage, descent
Whānau	Smallest social group in traditional Māori society, the extended family
Whare	House, building
Whare Tapa Whā	House with four walls, the metaphor of the Mason Durie model for health and well-being

REFERENCES

Berthrong, J. (2008). Master Zhu's wisdom. In M. Ferrari & G. Potworowski, G. (Eds.), *Teaching for wisdom: Cross-cultural perspectives on fostering wisdom* (pp. 93–112). Warren, MI: Springer.

Clandinin, J., & Connelly, M. (1994). Personal experience methods. In N. Denzin & Y. Lincoln (Eds.), *Handbook of qualitative research* (pp. 413–427). Thousand Oaks, CA: Sage.

Curnow, T. (2008). Introduction: Sophia's world: Episodes from the history of wisdom. In Ferrari, M. & Potworowski, G. (Eds.), *Teaching for wisdom: Cross-cultural perspectives on fostering wisdom* (pp. 1–22). Warren, MI: Springer

Drucker, P. (2001). *The essential Drucker.* New York, NY: Harper Business.

Durie, M. (1998). *Whaiora: Maori health development* (2nd ed.). Aukland, New Zealand: Oxford University Press.

Finlay, L. (2002). Negotiating the swamp: The opportunity and challenge of reflexivity in research practice. *Qualitative Research, 2*(2), 209–230.

Hamlin, J. K., Wynn, K., & Bloom, P. (2007). Social evaluation by preverbal infants. *Nature, 450,* 557–559.

Henare, M. (1998, July). *Te tangata, te taonga, te hau: Maori concepts of property.* Paper presented to the Conference on Property and the Constitution, Wellington for the Laws and Institutions in a Bicultural Society Research Project, Waikato University, Hamilton, New Zealand.

Henry, E., & Pene, J. (2001). Kaupapa Māori: Locating indigenous ontology, epistemology and methodology in the academy. *Organization, 8*(2), 234–242

Higgs, J. (2012). Realising practical wisdom from the pursuit of wise practice. In E. Kinsella & A. Pitman (Eds.), *Phronēsis as professional knowledge: Practical wisdom in the professions* (pp. 73–86). Rotterdam, The Netherlands: Sense.

Ka'ai, T., & Higgins, R. (2004). Te Ao Māori: Māori world view. In T. Ka'ai, J. Moorfield, M. Reilley, & S. Mosley (Eds.), *Ki Te Whaiao: An introduction to Maori culture and society* (pp. 13–25). Auckland, New Zealand: Pearson Longman.

Kemmis, S. (2010). Research for praxis: Knowing doing. *Pedagogy, Culture, & Society, 18*(1), 9–27. DOI: 10.1080/14681360903556756

Kemmis, S. (2012). Phrōnesis, experience and the primacy of praxis. In E. Kinsella & A. Pitman (Eds.), *Phrōnesis as professional knowledge: Practical wisdom in the professions* (pp. 147–162). Rotterdam, The Netherlands: Sense.

King, M. (2003). *The Penguin History of New Zealand.* Auckland, New Zealand: Penguin Books

Learmonth, M., & Humphreys, M. (2012). Autoethnography and academic identity: Glimpsing business school doppelgängers. *Organization, 19*(1), 99–117.

McKenna, B., Rooney, D., & Kenworthy, A. (2013). Introduction: Wisdom and management—a guest-edited special collection of resource reviews for management educators. *Academy of Management Learning & Education, 12*(2), 306–311.

Morrison, A. (1999). *Space for Māori in tertiary institutions: Exploring two sites at the University of Auckland.* Unpublished thesis, Masters of Education, University of Auckland.

Ngata, P., & Pomare, E. W. (1992, June) Cultural factors in medicine taking. *New Ethicals,* 43–50.

Park, N., & Peterson, C. (2008). The cultivation of character strengths. In M. Ferrari & G. Potworowski (Eds.), *Teaching for wisdom: Cross-cultural perspectives on fostering wisdom* (pp. 59–78). Warren, MI: Springer.

Prusak, L. (2013). Book review of *A Handbook of Practical Wisdom: Leadership, organisation and integral business practice. Academy of Management Learning & Education, 12*(2), 312–313. doi:10.5465/amle.2013.0113

Simmons, D., & Voyle, J. A. (2003). Reaching hard-to-reach, high-risk populations: piloting a health promotion and diabetes disease prevention programme on an urban marae in New Zealand. *Health Promotion International, 18*(1), 41–50.

Spiller, C., Pio, E., Erakovic, L., & Henare, M. (2011). Wise up: Creating organisa-tional wisdom through an ethic of Kaitiakitanga. *Journal of Business Ethics, 10,* 223–235

Sveiby, K-E., & Skuthorpe, T. (2006). *Treading lightly: The hidden wisdom of the world's oldest people.* Sydney, Australia: Allen & Unwin.

Tane-nui-a-Rangi. (1988). *Auckland University Marae.* Auckland: University of Auckland.

Wynn, K. (2008). Some innate foundations of social and moral cognition. In P. Carruthers, Laurence, S. & Stich, S. (Eds.), *The innate mind: Foundations and the future.* Oxford, England: Oxford University Press. Retrieved from http://psychology.yale.edu/faculty/karen-wynn

PART II

BELONGING AND RELATIONALITY

CHAPTER 5

SHINTO, BUDDHISM, AND CONFUCIANISM

Japanese Culture and Management Thought and Their Links to the World

Hiroshi Takeda

Japan has one of the longest histories of culture in the world, as testified by the oldest earthenware vessels, the Japanese Jōmon pottery (literally "cord marked"), produced circa 12,500 BC (British Museum, 2003).

One of the characteristics of Japanese culture is its multilayered structure, which refers to that a culture coming from somewhere else being stored in old cultures belonging to a particular place (Kodera, 2011). In adopting foreign cultural elements, the Japanese did not accept them all unconditionally but incorporated them selectively into Japanese culture and demonstrated their creativeness in changing them into what they wanted. For example, while the Japanese did not have any characters before adopting kanji (Chinese characters) sometime in the sixth century (Kodansha International, 1998), they developed two separate phonetic scripts, hiragana and katakana, from Chinese characters. The Japanese writing

Indigenous Spiritualities at Work, pages 71–75
Copyright © 2015 by Information Age Publishing
All rights of reproduction in any form reserved.

system today uses four scripts—kanji, hiragana, katakana, and Roman letters, which Japanese began to use after the Meiji Restoration in the 19th century. For instance, Toyota of Toyota Motor Corporation is written in Roman letters, and トヨタ自動車株式会社 (Toyota *jidosha kabushikigaisha*) in Japanese is a combination of katakana トヨタ, which signifies Toyota, and kanji 自動車株式会社, which stands for a motorcar corporation.

Similarly, Japanese thought and religion have been formed by interactions between Shinto, Japan's Indigenous religion, and Buddhism, Confucianism, and Western civilization. Among them, the worship of *kami* (神: the divinities) and Buddhism were central to Japanese culture (Sueki, 2006).

Since Japanese people worshipped *kami*, they had *matsuri* (祭: festivals) to welcome *kami* from the afterlife on a feast day, to offer them food, and to see them off to the afterlife. *Matsuri* were a cultural means of compensation for antagonism between human beings and nature and for avoiding *tatari* (祟り: curse) by *kami*, which were believed to cause natural disasters such as earthquakes, volcanic eruptions and typhoons (Yoshimura, 2000).

The worship of *kami* developed into Shinto after Buddhism was introduced from China through Korea in the sixth century (Sueki, 2006). Shinto has no founder, no canon, and no doctrine but conducts rituals for maintaining and developing communities (Yorizumi, 2000). The Shinto pantheon consists of the *yaoyorozu no kami*, 800 myriads of divinities, which include natural phenomena such as mountains, trees, water, wind, the sun and the moon, divinized ancestors, or great figures of the past. The central aspect of Shinto is purification, and community members need to purify both mind and body when they participate in *matsuri*. The purified mind was called *sei-meishin* (清明心), which was unselfish and read by other community members (Watsuji, 1962). The reason the unselfish mind was the mind read by other community members is that the selfish mind that was not read by others was considered against the community, since the community was an emotionally knit spiritual community.

Buddhism introduced Japanese people to the concept of good or bad from the viewpoint of *hotoke* (仏: Buddha); this let them take an objective view of their work in this world and ethically connected this world with that world, which was for them essentially unknowable (Yoshimura, 2000). It preached that people would go to heaven in that world if they had done good deeds in this world, or go to hell in that world if they had done bad deeds in this world. The introduction of Buddhism presented *kami* as controlled by *hotoke* and changed the character of *kami* (Sueki, 2006; Yorizumi, 2000). The Japanese people linked *hotoke* to *kami* and came to worship both. The harmonious relations between *kami* and *hotoke* are generally called *shinbutsu shugo* (神仏習合). The reasons *shinbutsu shugo*, harmonious relations, were generated are not only because Buddhism—fundamentally a doctrine for the salvation of each individual in India—had been adapted in China to become the guard of the nation (and therefore did not deny the development of communities, the aim of Shinto) but also because the Japanese regarded *hotoke* and *kami* as the same, since esoteric Buddhism, the most secular form in Mahāyāna Buddhism, had been widespread in Japan and both *hotoke* and *kami* were considered to work for the wishes of the Japanese people (Yorizumi, 2000).

The form of *shinbutsu shugo* can be observed in annual events such as *shogatsu* (正月: New Year's days). In order to greet the *toshigami*, Shinto divinity of the incoming year, Japanese people clean the whole house, decorate it in a traditional manner, and present food and sake to the *toshigami* at the end of the year. At midnight on New Year's Eve, many Japanese visit Buddhist temples to hear the tolling of temple bells 108 times to drive away the evils of the past year. *Shogatsu* are officially observed from January 1 through January 3, and all government and municipal offices and most companies are closed. During these holidays, people spend time with members of their family and visit a Shinto shrine or Buddhist temple.

Most fundamentals of Japanese Buddhism established in the early Heian period (794–1185) consist of *somoku jyobutsu ron* (草木成仏論), which did not exist in India and was born in China and then developed in Japan, which argues that not only the people but also even a weed or a single tree has a Buddha-nature (*bussho*: 仏性) and attains nirvana (Sueki, 1992). One aspect of *hongaku shiso* (本覚思想) acknowledges this concrete phenomenal world as it is as the world of enlightenment (Sueki, 1992). The distinctive characteristic of Buddhist thought, the principle of *ku* (空) in Mahāyāna Buddhism, is *in nen sei ki* (因縁生起), which means that all things follow the law of coming into existence by depending on cause (*in*: 因) and condition (*en*: 縁). The principle of *ku* eliminates perception based on conceptualization and verbal expression, since it makes all things fixed entities. However, described as *shin ku myo yu* (真空妙有), Buddhism recognizes the reality of experience and acknowledges only this phenomenal world (Izutsu, 1991; Sueki, 1992). In other words, *hongaku shiso* acknowledges nature as the ultimate world of Buddha (Sueki, 1992). Umehara (2011) explains that this Japanese deep-rooted belief since the Jōmon period (ca 12,500 BC–ca 300 BC), that weeds, trees, mountains, and rivers are alive, generated the *somoku jyobutsu ron*. Tsukio (2008) argues that the similarity between the *somoku jyobutsu ron* and the spirit of Māori is observed in their shared beliefs that all things in the universe have spirits.

Zen (禅), which originated in China out of interaction between Buddhism and Indigenous Taoist thought, developed in Japan during the Kamakura period (1185–1333) of warrior domination. The two major sects of Japanese Zen are the Rinzai sect (臨済宗), whose founder was Eisai, and the Soto sect (曹洞宗), whose founder was Dogen. Both sects regard the practice of Zen meditation (*zazen*: 座禅) very highly. Daisetz T. Suzuki

(1870–1966) introduced Zen Buddhism to the West through his numerous writings and lectures in North America and Europe and his strongest influence may be on the meditation movement today (Kodansha International, 1998). Zen is popular among businesspersons in the West. For example, Steve Jobs, co-founder of Apple, often talked about the influence of Zen on the design of his products ("The mindfulness business," 2013).

In addition to Shinto and Buddhism, Confucianism came to have great power, especially on the samurai in the Edo period (1600–1868), and the reciprocal relationships among Shinto, Buddhism, and Confucianism became central to Japanese culture (Sueki, 2006). Confucianism insisted on *toku* (徳) such as filial piety (*ko*: 孝), social harmony (*wa*: 和), loyalty to superiors (*chu*: 忠), and benevolence towards inferiors, which adapted well to the social system of the time.

These traditions of Japanese culture are alive today because of the multilayered structure of Japanese culture. They can be observed in management thoughts of Japanese successful entrepreneurs—for example, Kazuo Inamori (1932–), the founder of Kyocera Corporation and KDDI Corporation and the former CEO of Japan Airlines Co., Ltd. (JAL). Their management thoughts are called Kyocera philosophy, KDDI philosophy, and JAL philosophy respectively, and employees working in these corporations make a decision based on the respective philosophy (Takeda & Boyns, 2014). What is distinctive about their management thoughts is that they judge management issues by concepts of right or wrong rather than by profit or loss, asking, "What is right as a human being?" or "Is my motive virtuous?" These judgements are based on *toku* (徳) and reflections of Shinto, Buddhist, and Confucian thought. Inamori has taught his style of business management and has served without pay for more than 30 years at his private management school, *Seiwajyuku* (盛和塾), where more than 8,000 business owners and entrepreneurs not only from Japan but also from China, Brazil, and America attend (Inamori, 2013; Kitani, 2012). In particular, in China the number of business owners and entrepreneurs who have attended *Seiwajyuku* reached 1,335 as of December 2012 (Nikkei Top Leader, 2013, p. 165), since they have Confucian and Buddhist traditions and can understand the management thoughts of Inamori, and they are keen to learn principles of management from that successful entrepreneur.

In summary, the spirit of Japanese traditional culture is alive not only in Japanese companies but also in Chinese companies that learn management thoughts from Inamori, and in Western companies that utilize the spirit of Zen for their businesses. Therefore, when we consider transforming the spirit of business enterprise, it is worthwhile to study examples of Japanese management thoughts such as Kyocera philosophy, KDDI philosophy, and JAL philosophy, since they can harmonize Indigenous spiritualties at work in Japan with the spirit of business enterprises that survive in harsh global competitions.

REFERENCES

British Museum. (2003). *The British Museum: Japanese version.* London, England: Author. (in Japanese)

Inamori, K. (2013). *Mo e ru To-kon (A fighting spirit).* Tokyo, Japan: Mainichi Shinbunsha.

Izutsu, T. (1991). *I-shiki to Hon-shitsu (Consciousness and essence).* Tokyo, Japan: Iwanami Shoten.

Kitani, S. (2012). Inamori Kazuo no Keizai-Shiso to Gendai-teki-Igi (Economical philosophy of Kazuo Inamori and its contemporary significance). *Journal of Inamori Academy, 3,* 299–332. Kagoshima University.

Kodansha International. (1998). *Kodansha Bilingual Encyclopedia of Japan.* Tokyo, Japan: Author.

Kodera, S. (Ed.). (2011). *Mo ichi-do yo-mu yamakawa Rin-ri (Ethics).* Tokyo, Japan: Yamakawa Shuppansha. (in Japanese)

The mindfulness business. (2013, November). *The Economist, 409*(8862), 75.

Nikkei Top Leader. (2013). *Keiei-sha to wa (Kazuo Inamori and his followers).* Tokyo, Japan: Nikkei BP Sha.

Sueki, F. (1992). *Nihon Bukkyo Shi (The history of Japanese Buddhism).* Tokyo, Japan: Shinchosha.

Sueki, F. (2006). *Nihon Syukyo Shi (The history of Japanese religion).* Tokyo, Japan: Iwanami Shoten.

Takeda, H., & Boyns, T. (2014). Management, accounting and philosophy: The development of management accounting at Kyocera, 1959–2013. *Accounting, Auditing and Accountability Journal, 27*(2), 317–356.

Tsukio, Y. (2008). Sen-jyu min-zoku no Ei-chi (Wisdom of Indigenous people). *PHP Business Review, 5-6,* 42–48.

Umehara, T. (2011). Ten-dai hon-gaku ron to Kan-kyo mon-dai. *Shinran to Zeami (Shinran and Zeami).* Tokyo: Bungei syunjyu (in Japanese).

Watsuji, T. (1962). *Nihon-Rinri-Shiso-Shi Jyo (The history of Japanese thought in ethics).* In The complete works of Watsuji Tetsuro vol. 12. Tokyo, Japan: Iwanami Shoten.

Yorizumi, M. (2000). Shinto. In *Hikaku-Shiso Jiten (The encyclopedia of comparative thought)* (pp. 279–284). Tokyo, Japan: Tokyo Shoseki.

Yoshimura, H. (2000). Nihon bunka (Japanese culture). In *Hikaku-Shiso Jiten (The encyclopedia of comparative thought)* (pp. 437–438).Tokyo, Japan: Tokyo Shoseki.

CHAPTER 6

TAPU, MANA, MAURI, HAU, WAIRUA

A Māori Philosophy of Vitalism and Cosmos

Mānuka Hēnare

INTRODUCTION

If I were asked to say in two words how to sum up Māori philosophy, the answer would be humanism and reciprocity. The theme of this chapter is what vitalism and cosmos mean to Māori of Aotearoa New Zealand historically and spiritually, with reference to creation, ecology, the environment, and our East Polynesian heritage. The chapter is an exploration into the cosmic religious worldview and belief system of one group of Polynesian people of the Pacific Islands. Māori people have a common culture, a common language with dialects, one kinship system, and a common religious outlook and worldview. The focus is my own tribal region, called Te Tai Tokerau, which is the northernmost part of the main islands, from Auckland to the North Cape.[1] Māori are the Indigenous people of Aotearoa New Zealand, which are islands deep in the South Pacific, Aotearoa being the traditional

Indigenous Spiritualities at Work, pages 77–98
Copyright © 2015 by Information Age Publishing
All rights of reproduction in any form reserved.

name for our country. Today, a population of some 815,000 Aotearoa Māori are found worldwide (Kukutai, as cited in Collins, 2011), with 668,724 living in New Zealand, making up 17.5% of the New Zealand population; 84% percent of Māori live in urban areas. Pacific Island people, mainly other Polynesians, make up a further 6.9% of the New Zealand population (Statistics New Zealand, 2014). This means that about 24% of New Zealanders are Polynesian.[2]

Oral histories inform us that Māori are people of the Pacific Ocean, which traditionally is called Te Moana Nui a Kiwa—the Great Ocean of Kiwa. Kiwa is one of the children of Sky Father and Earth Mother and has the domain of the oceans under its care (Best, 1982). Pacific Island cultures emerged during thousands of years of constant habitation on small islands, atolls, and reefs that are spread over thousands of kilometers of an oceanic world and its multiplicity of ecosystems and species diversity (Rappaport, 1979; South Pacific Regional Environment Programme, 1992). In this environment, distinctive human cultures developed and are often referred to as Micronesians, Melanesians, and Polynesians. Māori of Aotearoa are Polynesians.[3]

The cosmic religious worldview of Māori is as old as the culture itself and constitutes a philosophy, which is a love of wisdom and search for knowledge of things and their causes (Schrempp, 1992; Williams, 1983). In traditional belief, creation is described as a dynamic movement, which is expressed in Māori as "i te kore, ki te pō, ki te ao mārama," and rendered as "out of the nothingness, into the night, into the world of light" (Shirres, 1997, p. 16). At the heart of this view of the creation process is an understanding that humanity and all things of the natural world are always emerging, always unfolding (Johansen, 1954). Within this knowledge and enlightenment-seeking framework, Salmond (1997) explains that Māori and other peoples of the Pacific have "their own ideas on how relations between people and between people, earth and sea must be conducted" (p. 176). In traditional cosmological chants is found an ordering of the world by "networks of kinship and alliance . . . animated by reciprocal exchanges" (p. 509):

> [T]he cosmos began with a surge of primal power. From this, thought emerged, followed by memory, the mind-heart, knowledge, darkness and the kore (the nothingness, potential forms of existence). Tapu, or cosmic power, was the source of all creation. It brought complementary forms of life together, generating new beings. (Salmond, 1997, p. 401)

Intriguingly, Māori artists trained in the traditional schools of learning have presented, in wood and bone carvings, body tattoos, and hand-painted scrolls, the cosmos process as a double spiral, which swirls into and out of a primal center. The chevrons etched into the spiral represent a key link in the unfolding of the cosmos. The naturalistic images utilized are unfolding fern fronds, the swirling power of a whirlpool, and a whirlwind—all of which depict life as a dynamic force that is sometimes creative and sometimes destructive (Salmond, 1985, 1997). Māori art is vitalistic in its expression of religion and philosophy, particularly where it is the intention of the artist to enhance vital potential. The art is said to be alive (Arieti, 1976). For, as Leonardo da Vinci is reputed to have said about his sculptured monuments, you can compress into an image more than you can ever say (Werner, 2000).

Pacific languages are languages of metaphor and symbols, where words and phrases often have layers of meaning and context is important. They are also vitalistic languages expressive of life forces, metaphysics, and cosmic energy. Māori is no exception in such narrative, where primary sources of knowledge and history in oral form have been passed down to the present from ancestors (Ricoeur, 1991).[4] The oral form of transmitting knowledge is Māori literature, wrote Sir James Hēnare (1987),[5] a leading elder, orator of Te Tai Tokerau, farmer, historian, and sage of the 20th century, in a booklet of tribal sayings and proverbs. He articulated an Indigenous philosophy and a hermeneutics of oral literature when he wrote that such literature was for:[6]

> [C]enturies preserved only by memory which naturally influenced the development of different forms of literary art, such as proverbs, poetic allusions, metaphor, epics and songs to name but a few. These were handed down from one generation to another in which wise sages embodied the results of their experiences and judicious observations. (Hēnare, 2987, Foreword)

These literary art forms, he said, are exemplified in the oral traditions, which are "a veritable treasure house of genius, wit, condensed wisdom and silent telepathy in the storied souls of our ancestors calling across the ages to their descendants struggling towards the cultural light." (Hēnare, 1987, Foreword).

The foundations of Māori religion, metaphysics, and philosophy are inextricably linked to those of the material, oral, and psychological aspects of the culture, which all developed over time. There is no known founder prophet like Mohammed, nor is there a sacred written text such as the Christian Bible, but the religion is an observable phenomenon. Māori religion is a belief in spiritual beings and is both a way of life and a view of life (Schreiter, 1985; Tylor, 1871). It is found in rituals, ceremonies, religious objects, sacred places and sites, in art forms and carvings, in songs and dances, proverbs, wise sayings and riddles, in the naming of people and places, in myths and legends, and in customs, beliefs, and practices (Mbiti, 1975). For example, traditional oral sources are replete with detailed accounts of the religious preparations for crossing the Ocean of Kiwa from a mystical homeland of Hawaiki to Te-Ika-a-Māui, the great fish of Māui, which upon first sighting by humans was named Aotearoa—the Land of the Long White Cloud.

Fundamental religious and metaphysical concepts, such as *tapu, mana, mauri, hau,* and *wairua,* all life and spiritual forces of the cosmos, did not originate in Aotearoa, having come in the hearts and minds and rituals of the founding ancestral East Polynesian explorers who discovered and settled the islands. This religion of the Pacific, with its philosophy and metaphysics, blossomed in the new complex environment in which the older, narrower worldview was transformed. Traditional Indigenous religious beliefs are the core of contemporary Māori worldview (Hēnare & Kernot, 1996).

RITUAL OF GREETING

Before progressing further in an exploration of Pacific vitalism and cosmos, first let me say that it is customary on occasions in the Pacific Islands to greet, according to ritual, friends and strangers. The following ritual greeting is the type given in hundreds of settings, big and small, each day.[7] So, in traditional Māori language and using the words and thoughts of the elder, Sir James Hēnare (1981), the following greeting is extended to the reader:

> E mihi ana kia koutou katoa,
> e tangi ana ki te whenua,
> taonga tuku iho a ngā tūpuna,
> ki te whei ao ki te ao mārama.
> Tuia te kawe, tairanga te kawe.
> Te kawe oi, te kawe o te haere
> Nau mai, haere mai.
> Tīhei, mauriora.

The elder gave the greeting in 1981 when invited to speak to a local law society on the theme of what land meant to Māori, historically and spiritually, from the time of Kupe, the great Polynesian and Pacific explorer, to 1840. The significance of the year 1840 is that this is when 540 Māori leaders signed a treaty of friendship with the British queen, Victoria, which they believed formalized a close relationship between themselves and the queen. The elder explained what the greeting means:

> Greetings to you all,
> I weep for the land,
> handed down by our ancestors,
> 'tis dawn, it is daylight.
> Make the shoulder pack,
> take up the shoulder pack, and come.
> Welcome. Ah 'tis life.

WORLDVIEW AND COSMOS

The greeting narrative is an introduction to the Māori worldview. In explicating the deeper meanings of the words of this elder, some insight into Māori thought is gained. However, no suggestion is being made here that one elder stands for the diversity and richness of Māori thought. This elder said, "Ki te whei ao ki te ao mārama" and explained it as "'tis dawn, it is daylight." The dawn, *whei ao,* refers to the unfolding of the world of light, whereas daylight, *ao mārama,* refers to the world of light itself, which is a way of referring to a state of enlightenment. *Whei ao* is a transitional or liminal state between darkness and the world of light and, according to Māori thought, in every facet of life there exist various conditions of *whei ao.* The first example of it is seen in the creation account of the world. It was during the time of Sky Father and Earth Mother, who were lovers and inseparable in a permanent embrace. The children, through separating the parents in the period known as *te whei ao,* made possible their own escape into the world of light (Barlow, 1991; Hēnare, 1981; Kant, 1987).[8] Creation accounts are the foundations upon which Māori of the Pacific have built a cosmological, religious philosophy and metaphysics. They are the bases for a Māori philosophy of vitalism, the idea that in all things in creation, whether material or nonmaterial, there is a life that is independent of the thing itself, and there is an original source of life itself.

Worldview, values, ethics, morals, and associated cultural practices are integral components of Māori ancestral legacy that preserve both unity and identity with roots in and continuity with the past. They are the signal of where Māori are in the present. According to two Māori writers (Marsden & Hēnare, 1992), Indigenous worldviews transmit certain crucial features. First, myth and legends are neither fables nor fireside stories; rather, they are deliberate constructs employed by the ancient seers and sages to encapsulate and condense into easily assimilated forms their views of the world, of ultimate reality, and of the relationships between the Creator, the universe, and humanity. Worldviews, then, are at the heart of Māori culture, touching, interacting with, and strongly influencing every aspect of it.[9]

From the early 19th century, with the arrival of European explorers, traders, and Christian missionaries, a religious encounter began and continues today. While Christian dogma, teachings, rituals, and church institutions and denominations became an accepted part of Māori society and culture, Māori Christianity is recognized as distinctive when contrasted with the Christianity of the European settler society. Neither the religious nor the colonial encounter led to the demise of traditional religion, many of its ritual practices and beliefs, and its worldview (Hēnare, 1990).

Philosophically, Māori do not see themselves as separate from nature, humanity, and the natural world, being direct descendants of Earth Mother.

Thus, the resources of the earth do not belong to humankind; rather, humans belong to the earth. While humans as well as animals, birds, fish, and trees can harvest the bounty of Mother Earth's resources, they do not own them. Instead, humans have "user rights" (Marsden & Hēnare, 1992, p. 18). Māori have recorded their user rights in their cosmic and genealogical relations with the natural world.

The ritual greeting, though brief, is full of the very best of metaphor and symbolism, which alludes to Māori history and fundamentals of cosmological thought. In his address, the elder spoke of Māori history, which began in the time before creation progressed to the birth of the mythical and original homeland of Māori called Hawaiki, a place distant in time and space, which is the link with the spirit world. In this sense, Hawaiki is a cosmic place. After the birth of Hawaiki, the gods were created. Rangi, the Sky Father, and Papatūānuku, the Earth Mother, were lovers locked in an age-long embrace, during which they had many children. The offspring lived between them, becoming the spirit beings of the sea, winds, forests, wild foods, crops, and humanity. In fact, the children are the progenitors of the world and its environment as we know it. The growing children lived in continuous darkness and in the confined space were crushed by their parents. The children decided it was enough and that their circumstances had to change. They separated the parent lovers and created a world of light. One of the children, called Tāne, the spirit being of forests, tore Sky Father from Earth Mother and so the New World, called Te Whenua Hawaiki, came into being. The earthly Hawaiki exists. It was light at last.

Like Tāne, the other children were allocated domains of the natural world for which they were each responsible, and thus humanity and a diverse natural world were born. In an oratorical way, the elder called confidently, triumphantly, "Tīhei mauriora!—Ah 'tis life." According to the elder, affection for and attachment to the land and environment historically commenced.

Philosophically and metaphysically, the sundering of the parents and the concomitant burst of light into the cosmos was the spark that started life for plants, fish, birds, and people. Like a wind, says Salmond (1997), it swept through the cosmos, bringing freedom and renewal. Once established in the new milieu, the power could be called upon by humans and transmitted through ritual pathways into receptacles such as stones or people. According to Māori thought, the cosmos started with a burst of primal energy.

The narrative of the elder then moved to the time of Māui, a Pacific hero who was half human and half spirit and who, though scorned by his brothers, earned the respect of humanity by taming the sun, capturing fire, and attempting to conquer death. But, above all, said the elder, Māui fished up Te-Ika-a-Māui, the Great Fish of Māui that is the North Island of Aotearoa, using his grandmother's potent jawbone. Much, much later in another time, one of the descendants rediscovered the island of Māui (Hēnare, 1981).

Kupe, the Polynesian explorer, and his wife, Kuramārōtini, voyaged the eight thousand kilometers from the northeast Pacific, thought to be the direction of the earthly Hawaiki, in their canoe Matawhaorua. It was Kuramārōtini who, upon sighting a long, large, white cloud, excitedly pointed to the land, naming it Aotearoa—the Land of the Long White Cloud. On arrival, they were confronted with a large, complex ecosystem and environment spanning sixteen hundred kilometers from north to south that was alien to the ecosystem of Hawaiki. Large trees, later identified and named by other generations of Māori, provided the canopy covering the main broad-leafed species. In the coastal areas they would have sighted for the first time the ancestral native trees, particularly the pohutukawa (*Metrosideros exceisa*), all much revered today, and, along the muddy margins of the coast, mangroves.[10]

As they traversed the valleys seeking food and fresh water, they found swamps of flax and bulrushes, orchids, ferns, fungi, mosses, and lichens. Abundant bird life was everywhere, and in the undergrowth were to be found astonishing insects and invertebrates unknown to the explorers. While fishing or fetching seafood they would have spotted the endless supply of new fish species living along the larger continental shelf of the islands (Department of Conservation, 1989).

After circumnavigating the islands of Aotearoa, Kupe and family returned to Hawaiki. In time his descendants decided to migrate to the new land, and it was settled according to family groups and tribes. In these early encounters and migrations, the love for the land was consummated, said the elder, and became the foundation upon which the tribes prospered (Hēnare, 1981). The historical human link to land and environment was established. Over the centuries there was no buying or selling of land: it was not considered a commodity, a development opportunity, or an article for exchange. It was, according to the elder, his or her very being; as he said, "on and by the land the people lived and died." (Hēnare, 1981). It became the task of these early communities to begin the identification and naming of the creations of Sky Father and Earth Mother and their children. Names given in the founding times remain important today for local communities, who identify themselves with the history of their ancestors (Hēnare, 1997).

MĀORI VITALISM AND THE NATURAL WORLD

After the elder established the historical links, he spoke next of the spirituality of land and its human relations. This spiritual, humanistic value of land and environment makes things vital, holy, and sacred in Māori understanding. A philosophy of vitalism is expressed in a number of terms in

Māori and constitutes an assembly of life forces: namely, *tapu, mana, mauri, hau,* and *wairua.* There are problems associated with translating Māori terms into English, especially where Māori terms have multiple meanings. Typically, it is the context in which Māori terms are used that clarifies the metaphysical and spiritual intentions of terms.

Māori vitalism can be suggested as being the belief in an original singular source of life in which that life continues as a force that imbues and animates all forms and things of the cosmos. Accordingly, life itself cannot be reduced to matter or form, and in Māori thought, life itself is independent of form (Beckner, 1996; Bergson, 1913, 1998; Manier, 1967; Mondin, 1985; Wachowski, 1967). In Western theorizing on traditional religions and cultures of Indigenous peoples, the religions are often categorized as static and as closed systems not open to quests for new knowledge (Bergson, 1986; Salmond, 1985, 1997; Schreiter, 1985).

These are provocative judgments and not accurate when applied to the Pacific. Neither do Pacific Islanders share such views about themselves. Salmond (1997) has observed that Māori have their own ideas on how relationships are to be conducted between peoples and between humans and creation. In her studies of the meanings of Māori cosmological chants, she sees described an ordered world of reciprocity, a "generative relation" (p. 176) that exists between individual human hearts and minds, as well as between human beings and matter.

In his greeting and speech to the lawyers, the elder spoke of weeping for the land handed down from ancestors of the past. Remembrance of the mythic history that came before people links humanity to the environment. His narrative informs us of the continuing personal relationships of the living with the ancestors and with the land. His words remind us that the land and the resources are a sacred gift passed on to the present generation from the human and spiritual ancestors.

At a deeper affective level, the *tangi,* the weeping, is a declaration about and a reference to the tragedy of land loss and cultural identity. *Tangi* flows from the remnants of land in which resides the wounded soul handed down by ancestors. Such weeping is not just for the immediate material loss, but also for lost potential and the diminution of spiritual and cultural identity. In the Māori mind, there is an ongoing connection between the health of Earth Mother and the well-being of humans in communities with rights and obligations. For generations, it has been considered that psychological and social illnesses can be attributed to the mistakes and evils of the past associated with the loss of land and the abuse of Earth Mother. In the context of the elder's narrative to the law society, this is particularly poignant. He reminds all who will listen that Māori have lost most of the land to others, often for unjust reasons, but also to a lesser degree through ill-informed decisions of Māori.

The history of Māori encounters with white settlers, which has significant different interpretations, involves considerations of religion and ecology. The Māori view of recent history has, following Pocock (1998), "shaped assumptions and structures, the ideologies, mentalities and discourses" (p. 484) by which Māori define themselves, others, and the world.[11] The maintenance of a historical sense and a willingness to learn from experience has ensured the resilience of the traditional worldview and religion—and this despite major changes in elements of Māori culture, in social organization, in the systematic undermining of kinship groups by the state, in transformations in material culture, and in political and economic activity. Yet all of these features have abiding elements that remain embedded in traditional Māori metaphysics and religious outlook (Hēnare & Douglas, 1988; Orange, 1990).[12] In the 20th century, traditional Māori religion has been lived and practiced as an implicit religion, yet in an increasingly Christian or secularist, utilitarian, and positivist society.[13] Māori worldview values emphasizing the mythico-historical origins of vital life, of the human, and of reciprocity as central to being Māori were bound to clash with the settlers' Christian or secular utilitarianism and positivism.

The story of the 20th century is one of Māori agency initiating a cultural, social, and political renaissance. This rebirth coincides with a dramatic movement away from rural to urban living, where access to improved housing, education, healthcare, and employment played a major part in survival and development. In this century, consistent campaigns were waged for cultural and religious enhancement, kinship group development, land retention and use, language survival, and political and economic rights. Noticeable changes occurred in the 1970s, when the courts and Parliament acknowledged that Māori rights and duties were of a constitutional order. With the establishment of the Waitangi Tribunal, Māori rights under Te *Tiriti*, the Treaty of 1840 could be given a modicum of effect. The tribunal, a court of enquiry, continues to hear Māori claims against the Crown government and whether its actions or non-actions are in accordance with the principles of the 1840 *Te Tiriti o Waitangi*: Treaty of Waitangi. Successful claims have led to attempts at social and economic relief. These include the recognition of Māori language as an official language of New Zealand, some land being restored to the descendants of original owners, and the recognition in law of aspects of Māori customs and values pertaining to forests, fisheries, broadcasting rights, and resource management (Durie, 1998; Orange, 1997).

With the idea of land and environment as gifts, glossed in Māori as *taonga*, go duties and the responsibility of guardianship. In his speech the elder described why this is so. He said:

> The Māori word *'whenua'*—land—is the term used for both the land and the placenta or afterbirth, therefore, the land for Māori people has the same deep

significance as the placenta, which surrounds the embryo. Giving it warmth and security, a *mauri*, a life force that relates to and interacts with Mother Earth's forces. (Hēnare, 1981, p. 18)

Here, the sage introduces us to one of the essentials of a Māori philosophy of vitalism. He acquaints us with *mauri*, which he describes as an interactive life force. He states another fundamental Māori understanding of the purpose and the source of life itself that has metaphysical, psychological, and philosophical implications. He informs us that *mauri*, having been imbued in the embryo at conception, interacts with Mother Earth's forces, the immediate source of life. The land is the nurturing source of human physical existence, just as the placenta is for the newborn child. In Māori cosmological thought, the *mauri*, together with *tapu, mana, hau*, and *wairua*, came from Io, the Supreme Cosmic Being that existed before Sky Father and Earth Mother and from which emanates the cosmos we know and understand. The land as the system of ecological interactions is a placenta that nurtures and sustains humanity. Humans reciprocate in special obligatory roles both to the source of their life and to the "placenta" or ecology that nourishes them.

Since mid-19th-century colonization, Māori have consistently asserted in New Zealand's political and environmental arenas an understanding of the symbiotic relationships between humanity, the physical world of nature, and the spiritual world.[14] Understanding the contemporary significance of *mauri* requires some familiarity with such associated terms as *tapu, mana, hau*, and *wairua*.

Tapu is a cosmic power imbued in all things at the time of creation and would normally remain for the duration of a thing's existence, its being. In the Sky Father and Earth Mother account, each of the children were conceived with the *tapu* of the parents, and they in turn are the sources of the *tapu* of all the domains and things of creation ascribed to them. Persons, places, or objects are *tapu* and are therefore in a sacred state or condition (Marsden, 1975). Philosophically, *tapu* is linked to the notion of *mana* and is "being with potentiality for power" (Shirres, 1997, p. 79). In its primary meaning, *tapu* expresses the understanding that once a thing is, it has within itself a real potency, *mana*. Each being, material or nonmaterial, from its first moment of existence, has this potentiality and its own power and authority. Coupled with the potential for power is the idea of awe and sacredness, which commands respect and separateness. It is in this sense that *tapu* can mean restrictions and prohibitions (Shirres, 1997). However, *tapu*, a core part of Pacific belief systems, was glossed as taboo by earlier Western observers and recognized largely in terms of restrictions or prohibitions. Unfortunately, it is the limited and negative understanding that is used to explain *tapu*, but this is only one aspect of its meaning.

Mana is religious power, authority, and ancestral efficacy. Together with *tapu* it derives from the creation parents and children, and ultimately from Io. It is humanity's greatest possession. *Tapu* is traditionally applied to many things and there are, therefore, many types of *tapu*. All children are *tapu*, individuals and groups are *tapu*. Houses and gardens are *tapu*, trees and birds are *tapu*, as are rivers, lakes, and oceans. Ecosystems and the environment as a whole are therefore *tapu*. *Tapu* needs to be treated with respect, awe, and sometimes fear, but it depends on the relationship of one's own *tapu* to the *tapu* belonging to other persons and life systems in the environment. A respectful relationship ensures harmony, balance, health, and well-being, but a bad relationship of abuse often leads to disharmony and imbalance. This applies to the *tapu* of distinct features of ecosystems. They need to be protected, strengthened, and constantly confirmed so that balance, harmony, and potentialities can be fulfilled (Johansen, 1954; Marsden, 1975; Salmond 1997).

Whatever complexities may be involved in understanding *tapu*, it is a significant and distinct concept in Māori thought. However, *tapu* cannot be separated from *mana*. Below, I discuss *tapu-mana* relations, using the metaphor of a spiral to point toward a core of Māori ethics that mediates human behaviour and the natural world. These are entry points for a broader discussion of Māori-Polynesian world view values.

Mauri is variously described as a unique power, a life essence, a life force, and a vital principle. *Mauri* refers to the vital spark, originally possessed by Io, the Primary Life Force and Supreme Cosmic Being. It is a force transmitted by Hauora, one of the children of the creation parents, who is responsible for *hau* and *mauri* and, therefore, life in all creation. It is intimately related to other metaphysical powers— *tapu, mana, hau,* and *wairua*—and all of these forces are essences of forms of life in persons, objects, and non-objectified beings. They endow a thing with its special character, which must correspond to its nature (Hēnare, 1995; Hēnare & Kernot, 1996; Johansen, 1954; Marsden, 1975; Salmond, 1997). *Mauri* is a concentration of life itself, like the center of an energy source and, because of its power and energy, its purpose is to make it "possible for everything to move and live in accordance with the conditions and limits of its existence" (Barlow, 1991, p. 83). Everything has its own *mauri*, its own nature—people, tribe, land, mountains, stones, fish, animals, birds, trees, rivers, lakes, oceans, thoughts, words, houses, factories—that permits these living things to exist within their own realm and sphere (Barlow, 1991; Makereti, 1986).

All *mauri* may be violated, abused, or diminished through neglect or attack. Thus, trees and plants, rivers, lakes, and oceans may not produce in limitless abundance. Fruits would be scarce, there would be fewer birds, animals, or fish (Makereti, 1986). From a Māori perspective, forests, rivers, and oceans can have their *mauri* restored through rituals of conservation accompanied by appropriate ritual prayer forms and ceremonies. The restored *mauri* would ensure that depleted food supplies, such as fish, shellfish, or birds, would be abundant again.

The Māori explanation of life and growth is illustrated in the poetry and sayings of the ancestors, as well as in the arts and crafts of artists. In both perspectives the seed of life is with the male, and the woman represents the sheltering and nurturing receptacle for the seed. Thus, conception and growth are possible where this gender mutuality occurs. The Māori term *kunenga* denotes the life-forming process of "conception, the assuming of form and the commencement of the acquirement of form." (Best, 1975, p. 11). Accordingly, the eyes are said to be the first parts of the embryo to acquire form. The *wairua,* a spirit akin to a soul, is implanted in the embryo when the eyes assume form, but something else is given in the nature of an impetus. With the establishment of the *wairua* also comes the dawn of intelligence (Best, 1975).

The implanted spirit, the *wairua,* must remain with the embryo and the developing human body, *tinana,* in order for the body to continue growing. *Wairua* is necessary for the existence of the body. Its conspicuous feature is that it is the part of the human being that dreams, and if the person is threatened, it is the *wairua* that experiences the threat. It is the *mauri* that binds the *wairua* and the embryo-body (*tinana*) together, and in this integral entity life exists.

Mauri is life itself. Together, the body, *wairua,* and *mauri* constitute a living being. While the *wairua* is something of a free spirit and can move away from its material resemblance, the body, it must return to it. The *wairua* of humans protects the body by sensing the evil thoughts and presence of others and alerting it to potential danger (Johansen, 1954). However, another force is essential to the totality of life as understood by Māori. The *hau,* a cosmic power and vital essence, is infused also into the embryo and is another set of specific qualities closely allied to the *mauri,* yet both are decidedly distinct. *Hau* is often referred to as the breath of life or alluded to as the wind, which is sometimes the phenomenon identified as the manifestation of the life force. The *hau* is called up by the priestly leader at birth and bound in humans. With the *hau* is the *tapu* and *mana* of their ancestral spirit being, which are present also at conception and remain with the form in life and in death (Salmond, 1997).

What then is the understanding of death? Māori thought has it that death occurs when the *mauri* is no longer able to keep body and *wairua* bound together and so guarantee continued life. A separation takes place and, as a consequence, the body is considered dead. The funeral ritual, called a *tangihanga,* is organized and often lasts three or more days during which kinfolk and friends gather to pay their respects, which are expressed in speech making, formal prayer, and much discussion about the person. This ritual includes a retelling of the deceased's genealogical and tribal history.

While the social imperatives are important, the primary purpose of the ritual is to ensure that the body is cared for prior to burial and that the *mauri* and the *hau* have departed and returned to their source, Io. At the same time, the ritual ought to ensure that the spirit, *wairua*, is freed of earthly attachments so as to return to Hawaiki safely and join the great body of ancestors. It is believed that, should the ritual be held inappropriately, things can go wrong, especially for the *wairua*, which may linger on earth; in this state the *wairua* is referred to as a *kehua*, and is capable of returning in a malevolent mood or approaching the living to seek ways to return to Hawaiki. Having completed the ritual of burial, those remaining continue their daily lives.

These elements of the life-death process also apply to the natural world—land, mountains, rivers, seas, trees, animals, and insects. According to Māori, all things in creation have had a *tinana*, a *wairua*, a *mauri*, and a *hau*. This fundamental assembly of life forces gave "form and energy to all matter" (Salmond, 1997, p. 510). For instance, a tree is first formed as a seed resplendent with the *mauri* and *hau* of Tāne, the child who separated Earth Mother and Sky Father. The seed now has a being with potential to be a living, creating process that is the *mana* of Tāne. In time the form, the seed, is transformed into a trunk, a body, which has a *wairua*, a spirit, and these are bound together by a *mauri*, which, when separated from the tree, causes the tree to die. Thus, in using parts of trees or in cutting down trees, appropriate rituals and customs ought to be followed. If not, there may be malevolent tree spirits in the forest. "All things possess a wairua; otherwise they could not exist. Matter cannot exist without such a principle," says one Māori (as cited in Johansen, 1954, p. 261).

Hau, furthermore, is a cosmic power and vital essence embodied in all persons and things and often described as the very essence of vitality. It has an extraordinary range of applications and, when considered in terms of its relationships, it can be seen as "a part of life" that influences the whole (Johansen, 1954, p. 117). When applied to all aspects and dimensions of the natural world, it is a life force that is closely linked to the *mauri*. Its purpose is toward goodness. All rivers, lakes, oceans, forests, and mountains have this life principle that must be protected by good acts and nurtured because of the association with food and other supplies. The *hau* of tribal land and forests is their vitality and fertility, which are also signs of their *mana*, their honor, prestige, and power. However, if they are not cared for or are neglected or abused, the land can be rendered infertile and the forests unproductive. The vitality of trees, and this vitality's power, is the agency for attracting birds (Best, 1909; Gathercole, 1978; Hēnare & Kernot, 1996). It is a gift from Hauora. The significance of the *hau* and its potency is illustrated by the account of the argument of the children over the rights and wrongs of separating the cosmic parents. At one time, each tried to destroy the *hau* of the others, thus attempting to nullify the power and authority of the others to act.

Religious rituals play an integral role in nurturing and protecting the *hau* of the natural world. One ritual is called "feeding the *hau*" and entails making offerings to the sea, river, lake, or forest. It can be the first catch of fish or birds or the first crop of potatoes that are returned to its source or put aside for ritual use. Like the close association of *tapu-mana*, so with *mauri* and *hau*, in which the *hau* is thought to rest in the *mauri*. The *mauri* protects the *hau* in the same way that the *wairua*, spirit, protects its physical basis, the body. In returning the first catch, the fundamentals of reciprocal exchange are identified. By means of these rituals of feeding, *hau* and *mauri* are returned to the original source (Best, 1982; Salmond, 1997). Over the millennia *hau* was established as a complex totalizing system of obligatory gift exchange infusing Māori social, economic, and religious life with profound implications for the management and guardianship of the natural world (Godelier, 1999; Mauss, 1990; Schrift, 1997). Climate change, changing ecosystems, the decline of native forest reserves, declining coastal flora, inshore and deep-sea fisheries, and waterway and land uses are the central Māori environmental issues of the 21st century. When considered as a unity, *mauri*, *hau*, and *wairua* appear to protect *tapu* and so maintain the *mana* of the person or group, the tree or forest, the dandelion or flower, the stream or ocean.

Such a holistic approach to environmental and ecological care and management has been impossible during the last 160 years for tribal regions such as *Te Tai Tokerau*. Māori have experienced externally imposed land management policies, which have been motivated by secularist, scientific, Cartesian dualist thinking. Management by quantitative analysis has critically impacted *Te Tai Tokerau* spirituality, culture, people, and environment. Alienation and disconnection from land, forest, rivers, streams, tributaries, pools, and seas has distanced people from Earth Mother and nature. Denial of the responsibilities of guardianship over creation and being unable to nurture and feed both the life forces *(mauri* and *hau)* of the diverse substances and forms of creation have profound implications both for humans and nature. The obligatory reciprocity between humanity and the natural world has not occurred and the spirit, *wairua*, of the region is sick—an illness that manifests itself in poor production, high unemployment, and other social ills of the century just past.

MĀORI ETHICS AND ECOLOGICAL AND ENVIRONMENTAL SUSTAINABILITY

In recent years there has been a movement toward clarifying the extent to which traditional practices and values can inform the present regarding an ethics relevant to humanity in meaningful relationship with the world. Māori claimants appearing in courts and other fora have articulated core values parallel to those informing the Waitangi Tribunal. According to the tribunal, a set of criteria underlie Māori thinking on the resources of the environment and constitute rules that ought to govern human behaviour in the environment. They are a reverence for the total creation as one whole, a sense of kinship with other beings, a sacred regard for the whole of nature and its resources as being gifts from the spiritual powers, a sense of responsibility for these gifts (taonga) as the appointed stewards and guardians, a distinctive economic ethic of reciprocity, and a sense of commitment to safeguard natural resources for future generations (Waitangi Tribunal, 1988). These criteria were reiterated in a further development when claimants articulated a set of core values, which the tribunal recognized as conceptual regulators associated with land rights and communal obligations when applied to the environment and land of *Te Tai Tokerau*. The values are also part of a general system for regulating human behavior. They are given as:

- kinship (*whanaungatanga*), which stresses the primacy of kinship bonds in determining action and the importance of genealogy in establishing rights and status
- compassion (*arohatanga*), which is a basis for peaceful coexistence
- hospitality (*manaakitanga*), which is a desirable character trait of generosity, care-giving, or compassion, and is generally about establishing one's *mana*
- reciprocity (*utu*), which concerns the maintenance of harmony and balance, and of *mana* (Waitangi Tribunal, 1997)

Finally, our study of Māori religion, metaphysics, and philosophy of vitalism and cosmos informs us of a spiral of ethics for life. Schweitzer (1929) wrote that, in the stillness of the primeval forest in Africa, he realized that worldview is a product of life view, not vice versa. For him, all profound world view is mysticism, and this is "the germ of all ideas and dispositions which are determinative for the conduct of individuals and society" (p. xviii). Following a restoration of a world view for life he found that "ethics too, are nothing but reverence for life" (p. xiv)

Outlined in Figure 6.1 is a matrix of ethics and morality that simultaneously presents t h e Māori worldview and acts as a check on that worldview. This is not a hierarchy of ethics; rather, this begins in the center of the spiral and, together with the above values, constitutes a Pacific Polynesian view of holism and way of linking humanity and environment in a relationship of reciprocity and respect (Hēnare, 1999).

- Tikanga te ao mārama: the ethic of wholeness, evolving, cosmos
- Tikanga te ao hurihuri: the ethic of change and tradition
- Tikanga tapu: the ethic of existence, being with potentiality, power, the sacred

- Tikanga mauri: ethic of life essences, vitalism, reverence for life
- Tikanga mana: the ethic of power, authority, and common good, actualization of tapu
- Tikanga hau: the ethic of spiritual power of obligatory reciprocity in relationships with nature, life force, breath of life
- Tikanga wairua: the ethic of the spirit and spirituality
- Tikanga tika: the ethic of the distinctive nature of things, of the right way, of the quest for justice
- Tikanga whānau: the ethic of family, tangata—the human person
- Tikanga whanaungatanga: the ethic of belonging, reverence for the human person
- Tikanga tiakitanga: the ethic of guardianship of creation, land, seas, forests, environment
- Tikanga hohou rongo: the ethic of peace and reconciliation, restoration
- Tikanga kotahitanga: the ethic of solidarity with people and the natural world and common good
- Tikanga manaakitanga-atawhai: the ethic of love and honor, solidarity, reciprocity (Hēnare, 2003)

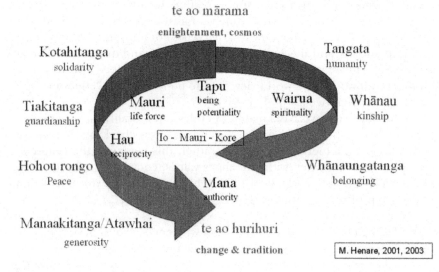

Figure 6.1 He korunga o ngā tikanga.

I end with the elder's words: "It is a pleasant thing that we meet, because we cannot meet without learning to know and understand one another better.... Tīhei mauri ora. Ah 'tis life!" (Hēnare, 1981).

NOTES

1. This chapter draws on fieldwork and archival research for interdisciplinary research projects on social, economic, and cultural sustainable development in the *Te Tai Tokerau* region. The projects were funded by the New Zealand Foundation for Research, Science and Technology. See Hēnare (1997, 1998).

2. Dr. Tahu Kukutai (as cited in Collins, 2011) has found that of the total 815,000 Māori population, 151,000 reside overseas, 140,000 in Australia. The 2013 New Zealand Population Census records that 668,724 people claim Māori descent of a total population of 4,242,048. Māori life expectancy has increased dramatically in the past fifty years. It is currently 75 years of age for women and 70 for men, and the gap between Māori and the national average is declining, currently at 7.3 years. The population is young, with 33% under the age of 15. While the phenomenon of urbanization is ancient, in Asia-Pacific history it continues as a significant factor for contemporary Māori society. Before the 1940s, more than 80% lived in rural areas, largely within their own tribal domains, but at the end of the 20th century, some 84% lived in urban areas. A majority now live outside their tribal boundaries. Social mobility appears to be an accepted part of Māori ethos and, together with new forms of urban living and easier access to improved housing, education, health care, and employment, has played a major part in Māori survival and social development. For further information see the Statistics New Zealand web site, http://www.stats.govt.nz.

3. The categories of Polynesian, Melanesian, and Micronesian are not Indigenous peoples' classifications.

4. Māori history consists of genealogies, kinship systems, poetry, myths, proverbs, songs, and ritual dances, which together constitute a narrative on identity. For Ricoeur (1991), narrative identity is "[the] kind of identity that human beings acquire through the mediation of the narrative function" (p. 188).

5. Sir James Hēnare was a leader in *Te Tai Tokerau*, Aotearoa New Zealand and Polynesia and was recognized as an authority on Māori oral history and Polynesian genealogy.

6. According to Paul Ricoeur, we can understand human beings and human possibilities through an analysis of symbols and texts, which attest to that existence. He claims that it is only through stories and histories that we gain a catalogue of the humanly possible (Ricoeur, 1993; Vanhoozer, 1991).

7. Shirres (1997) studied Māori ritual, particularly ritual prayer forms, their structures, and how ritual is a means of being human. In a broader study, Rappaport (1999) persuasively argues: "first on ritual's internal logic, next on the products (like sanctity) that its logic entails, and on the nature of their truth, and... on the place of ritual and its products in humanity's evolution" (p. 3).

8. Māori enlightenment is, in the spirit of Kant (1987), liberation from superstition.
9. Other Indigenous people explain worldview in a similar way: according to Ortiz (as cited in Beck, Walters, & Francisco, 1990), "The notion 'world view' denotes a distinctive vision of reality which not only interprets and orders the place and events in the experience of a people, but lends form, direction, and continuity to life as well. World view provides people with a distinctive set of values, an identity, a feeling of rootedness, of belonging to a time and place, and a sense of continuity with a tradition which transcends the experience of a single lifetime, a tradition which may be said to transcend even time" (pp. 5–6).
10. The trees are the pohutukawa, tōtara (Podocarpus tōtara), kauri (Agathis australis), karaka (Corynocarpus laevigata), and *kōwhai* (Sophora tetraptera). The pohutukawa is the national plant of Aotearoa New Zealand and the kiwi is the national bird.
11. Pocock (1998), as a New Zealander, examines the politics in New Zealand arising from the revivification of the Treaty of Waitangi. He considers historiographical consequences that follow the redefinition of a nation's sovereignty and treaty relations between differing concepts of sovereignty and history.
12. The colonial history and Māori experience of it, and New Zealand society's attempts to deal with its past and make a new present so as to move into the future, represent a new experience. Three dimensions of time, past, present, and future are embedded in Māori worldview: The past is like a pathway in front of the present, which leads to the future. The past is never behind but is considered as always being in front of the present. Māori relive the past in the present and, in so doing, find the future. The elder in his ritual greeting to the lawyers referred to past ancestors as if they are standing before the group. He was pointing toward the necessity of the struggle for cultural integrity, including environmental spirituality.

    Māori became a minority population in the 1860s and experienced the onslaught of colonization, forced poverty, destitution, famine, and near extinction. This loss of control over the country and destiny came about despite a Māori Declaration of Independence in 1835, He Whakaputanga o te Rangatiratanga o Nu Tīreni, and an 1840 treaty of friendship with the British Crown, which Māori considered to guarantee their sovereignty and way of life. However, the British Crown and later New Zealand governments considered that sovereignty was ceded in perpetuity. The 19th century was one of high political and military activity around claims to sovereignty, and the 20th century one of encounter against assimilation and integration as espoused by the dominant European society. However, minority status was not always the norm. The 1840 population estimates put Māori society at l00,000, constituting the dominant group. It is also the beginning of colonization and European settlement, largely from Great Britain. However, with the first encounter of Māori and European in 1769, the introduction of measles, tuberculosis, typhoid fever, and venereal and other diseases new to Māori when coupled with forced poverty, hunger, and famine became a significant factor in population decrease into the 20th century. By the end of the 19th century, observers considered Māori a dying race, when the population had been reduced to 45,549 people by 1901. The alienation of land to settler ownership was almost complete, with some 66 million acres in 1840 to about 3 million acres in Māori control (Hēnare & Douglas, 1988; Hēnare, Middleton, & Puckey, 2013; Orange, 1990).

13. Grateful thanks are extended to the Reverend Edward Bailey (personal communication, February, 2000) of the Centre for the Study of Implicit Religion and Contemporary Society, Middlesex University, for a discussion on implicit religions, which are active in societies.

14. For instance, a worldview and belief in life forces and their significance in society and nature were highlighted in the Waitangi Tribunal *Muriwhenua Land Report* (1997). After hearing both oral and written evidence from Muriwhenua people (who live in the northernmost part of *Te Tai Tokerau*), anthropologists, and historians, the tribunal summed up the tribal claimant's relationship with the land and seas as follows: "The people's accounts started before time began, at Matangireia, home of the first being, Io-matua-kore, and proceeded from there on a mental and spiritual journey through aeons. It told of an enterprising people, pragmatic but deeply religious, so intimately tied to land, sea, and space that in their cosmos all life forms, and phenomena like the sky, sun, wind and rain, are bound to them by treasured links in ancient genealogy. Māori thus see themselves as descendants of gods, and as partners with them in a physical and spiritual universe" (p. 15). Io-matua-kore, glossed as Io who had no parents, is one of many such attributes used to describe this numinous Supreme Being. Other attributes are Io matua, Io who is the parent of all, and Io wānanga, Io who is knowledge. In the cosmological accounts there are twelve heavens, of which Matangireia is the highest and is the abode of Io (Best, 1976; Shirres, 1997). Finally, in the two separate reports to the government on claims over sea, coast and fish, and land, the Waitangi Tribunal found in favor of Muriwhenua Claimants (Waitangi Tribunal, 1988). For other reports and summaries of findings, see also the tribunal's web site, http://www.justice.govt.nz/tribunals/waitangi-tribunal.

REFERENCES

Arieti, S. (1976). *Creativity: The magic synthesis.* New York, NY: Basic Books.

Barlow, C. (1991). *Tikanga whakaaro: Key concepts in Māori culture.* Auckland, New Zealand: Oxford University Press.

Beck, P. V., Walters, A. L., & Francisco, N. (1990). *The sacred: Ways of knowledge, sources of life.* Tsaile, AZ: Navajo Community College Press/Northland Publishing.

Beckner, M. (1996). Vitalism. In P. Edwards (Ed.), *The encyclopedia of philosophy* (pp. 253–256). New York, NY: Macmillan.

Bergson, H. (1913). *An introduction to metaphysics* (T. E. Hulme, Trans.). London, England: Macmillan.

Bergson, H. (1986). *The two sources of morality and religion* (R. A. Audra & C. Brereton, Trans.). Notre Dame, Ind.: University of Notre Dame Press. (Original work published 1932).

Bergson, H. (1998). *Creative evolution* (A. Mitchell, Trans.). New York, NY: Dover. (Original work published 1911).

Best, E. (1909). Māori forest lore. *Transactions of the New Zealand Institute, 42,* 434–481.

Best, E. (1975). *The whare kohanga (the "nest house") and its lore.* Wellington, New Zealand: Government Printer. (Original work published 1929)

Best, E. (1976). *Māori religion and mythology (vol. 1).* Wellington, New Zealand: Government Printer.

Best, E. (1982). *Māori religion and mythology (vol. 2).* Wellington, New Zealand: Government Printer.

Collins, S. (2011, November 29). 18 per cent of Māori now live overseas. *New Zealand Herald.* Retrieved from http://www.nzherald.co.nz/nz/news/article.cfm?c_id=1&objectid=10769488

Department of Conservation (New Zealand) [DOC]. (1989). *The story of the Bay of Islands Maritime and Historic Park.* Russell, New Zealand: Bay of Islands Maritime and Historic Park.

Durie, E. T. (1998, July). *Ethics and values.* Paper presented at Te Oru Rangahau Māori Research and Development Conference, Massey University, Palmerston North, New Zealand.

Gathercole, P. (1978). Hau, mauri and utu: A re-examination. *Mankind 11*(3), 334–340.

Godelier, M. (1999). *The enigma of the gift* (N. Scott, Trans.). Chicago, IL: University of Chicago Press.

Hēnare, Sir James. (1981, July 4). *Address to Auckland District Law Society.* Photocopy of typescript.

Hēnare, Sir James. (1987). Foreword. In J. McRae (comp.), *He pepeha, he whakatauaki no Taitokerau [Tribal sayings and proverbs of North Auckland].* Whāngārei, New Zealand: Department of Māori Affairs.

Hēnare, M. (1990). Christianity: Māori Churches. In P. Donovan (Ed.), *Religions of New Zealanders.* Palmerston North, New Zealand: Dunmore Press.

Hēnare, M. (1995). Human labour as a commodity—A Māori ethical response. In P. S. Morrison (Ed.), *Labour, employment and work in New Zealand, 1994: Proceedings of the Sixth Conference, November 24 and 25, 1994* (pp. 214–222). Wellington, New Zealand: Department of Geography, Victoria University of Wellington.

Hēnare, M. (1997). The mana of Whangaroa. In *Sustainable development in Tai Tokerau. Case study three—Whangaroa* (pp. 213–239). Auckland: James Henare Māori Research Centre, University of Auckland.

Hēnare, M. (1998). The mana of Ngāpuhi. In *Sustainable development in Tai Tokerau. Case study four—Ngāpuhi* (pp. 669–693). Auckland: James Henare Māori Research Centre, University of Auckland.

Hēnare, M. (1999). Sustainable social policy. In J. Boston, P. Dalziel & S. St John (Eds.), *Redesigning the welfare state in New Zealand: Problems, policies, prospects* (pp. 39–59). Auckland, New Zealand: Oxford University Press.

Hēnare, M. (2003). *Changing images of nineteenth century Māori society—From tribes to nation.* Unpublished PhD thesis. Victoria University of Wellington, Wellington, New Zealand.

Hēnare, M., & Douglas, E. (1988). Te reo o Te Tiriti mai rā anō: The Treaty always speaks. In *Future Directions. The April report: Report of the Royal Commission on social policy,* (vol. 3, pt. 1, pp. 79–220). Wellington, New Zealand: Royal Commission on Social Policy.

Hēnare, M., & Kernot, B. (1996). Māori religion: The spiritual landscape. In J. Veitch (Ed.), *Can humanity survive? The world's religions and the environment* (pp. 205–216). Auckland, New Zealand: Awareness Book.

Hēnare, M., Middleton, A., & Puckey, A. M. A. (2013). *He Rangi Mauroa Ao te Pō: Melodies Eternally New. Ngā Rangi-Waiata a Te Aho: Ngā Waiata o te Māramatanga. Songs of Te Aho: Songs on the theme of knowing.* Wellington, New Zealand: Crown Forestry Rental Trust (CRFT). Contract, Uniservices Ltd.

Johansen, J. P. (1954). *The Māori and his religion in its non-ritual aspects.* Copenhagen, Denmark: Ejnarn Munksgaard.

Kant, E. (1987). *Critique of judgement* (W. Pluhar, Trans.). Cambridge, MA: Hackett Publishing. (Original work published 1790).

Makereti (1986). *The old-time Māori.* Auckland, New Zealand: New Women's Press. (Original work published 1938).

Manier, A. E. (1967). Vitalism. In *New Catholic encyclopedia* (Vol. 14, pp. 724–725). New York, NY: McGraw-Hill.

Marsden, M. (1975). God, man and universe: A Māori view. In M. King (Ed.), *Te Ao Hurihuri: The world moves on* (pp. 117–137). Wellington, New Zealand: Hicks Smith.

Marsden, M., & Hēnare, T. A. (1992, November). *Kaitiakitanga: A definitive introduction to the holistic world view of the Māori.* Wellington, New Zealand: Ministry for the Environment. Typescript.

Mauss, M. (1990). *The gift: The form and reason for exchange in archaic societies* (W. D. Hall, Trans.). London, England: Routledge.

Mbiti, J. S. (1975). *Introduction to African religion.* London, England: Heinemann Educational.

Mondin, B. (1985). *Philosophical anthropology: Man, an impossible project?* (M. A. Cizdyn, Trans.). Rome, Italy: Urbania University Press.

Orange, C. (1990). *An illustrated history of the Treaty of Waitangi.* Wellington, New Zealand: Allen and Unwin, in association with Port Nicholson Press.

Orange, C. (1997). *The Treaty of Waitangi.* Wellington, New Zealand: Bridget Williams Books. (Original work published 1987)

Pocock, J. G. A. (1998). Law, sovereignty and history in a divided culture: The case of New Zealand and the Treaty of Waitangi. *McGill Law Journal, 43*(3), 481–506.

Rappaport, R. A. (1979). *Ecology, meaning, and religion.* Richmond, CA: North Atlantic Books.

Rappaport, R. A. (1999). *Ritual and religion in the making of humanity.* Cambridge, England: Cambridge University Press.

Ricoeur, P. (1991). Narrative identity. In D. Wood (Ed.), *On Paul Ricoeur: Narrative and interpretation* (pp. 188–199). London, England: Routledge.

Ricoeur, P. (1993). *The rule of metaphor: Multi-disciplinary studies of the creation of meaning in language* (R. Czerny with K. McLaughlin & J. Costello, Trans.). Toronto, ON: University of Toronto Press. (Original work published 1975)

Salmond, A. (1985). Māori epistemologies. In J. Overing (Ed.), *Reason and morality* (pp. 240–263). London, England: Tavistock.

Salmond, A. (1997). *Between worlds: Early exchanges between Māori and Europeans, 1773–1815.* Auckland, New Zealand: Viking.

Schreiter, R. (1985). *Constructing local theologies.* Maryknoll, NY: Orbis Books.

Schrempp, G. (1992). *Magical arrows: The Māori, the Greeks, and the folklore of the universe.* Madison, WI: University of Wisconsin Press.

Schrift, A. D. (Ed.). (1997). *The logic of the gift: Toward an ethic of generosity.* London, England: Routledge.

Schweitzer, A. (1929). *Civilization and ethics: The philosophy of civilization Part II.* Dale Memorial Lectures 1922 (vol. 2) (C. T. Campion, Trans.). London, England: A. and C. Black.

Shirres, M. P. (1997). *Te tangata—The human person.* Auckland, New Zealand: Accent Publications.

South Pacific Regional Environment Programme. (1992). *The pacific way: Pacific Island Developing Countries' report to the United Nations conference on environment and development.* Noumea, New Caledonia: Author.

Statistics New Zealand. (2014). Statistics New Zealand. Retrieved from http://www.stats.govt.nz/

Tylor, E. B. (1871). *Primitive culture: Researches into the development of mythology, philosophy, religion, art, and custom* (Vols. 1-2). London, England: J. Murray.

Vanhoozer, K. (1991). Philosophical antecedents to Ricoeur's time and narrative. In D. Wood (Ed.), *On Paul Ricoeur: Narrative and interpretation* (pp. 34–54). London, England: Routledge.

Wachowski, H. E. (1967). Biology, II current status—vitalism. In *New Catholic encyclopedia* (Vol. II, pp. 570–573). New York, NY: McGraw-Hill.

Waitangi Tribunal. (1988). *Report of the Waitangi Tribunal on the Muriwhenua Fishing Claim.* Wai-22. Retrieved from http://80-www.waitangi-tribunal.govt.nz.info.lbr.auckland.ac.nz/reports/northislandnorth/wai22/wai022asp.asp

Waitangi Tribunal. (1997). *Muriwhenua Land Report.* Wellington, New Zealand: GP Publications.

Werner, M. (2000, January 24). Start of the week [Radio]. London, England: BBC Radio 4.

Williams, R. (1983). *Keywords: A vocabulary of culture and society* (rev. and expanded). London, England: Fontana Paperbacks.

CHAPTER 7

THE AYNI PRINCIPLE

An Indigenous Theory of Value Creation

Mariaelena Huambachano

INTRODUCTION

The literature reveals that "sustainability" is not a new concept but rather an enduring principle that requires ongoing attention to maintaining a balance between ecological, economic, and social systems (Berkes, 1993; Cajete, 2000; Spiller, Pio, Erakovic, & Hēnare, 2011). However, from a business point of view, sustainability is about ensuring that a business is innovative, competitive, and profitable in a world that is facing major environmental and social changes (Epstein, 2008; Henriques, 2007). In contrast, one of the salient characteristics of Indigenous people's way of life concerning sustainability is their collectivistic, holistic, and spiritual approach to a "good living" philosophy (Dávalos, 2008; Gorjestani, 2000). The Indigenous philosophy of good living by the Andean people provides a case in point (LaDuke, 2005; Lajo, 2005; Nelson, 2008). The good living philosophy of "Sumaq Kawsay"[1] embraces the Andean worldview of collective knowledge represented in the tenets of reciprocity, duality, and equilibrium (Dávalos, 2008).

Indigenous Spiritualities at Work, pages 99–115
Copyright © 2015 by Information Age Publishing
All rights of reproduction in any form reserved.

In particular, the Ayni[2] principle is a humanistic and spiritual expression of "collective common good" that is achieved by working collectively in order to attain a "good living" in accordance with Sumak Kawsay philosophy (Argumedo & Wong, 2010). This has been the guiding sustainable philosophy of the Andean civilization for thousands of years, and has led to the success of value creation seen through an Indigenous lens. Value creation involves recombining a large number of existing elements such as vision, strategy, and leadership (Bovée & Thill, 2013). Peruvian mythology reveals how the Andean people's spiritual leadership embodied in the Ayni tenet and the adoption of the Ayni system in their agricultural practices was able to satisfy the hunger of their people (Espinoza, 2011). This is a coherent theory of value creation taking place.

In this chapter, I posit the question, "How can we adopt the Sumaq Kawsay[3] approach, in particular the Ayni principle, as Indigenous people have done in the past?" Subsequently, I explore Ayni as a guiding principle for companies that seek to create value. I argue that the Ayni concept was not simply an act of business transaction between families, but more importantly an Indigenous theory of value creation that embodies the Andean worldviews with regard to business ethics and human well-being for the benefit of all stakeholders.

Subsequently, Indigenous stakeholder principles form the basis of my proposed Corporate Indigenous Theory since they have led the Andean peoples to the attainment of what I describe as an Indigenous theory of value creation. The same Indigenous principles can be extended to the management of business in today's society.

I begin with an overview of the contemporary context of business philosophies. Then I describe the Andean Sumaq Kawsay or Good Living philosophy that elucidates Indigenous principles and values embedded in Andean people's cultural identity. Finally, I introduce and detail the Corporate Indigenous Theory.

BACKGROUND

The view that the objective of a business is simply to generate profit and to retain it in order to improve capital investment levels was vigorously supported by economists such as Milton Friedman (Payne, 2007). In his book *Capitalism in Freedom*, Friedman (1962) stated that a business's sole purpose is to generate profit for its shareholders. While profit maximization is still targeted by businesses, this approach has evolved in the past few decades. Now a more holistic management view that takes into account the embedding of sustainability into business practices as well as profit making has become part of many companies' agenda (Ganesh, 2007; Kleine & Hauff,

2009). Barr (2003) and Epstein (2008) point out that the embracing of "managerial leadership" has played a crucial role in businesses implementing sustainable development strategies into their management strategy.

Industrialization, which began in the late 1800s, was driven by a growth imperative. Consequently, in the 1980s, businesses operated with what can be understood as a growth imperative mindset when adopting foreign market entry strategies. They assumed that the emerging markets in developing countries were markets for their old products. They foresaw a bonanza in incremental sales for their existing products or the chance to squeeze profits out of their sunset technologies (Giddings, Hopwood, & O'Brien, 2002). This dominant thinking prevented them from understanding that the cornerstone of a healthy organization is its reciprocal relationships with other stakeholders, not only shareholders (Epstein, 2008; Montiel, 2008). Stakeholders are defined as any person or group that has a stake in or claim on the firm or business, ranging from customers and employees to the local community (Freeman, 1984). As a result of this growth-imperative mindset, organizations have undermined the business ethics controversies and anti-lobbying campaigns by stakeholders over the long haul, have failed to create value, and have achieved only limited success (Henriques, 2007).

In a paper entitled *Free, Prior and Informed Consent (FPIC): Making FPIC work for forests and peoples*, Colchester (2010) expressed her views on corporations' respecting of Indigenous peoples' rights as not just a moral imperative, but also a business necessity. Similarly, Yunus and Weber (2011) describe a new "social business" approach whereby a company should not support a profit maximization goal but rather adopt a series of business responsibilities towards the well-being of shareholders, thus introducing social benefit. "Social" in this context means that "the business serves to benefit a broad group of people rather than being focused purely on the shareholder's monetary gain" (Yunus & Weber, 2011, p. 10). The social business approach as argued by Yunus and Weber contrasts with Anglo-Western stakeholder theory but resonates with Indigenous stakeholder principles. These two ideologies will be explored in detailed below.

Anglo-Western Stakeholder Principle

In the Anglo-Western view, the nature of a business is simply to generate and retain profits to improve capital investment levels. Economists such as Milton Friedman vigorously supported this thinking (Cherni, 2002). This view is contested by the stakeholder theory, which argues that the success of a business can be achieved at a high level by focusing on the best interests of stakeholders (Freeman, 1984).

The argument goes further in that multinational enterprises have a role in global development not only through capital investment but, more importantly, by investing in human capital and providing local people with the tools to drive their own economic development (Montiel, 2008). Debate has been generated in regard to socially responsible practice by businesses, which has implications for their management practices (McIntosh, 2003). In light of codes of ethics, charters, compliance and legislative requirements, businesses are now under pressure to exhibit a moral obligation to the societies in which they operate. They are held accountable and are urged to be responsible for their performance in social and environmental arenas.

For example, Indigenous communities living in protected forested areas face the alarming social and environmental impacts of oil extraction projects in the region (Barandiaran, Gamboa, & Cueto, 2011; Oxfam, 2011). Melendez and Leon (2008) state that one of the main issues derived from the extraction of natural resources from Indigenous traditional territories is the displacement of the Indigenous people from their titled territories and from the reserves where they were living in voluntary isolation. This places them under grave threat. This is a clear example of how the well-being of stakeholders is not being fulfilled.

On the other hand, other economic scholars follow the capitalist concept that the nature of a business is simply to maximize profits. As Bartol and Martin (1991) state, in a capitalist economy economic activity is governed by market forces, and the means of production are privately owned by individuals, either directly or through corporations. One of the most important questions of our time is whether corporations are acting in the public interest, or even whether they *can* act in the public interest. This is a concern that has increased over the past few decades since assets and power around the world have shifted massively from governments to the private sector, and with this shift have come expectations of great benefits to society (Epstein, 2008; Jones, Felps, & Bigley, 2007). However, economic crises such as the financial meltdown experienced on September 14, 2008 in the United States of America caused a detrimental financial impact, leading to a global financial crisis in which overseas financial confidence and stock markets plummeted in a matter of seconds (Bennet, 2008). These concerns, coupled with economic, social and environmental issues, have cast doubt on business's ability to deliver on its promises in meaningful ways.

Consequently, public opinion is questioning the business practices that organizations have adopted in their drive to achieve profits. Such incidents have caused politicians, citizens, and business leaders to evaluate the impact of business actions on society and on the ecosystem (Eweje, 2006). I, along with many other advocates of sustainability in business, argue that corporations have an obligation to protect the well-being and environmental habitat of all stakeholders above and beyond what is required by law and regulations regarding safety, financial integrity, and so forth. Businesses should cooperate and interact with governments and stakeholders to establish a framework of social, political, and environmental responsibilities with a view to supporting the well-being of society at the local, national, and international level (Elkington, 1994, 1999). Otherwise, businesses will continue to face the dilemma that their pursuit of profit maximization is inconsistent with social considerations.

Indigenous Stakeholder Principles: The Sumaq Kawsay—"Good Living"—Principle

By contrast, the Indigenous world view of the "good living" philosophy can arguably represent an Indigenous theory of value creation. Indigenous scholars (see Cajete, 2000; LaDuke, 1994; Nelson, 2008) argue that Indigenous societies from the Arctic to the Andes are exemplars of sustainable living. The good living principle is found, for example, in North America among the *Anishinaabeg* people, in South America among the Andean people, and in New Zealand among the Māori people. In spite of colonization and today's modern world, these Indigenous groups' values and beliefs have remained intact (Argumedo, 2010; Smith, 2012; Spiller et al., 2011).

According to Lajo (2011), the Andean world view of "El Buen vivir" or *Sumaq Kawsay* is one of the legacies of the Indigenous people of the Abya Yala that is unique in the world. In the Kuna Indigenous language, which is specifically used to refer to the language of the Americas continent before the arrival of Christopher Colombus, Abya Yala means "land in its full maturity" or "land of vital blood." In the Andean worldview, the good living philosophy or Sumaq Kawsay has been passed on from one generation to the other through oral history (Espinoza, 2011).

The Spanish terms used to describe the Sumak Kawsay (Quechua) or Sum Qamaña (Aymara), which expresses the *good living* philosophies in Peru and Ecuador and *living well* philosophy in Bolivia, are exemplified in the phrase *living in harmony and equilibrium within yourself, within community and with Pachamama*[4] (Lajo, 2011).

However, one of the most accurate translations of Sumak Kawsay/Sum Qamaña from the Aymara's cosmovision is composed from the words below:

Sum: sublime, superb, magnificent, beautiful
Qamaña: living, to be, spatial time

Therefore the most accurate translation of "Suma qamaña" is "living well." Conversely, the Quechua translation of Sumaw Kawsay, meaning "good living," is composed from the following words:

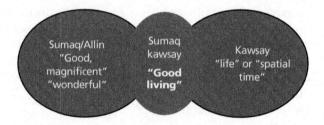

Figure 7.1 Illustration of the origins of Sumaq Kawsay (*Source:* Adapted from Lajo, 2012).

Sumaq: Good, magnificent, wonderful
Kawsay: life, spatial time

As illustrated in Figure 7.1, the combination of these two Quechua words leads to the meaning of the Sumaq Kawsay concept and represents the good living principle of the Andean-Amazonian Peoples (Association for Conservation of Nature and Sustainable Development, 2012; Argumedo, 2013; Lajo, 2005). Moreover, the Sumaq Kawsay concept encapsulates three main Andean tenets that, in the Andean worldview, are considered to be the most important obligations between humans and Pachamama (Earth Mother) (Jaramillo, 2010). Lajo (2011) details the three tenets that define the Sumaq Kawsay or good living concept as:

Allin Ruay: This principle means "do good deeds" through ethical behavior at all times.
Munay Allin: This principle expresses the view that to achieve good living, humans ought to deeply love non-humans (sea, mountains, and rivers) in order to co-exist in harmony with Pachamama.
Allin Yachay: This principle refers to thinking wisely or to being a wise person to ensure social fairness within communities.

DISCUSSION

Andean Worldviews and Philosophy

A worldview is an "overall perspective from which one both sees and interprets the world around them including events, or a worldview is simply a collection of beliefs about life and the universe held by an individual or group" (Worldview, 2006, p. xxvii).

Worldview is further explained by Marsden as follows:

> Cultures pattern perceptions of reality into conceptualizations of what they perceive reality to be; of what it is to be regarded as actual, probable, possible or impossible. These conceptualizations form what is termed the "world view" of a culture. The worldview is the central systemization of conceptions of reality to which members of its culture assent and from which stems their value system. The worldview lies at the very heart of the culture, touching, interacting with and strongly influencing every aspect of the culture. (2003, p. 56)

According to Hēnare (2003), worldviews are the ethical and moral approach to life. The epistemological worldviews of the Andean people are represented in a reciprocal or dual relationship with nature, exemplified in the interconnection of their spiritual life represented by the tenet of reciprocity, material life (equilibrium), and social life (duality), which is encapsulated in the kinship with their Pachamama (Earth Mother) in the Andean worldviews (Argumedo, 2013; Espinoza, 2011; Quijano, 2011).

In the Andean philosophy of Sumaq Kawsay, the verb *to work* was not imposed on the Ayllu (community) as a means of survival but as a way of connecting with Pachamama through songs and rituals offered to her at the beginning and at the end of receiving fruits that were offered by Pachamama (Argumedo, 2013). For example, in the society of the Andean people or Tahuantisuyo,[5] when they practiced Ayni (that is, working collectively together, loving and honoring Pachamama), their human needs for food, clothing, and shelter were met. Conversely, in today's business practices, although some businesses are adopting sustainability practices as part of their business strategy (McIntosh, 2003; Willard, 2002), there is only very limited literature on business strategy that provides evidence of the systematic application of the Ayni principle as a coherent theory of value creation in today's companies (Yunus & Weber, 2011).

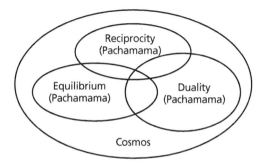

Figure 7.2 Andean worldviews. (*Source:* Author, based on Argumedo, 2010).

Ayni—Reciprocity

Indigenous perspectives offer important insights into how Indigenous peoples were able to lead a sustainable life without compromising their tradition, beliefs, and connection with Earth Mother (Cajete, 2000; Spiller, 2010; Wolfgramm, 2007). In this chapter, I describe the key tenets of Sumaq Kawsay (Table 7.1), with a special focus on the "reciprocity" or Ayni tenet, due to the fact that the Ayni played a key role in guiding the Andean people's ethical principles and beliefs when working in the Tahuantisutyo.

To illustrate the tenet of reciprocity from the Indigenous peoples of North America's viewpoint:

> A hunter always speaks as if the animals are in control of the hunt. The success of the hunt depends on the animals; the hunter is successful if the animal decides to make himself available. The hunters have no power over the game; animals have the last say as to whether they will be caught. (Anishinaabeg people—North America)

In this illustration, for Indigenous people the fish is considered to be a person too, and as such is assumed to have an intellectual capacity to identify the danger from being hunted. Therefore, if the fish were to be caught, it can also be assumed that it was its own decision to be caught (LaDuke,

TABLE 7.1 Andean Worldviews Embedded in the Sumaq Kawsay Concept

Reciprocity (Ayninakuy)	Duality (Yanantin)	Equilibrium (Rakinakuy)
What is received must be returned in equal measure. Ayni is defined as mutual assistance and can be applied both to people and to elements of nature, including human beings. This principle is illustrated in the seed exchanges among the communities and in the distribution of agricultural work.	Comprises rights and obligations from both men and women, which, while differentiated, do not denote superiority or subservience, but mutual interdependence, with the view to meet and achieve harmony and maintain equilibrium. These principles are exemplified in the transmission of knowledge related to agricultural practices, where the roles of women and men complement each other.	Refers to the proportion and harmony with nature, Pachamama, and the cosmos, and among community members. For example, respect for nature, mountain gods, and the resolution of conflicts to restore social harmony and complementarity, including between ecological niches.

Source: Adapted from Argumedo (2010).

1999). Hence the metaphor of the prey "giving itself to you" (Berkes, 1993) is useful in understanding the concept of gratitude to the fish who gave its life to the hunter, as well as the hunter honoring the death of the fish or other nonhuman life form.

Similarly, the principle of Ayni—reciprocity—is one of the key tenets of the Andean people's philosophy of good living or Sumaq Kawsay that still plays a key role in their cultural identity. Espinoza (2011) explains that Ayni has its origins in the Andean peoples' worldview of maintaining and reciprocating their intimate and sacred relationships with their gods, the earth, the sky, and the sea. For example, the Andean people would 'reciprocate' the gifts given by their gods—sea (fish), earth (food crops), and sea (water)—not only by conducting offerings and rituals before the beginning and at the end of their harvest festival season, but also by applying this Indigenous philosophy in their daily lives.

The Ayni or common good principle is connected to the protection and ethical use of the community's natural resources and Indigenous knowledge such as the knowledge and practices of food production and sustainable living (ANDES, 2012). The resilience of the Andean people in the adoption of agricultural practices despite the geographical complexity and unpredictable ecological conditions of the Andes has enabled them to develop Indigenous innovation systems.

For example, the large-scale irrigation system of canals built up by the Andean peoples of Peru to divert water from rivers descending from highland areas to irrigate foothill slopes is a clear example of a sustainable traditional farming system (Altieri & Merrick, 1987; Crabtree, 2002). Also, they have developed a variety of ecological and agricultural strategies such as the rotation-of-cropping system in order to preserve 'Pachamama' or 'Mother Earth' (Beddington, 2010). This is a clear example of their strategic vision and leadership, or value creation.

To illustrate the notion of "value creation" from an Indigenous perspective, Inca society used the Andean agricultural system, which was characterized by the development of complex irrigation systems and traditional farming techniques. This enabled the Inca to maintain a steady growth of sustainable agricultural production and food security (Grim & Tucker, 2011). "Many Indigeneity elements, practices, strategies, and symbols both material and non-material, make up the sum of 'Lo Andino' (Andean worldviews)" (Gade, 1999, p. 36).

Furthermore, the Ayni or reciprocity principle functions as the link within a community's cooperation system that ensures the social inclusion of community members with a view to embracing equality and social fairness (Dávalos, 2008; Espinoza, 2011). According to Argumedo and Wong (2010), in the Andean agricultural system the Ayni principle is exemplified in the exchange of community work between families, commonly referred to in

Quechua as *ayllus*. These authors further suggested that the Andean communities succeeded in satisfying the hunger of their people due to the adoption of the Ayni system in their farming practices. The Ayni was not simply an act of trade-off between families, but more importantly it encapsulated a set of Indigenous values and beliefs with regard to business ethics and human well-being with sustainability, transparency, and accountability values being reflected in the Ayni, or reciprocity, principle (ANDES, 2012; Lajo, 2011).

For the purpose of illustrating how the principle of Ayni was used in crop-rotating systems between Inca families, consider the following subjective example:

> The Huambachano family from the Wari community in Southern Peru was required to grow a hectare of quinoa in 6 months' time for the Mamani family. Consequently, the Huambachano family focused on this vegetation diversification technique by working collectively towards achieving this goal. In return the Mamani family provided the Huambachano family with food, drinks, and gifts as an expression of respect and gratitude towards them. The food and drinks as well as gifts were presented to them in ritual ceremonies to Pachamama recognizing their sheer work, commitment, and work ethics. They embraced the belief that "all you give must be returned to you in its pure form" therefore encapsulating the philosophy of reciprocity. (N. Ramirez, personal communication, April 3, 2013)

In addition, Ayni was considered not only an act of good faith between Indigenous farming communities but more importantly an act of business ethics (Argumedo & Wong, 2010). The success of the Ayni depended on the community's knowledge cooperation system that incorporated the values of trust, solidarity, reciprocity, and work ethics of community members. The colloquial Spanish phrase "un dame y toma sin fin" ("give and take without end"), or in Indigenous philosophy, "indefinite reciprocity," was widely recognized as the core value of Ayni within Andean farming communities. This led to the Inca Empire developing one of the most organized and sustainable agricultural production systems (Argumedo, 2010; Lajo, 2011).

Indigenous Theory of Value Creation: The Ayni

As mentioned above, I argue that the Ayni principle characterizes the Indigenous theory of value creation. Zenger (2013) introduces the concept of *corporate theory*. He argues that a "leader's most vexing strategic challenge is not how to obtain or sustain competitive advantage—but rather, how to keep finding new, unexpected ways to create value" (p. 74). Therefore, for businesses to sustain value they must develop a corporate theory that elucidates the company's vision of how value can be created and sustained in the long run, as opposed to focusing purely on competitive advantage with the view of profit maximization or a company's growth (Porter & Van der Linde, 1995; Zenger, 2013).

For the Andean people, the notion of "corporate theory" is embodied by the principle of Ayni. The practice of Ayni is more than a strategy to attain Sumaq Kawsay: rather, it is a guiding principle for the selection of strategies to sustain growth for the collective common good of the ayllus. Espinoza's 2011 book *The Incas* states that the Ayllus is where the Andean people communicate with their three cosmic brothers: sun, moon, and rain. Thus, labor was performed collectively and was enjoyed by everyone from the Inca to the commoner, from the child to the grandfather, the man and the woman. There was no one person living and enjoying other people's work; rather, it was collectively shared together.

Consequently, I introduce the Corporate Indigenous Theory exemplified in the theoretical guiding framework and explained in detail in Figure 7.3.

The proposed Corporate Indigenous Theory elucidates the Indigenous "good living" or Sumaq Kawsay philosophy, in particular the Ayni principle,

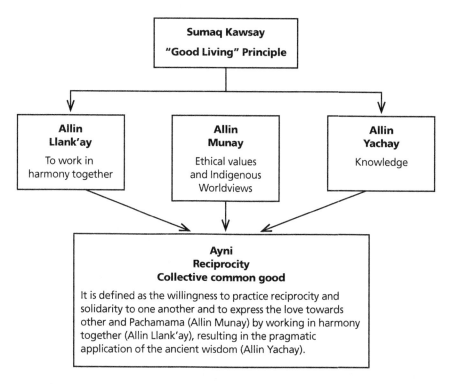

Figure 7.3 Corporate Indigenous theory: Theoretical guiding framework. (*Source:* Author, based on Argumedo, 2010 and Lajo, 2011).

ingrained in traditional narrative as illustrated below. According to Lajo (2011), the Ayni principle embodies the Andean cultural identity, and metaphorically expresses that "the act of working collectively" is like the moon being married to the sun, where both simply lead a life of spiritual equilibrium and complementarity with each other, including nature, cosmos, and the community. Dávalos (2008) argues that the Indigenous philosophy of Ayni is attributed to the Andean people's state of happiness because labor was performed in a joyous and collective manner. Thus, in the Tahuantisuyo "labor" was not considered a commodity but rather a symbol of happiness. The same philosophy is still practiced in the Ayllus. This is a coherent theory of value creation in action.

Furthermore, Espinoza (2011) explains that because the Andean people regarded communal working days as festive holidays, they would cross the mountains dancing and singing joyfully. They would ask permission from their cosmic brothers, especially those that directly affected land cultivation and growth of arable crops. They would perform rituals, called Sata Qallta, to the sun, rain, earth, and air in the form of dances, chants, and the sharing of food among community members. These were performed according to the Inca calendar at the end of September. Also, it was a tradition for the Inca to declare the harvest season by digging into the ground with a Chaquithajlla (golden stick), although the translation in Quechua of Chaquithajlla is *chaqui*—foot, *thajlla*—land (N. Ramirez, personal communication, December 15, 2013). This would be followed by four women wearing beautiful and brightly colored *polleras*, which are traditional Andean garments made of cotton or wool with several embroidered underskirts illuminating the vibrant soul of the Andean woman.

The four women represented their four cosmic brothers; sun, rain, earth and air, and each would start the pollination of native seeds by planting male and female seeds and germinated together resulting in nutritious food. They have performed this ritual by putting into practise the principle of duality or *yanantin*, as mentioned in Table 7.1. Afterwards the women would greet their four cosmic brothers with joyful dances and chants and would swing their colorful *polleras* around, giving the crowd the impression of a colorful rainbow (Argumedo, 2010; Dávalos, 2008).

Then it would be the men's turn to form four groups of four, representing the four basic principles of life: space, time, matter, and energy. By dancing together and digging in the *Chaquithajlla* they would look forward to the new harvest season. At present, the Ayllus awaits anxiously for the festivities of the Sata Qallta or the harvest festival. As a result, the well-being or good living of the community was paramount for them, and this was achieved by seamlessly respecting, loving, and honoring Pachamama and their four cosmic brothers.

Yunus and Weber (2011) argue that that a new paradigm is required to move beyond the confines of conservative thinking in organizations and suggest the adoption of a "social business" approach. They further argue that this new paradigm may well be the rediscovery and renewal of an old paradigm that is deeply embedded in traditional wisdom. The Indigenous worldview lies beyond contemporary business practices where stakeholders are enmeshed in a materialistic, individualistic economic environment (Argumedo, 2013; Cajete, 2000; Spiller et al., 2011).

CONCLUSION

In this chapter I have reviewed the contemporary business challenges, particularly in the context of stakeholder theory, that have led multinational enterprises to shift their business thinking from profit maximization only to a more holistic approach to doing business that takes into account principles of sustainability. Then, I explored the Andean people's philosophy of good living, specifically the Ayni principle, as a source of value creation by drawing on the collective common good principle of the Andean civilization. I have elucidated how ethical values and beliefs, developed by Indigenous peoples over the millennia in relation to their worldviews, enlighten their beliefs and their business ethics, as represented in the Ayni tenet, resulting in the conscious creation of Sumaq Kawsay. The Andean peoples still embrace this concept through their adoption of sustainable agricultural practices within the high altitudinal belts of the Andes, which has enabled them to achieve food security.

The attainment of Sumaq Kawsay is achieved through the realization of three main tenets in the Andean worldviews: reciprocity, equilibrium, and duality that exemplify their kinship—love of and respect for Pachamama. The reciprocity principle is considered one of the main tenets for the Andean peoples since it is a symbol of their cultural identity and has been passed on from one generation to the next. The metaphor of "the act of working is like the moon being married to the sun" is still regarded as a unique expression for their intimate and sacred relationships with their gods: the earth, the sky, and the sea. The Ayni or "common good" principle is connected to the protection and ethical use of the community's natural resources and Indigenous wisdom, such as the knowledge and practices of sustainable living and food production.

The Ayni principle described in this chapter takes a holistic view that businesses can be the masters of coherent value creation by adopting a holistic view that takes into account the intrinsic worth of the stakeholders—that is, the principle of Sumaq Kawsay. The Sumaq Kawsay or good living approach as mentioned above entails having collective knowledge of values, beliefs, and principles practiced together with a view to consciously creating a "good living" for all stakeholders. In the act of doing so lies the essence of a coherent theory of value creation.

Businesses can evolve from their contemporary management view of material wealth only towards a more holistic management view of creating a good living by adopting the same views of the Corporate Indigenous Theory. Thus they can foster value creation along the continuum and in the realm of a collective common good.

NOTES

1. Sumaq kawsay: The good living, Buen Vivir, philosophy.
2. Ayni: 'Reciprocity"—What is received must be returned in equal measure.
3. Sumaq Kawsay: The good living, Buen Vivir, philosophy.
4. Pachamama: In the Andean world views "Pachamama" is the fertility goddess who presides over planting and harvesting, and she is also known as "Mother Earth." In Inca mythology, Pachamama is the wife of Pachakamac, the water god, and her son is Inti, the sun god, and Killa, the moon goddess (Espinoza, 2011).
5. Tahuantisuyo: The Inca Empire in Peru was the largest and most influential Andean culture since it expanded the Andean world views to what now represents the countries of Bolivia, Ecuador, Argentina, Chile, and South of Colombia—this Inca territory is referred as "Tahuantisuyo" (Inca Empire) (Espinoza, 2011).

REFERENCES

Altieri, M. A., & Merrick, L. (1987). In situ conservation of crop genetic resources through maintenance of traditional farming systems. *Economic Botany, 41*(1), 86–96.

Association for Conservation of Nature and Sustainable Development (ANDES). (2012). *Communities of the Potato Park sign a new Repatriation Agreement with the International Potato Centre for the repatriation of native potatoes and recognition of rights over associated traditional knowledge.* Retrieved from http://www.andes.org.pe/en/home/24-andesen/news/80-potatopark.html

Argumedo, A. (2010). Descolonizando la investigación: El protocolo biocultural del parque de la papa para la distribución de beneficios. *Aprendizaje y Acción Participativos, 65*(7), 99–108.

Argumedo, A. (2013). *Collective trademarks and biocultural heritage: Towards new indications of distinction for indigenous peoples in the Potato Park, Peru.* London, England: IIED.

Argumedo, A., & Wong, B.Y.L. (2010). *The Ayllu system of the Potato Park, Cusco, Peru: The Satoyama Initiative.* Retrieved from http://satoyama-initiative.org/en/case_studies-2/area_americas-2/the-ayllu-system-of-the-potato-park-cusco-peru/

Barandiaran, A., Gamboa, C., & Cueto, V. (2011). Diagnóstico Situacional del Nivel de Cumplimiento de los Compromisos. Derecho Ambiente y Recursos Naturales (DAR). Retrieved from http://biblioteca.ana.gob.pe/biblioteca/catalogo/ver.php?id=24881&idx=14335

Barr, S. (2003). Strategies for sustainability: Citizens and responsible environmental behaviour. *Royal Geographical Society, 35*, 227–240.

Bartol, K. M., & Martin, D. C. (1991). *Management.* New York, NY: McGraw-Hill.

Beddington, J. (2010). Global food and farming futures. *The Royal Society of Biological Sciences, 365*(1554), 2767–2792.

Bennet, A. (2008, September 17). Economy at threat as crisis deepens. *The New Zealand Herald*, 28.

Berkes, F. (1993). Traditional ecological knowledge in perspective. *In J. Inglis (Ed.), Traditional ecological knowledge: Concepts and cases* (pp. 1–7). Ottawa, ON: TRI-US Design.

Bovée, L., & Thill, J. (2013). *Business in action.* Englewood Cliffs, NJ: Pearson Education.

Cajete, G. (2000). *Native science: Natural laws of interdependence.* Santa Fe, NM: Clear Light Publishers.

Cherni, J. (2002). *Economic growth versus the environment: The politics of wealth, health and air pollution.* New York, NY: Palgrave Publishers ltd.

Colchester, M. (2010). Free, Prior and Informed Consent (FPC): Making FPIC work for forests and peoples. Retrieved from http://www.forestpeoples.org/sites/fpp/files/publication/2010/10/tfdfpicresearchpapercolchesterhi-res2.pdf

Crabtree, J. (2002). The impact of neo-liberal economics on Peruvian peasant agriculture in the 1990s. *Journal of Peasant Studies, 29*, 131–161.

Dávalos, P. (2008). El Sumak Kawsay (Buen Vivir) y las censuras del desarrollo. Retrieved from http://alainet.org/active/23920

Elkington, J. (1994). Towards the suitable corporation: Win-win-win business strategies for sustainable development. *California Management Review, 36*(2), 90–100.

Elkington, J. (1999). *Cannibals with forks.* Oxford, England: Capstone.

Epstein, M. (2008). *Making sustainability work.* Sheffield, England: Greenleaf.

Espinoza, S. (2011). *Los Incas: Economia Sociedad y Estado en la era del Tahyantisuyo.* Lima, Peru: AMARU editores.

Eweje, G. (2006). The role of MNEs in community development initiatives in developing countries: Corporate social responsibility at work in Nigeria and South Africa. *Business & Society, 45*, 93–129.

Freeman, R. E. (1984). *Strategic management: A shareholder approach.* Boston, MA: Pitman/Ballinger.

Friedman, M. (1962). *Capitalism and freedom.* Chicago, IL: University of Chicago Press.

Gade, D. W. (1999). *Nature and culture in the Andes.* Madison: University of Wisconsin Press.

Ganesh, S. (2007). Sustainable development discourse and the global economy: promoting responsibility, containing change. In S. May, G. Cheney & J. Roper (Eds.), *The debate over corporate social responsibility* (pp. 379–390). New York, NY: Oxford University Press.

Giddings, B., Hopwood, B., & O'Brien, G. (2002). Environment, economy and society: Fitting them together into sustainable development. *Sustainable Development, 10,* 187–196.

Gorjestani, N. (2000). Indigenous knowledge for development opportunities and challenges. Retrieved from www.worldbank.org/afr/ik/ikpaper_0102.pdf.

Grim, J., & Tucker, M. E. (2011). Intellectual and organizational foundations of religion and ecology. In W. Bauman, R. R. Bohannon II, & K. J. O'Brien (Eds.), *Grounding religion: A field guide to the study of religion and ecology* (p. 81). New York, NY: Routledge

Hēnare, M. (2003). *The changing images of nineteenth century Māori society: From tribes to nation.* Unpublished doctoral thesis, Victoria University of Wellington. Wellington, New Zealand.

Henriques, A. (2007). *Corporate truth: The limits to transparency.* London, England: Bath Press.

Jaramillo. E. (2010). Mother earth and 'living well'—New analytical and strategic paradigms for Indigenous struggles. Retrieved from http://www.iwgia.org/publications/search-pubs?publication_id=470

Jones, T., Felps, W., & Bigley, G. (2007). Ethical theory and stakeholder related decision: The role of the stakeholder culture. *Academy of Management Review, 32*(1), 137–155

Kleine, A., & Hauff, M. (2009). Sustainability driven implementation of corporate social responsibility: Application of the integrative sustainability triangle. *Journal of Business Ethics, 85,* 517–533.

LaDuke, W. (1994). Traditional ecological knowledge and environmental futures. *Journal of International Environment and Policy, 5,* 127–135.

LaDuke, W. (1999). *All our relations: Native struggles for land and life.* New York, NY: South End Press.

LaDuke, W. (2005). *Recovering the sacred: The power of naming and claiming.* Cambridge, MA: South End Press.

Lajo. J. (2005). *Qhapaq Ñan: La ruta inka de la sabiduría.* Lima, Peru: Centro de Estudio Nueva Economica y Sociedad.

Lajo. J. (2011). Un model Sumaq Kawsay de gobierno. Retrieved from http://alainet.org/active/49164&lang=es

Lajo. J. (2012). Cosmovision Andina: Sumaq Kawsay-ninchik o Nuestro Vivir Bien. Retrieved from http://alainet.org/active/59345&lang=es

Marsden, M. (2003). *The woven universe: Selected writings of Rev. Māori Marsden* (Estate of Rev. Māori Marsden). Otaki, New Zealand: Estate of Rev. Māori Marsden.

McIntosh, M. (2003). *Raising a ladder to the moon: The complexities of corporate social and environmental responsibility.* New York, NY: Palgrave Macmillan.

Melendez, C., & Leon, C. (2008). El juego de ajedrez de la gobernabilidad en partidas simultáneas. *Revista de Ciencia Política, 29,* 591–609.

Montiel, I. (2008). Corporate social responsibility and corporate responsibility: Separate pasts, common futures. *Organisation & Environment, 21*(3), 245–269.

Nelson. M. (2008). *Indigenous teachings for a sustainable future.* Rochester, VT: Bear & Company.

Oxfam. (2011). *Land and power: The growing scandal surrounding the new wave of investment in land.* Retrieved from www.oxfam.org/en/grow/policy/land

Payne, R. (2007). *Global issues: Political, economics and culture.* Upper Saddle River, NJ: Pearson Education.

Porter, M., & Van der Linde, C. (1995). Green and competitive. *Harvard Business Review, 16,* 120–134.

Quijano, A. (2011). ¿Sistemas alternativos de producción? *Producir Para Vivir: Los Caminos De La Producción no Capitalista, 8,* 369–399.

Smith, L. T. (2012). *Decolonizing methodologies: Research and Indigenous peoples* (2nd ed.). London & Dunedin: Zed Books Ltd. & University of Otago Press.

Spiller, C. (2010). *How Māori cultural tourism business create authentic and sustainable well-being.* Unpublished doctoral thesis, The University of Auckland, Auckland, New Zealand.

Spiller, C., Pio, E., Erakovic, L., & Hēnare, M. (2011). Wise up: Creating organizational wisdom through an ethic of kaitiakitanga. *Journal of Business Ethics, 104*(2), 223–235.

Willard, B. (2002). *The sustainability advantage: Seven case benefits of a triple bottom line.* Gabriola Island, BC: New Society Publishers.

Wolfgramm, R. M. (2007). *Continuity and vitality of worldview(s) in organisational culture: Towards a Māori perspective.* Unpublished doctoral thesis, The University of Auckland, Auckland, New Zealand.

Worldview. (2006). In *American Heritage Dictionary of the English Language.* New York, NY: Houghton Mifflin Company.

Yunus, M., & Weber, K. (2011). *Building social business: The new kind of capitalism that serves humanity's most pressing needs.* New York, NY: Public Affairs.

Zenger, T. (2013). What is the theory of your firm? Focus less on competitive advantage and more on growth that creates value. Retrieved from http://hbr.org/2013/06/what-is-the-theory-of-your-firm/ar/1

CHAPTER 8

BELONGING IN THE COSMOS

Jane Riddiford

ABSTRACT

Developing a deep time relationship to the creative process of who I am and what I am a part of has brought me home—to a deeper connection, not only to myself, but also to New Zealand, where I was born, and to the people I now work with 12,000 miles away in the UK.

The ground under our feet reveals the creative and connective impulses of how all of life came to be. Evolution and ecology are written everywhere, even in the harsh and concrete terrain of a construction site, where much of my work as director of Global Generation is based. Through a range of sustainability initiatives, we link young people of diverse cultural and social backgrounds to the businesses that are making and moving into the area and to the ground under their feet. This chapter explores how the notion of being Indigenous to the cosmos is a generative foundation for participative and ethical leadership.

Land-based experiences evoke a different sensibility in me; my pace slows, I trust, I connect, I embrace the rhythm of change. As I was growing up, and still now, I take myself into wild places and almost intentionally try to get lost. Gravity pulls me to the hidden land ... still and moving, it reminds me that all things are distinct but not separate; the intertwining growth of grass

Indigenous Spiritualities at Work, pages 117–135
Copyright © 2015 by Information Age Publishing
All rights of reproduction in any form reserved.

underfoot, the sound of a solo bird, the sky. Land provides a doorway to the story of the universe.

Holding questions about how I and all of life came to be within the context of the universe story has brought about a shift in me, from a limited to a more expanded identity that makes room for facing into inherited fault lines, and this in turn surfaces connections. This chapter explores how developing a more porous identity that I refer to as being *Indigenous to the cosmos* generates a different relationship to the land than my New Zealand forebears had. This provides a metaphorical and philosophical foundation for cultivating a participatory and ethical style of leadership. I reflect upon my experience as a Pākehā from a pioneering farming family and my journey into process theology and aspects of Māori philosophy. I consider how awareness of the past, both New Zealand and cosmic-geological history affects my work as leader of Global Generation, a UK-based environmental education charity. Māori are the Indigenous peoples of New Zealand, and Pākehā refers to non-Māori New Zealanders, in my case of European descent.

CONNECTING TO THE COSMOS

I sense that the core of the universe is my core; it is nothingness becoming something. I often wear a locket around my neck that I choose to leave empty. It is a reminder that creativity grows through listening from an empty space of not knowing inside oneself. Māori refer to the empty ground that holds the potential for everything in the universe as *Te kore te wiwia* (unpossessed nothingness) and *Te kore te rawea* (unbound nothingness) (Hēnare, 2003). "At the heart of this view of the creation process is an understanding that humanity and all things of the natural world are always emerging, always unfolding" (Hēnare, 2001, p. 198). This ground is a place before anything happened and it opens the way to a kind of Indigeneity that is common to all of us. Regular meditation practice has helped me to find my core, to find home in nothingness.

It can be a challenge for those of us trained in rational ways of thinking to meaningfully connect with the evolution of the universe as our story. Consideration of the universe is often an exclusively physical endeavor (Berry, 1988) and an invitation to understand the universe through looking inward is unfamiliar. Back in the mid-1950s, when our concept of the universe was of a mere 5-billion-year event, Teilhard de Chardin (1955) explained how the technique of analysis and objectification that we have inherited from scientific method means we depersonalize reality automatically. This is compounded, he argued, by scientific revelations of the vastness of outer space, which can have the effect of dwarfing the human in relationship to the cosmos. In her commentary on de Chardin's thinking about ecological spirituality, Mary

Evelyn Tucker offers an antidote to the sense of disconnection that so many of us feel, "to rediscover meaning for the human venture we must first rediscover the personal in the cosmos" (Tucker, 1985, p. 13).

As I see it, the process of becoming *Indigenous to the cosmos* is about fostering an inner and personal relationship to what science is now revealing about how the universe was created. To this end, my partner Rod Sugden and I encourage Global Generation participants of all ages to personify different aspects of the universe as themselves. One way of doing this is to connect our own values with the characteristics of the universe. In our workshops with young people, we often ask them to begin by being still and silent, which is a simple way of opening up a space of meditation—a space before anything happened. We then ask them to write about the universe in a "free-fall" (Turner-Vesselago, 2013), unedited and first-person way. The following are excerpts of free-fall writing from the journals of our workshop participants:

> I am the silence. It's so quiet. I am feeling very tranquil. I have to be patient as my creation develops around me. (Tegan, 10 years)

> Commitment has been around for a long time—from the beginning of the timeline until today. It has been around for so long it has even grown inside of us. The commitment of the universe is boiling in my blood. This shows me that we are all the universe, contributing to a bigger picture. (Xafsa, 17 years)

Leadership and Practice

Global Generation brings together urban young people and business employees at our campsite on an organic farm in Wiltshire and in urban agriculture and vocational projects in London. Our home is in the middle of the new King's Cross development, which is currently one of the largest construction sites in Europe.

> King's Cross is a bit like a sandwich. On either side are people who live in the area, some of them for one or two generations at most. In the middle is formerly disused railway land. It is the size of 67 football fields. Now, new offices, a university and accommodation are being built. Big business is moving in. It could all too easily stay an out-of-bounds area for the many people who live on either side. (Riddiford, 2013, p. 159)

As a metaphor, the diverse and evolving nature of the universe gives room for people of different ages and different worldviews to learn from each other, and in this way a new space is created beyond the constraints of what each of us already knows. This emergent way of working speaks to what I consider to be participatory leadership. One of our participants describes how she experiences our workshops in the Skip Garden:

> Letting young people, business volunteers and others work collectively in a way that respects one another, opens each other's eyes to different thinking creates a collective learning experience. (Project Manager, Argent LLP, King's Cross Developers)

The integration in Global Generation's work does not occur only between diverse groups of people. Integrating different ways of knowing within oneself is foundational to the way I endeavor to lead the organization and the way my colleagues and I lead our workshops. Niki Harré writes about "authentic leadership" and describes a process that brings together three ways of knowing: "First, the intellectual form of knowing; second, the intuitive, values-based or metaphorical way of knowing; and third, the knowing that comes from practice" (Harré , 2013, p. 122).

Having begun university studies in my mid-40s, confidence in intellectual knowing has come late for me. For the most part I have learned by doing. In my work with Global Generation, I encourage both a practical and a reflective approach. Through a range of sustainability initiatives, such as a biodiverse food-growing garden in a series of skips (dumpsters), an associated café and up-cycled wood workshops, young people link to the businesses that are making and moving into King's Cross. I use dialogue, creative writing, and mythic narratives (which I share later) to encourage reflection and bring forth a less tangible dimension of life. This nonmeasurable territory is the unbroken ground under my feet.

Tūrangawaewae

I often tell the young people I work with that it is important to stand in one's own shoes. I look to my own shoes and to the ground I stand on. Is it whole or is it broken? How does this affect my actions? In discussing what gives leaders "the sense of agency, the resources, the awareness, the approach and the crafts of practice to take action of some kind in the service of a more socially and environmentally sustainable and socially just world," Marshall, Coleman, and Reason (2011, p. 6) write, "sufficiently robust change means questioning the ground we stand on." In this light, the Māori concept of *tūrangawaewae*, the place where you stand—from *tūranga* (place) and *waewae* (feet)—can be seen as a cornerstone of leadership.

My sister and I spoke of *tū*rangawaewae as we returned from an early morning walk across the land where I spent a large part of my childhood. "Tūrangawaewae is the standing and identity of a people" (Walker, 1990,

p. 70). It is the ground on which one feels empowered and connected. As we talked, we watched the sunrise outline the sharp upward reaching shapes of the Tararua ranges in the distance. Our conversation went deeper when my sister said, "Rather than exploring the source of your inspiration, it's about actually seeing where you stand right now. Tūrangawaewae for Māori is the place where they know who they are. This includes your family grouping. You, Jane, know where you come from, but where do you stand now?" I sensed this was pointing to ground from which generative change can grow. For me, this has meant digging more deeply into my family background so that I could go beyond conflicting feelings that I have held to in relation to my country and particularly the land. I needed to know the soil that I grew up with and a colonial past that colors my emotions in the present.

I come from a fifth-generation farming family who arrived in New Zealand in the late 1800s. It wasn't the birthright of my ancestors to own land in England. Coming out of the harshness of the industrial revolution, their hopes for a better life lay in the promise of New Zealand as a "Garden of Eden" (Park, 1995, p. 324) where they, like others of similar circumstance, could become landowners. The early settlers arrived to find a people, New Zealand Māori, who were steeped in a mythological way of thinking, in which land and people were not separate. By mythological I mean working with metaphorical stories that connect us to intangible forces of the natural world and help us find our place and purpose in the universe. William Doty describes how mythic narratives "are not little but big stories, touching not just the everyday, but sacred or specially marked topics that concern much more than any immediate situation" (2000, p. 15). Manuka Hēnare contextualizes the consequence of identity that connects us mythically to the natural world: "Philosophically, Māori people do not see themselves as separate from nature, humanity and the natural world, being direct descendants of Earth Mother. Thus, the resources of the earth do not belong to humankind; rather, humans belong to the earth" (2001, p. 202).

Like their contemporaries, I imagine my forebears held the notion that we live on an unconscious and mechanical planet and that it was their responsibility to manipulate it for the economic betterment of human kind (Tarnas, 1997). Novelist Fiona Farrell writes, "those that arrived in New Zealand brought with them religious notions of human supremacy over nature, a fierce determination to reshape the land to fit it for participation in new forms of global trade" (Farrell, 2007, p. 217).

This was a recipe for owning and stripping the land bare in the service of farming, which has had generational consequences for land and people. The Māori notion of reciprocity was "bound to clash with the settlers' Christian utilitarianism and positivism" (Hēnare, 2011, p. 206). More immediately, I felt that if I didn't reconcile the different worldviews within me I would continue to stand on divided ground.

As my sister spoke, a glimpse of an underlying fault line opened inside me and I said, "Living away for the last 20 years, I have maintained a kind of romantic relationship to New Zealand, which posed a clash with my deeper values. There have been two parallel threads running in me. The opportunist spirit of the pioneer is well and truly alive within me, which at times creates ambivalence about giving over to deeper values of wholeness. I couldn't feel fully connected as there was this division going on."

This was an opportunity to take the conversation further, and my sister said, "It's like an earthquake, shifting forces on shifting ground. Up until now, you have had a nice little story about where you come from, before you talk about who you are now. Whereas the sort of work you are doing and the things you are grappling with need to be reconciled with motivations that lie at a very deep part of your being."

The truth of what was being said landed. "Yes," I replied, "it is about making sense of it. I need to find out where the rifts that are within me come from; what are the deeper seismic shifts?" My sister agreed and said in a quiet voice, "It is something that Pākehā struggle to do. . . . We are talking about fault lines." This comment echoes Rosemary Anderson, who describes how in intuitive inquiry "explorations along the fault lines of the personality tend to invite change and transform openings" (Anderson, 2006, p. 9).

Drawing Threads Together

Dwelling within inherited fault lines reveals why I feel compelled to bring the natural life of the soil to a concrete construction site, creating both an excuse and a metaphor for how different cultures within a local community can work together. As I experience it, connecting land and people is generative for the business of the two intertwined processes of growing an organization and nurturing a participative community. While it is not explicit, there is a sense of personal and generational resolution in this work.

One of my challenges has been that many of the ways Global Generation works with young people and local business employees come from my own spiritual journey. Consequently, an ongoing and open inquiry for me is how I can create the space for others, who have taken a different journey than I have, to feel ownership for the work we are doing together.

This has led me to a consideration of how I do or don't do leadership and what leadership is in service of. Ten years ago, one of my colleagues in another organization commented, "The problem with you, Jane, is that you want to change the world." Those words haunted me. I kept thinking, "What's wrong with that?" My interest in leadership is born of an ethical motive, the pressing sense that environmental and social change is needed in the world. It seems that these things are not automatically connected. As Donna Ladkin writes, "Although I routinely encounter the question, 'What is leadership?' I rarely stumble upon the query, 'What is leadership for?' This question raises issues of purpose and meaning" (Ladkin, 2010, p. 3).

It has been a slow, unfolding process of learning to feel comfortable applying the word "leadership" to myself and my colleagues. It has also been a slow process to create the conditions in which to enable others to discover the power of our cosmic story for themselves. Rather than focusing on grand notions of changing the world, increasingly I feel the real work is about our internal culture within the organization, and from that foundation we will act generatively in the wider world. The word "culture" can be confusing in that it holds a plurality of meanings. I choose to reclaim the spirit of its original meaning, in which culture was an agricultural term strongly connected to the land:

> In his classic text *Culture*, historian Raymond Williams traces the meaning of the word back to its early use as a noun denoting a process: the culture (i.e., cultivation) of crops, or the culture (i.e., rearing and breeding) of animals. In the sixteenth century this meaning was extended metaphorically to the active cultivation of the human mind. (Capra, 2002, p. 75)

My sense of leadership has associations with the rhythms of the land, and, as I mentioned earlier, land is for me a doorway to the story of the universe. Do I have a reciprocal or a utilitarian approach to the land? How does this affect my relationships?

The Three Baskets of Tāne

Along with the concept of *tūrangawaewae*, my sister also introduced me to the story of Tāne's three baskets. This traditional Māori legend speaks directly to my spiritual journey and the context of what Global Generation is endeavouring to awaken in young people—that is, a deeper and more connected sense of who we all are, which I feel is a generative foundation for any kind of leadership.

While I have come across different interpretations of the story, the common thread is that Tāne, the god of the forest, is asked by

> Io, the Supreme Being, to journey through the twelve heavens to retrieve the knowledge that will guide human existence on earth. The knowledge he received came in the form of three kete mātauranga—baskets of knowledge— along with two stones for assimilation of knowledge to ensure that what is

selected from the baskets is used wisely and not simply for personal gain, but for all. (Spiller, 2011, p. 127)

I have reworked the following excerpt based on a play written by James Barnes (2004) with interpretation of the three baskets from Rev. Māori Marsden (2003):

> Tāne crossed a silver bridge made from billowy vapor. As the vapor cleared Tāne saw in front of him a beautiful woman. She looked up at Tāne and her eyes shone like greenstone in the sunlight. Tāne thought she must be a messenger from Io and so knelt before her and spoke, "I have come to receive the three baskets of the sacred knowledge. Can you tell me where I can find them?"
>
> The woman looked at Tāne and her words penetrated deep inside him. "I will show you the three baskets, but you must promise to always carry them," and Tāne agreed that he and all of his children and his children's children would be the guardians of the knowledge. "Look into my eyes—what do you see?" said the woman. Tāne looked into her dark shiny eyes. He was shocked; he saw himself staring back at him, all of his hopes, his fears, his attributes, his challenges, and he described this. "That," said the woman, "is the first basket, knowledge of oneself as one truly is."
>
> "Look again," said the woman. This time Tāne saw the woman and he saw the reflection of the sky, the rocks, the plants, the birds and the trees, and he said, "I see you and I see all that has passed in all that is present in the physical world around me."
>
> "That is the second basket of knowledge," said the woman, "knowledge and respect of everything around us. Now I will show you the third basket and this is the most important one. In the future if people forget this they will lose their way." Tāne looked again and this time, he saw the woman, the plants, the animals, the sky, the sea, and he saw himself. He described how he saw everything as one thing. The woman smiled and said, "To see one's own reflection as the connective energy upon which the universe is built—this is the third basket, Kete Tūātea."

As previously mentioned, integrating different ways of knowing and different dimensions of experience has been central to Global Generation's approach in supporting youth development and community building. For some years now I have framed this as "I, We, and The Planet" (cf. Wilber, 1996). This approach provided fertile ground in which the Three Baskets of Knowledge landed:

I: a deeper and more connected sense of identity
We: the emerging potential between people and all of life
The planet: leaving a positive legacy in the physical environment

The mythic quality of telling a story has been a powerful way of going beyond the cover story of life as usual with diverse groups of participants. Nonetheless, working with Tāne's story, I felt a degree of trepidation; did I as a Pākehā have the right to presume understanding of a Māori myth? "This legend is part of the corpus of sacred knowledge and as such was not normally related in public" (Marsden, 2003, p. 57). The traditional version is full of rich metaphor. In line with Armstrong (2009), who describes how myth carries a universal license to be told in different ways, I usually choose to tell the story using images and characters drawn from the urban setting that I work in. When I first came across the story, I was aware of the sacredness of Tāne's journey slowing me down. Following the recommendation of Marsden, that Māoritanga can only be understood "through a passionate, inward, subjective approach" (Marsden, 2003, p.23), I felt called to unmask myself. Tāne's story has given me a fresh opportunity to explore more deeply the forces that drive me.

The First Basket of Knowledge: Kete Tūāuri

My Journal, 1983

Come to the sea
Come to where the tide rides and you can ride to
The waters today move gently and so must we
Listen to the Morepork[1] calling
Listen to the Morepork calling
Calling on the place within where the caterpillar of truth lies
Waiting forever waiting, metamorphically straining
Revelation the prize of the path being clear

The first basket of knowledge I speak to is Kete Tūāuri, which raises questions of identity that speak to a spiritual calling that has been burning within me for most of my life. It is what stirred in me as a child when I lay in bed and heard the sound of the Morepork calling. By my teenage years, I had begun to recognize in myself a spiritual current that ran deeper than who I thought I was supposed to be.

Acknowledging, let alone prioritizing, spirit runs against what the dominant myth in Western culture looks like. Helena Kettleborough sums it up: "[W]e have a story but it's very one-sided: you go to school, you get a job, you work and you buy stuff. Then you die. The trouble with this story is that it's not satisfying. There's no oomph in it. It's not the whole story either; there's more" (Kettleborough & Kettleborough, 2013, p. 149). By the time I was twenty, I realized that there was more to life than I was being told. This was the catalyst to begin a life-long exploration into meditation and other aspects of eastern and evolutionary spirituality. Now, whenever I hear the Morepork, I am reminded of the spiritual ground I stand on.

The Second Basket of Knowledge: Kete Aronui

Everything we can see, hear, taste and touch is held in the second basket of knowledge. "This is the natural world around us apprehended by the senses" (Marsden, 2003, p. 61).

Land acts as a mirror for the forces that drive me. In terms of setting up an organization, I have drawn on the 'can do', 'go out and get it' approach of the pioneer. However, there is also pathology in the pioneer that has created generational consequences for land and people. Human ecologist Alistair McIntosh writes, "The proper use of land poses not a technical nor an economic, but primarily a metaphysical problem" (2001, p. 81). In 1940 Monte Holcroft forecast that until we found reconciliation with the forest, "New Zealanders would remain cut off from any real depth of spiritual life" (as quoted by Park, 1995, p. 310). A recent experience surfaced the inherited fault line of a disconnected approach to the land. I felt the clash in myself between the opportunistic values of the pioneer and an approach to life that is more focused on connection and responsibility for the whole.

It took me several days to digest what I had seen; before me, grey skeletons stretched across a hundred acres of steep hillside. "What is it with the trees?" I asked. The kānuka (New Zealand native trees) had been poisoned by helicopter so they could be replaced with *new* trees. Minus their foliage, the remains of the native bush would make a windbreak for 80,000 exotic species. Lured by the economics of a government grant, the landowner had gone all out—a grant justified on the premise of environmental sustainability. The thinking is that as new trees grow they will capture and store carbon. This enables governments the world over to play the global game of carbon credits, a means of checking boxes to enable people to continue life as usual.

It takes a certain kind of determination advance one's own schemes against the forces of nature. I acknowledge that in the face of climate change there are no easy answers. However, the dubious intent of taming the land seems to require a denial of the whole of one's experience. The carnage of the kānuka forest, rough and raw, eclipses the laws of connectedness.

I think about how we need to draw upon the potentials of Indegeneity within landscapes that are broken. Studying horticulture in the early 1990s, I learned the ecological story of gorse in New Zealand. This story has provided a foundational metaphor for my work over the last twenty years. When European settlers arrived in New Zealand, they burned and cleared the native forest. In their efforts to feed themselves and recreate the familiar, they introduced animals to hunt and stripped the hillsides bare. They planted grass for sheep and cattle to graze and yellow flowering gorse (*Ulex uropaeus*) for hedges. Without the red juicy berries of the original forest cover to feed on and preyed on by ferrets and other imported predators, the native birds were silenced. The settlers had unknowingly "switched off each district's dawn chorus" (Park, 1995, p. 310). The soil on the naked hillsides began to slide. Erosion became the face of the jagged hills that rose up out of the river valleys into the sky.

As a child, my memory is of long car journeys looking up at hillsides covered in the bright yellow flowers of the shrubby, prickly, hardy gorse. It was known across the country as a noxious weed. In time, thriving in its new home, gorse began to play a restorative role, as the colonizer of open ground. Some of the farmers still tried to graze the hillsides. They would burn the gorse annually. The seedpods of the gorse would crack open and germinate; growth became all the more vigorous. Eventually the fires stopped and the gorse was left to grow.

Gorse is a legume: the nodules on the roots of the gorse captured atmospheric nitrogen and the soil became nutritious. Gorse also provided shelter from the wind and the harsh rays of the sun. While by no means a replacement for the loss of native *mānuka* (*Leptospermum scoparium*), gorse left to its own devices served a similar function to mānuka as the nurse crop for the climax layer of the forest, which includes trees like the softwood rimu and tōtara and the hardwood tītoki and pūriri. The conditions needed to be right for the forest to grow again. They included leaving gorse to grow, controlling predators so the native birds that disperse seeds could return and willing volunteers across the country to plant large tracts of land in native plant species. When I return to New Zealand, I notice hills around Wellington, once yellow, now clothed in the dark green mantle of the native bush. It's a tentative process, but in some places the berries and the birds are returning; nature, given a chance, is bringing life back to the land (Gabites, 1993; Magesan, Wang, & Clinton, 2011).

In Global Generation's work of bringing life to an intense urban environment in the heart of London, I often have the sense of uncovering "a map of connectedness, that is already there, just not visible" (Riddiford, 2013, p. 159). The potential for growing a new and positive culture is there and, like the nurse crop, it is up to us to create the right conditions for life to grow.

The Third Basket of Knowledge: Kete Tuatea

To see one's own reflection as the connective energy upon which the universe is built is the third basket, Kete Tuatea. The third basket of knowledge connects with the notion of *whakapapa*, "a genealogical narrative, a story told layer upon layer, ancestor upon ancestor up to the present day" (Te Rito, 2007, p. 1). To know oneself is to know one's *whakapapa*. To know about a tree, a rock, or the fish in the sea is to know my *whakapapa*. It is an invitation to experience connection with the whole of life.

Williams writes of learning to be Indigenous in a global context: "[E]very person on this planet has the innate human capacity to be Indigenous; that is, to be in intimate relationship or resonance with the world of sprit, the earth, and other human beings" (2012, p. 92). Being *Indigenous to the cosmos* brings an authority that goes beyond the boundaries of the land one was born on or even the planet into the power of a deep time connection, as described by Joanna Macy:

> Now is the time to clothe ourselves in our true authority. Every particle in every atom of every cell in our body goes back to the primal flaring forth of space and time. In that sense you are as old as the universe, with an age of about 14 billion years. (2013, p. 8)

It is not the naming of separate things that draws me but a deeper current which flows through all things. In his ground-breaking book *Creative Evolution*, process philosopher Henri Bergson (1911/2005) describes a vital force that flows through all of life. A vitalist ontology is central to traditional Māori philosophy: "the belief in an original singular source of life in which that life continues as a force which imbues and animates all forms and things of the cosmos" (Hēnare, 2001, p. 297).

Sitting with the Generators, Global Generation's youth leaders, I return to our organization's roots. What is the meaning of the word global? More than the physical planet, it is a perspective, a view of life that is whole and without division. What is generation? It is all that has been handed down and all that will be passed on, and it is the vital energy from which life can flourish. This contemplation segues into a consideration of what the word "nature" might really mean. The conversation starts with bugs and bushes, and ends in purpose—deep time purpose. Swimme and Tucker refer to this as "a new kind of sight— insight into deep evolutionary time" (2011, p. 63).

One of the Generators articulates the benefit of discovering the creative journey of how all of life came to be: "Knowing the back story helps you feel a purpose in life and gives you something to work for" (Liz, 15 years).

The ground under our feet reveals the creative and connective impulses of how all of life came to be; evolution and ecology are written everywhere. As Swimme writes, "the crust of the earth holds the story book of life's great adventure" (1991, p. 101). Even in intense urban environments, that ground is available.

A FRESH DOORWAY INTO SUSTAINABILITY

One of my favorite sessions in the Skip Garden is when we have a chance to work with the people who are involved in making the roads and buildings in this new part of London. In a recent workshop with young construction apprentices, I introduced them to the notion that in times of crisis the universe becomes more creative. Metaphorically speaking, one might say that in the beginning, particles were at war with each other, until they learned to collaborate and create hydrogen gas, atoms, stars, and galaxies. Similarly, when our hunter-gatherer ancestors were in danger of running out of food, it was their creativity in learning how to grow food that saved them.

This is a natural starting place to discuss our role in creating the future. As one of the apprentices asked, "In the next two thousand years how might we be different?" The question is, would we be different in the way we looked or would it be our values that change?

Traveling With the Three Baskets

Niki Harré describes how authentic leadership is iterative in that "one is always open to new information from each source of knowledge" (2013, p. 125). Harré goes on to explain how she is open to learning from others, which strengthens leadership and "hands on leadership to others" (pp. 127–128). It has been an iterative process for me to introduce mythic ground in the facilitation of sustainability and youth development workshops. I have traveled to the metaphorical realm through the Three Baskets of Knowledge, which has been rewritten many times by me and others connected to Global Generation, changing each time to suit the context in which it is being told. As I shared the legend of Tāne with others and they began telling it in their own way, understanding, respect, and independence grew between us.

The following account is from a camp that Global Generation held for twelve young people on Pertwood Farm in Wiltshire. For some, it was a first step into being a Generator (on Global Generation's youth leadership program). It was also the first time they had been out of London. On the train, I sat beside Lily, one of our Senior Generators. All the way, she wrote. What emerged was her version of the Three Baskets of Knowledge that would provide an overarching narrative throughout the camp. This time, the protagonist of the story was a teenager, like Lily, plugged into thumping music, aware of the contradictions of school policies of equality, as racist comments still fill the hallways. She dreamed of a friendship between a spider and a seagull; she wished she could lead a life that was worth more. The next morning, the seagull appeared in front of Lily and she flew with the seagull out of the city to a gorse and hawthorn copse, with a fire pit and a yurt. As she looked into the seagull's eyes, she saw herself and learned about the first basket of knowledge... her hopes and her fears, her challenges and the values that would help her find a way forward.

As we sat together that night in the Pertwood yurt, on our first night of camp, Lily told her story. This was an invitation for the Generators to introduce themselves to each other through the values they had expressed by coming. With their journals in hand, they learned about themselves as they wrote about what it meant to them to leave London behind:

> Camping is very difficult—I don't know if I will be able to sleep at night. I will worry about my family who I am so far away from. There is no turning back; I just have to make the best. (Nazifah, 15 years)

> Our tent is filled with bugs and it is cold; the toilet has no light or heater. Many like it, but this has made me realise how much I miss the city, the loudness, the fact that there's always someone creating havoc. (Kulshum, 16 years)

The next morning, the clouds hung heavy in the sky. Yet, undeterred, the Generators set off up the track. Slowly, they made their way up to the big stone circle, each of them taking a place by the stones, standing in silence; not one flinching from the wind and the rain that was now coming down, even if . . .

> . . . it was too silent; it was nice being on your own for a bit, but I still prefer being in a room full of people or a city. (Kulshum)

> As a city kid walking over the hills in the rain was quite a journey for me— seeing all the valleys becoming distanced. The different shades of green looked like a small section of a rainbow. (Nazifah)

During the day, we explored the second basket of knowledge, the reflection in the gull's eyes of everything around us, be it rock, person, animal, or tree. In the blackness of the night, we became animals as we left our torches behind and silently threaded through the forest. By the morning, the Generators were ready to stand in the footsteps of the land. . . . What might it mean to imagine ourselves as the sky, the earth, and all that lies between?

> I am the sky, I am so beautiful in the daytime with white fluffy clouds and at night I come out with the prettiest stars, but even I have my ugly days, especially when the rain is about. You can always look up to me, whether you are happy or sad, whether you are scared or confident, anything . . . (Kulshum)

On our last day, a local farmer brought a falcon for the Generators to see. The black shiny eyes of the falcon were a reminder of the three baskets. As we approached the final circle, Kulshum said, "Can you tell us the last part of the story—what is in the third basket of knowledge? I want to get into that zone again."

This was an opportunity to reflect on all that we had experienced over our time together. As Lily asked the gull what was in the third basket, the gull transformed into the falcon we had just seen. She looked into the falcon's shiny eyes. She saw the falcon, she saw herself and everything around her. In their own ways, the Generators understood and expressed the third basket of knowledge—the interconnective and creative energy upon which the universe is built. Their free-fall writing speaks to what belonging in the cosmos might mean.

> I am the wind that howls and I am the movement of grass that sways side to side. I am what makes and creates things to grow and flourish as I am the ground beneath your feet. I am the soul within you deep. I am the stream in which you fish. I am the world in which you live. I am your home. (Nazifah)

> When I first got here I hated it. I tried to like it but I didn't—the silence, the atmosphere. It wasn't for me...then I thought I am only here for another day. Let me make the most of it. That's when I started to understand what nature is—nature is beautiful. Now I feel a part of nature. I am a city girl with a hint of country girl. (Kulshum)

The Needle of Inquiry

For some years now, I have identified the unfolding cosmic process as core to who I am. However, it was through my journey into Māori philosophy that I began thinking of myself as being *Indigenous to the cosmos*. Viewing experience within this large and interconnected frame helps me see different rifts running within me as all part of the ongoing universe story. It brings me into relationship with the past—not only my deep time past but also the lives of my immediate ancestors. Rather than vilifying actions, such as deforestation, which in today's light seem harsh and misguided, I have tried to understand the worldview of my forebears within the context of evolutionary process.

In her summary on Teilhard de Chardin's ecological spirituality, Mary Evelyn Tucker writes of an imperative to shift from human historical time to cosmic and geological time, which helps re-situate the polarization of good and evil that is present within the Judeo-Christian heritage. Tucker describes a movement from a radical separation of good and evil in nature and in the human to that which sees these two forces as the dynamizing drive of evolution itself (1985, p. 10).

The energizing drive, for me, takes the form of inquiry: and it is a collaborative inquiry. My sister describes it like this:

> Weaving is the gathering together of threads and this is the role you play in the family. You are promoting a sense of connection with each of us. You are driven by the needle of your inquiry, taking it down and up, down and up

through the warp and weft of the family fabric and this is opening up the inquiry for the next generation to break the mould and take risks.

The journey has also been one of reconnection to my Catholic roots. I am now part of a worldwide community of universe story practitioners (www.deeptimejourney.org); a number of them are Catholic nuns. Like me, they have been inspired by the vitalist and unitary spirit of radical Catholic thinkers such as Teilhard de Chardin and Thomas Berry. Many of the young people Global Generation works with are from Muslim and Christian backgrounds. As a facilitator, I choose not to focus on religious or any other kind of divide. I notice that engagement in the universe story inquiry often helps our young participants bring together their interests in science and religion and fosters broader intercultural understanding. We are sharing their journey on www.universestory.org.uk.

It has been important to spend time in the forests, in the soil of Aoteoroa New Zealand. Considering what it means to be *Indigenous to the cosmos* has been an invitation to locate leadership within the context of the land. I now ask, "What does the land have to say to me?"—a question my pioneering forebears would have dismissed as superstitious and animistic. I am also curious about my ancient ancestors; how did their creation stories inform their relationship to the land and to each other? As I described earlier, I entered the metaphorical story of Tāne slowly and carefully. I asked myself if my actions were yet another form of cultural appropriation (Johnston, 2006; Tuhiwai Smith, 2012). This hasn't been a journey I was consciously looking for; it came up to meet me. I have reached into Māori culture and pulled out features that I can identify with. This is a criticism leveled at the historian Michael King and other Pākehā writers (King, 1985). Like King, I am not trying to be Māori. My interest is in sharing values that I feel are integral to our shared 14-billion-year story—a story that was being written long before the features of Māori and Pākehā evolved. However, as a New Zealander, it has been particularly powerful to find elements of this story expressed in Māori mythology that developed under the same sky, the same soil that raised me. It has also been important and encouraging to have the support of people I consider to be my Māori mentors, especially Chellie Spiller and Manuka Hēnare, They have helped me clarify the implications of a vitalist view as expressed by thinkers both Māori and non-Māori.

CONCLUDING THOUGHTS

"We live in an ecological world and at the heart of ecology is mythology" (Shaw, 2011, p. 7). With this in mind, I would like to close this chapter by sharing more of the mythology surrounding the Three Baskets of

Knowledge. This legend speaks to a participatory and ethical ground for leadership and community building that I have endeavored to convey in this chapter. I use community in a full sense of the word, in which not only humans, but also "soils and waters, plants and animals are fellow members" (Leopold, 1949, p. 240).

In the way I usually tell it, I make a small addition to the traditional legend. Io, the supreme God who dwelt in the void of *te kore* (Marsden, 2003, p. 16), has a messenger who is a bird. It could be any bird, a morepork or a falcon, depending on where I am. I choose a bird because the loss of bird life and the consequent silencing of the land is one of the first signs that the third basket of knowledge has been forgotten. In other words, the vital interconnection upon which the universe is built is being disregarded. In less than 150 years, New Zealand experienced "a record of extinctions of bird species, without equal anywhere in the world" (Farrell, 2007, p. 217). Thankfully, in my lifetime this is beginning to change. Native forests are no longer viewed as "a primeval wasteland awaiting cultivation" (Park, 1995, p. 311), and huge efforts are being made to restore them and native bird populations.

My journey has been about grappling with different worldviews in the people I am involved with and in my own immediate cultural heritage. Birds weave their nests out of different materials and, in many cultures, as in Māori culture, "Weaving is embodied with spiritual values" (Puketapu-Hetet, 1989, p. 40). The way I see it, the art of weaving brings together different dimensions of our experience, the visible and the invisible, the physical and the spiritual. Weaving together these different forces creates a container that is flexible and strong. Birds lay their eggs in the empty space in the middle of the nest. It is a primordial place before anything happened, before there was a problem. A space that is full of potential in which new life can flourish.

Regardless of the physical ground we stand on, if we are still and quiet and if we really listen, we can find a shared sense of Indigeneity. In this way we can connect in a different and perhaps more personal and meaningful way to the cosmic story which is our collective story.

NOTE

1. Morepork is the English word for Ruru, the New Zealand Owl

REFERENCES

Anderson, R. (2006). *Intuitive inquiry: The ways of the heart in research and scholarship.* Retrieved from http://www.wellknowingconsulting.org/publications/pdfs/intuitive_inquiry_final.pdf

Armstrong, K. (2009). *A case for God.* London, England: Vintage Books.

Barnes, J. (2004). *Sea songs: Readers theatre from the South Pacific.* Westport, CT: Teacher Ideas Press.

Bergson, H. (2005). *Creative evolution.* New York, NY: Cosimo. (Original work published in 1911)

Berry, T. (1988). *The dream of the earth.* San Francisco, CA: Sierra Club Books.

Capra, F. (2002). *The hidden connections: A science for sustainable living.* London, England: Harper Collins.

Doty, W. G. (2000). *Mythography: The study of Myths and Rituals.* Birmingham, AL: The University of Alabama Press.

Farrell, F. (2007). *Mr Allbone's ferrets.* Auckland, New Zealand: Random House.

Gabites, I. (1993). *Wellington's living cloak: A guide to the natural plant communities.* Victoria, Australia: Wiley Publishers

Harré, N. (2013). *Authentic Leadership: Demonstrating and encouraging three ways of knowing.* In D. Ladkin & C. Spiller (Eds.), *Authentic leadership: Clashes, convergences and coalescence* (pp. 120–130). Cheltenham, England: Edward Elgar.

Hēnare, M. (2001). *Tapu, Mana, Mauri, Hau,Wairua: Māori philosophy of vitalism and the cosmos in Indigenous traditions and ecology: The interbeing of cosmology and community.* Cambridge, MA: Harvard University Press.

Hēnare, M. (2003). *The changing images of nineteenth century Māori society: from tribes to nation.* Unpublished doctoral thesis, Victoria University, Wellington, New Zealand.

Johnston, A. M. (2006). *Is the sacred for sale? Tourism and indigenous peoples.* Sterling, VA: Earthscan.

Kettleborough, H., & Kettleborough, N. (2013). Discovering that we live in an ancient and beautiful universe. In P. Reason & M. Newman (Eds.), *Stories of the great turning* (pp. 149–158). Bristol, England: Vala Publishing Cooperative

King, M. (1985). *Being pakeha: An encounter with New Zealand and the Maori renaissance.* Auckland, New Zealand: Hodder and Stoughton.

Ladkin, D. (2010). *Rethinking leadership: A new look at Old Leadership Questions.* Northampton, MA: Edward Elgar.

Leopold, A. (1949). *A Sand County almanac.* Oxford, England: Oxford University Press.

Macy, J. (2013). Playing our part in the great turning. In P. Reason & M. Newman (Eds.), *Stories of the great turning* (pp. 5–8). Bristol, UK: Vala Publishing Cooperative.

McIntosh, A. (2001). *Soul and soil: People versus corporate power.* London, England: Aurum Press.

Magesan, G. N, Wang, H, Clinton, P. W. (2011). *Nitrogen cycling in gorse-dominated ecosystems in New Zealand.* Retrieved from http://www.newzealandecology.org/nzje/

Marsden, M. (2003). *The woven universe: Selected writings of Rev Māori Marsden.* Masterton, New Zealand: Mauriora-ki-te-ao.

Marshall, J., Coleman, G., & Reason, P. (2011). *Leadership for sustainability. An action research approach.* Sheffield, England: Green Leaf.

Park, G. (1995). *Ngā uruora (The groves of life): Ecology and history in a New Zealand landscape.* Wellington, New Zealand: Victoria University Press.

Puketapu-Hetet, E. (1989). *Māori Weaving*. Auckland: Pitman.[Online] Available at: http://maaori.com/misc/raranga.htm [Accessed: 28.02.14]

Riddiford, J. (2013). Cabbages and Cranes. In P. Reason & M. Newman (Eds.), *Stories of the great turning* (pp. 159–168). Bristol, England: Vala Publishing Cooperative.

Shaw, M. (2011). *A branch of the lightning tree. Ecstatic myth and the grace.* Ashland, OR: White Cloud Press.

Spiller, C. (2011). Tane's journey to retrieve knowledge. In J. Marques & S. Dhiman (Eds.), *Stories to tell your students: Transforming toward organizational growth* (pp. 127–131). New York, NY: Palgrave Macmillan.

Swimme, B. (1991). *The universe is a green dragon: A cosmic creation story.* Sante Fe, NM: Arcana.

Swimme, B., & Tucker, M. E. (2011). *Journey of the universe.* New Haven, CT: Yale University Press.

Tarnas, R. (1997). *The passion of the western mind. Understanding the ideas that have shaped our world view.* London, England: Pimlico.

Teilhard de Chardin, P. (2008). *The Phenomenon of Man.* New York: Harper (originally published in French as Le Phénomène humain, 1955).

Te Rito, J. S. (2007). Whakapapa: A framework for understanding identity. *MAI Review*, Issue 2, Article 2. Retrieved from http://www.review.mai.ac.nz

Tucker, M. E. (1985). *The ecological spirituality of Teilhard.* Chambersburg, PA: Anima Publications.

Tuhiwai Smith, L. (2012). *Decolonising methodologies: Research and Indigenous peoples* (Rev. Ed.). Dunedin, New Zealand: Otago University Press

Turner-Vesselago, B. (2013). *Writing without a parachute: The art of freefall.* Bristol, England: Vala Publishing Cooperative.

Walker, R. (1990). *Ka whawhai tonu matou, Struggle without end.* Harmondsworth, England: Penguin.

Wilber, K. (1996). *A brief history of everything.* Boston, MA: Shambhala.

Williams, L. (2012). He Whanaunga Tera: The politics and practice of an Indigenous and intercultural approach to ecological well being. In L. Williams, R. Roberts, & A. McIntosh (Eds.), *Radical human ecology: Intercultural and Indigenous approaches* (pp. 397–349). Farnham, England: Ashgate.

CHAPTER 9

AFRICAN SPIRITUALITY
Insights from the Cradle of Mankind

Rica Viljoen and Loraine I. Laubscher

The time to build is upon us. We have at last achieved our emancipation. We pledge ourselves to liberate all our people from the continuing bondage of poverty, deprivation, suffering and discrimination. Let freedom reign. The sun shall never set on so glorious a human achievement. God bless Africa.
—Nelson Mandela, 10 May 1994

INTRODUCTION

Africa is the home of many peoples, tribes, and beliefs. The decolonization of Africa contributed to the awareness of the diversity of cultures on the African continent. The dismantling of Apartheid in South Africa in 1994 raised awareness and anticipation about African leadership internationally. Globalization blurred boundaries between continents, technology collapsed time zones, and rising levels of consciousness internationally added to the multicultural diversity of today's workforce.

Paradoxically, these changes in the international psyche simultaneously crystalize the gifts of African spirituality discussed in this chapter. They also emphasize fundamentalism as is evident in recent events of terrorism such

Indigenous Spiritualities at Work, pages 137–158
Copyright © 2015 by Information Age Publishing
137

as Boko Haram in Nigeria, armed robberies reported on in the news, and bomb blasts in shopping centers.

Although the different countries in Africa share common characteristics such as poverty, high birth rates, and economic dependence compared to advanced countries, a surprise awaits those who can find magic in self-organization and chaos, those who can see past the surface and acknowledge the underlying humanity that is visible to all travelers who linger a bit. This chapter explores the dynamics created by the thinking systems of Indigenous Africans.

It is an impossible task to describe the diversity that plays out in the African arena in one chapter. An attempt is not made to describe the differences in diversity of thought of the various groupings in Africa. Rather, human niche theory as described by Laubscher (2013) and Viljoen (2014), with deep roots in Spiral Dynamics (Graves, 1974; Beck & Cowan, 1996, 2013), is used as lens to describe the ontological sameness in Indigenous African people.

The African Philosophy of Ubuntu

> *There is no alternative to global cooperation on the basis of our humanism:*
> *without it we are doomed.... Ubuntu is far superior to modern notions of systematic*
> *interdependence because it carries the weight of ethical tradition with it.*

—Khoza (2011, p. 27)

The uniquely African concept of Ubuntu captures the philosophical premise of this chapter and offers a generous philosophy that opens to researchers an integrative understanding of life within Africa (Forster, 2006). The concept of Ubuntu or botho—loosely translated as "humanness"—is a comprehensive philosophical, anthropological, sociological, and cultural premise for African thinking about human identity and consciousness (Mbigi, 2005; Mbiti, 1990; Vilikati, Schurink, & Viljoen, 2013). This concept is encapsulated by the Southern African Zulu maxim, "Umuntu ngumuntu ngabantu" (A person is a person through other persons).

Mangaliso (2001, p. 24) defines *Ubuntu* as "humaneness—a pervasive spirit of caring and community, harmony and hospitality, respect and responsiveness—that individuals and groups display for one another. *Ubuntu* is the foundation for the basic values that manifest themselves in the ways African people think and behave towards each other and everyone else they encounter."

Mutwa (1997) explained, "[W]hen people feel with each other, when people feel for each other, when people are connected...that is *Ubuntu*." Mnyandu's conception of *Ubuntu* provides a helpful hint of the promise of leadership mastery from an African perspective: "Ubuntu is not merely positive human qualities, but the very human essence itself, which lures and enables human beings to become abantu or humanised beings, living in daily self-expressive works of love and efforts to create harmonious relationships in the community and the world beyond" (1997, p. 81).

The philosophy of *Ubuntu* is key to all African values and involves collective personhood and collective morality (Van der Colff, 2003). African leaders must display an element of sacrifice for the followers to realize their collective goals, Benjamin (2013) stresses. Time, energy, money, or friendship may be sacrificed for the benefit of the collective. Later in the chapter, a specific human niche or thinking system, named PURPLE, will be applied to describe this worldview.

Ubuntu is deeply ingrained as ontology in the African psyche. It is a lived philosophy that is made manifest through stories, wisdoms, behaviors, and beliefs. We share insights that arise from this philosophy. For example, one African saying is that it takes a whole community to raise a child. Much more is communicated than only the words of the saying—the idea of instilling good values, ethics, and spiritual development from childhood is implied. From Africa we can learn the gift of connectedness, humanness, and belonging. Young Africans are the children of every mother and father in the village where they grew up. The grown-ups share the responsibility of raising the children. Children are then the sum product of the community in contrast to the product of a single household, Benjamin (2013) explains. In times of hunger, disease, and drought, the community relies on the grown children to support the village. Older brothers and sisters who work in corporate settings are often expected to contribute financially to the community.

Broodryk (2004, p. 1) sheds further light on the spiritual nature of this philosophy:

> Man [sic] was declared "human" as soon as the element of "divine" (image) goodness (likeness) was instilled in him. This divine element that transformed man (matter) into a human being was nothing but a humanness, "Ubuntu," that manifested the image and likeness of God in each individual person of the human race.

The philosophy of *Ubuntu* encompasses the wisdom for understanding humanness, divine spirituality, and a relational way of thinking and being African. We adapt *Ubuntu* as an archetype that encapsulates the spirit of Indigenous Africa, explored through a human niches' lens.

African Spiritual Consciousness

> *Wisdom is like a baobab tee; no one individual can embrace it.*
>
> —Akan Proverb

The concept of African spiritual consciousness, according to Vilikati et al. (2013) allude to an appreciation of the African worldview. To understand African consciousness and personhood, one needs to be baptised into the rich ambience of the African people's cultures, language, geography, mythology, and oral tradition, and touch the real-world practices of the people (Mbiti, 1990). An immersion into the African existence reveals a particular cosmology and hierarchy that fashions their world. The following argument put forward by Forster offers a point of departure towards conceptualizing African Spiritual Consciousness:

> The question "who am I" (subjective) is intricately related to who you say that I am (objective), and who we are together (inter-subjective). Instead of being a lone subject, or a quantifiable and containable object, we are all "intersubjects," fundamentally interwoven into a common cosmic identity and being that is run through with sacred dignity. It is not just me, it is not just you, it is not just the material reality, neither is it just the spiritual reality; true reality is a sacred interweaving of all these things—true reality is beyond one single quantifiable truth, it is generous. Identity, in this sense, is a dynamic engagement and discovery of mutual identity and shared dignity—that is, a generous ontology. (2010, p. 12)

Setiloane (1998), Mbigi (2005), Ramose (1999), and Vilikati (2012), who support an integrative research approach, emphasize that the African worldview is a holistic one in which the internal, external, and transcendent aspects of being are interwoven into the same cosmos. Mbigi (2005) goes further to say that the essence and spirit of African consciousness is characterized by the values of connectedness, harmony, compassion and empathy, and a respectful relationship with creation.

Vilikati (2012) explains that in Africa life is not compartmentalized. When people are reduced to competencies, they become disconnected from their existential purpose and motivation. The content of relationships is important in Africa. Good relationships result in a sense of connectedness. Interpersonal relationships at work are viewed as important, as the organizations can be viewed as additional tribes to which African people belong.

HUMAN NICHES— DIFFERENT THINKING SYSTEMS AT PLAY

Sticks in a bundle are unbreakable
—Bondei Proverb

Clare Graves (1974) developed a bio-socio-psycho model of adult development that describes different worldviews or thinking systems. This model, later called spiral dynamics by Don Beck (2013) has been used successfully in Africa to explain differences in thinking systems in this diverse country. Together with Beck, Loraine Laubscher (2013) applied Gravesian thinking systems to African dynamics, contributing a deep appreciation of the African spirituality (Viljoen, 2014). Laubscher (2013) coined human niches as spiral dynamics for Africa.

Human niches detail the thinking systems in which people excel as an outcome of specific thinking patterns. Different questions of existence result in different thinking systems that lead to a human niche—something that an individual or culture excels at. On one of his 64 visits to South Africa Beck introduced the use of colors to identify the different thinking systems (Laubscher, 2013). The different thinking systems are explained in Table 9.1.

Human niches inform:

- How do I/we view the world?
- What do I/we see as the permanent parts of being me?
- How do I/we see the future?
- What information do I select or receive to see my world?
- What do I do daily (spend my time and attention on)?

Different human niches will answer the abovementioned questions differently.

A thinking system that sacrifices the self for the group is an indication of a collectivist worldview, according to Graves (1974). The different human niches oscillate between individualism and collectivism—between thinking systems that ask expressive questions of existence and thinking systems with a self-sacrificial intent. Conflicts between individualism and collectivism can explain some of the tension, social uprising, and tribal feuds currently seen in Africa.

Although Africa is a continent where all these thinking systems are manifested in its kaleidoscope of people, Viljoen (2014) found in her research, which is based on more than 50,000 participants, that more than 60% of

TABLE 9.1   Different Human Niches

Human Niche	Type of Question	Question of Existence
BEIGE	Individualistic	How do I survive?
PURPLE	Collectivistic	How can we sacrifice for the community or elder (chief)?
RED	Individualistic	How can I get power?
BLUE	Collectivistic	How can we sacrifice for the future?
ORANGE	Individualistic	How can I achieve success?
GREEN	Collectivistic	How can we sacrifice for the earth/globe?
YELLOW	Individualistic and Collectivistic	How can you and I survive?

Source: Adapted from Loraine Laubscher (2013).

the African population can be described as PURPLE. A further finding in the study that stretched over 42 countries is that internationally, leadership is mostly BLUE and ORANGE, but workers are mostly PURPLE and RED. Laubscher (2013) explains that BLUE and ORANGE ways "just glide off PURPLE"—the thinking systems are too far removed to understand each other spontaneously. Translation between thinking systems is needed. Leaders need all the different thinking systems to be optimized collectively in an inclusive manner for a geopolitical region to progress.

The Self Concept in African Spiritual Consciousness

If you want to walk fast, walk alone.
If you want to walk far, walk together.
—African Proverb

The term "African" is a vaguely defined concept. Part of what creates the definitional complexity is that Africa is made up of different cultures and subcultures. Vilikati (2012) warns that the risks of crystalizing a definition for Africa may lead to losing the very essence of it, because definitions are often used in a commercialized sense in our modern context. He continues as follows:

> For me African would refer to the simple little thing—how African people define for themselves what life is about—our notion of existence as living because others are living. Being alone and disconnected in the African worldview is almost equivalent to death. Death is a state of being alone. The worst form of punishment in African society is not even the death penalty but exclusion. Throwing somebody out of the community destroys their sense of identity and their primary focus of existence—it is a state of death. (Vilikati, 2012, p. 23)

The Zulu word *sawubona*, from Southern Africa, explains it well. It is one of those tribal words that explain that eyes are connected to an ancestral reality. "We see" in this sense, means that we see you and your ancestors. Seeing in this sense establishes everyone as a witness. We see each other. It becomes an obligation to investigate what this moment in time gives each other. Greeting someone in this way invites dialogue. It obliges each to share what is needed in that moment.

Identity is not anchored in the individual, but in relation to others (Vilikati, 2012). Identity is also not individualized or conscious (Viljoen, 2014). Organizational development interventions in organizations should take cognizance of how identity is conceptualised in Indigenous Africans.

Mbeki (1998), Young (1990), Biko (1978), and Vilikati (2012) all alluded to how political, economic, and sociocultural injustices in the South African past suppressed, erased, and misappropriated the identity of African people. Scientific imperialism emphasizes the impact on identity even more (Viljoen, 2014). Western role models (BLUE and ORANGE human niches) are often portrayed on television programs and movies.

Africans leaders often struggle to maintain their deep Indigenous PURPLE roots, rather than adapting a BLUE or ORANGE working persona and rejecting the old ways (Laubscher, 2013).

The human niche of PURPLE presents the gift of humanness and spirit. Ways should be found to remember the old ways (Laubscher, 2013; Mutwa, 1997; Watson, 1982). An evolvement and synthesis of worldviews can rather occur that may lead to integration and higher levels of consciousness.

The Interrelatedness of African PURPLE

Laubscher (2013) used ethnographic content analysis to describe the phenomenon of African PUPRLE from data gathered through lived history from actively working with spiral dynamics in Africa for more than 40 years. Four domains emerged in an attempt to describe the nature of being African. The four domains, namely the human domain, the sacred domain, the physical domain, and the external present domain (Figure 9.1) are closely

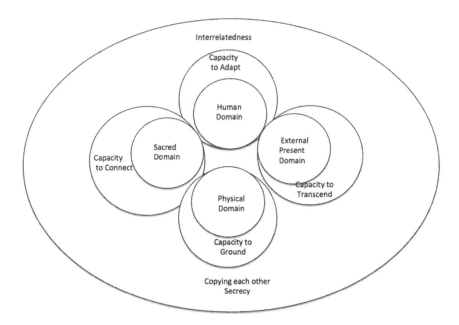

Figure 9.1 The interrelatedness of African PURPLE, adapted from Laubscher (2013).

knitted together and weave the integral whole of the collective experience of being African.

Identity in African PURPLE, says Laubscher (2013), is constructed not as an individual sense of self but a deep interrelated sense of belonging to the human domain, the sacred domain, the physical domain, and being part of the past as it is manifested in the present. In African PURPLE, members of a community copy each other. The analogue thinking system of this human niche ensures that stories, metaphor, and parables are particularly effective in conveying messages.

The human domain describes how an Indigenous PURPLE African adapts—namely in relation to others in the community. The sacred domain refers to the way in which Indigenous PURPLE African people connect with their roots, their spirituality, and the world. In the physical domain, the groundedness to mother earth of an Indigenous African PURPLE person is conceptualized. In traditional African-ness, the ability to transcend time and space and be very aware of predecessors and ancestors in daily life is deeply integrated in the psyche. These dynamics are discussed under the external, present domain as described by Laubscher (2013).

Ubuntu is the philosophy that binds the domains together. Each of these domains that draw deeply on Indigenous wisdom is discussed briefly below.

The Human Domain of African PURPLE

> *You are just as welcome in a place as the size of your foot.*
> —Ghanaian Proverb

The human domain forms a key cornerstone in an exploration to understand the phenomenon of African interrelatedness. The following subcomponents form part of this domain:

- People relations
- Family relations
- Rules of behavior
- Ceremonial or ritual behavior

It must be noted that, as discussed in the previous section, the self is not identified in African PURPLE at an individual level but collectively, and that identity does not reside with the individual but in an interplay between the self, the human domain, the physical domain, and the sacred domain. In Figure 9.2, the subcomponents of the human domain are presented.

In Figure 9.2 the phenomenon of people relations in the context of Africa are contextualized as collective and through others. It is critical to

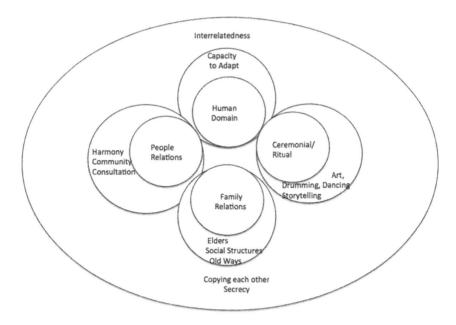

Figure 9.2   The human domain of African PURPLE, adapted from Laubscher (2013).

remain in harmony with others, with the tribe, and with nature. The community comes first, says Laubscher (2013). All decisions must be made by way of consultation (Benjamin, 2013).

In terms of people relations, family structures are critical. The role that the mother or the father plays in the life of their children is profound. Both parents have lessons that they must transfer from generation to generation (Mutwa, 1997). The elders must always be respected (Viljoen, 2014). The old ways, the oral history, and the ways to live are shared through family relations.

Ubuntu as a philosophy becomes very real in this domain. Humanness forms the basis of relationships. It is also in this domain that punishment is meted out. Parents are ashamed when their children are disobedient. Laubscher (2013) elaborates that the worst punishment in African PURPLE is public shame.

Another aspect that forms part of the integral collective experience is the unspoken rules of behavior in the specific society. In Africa secrecy is important (Mutwa, 1997). People have to save face and not expose elders, managers, or seniors (Viljoen, 2015). They do not want others to be concerned and underplay the impact of negative stories.

Social structures must be respected. The practice is that if a person visits the chief, a present must be taken (Laubscher, 2013). There is a strict way in which things are to be done—and that way must be followed or copied.

However, humanness in African leadership also considers the poor, who are also allowed to visit the leaders. The implications of reciprocal exchange are discussed later in this chapter.

The ceremonial or ritual domain forms an integrated part of the sense of African identity (Benjamin, 2013). There are special festivals in which one must participate. Drumming is not only used as music, it is also a way of communicating with each other's domain and with the spiritual domain. PURPLE Africans love theatre and art. They are adept at interpreting metaphors. Storytelling is a gift that contributes to a sense of community, and the art of storytelling is truly valued (Laubscher, 2013; Mutwa, 1997; Viljoen, 2014).

Most native Africans believed in a Great Mystery or Great Spirit that underlay the complexity of all existence, as well as in many other spiritual powers that influenced the entire life they engaged in according to a variety of rituals (Mutwa, 1997). As a person passed through the stages of the life cycle—obtaining a name after birth, seeking a guardian spirit at puberty, setting off at death for the journey to the afterlife—rituals marked the passages. In prayer, Africans used gestures and words as well as songs and dances to communicate with the spirits (Watson, 1982). Ceremonial observances of prayer and thanksgiving took place at critical stages in the agricultural or hunting season. The ancestors provided protection and looked after the well-being of the offspring.

Africans often receive their training from life. The Sotho, from Southern Africa, call life *moya*. It translates directly into breath, soul, spirit, or life. It may come from gods or spirits, or it may simply exist. The life and spirit that one finds alive and well in Africa can be described as the spirit of PURPLE and should be protected and celebrated.

It must be noted that by forming such a tight community through family and tribal relations, in and out groups are formed. Belonging to a specific group or tribe is important for the identity of African PURPLE. Paradoxically, inclusion in a tribe means exclusion from other groupings.

The Physical Domain of African PURPLE

In Figure 9.3, the physical domain of African PURPLE is visually presented. The following aspects constitute a sense of connection or groundedness with the earth, the animals, the sky, and the land. African PURPLE people speak a language that is older than words, Mutwa (1997) and Laubscher (2013) explain. There is an acute awareness of the interconnectedness of things that is an outflow of their ability to form deep relationships with the physical world, animals, the land, and the sky.

In Figure 9.3 the different aspects of the physical domain of African PURPLE are described. The spirit of animals is acknowledged and celebrated in African PURPLE, Benjamin (2013) explains. Different tribes often adapt an animal totem. The spirit of this animal (such as a baboon or lion)

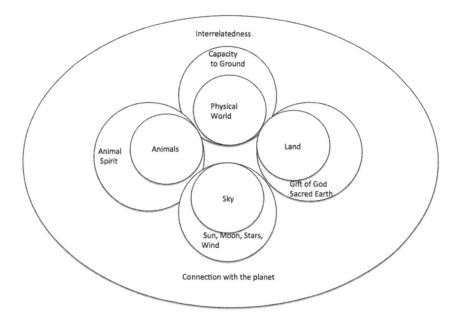

Figure 9.3 The physical domain of African PURPLE, Laubscher (2013).

then represents the spirit of the tribe. It is believed in Indigenous African PURPLE that all living organisms have a traceable spirit, which influences who we are as human beings. Benjamin (2013) applies this metaphor to leadership and argues that leadership internationally forms a tribe that should share universal values to be effective.

There is a real awareness of the elements of the sky in African-ness. The sun, the moon, the stars, and the wind, Mutwa (1997) explains, all play a role in all the communities to a larger or lesser extent. Often festivals are held to celebrate the change of seasons or the solstices (Laubscher, 2013). The sky is watched closely for agricultural purposes. Often the land is worshipped as sacred, explains Viljoen (2014). It is viewed as God's land, and therefore no human can ever really own land. The earth should be respected and taken care of. Living off the earth is valued and seen as a life of quality. Living close to the physical world serves a grounding function.

The Spiritual Domain of African PURPLE

The third domain of African PURPLE deals with the sacred or the spiritual domain. The aspects that contribute to this dynamic ability to connect are magic, ancestors, stories, and time orientation. In Figure 9.4, the sacred or spiritual domain is displayed.

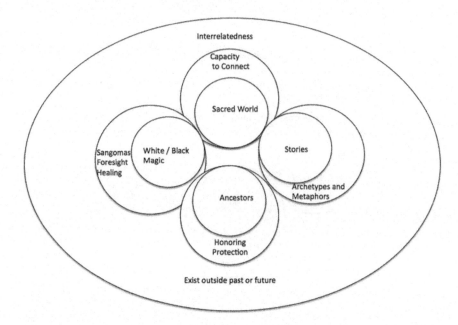

Figure 9.4 The sacred/spiritual domain of African PURPLE, adapted from Laubscher (2013).

In Figure 9.4 the aspects that impact the sacred and spiritual domain of African PURPLE that contribute to the capacity to connect are shown. Typically there are elements of magic—white or black magic or superstition—that impact the daily life of an Indigenous African across boundaries of different tribes (Laubscher, 2013). Sometimes it manifests in a sense of knowing or foresight (Mutwa, 1997). In some cases where religion is alive and well, a very real sense of karma is experienced: "We must treat a stranger well, it could have been an angel" (Viljoen, 2014). It is a combination of all the senses, an extension that leads to other understandings. Worshipping the ancestors is an integral part of being African PURPLE. If one does not do this, it is believed that one's efforts will not be blessed. Honoring the ancestors includes offering them beer, food, and prayer during sacred rituals (Mutwa, 1997). Benjamin (2013) contributed significantly to the documentation of the impact that music and dancing have during rituals in some African tribes.

African PURPLE culture makes a definite difference between a traditional healer or a *sangoma* and a witchdoctor or a witch. Among the Kwazulu/Natal people of South Africa, for instance, sangomas are healers and deeply valued. They are the keepers of the old ways, the old stories. Witches are viewed as inherently evil. Their powers are inherited and form part of their organic constitution, and they are psychic. Watson explained the African belief that there is life on earth—one life that

> embraces every animal and plant on the planet. Time has divided it up into several million parts, but each is an integral part of the whole. A rose is a rose, but it is also a robin and a rabbit. We are all of one flesh, drawn from the same crucible. (1982, p. 19)

Storytelling is used to share old wisdom and Indigenous spiritual knowledge (Toendepi, 2012). Often the old ways are explained by oral history and transferred from one generation to another (Mutwa, 1997). Ritual (such as initiation) often forms part of a human niche, and a blood ritual (such as tattooing or slaughtering of an animal) is to be expected (Laubscher, 2013). The ability to live in the present, while the past and the present are simultaneously experienced, contributes to the sense of connection to a bigger force (Viljoen, 2014).

African spiritual consciousness can be expressed through an understanding of the PURPLE niche and by taking into account the interrelatedness of African PUPRLE domains. By remembering Indigenous knowledge, and by integrating it into consciousness, African spirituality is manifested.

The External Present Domain of African PURPLE

The last domain that Laubscher (2013) described is the external present domain of African PURPLE. To a degree, this domain is interwoven in the other domains. Here, the focus is on being present in the here and the now and how identity is conceptualized.

In certain parts of Africa, the same word is used for both "yesterday" and "tomorrow." The present moment is the center of time. The distance from the present is more important than the direction (Laubscher, 2013). The past and future are not seen as opposites, but merely as more remote forms of the present. This makes the ancestors very real. Although the focus is often on creating a better future for the children, energy is also spent on how to bury the dead and how to remember the old ways.

Often, the lifespan is shorter than is expected in a first-world country. Too many elders pass on before their stories are shared. The struggle for survival often distracts from long-term planning. Children are often educated in BLUE educational systems and often in English rather than the Indigenous languages. The struggle to maintain the old ways often rests with the older generation.

Western leaders can also find worth in hearing the whispers of their ancestors singing to them not to forget the old ways. This aspect complicates strategic planning and buy-in into long-term initiatives significantly in organizations. By linking business goals to aspects that enthuse PURPLE, really inclusive organizations can be built.

INDIGENOUS SPIRITUALITIES AND LEADERSHIP

Nature, spirituality, philosophy, and even politics, which are often mechanistically separated into different domains by Western cultures, are interrelated and viewed as an organic whole by Indigenous Africans.

There are, for example, lessons to be learned from the tribal institution. One can learn about concepts like authority from tribal structures. Humanness can also be observed. In tribal meetings, effort is often made to ensure inclusivity. Western managers can study the self-organizing nature of tribal ways and meet employees from these social systems where they are.

From Zimbabwe, the Shona word for leadership is *Utungamiriri,* which literally means to go in front and show the way. Benjamin (2013) explains that a person on whom this word is bestowed must give vision, direction, knowledge, and resources to get to the desired outcome.

Typically, leadership is passed on from one generation to another. Best practice in terms of leadership is passed from generation to generation by the great ancestors and through oral history. This practice can be adapted in the workplace. This social structure, however, presents a real challenge for organizations in which new leaders are appointed from outside the organization instead of relying on internal succession planning—thus promoting from the tribe. Organizations should take this dynamic into consideration in their induction and leadership development initiatives.

There is a real openness in PURPLE leadership to be reflective. In Ghana, the Sankofa is a symbol for the ability of a leader to look back and learn from his mistakes. It is never shameful to reflect and adjust one's ways. Another Western African saying explains that the person who cleans the land with a panga and walks in front often cannot see how straight they walk. Feedback is needed from the people who walk behind. These lessons from Indigenous spiritualities can be applied to leadership in organizations.

Leaders in the new world of work must be catalysts or shape shifters (Beck & Cowan, 1996; Laubscher, 2013). Leaders must become the new *sangomas,* or healers. One has to understand the background culture of each member of the group that one is working with. The leader also needs to have insight and to be sensitive to each participant's level of education as well as cognitive understanding of the work that is being presented. Leaders have to be able to help bridge the gap of understanding by way of analogies, metaphors and relevant storytelling. Through a process of inclusivity, real organizational transformation can happen (Viljoen, 2008). Acting contextually appropriately can enable leaders to bring out the best in their workforce and align the unseen human potential around organizational efforts.

Two aspects of African PURPLE that must be taken into account from a leadership perspective are the energy and rhythms of the different thinking systems and the dance of respect of African people. These aspects are described in the following paragraphs.

The Energy and Rhythm of Africa

Each African community has its own values and norms that result in a specific energy or rhythm in the community. This rhythm is expressed through the core processes and projects in the community and refers to the innermost aspirations, needs, and spiritual contentment of a society (Benjamin, 2013). Companies that want to extend their footprint into rural spaces must make very sure that they understand the rhythm of the local society.

Rhythm, however, is not only applicable metaphorically. In most African societies, weeding and singing take place synchronously, by interweaving the physical work and the invisible values and beliefs into an undeniable drumbeat of being in it together. Often dancing forms part of the ritual of growth (Benjamin, 2013).

The rhythms of different human niches are also different. There are self-organizing rhythms in PURPLE, but something does not necessarily happen according to a clock or a calendar. A great deal of consultation must take place before a collective decision can be made. RED is self-driven, with an expressive energy and a fast rhythm. Because a person may decide for himself or herself in RED, the impact is instantaneous. BLUE has a controlled rhythm, and life is structured by rules and regulations. The conservative risk profile in BLUE ensures that all rules are followed and all corporate structures are respected. ORANGE has an individualistic rhythm that looks out for opportunities and events that can contribute to its status. GREEN has a slower, yet accommodating, rhythm. It is slower as it needs to reach inclusivity.

The whole community is welcome at lunchtime, Laubscher (2013) says, and an excessive amount of food is available. Often in a corporate setting, a local manager will frown upon the loaded plate of food that a local African dishes up during a lunch break. In PURPLE, one does not know when one will eat again. The food of the parents (the company) is also the food of the people, and PURPLE people find it difficult to understand why they cannot take leftovers for their extended family at home.

It must be noted that there is also a strong RED human niche component in Africa. Nigeria, for example, has a lovely entrepreneurial buzz, and energy (Viljoen, 2014). The RED thinking system in its underdeveloped form is driven by instant gratification and power (Laubscher, 2013), and often leads to conflicts in the country and the continent.

Reciprocal Exchange—The Dance of Respect

Traditionally, the Indigenous PURPLE peoples of Africa perceived themselves as living in a cosmos pervaded by powerful, mysterious spiritual beings and forces that underlie and support human life. They believed that in order to survive, it was necessary to acknowledge these spiritual powers in every aspect of their lives. They did this by addressing the powers in prayer and song, offering them gifts, establishing ritual relationships with them, and passing down knowledge about them to subsequent generations, primarily through myths (Mutwa, 1997).

There is a wonderful tradition in most African tribes, where one will always take a gift when one goes to meet a senior person. This is done out of respect and to acknowledge the audience. The BLUE thinking system is concerned with truth, justice, and compliance. They declare gifts that are received in organizational gift registers. BLUE is concerned about the ethical implications of bribery. The interpretation of BLUE is that PURPLE thinking systems are corrupt.

The Nigerian President, Olusegun Obasanjo (1997), explained the dilemma of reciprocal exchange as follows:

> The gift is made in the open for all to see, never in secret. Where a gift is excessive, it becomes an embarrassment, and is returned. If anything, corruption—as practiced by exporters from the North as well as by officials in the South—has perverted positive aspects of this age-old tradition.

In Africa a gift is a concept of appreciation and hospitality and serves as a token of goodwill. It is not demanded, and the value is not in the material worth of the present but in the spirit of giving. It is critical to always understand the contextual dynamics while not violating universally accepted norms. In terms of ethics, the spiral truly assists in identifying the etiology of bias.

Hearing the Voices of Africa

The two human niches that are predominantly representative in Africa are PURPLE and RED. Laubscher (2013) stated that for PURPLE, questions of existence focus on solving the problem of shelter and food in the local tribe. It is sacrificing self for the group, the family or the tribe. Graves (1971) and Wilber (2010) described this value system as primitive (Beck,

2012; Wilber, 2010). Laubscher (2013) and Viljoen (2014) moved away from this positioning of spiral dynamics. The wisdom of storytelling, the lessons learned from remembering the old ways, and the true understanding of nature are not celebrated as they should be. The lovely energy that a healthy RED niche radiates and the heroic and warrior-like attributes that accompany this value system are often ignored. These attributes are gifts for a diverse society. The healing that must happen in the continent of Africa, and globally, there should not be an attempt to change the thinking systems of societies but an attempt to ensure that the specific human niches mature so that the gifts that are innate in that system blossom.

PURPLE often communicates via storytelling and oral history (Viljoen, 2014). Little is captured in writing, and limited literary work finds its way into mainstream published academic work. In current Western tradition, knowledge evolves incrementally. To hear the voices of Africa, leaders must pause and become aware of the self-organizing rhythm of Africa, become still and listen to the old ways that strangely also resonate within the soul of humankind.

BLUE countries come to Africa to help or to change PURPLE and RED through interventions, not taking into account that instead they could learn something from Africa—lessons of life and spirit that other societies have forgotten. Mutwa (1986, p. 792) pleaded that foreigners should please leave his Africa undefiled by their ideals, falsehoods, and hypocrisies. He continued as follows:

> [T]hey have not learnt—or they do not wish to learn—that one cannot expect people to be loyal to something alien to their customary ways and which they do not understand.... How can one expect a tribal-scarred Lukonde woodcarver to be loyal to a Parliament based on the British model? Could one expect an officer of the Guards to be loyal to his Battle Induna immediately after being forcefully transferred to an impi of Baluba warriors? ... Why must we be turned into soulless zombies?

The African philosophy, ontology, and context are often ignored in doing business with African companies and African employees (Viljoen, 20014). BLUE businesses cannot understand why procedures and strategies are not optimally implemented (Laubscher, 2013). PURPLE and RED thinking systems are often not understood by other human niches. Translation between thinking systems does not happen, and the benefits of inclusivity as described by Viljoen (2008) are not brought about.

Managers who hold senior positions in organizations often do not take time to listen to their workers (Viljoen, 2008). BLUE and ORANGE thinking systems want to improve PURPLE—as if something is wrong or backward. The rest of the world wants to fix Africa (Laubscher, 2013). The solution for African challenges must come from Africa.

The Challenge of Leadership in Africa

Leadership in organizations needs to understand how collectivism in PURPLE-ness functions in order to optimize the gifts that are presented by this human niche. In PURPLE, property is jointly owned. For example, cousins feel free to wear each other's clothes. Everything must be kept in the family. If a person has a job and a vacancy occurs he must recommend his brother or sister regardless of their qualifications or the job specifications. If there is a tender[1] and a person has discretionary power he is expected to allocate it to his family. These dynamics have real implications for organizational leaders trying to implement corporate governance and attempting to steer away from nepotism.

Due to the time orientation described above, in Indigenous African PURPLE, there is often no understanding of the future consequence of actions. The thinking system of Indigenous Africans takes a very limited view of the future, and what is going to happen in the future is typically not considered. These dynamics present a very serious challenge for strategy implementation in organizations and for other longer-term organizational practices such as implementing and measuring an employee's balanced score card.

Traditional organizational strategies, structures, and processes often have little impact in Africa. Other more inclusive and organic organizational design models are needed. Viljoen (2014) discussed African case studies where organizational strategy had to be translated very specifically to ensure congruence with the thinking systems of the employees.

Understanding human niches is critical, especially at national and regional levels. Leaders in Africa are faced with the following:

- Thinking of different human niches is not understood throughout the organization.
- We underestimate the wisdom of people who were not educated in traditional Western schooling systems.
- Other human niches often do not acknowledge, see, or sense the self-organizing capability of PURPLE.
- Social structures overrides the organizational structure.
- Questions that are not appropriate for using in one system of thinking may nevertheless fit into another system.
- Interventions should yield a multifaceted systemic approach at global level and involve the whole person-system at the individual level—thus body, mind, and soul.
- Controversy must be reframed—look at things from at least four levels.
- Leaders need to understand people in the worlds in which they live.

Other human niches are often trying hard to "fix or rescue" PURPLE, explains Laubscher (2013)—as if one grouping would ever be able to change the thinking system of another group. For example, attempts to implement quality improvement programs, behavior-based safety initiatives, and business optimization initiatives often fail because the underlying philosophy of these attempts is BLUE and is seldom translated into PURPLE terms. Western industrial society and the worldviews that go with this belief system lead inexorably to the kinds of global difficulties we now face. African spiritual consciousness as a philosophy searches for wholeness and a community with enhanced relationships. Perhaps an African ontology can be adapted to address the systemic issues the world is faced with.

The Gift of Africa

PURPLE human niches have spirit. Africa has spirit. Spirit becomes so controlled in BLUE and suppressed in ORANGE that the world may risk the loss of spirit (Laubscher, 2013). This is the gift that Africa can bring—that people do not have to reject their roots, their old manners, and the stories of their ancestors or forefathers. We should much rather remember those stories and manners while we continue on this journey we call life.

Powerful forces that shape our modern world such as technology, globalization, and aggressive nation-state politics focus on a dominating and aggressive model rather than on cooperation and intuition. PURPLE innately operates from intuition and in a cooperative manner. Consumerism has become the new ethic, and in the mass-consumption society there is a mindset that can be described as a "throw-away society." PURPLE does not accumulate earthly possessions. Burying their loved ones in a memorable way, living close to their ancestors and their community, and remembering the ways of the forefathers are at the top of their minds. Their organization does not cause pollution or global warming.

In *The Red Book*, Jung (2009) underlined the importance for the soul to go to the desert. In Africa, people live their symbols. Still today, various African tribes adopt a token animal, and the spirit of this symbol fulfills the purpose of describing the essence of the tribe. In Zimbabwe tribes associate with, for example, the monkey, the lion, or the great warrior. Indigenous Africans still today find an abundance of visions, fruits of the deserts and the wonderful flowers of the soul.

Africa teaches us that nature is healing. Nature helps us become grounded. To reconnect with nature one must go to the desert, sit and watch the waves of the ocean, or collect some shells. We must take a walk, pick some flowers, sit in the park, throw pebbles into a shallow stream, and enjoy the sunshine. We should lie on the grass, look up at the sky and the floating clouds. At night we should study the night sky and the majestic constellations. We must take deep breaths of fresh air, and smell the fragrance of blossoms, the greenery, and Mother Earth herself.

CONCLUSION

The challenge in Africa in the next decade will be not to resist shifts in thinking systems, nor will it be to change prematurely or for the sake of changing. We must rather process change with mutual cooperation and caring, which results in as little misery as possible. The importance of human development in organizations should not be underestimated. In Africa we need to revisit basic management skills such as how to plan, organize, lead, and control and to ensure that management depth is built.

African spiritual consciousness in its very nature understands human nature innately. Insights from African wisdom traditions can be directed to dealing with the rising levels of violence in Africa. Crime-ridden townships can benefit largely from management and skills development. Why are leaders not focusing the human energy in African Indigenous systems the way that elders or chiefs used to do? It might just be that the rest of the world can also grow by remembering the old ways, the ways of our forefathers, the way of humans.

To conclude, Watson (1982, p. 8) prompts us to "learn from people whose lineage perhaps runs more directly than ours to the roots of 'human beings', and who embody, in their way of seeing and in their system of belief, a philosophy that is older than our own—and which may be closer to the truth."

The answers to old problems will not come from the Western mind. Africa just might hold very specific wisdom for the world about humanity. Insights into new economic, political, and societal models just might emerge from Africa, the cradle of mankind.

NOTE

1. In Africa, it is required to *render a tender*—or a proposal for work. This is a compliance process used to minimize corruption.

REFERENCES

Beck, D. E. (2012). *The integral dance: How a master code pollinates and preserves the culture of bumblebees.* Retrieved from http:://www.integralleadershipreview.com/ 7174-the-master-code-spiral-dynamics-integral

Beck, D. E. (2013). *The master code. Spiral dynamics integral accreditation* (unpublished course notes). Santa Barbara, CA: Adizes Business School.

Beck, D. E., & Cowan, C. C. (1996). S*piral dynamics, mastering values, leadership and change.* Malden, MA: Blackwell.

Benjamin, E. (2013). *"Utungamiriri Misire": In search of the GENE of African leadership.* Unpublished doctoral thesis, Da Vinci Institute for Technology Management, Johannesburg, South Africa. Retrieved from http://www.davinci.ac.za/wpcontent/uploads/2014/03/EmekaEgbeonuFinalThesissubmission.Pdf

Biko, S. (1978). *I write what I like.* London, England: Heinemann.

Broodryk, J. (2004). *Ubuntu: Life lessons from Africa:* Pretoria, South Africa: Ubuntu School of Philosophy.

Forster, D. (2006). *Self validating consciousness in strong artificial intelligence: An African theological contribution.* Retrieved from www.spirituality.org.za/files/

Forster, D. (2010). A generous ontology: Identity as a process of intersubjective discovery An African theological contribution. *HTS Theological Studies, 66*(1), 1–12.

Graves, C. W. (1971, October). *Seminar on Levels of Human Existence.* Presented at the Washington School of Psychiatry, Washington, DC.

Graves, C. W. (1974). Human nature prepares for a momentous leap. *The Futurist,* April, 72–87.

Jung, C. J. (2009). *The red book; Liber novus* (M. Kyburz, J. Peck, & Shamdasani, Trans.; Introduced by Shamdasani). New York, NY: Norton.

Khoza, J. R. (2011). *Attuned leadership: African humanism as compass.* Johannesburg, South Africa: Penguin.

Laubscher, L. I. (2013). *Human niches: Spiral dynamics for Africa.* Unpublished doctoral dissertation, Da Vinci Institute for Technology Management, Johannesburg, South Africa. Retrieved from http://www.davinci.ac.za/wpcontent/uploads/2014/03/LoraineLaubscherHumannichesspiraldynamicsforAfrica.Pdf

Mandela, N. R. (1994, May 10). Inaugural Speech. Pretoria, South Africa. Available at www.africa.upenn.edu/Articles_Gen/Inaugural_Speech_17984.ht Accessed on 15/05/2015

Mandela, N. (1994). *The long walk to freedom.* London, England: Abacus.

Mangaliso, M. P. (2001). Building competitive advantage from *Ubuntu*: Management lessons from South Africa. *Academy of Management Executive, 15*(3), 23–32.

Mbeki, T. (1998). *Africa: The time has come.* Cape Town, South Africa: Tafelberg.

Mbigi, L. (2005). *The spirit of African leadership.* Randburg, South Africa: Knowledge Resources.

Mbiti, J. S. (1990). *African religions and philosophy* (2nd ed). London, England: Heinemann.

Mnyandu, M. (1997). Ubuntu as the basis of authentic humanity: An African Christian perspective. Journal of Constructive Theology, *3,* 77–91.

Mutwa, C. (1986). *Let not my country die.* Pretoria, South Africa: United Publishers International.

Mutwa, C. (1997). *African proverbs.* Cape Town, South Africa: Struik Publishers.

Obasanjo, O. (1997). *Issues in global governance.* Management Development and Governance Division, Bureau for Development Policy. Retrieved from http://www.pogar.org/publications/other/undp/governance/claywesc-speech97e.pdf

Ramose, M. B. (1999). *African philosophy through Ubuntu.* Harare, Zimbabwe: Mond Books.

Setiloane, G. M. (1998). Towards a biocentric theology and ethic- via Africa. In C. W. Du

Toit (Ed.), *Faith science and African culture: African cosmology* (pp. 73–84). Pretoria, South Africa: University of South Africa, Research Institute for Theology and Religion.

Toendepi, J. (2012). *A systemic perspective to wealth creation through learning and adaptation: an analysis of South Africa's competitiveness.* Unpublished doctoral thesis, Da Vinci Institute for Technology Management, Johannesburg, South Africa. Available at: http://group.aomonline.org/msr/msr_summer_2013.

Van der Colff, L. (2003). Leadership lessons from the African tree. *Management Decision. 41*(3), 257–261.

Vilikati, M. V. (2012). *African Spiritual Consciousness.* Unpublished master of philosophy dissertation, University of Johannesburg, South Africa. Retrieved from https://ujdigispace.uj.ac.za/handle/10210/7920

Vilikati, M. V., Schurink, W., & Viljoen, R. C. (2013, January). *Exploring the concept of African spiritual consciousness.* Paper presented at the Academy of Management Conference, Orlando, FL.

Viljoen, R. C. (2008). *Sustainable organisational transformation through inclusivity.* University of South Africa. Retrieved from http://uir.unisa.ac.za/handle/10500/726

Viljoen, R. C. (2014). *Inclusive organisational transformation.* Gover Transformation and Innovation Series. Farnham, England: Ashgate Publishers.

Watson, L. (1982). *Lightning bird: One man's journey into Africa.* New York, NY: Simon and Schuster.

Wilber, K. (2010). AQAL Glossary. Introduction to integral theory and practice: IOS basic and the AQAL map, Vol. 1, No. 3. Available at http://aqaljournal.integralinstitute.org/public/Pdf/AQAL_Glossary_01-27-07.pdf

Young, I. M. (1990). *Justice and the politics of difference.* Princeton, NJ: Princeton University Press.

PART III

IDENTITIES

CHAPTER 10

KARMA-MAKERS?

Organizations and Indigenous People in India

Edwina Pio

A night of stars enchanted the Adivasi boy as he hid in a tree to avoid the graveyard shift at the factory where his leave had been declined...for he must attend the early morning rituals to welcome the breath of spring in the air...

A day of pink dogs coloured by effluent in the local stream, evidence of the continuing impact of local Indian and foreign globalizing organizations...

A night of murder and rape by high-caste men, who in preserving atrocious boundaries render people mute in the corruption and bureaucracy that lace India's good laws...

A day of organizations in India imbued with the ethos of jal (water), jungle (forest), jameen (land)—an ethos that has been the life-blood of Adivasis for centuries...

The paradox of day and night and karma-makers...

Such paradoxes (Heredia, 2007; Roy, 2011; The Hindu, 2014) are liberally sprinkled in the lives of Adivasis, the original inhabitants of the land in India. This term is derived from the Sanskrit words *adi*, meaning earliest

Indigenous Spiritualities at Work, pages 161–166
Copyright © 2015 by Information Age Publishing
161

times/from the beginning and *vasi*, or resident/inhabitant (Adivasi, 2014). The constitutional and legal term used for Adivasis is Scheduled Tribes. The Scheduled Tribes are distinguished from the Scheduled Castes despite the fact that there is an overlap between the categories. Scheduled Castes is the legal and constitutional name collectively given to the groups who traditionally occupied the lowest status in Indian society—primarily from the Hindu religious point of view—and were outside the caste system and inferior to the castes. They have been variously termed untouchables, harijans, and dalits (World Directory of Minorities, 2008). However, categories change over time (Chaube, 1999): tribals were called Forest Tribes in the 1891 census; later they were classified as Hill Tribes and in the 1941 census as Tribes; and today they are known as Scheduled Tribes (Heredia, 2012).

My focus, in Karma-makers, is on the Scheduled Tribes or the Adivasis, the Indigenous people of India. Karma is often translated as destiny, and in this context organizations are sites of hope (Pio, 2014). Thus karma-makers or destiny-makers present relational possibility in organizational processes. Hope is not just wishful thinking, sunny advice, or hoping for the best. Rather, hope is a bidimensional construct composed of agency or a sense of will power and way-power or pathways to generate successful plans and alternatives irrespective of obstacles, to reach one's goals (Snyder, 2000). Therefore, acknowledging the virtuous aspects of Adivasis is a concerted effort, to offset and perhaps reduce the negative stereotypes rampant about Adivasis (Guha, 1999; Kujur & Minz, 2007; Nayak, 2007; Redford, 1999).

India's Adivasis are not homogeneous; they speak more than 100 different languages and vary vastly in their ethnic and cultural backgrounds. Adivasis number approximately 84 million, are from approximately 461 ethnic groups, and consist of numerous tribes such as the Warlis, Bhils, Santals, Chenchus, and Gonds (International Work Group for Indigenous Affairs [IWGIA], 2013). They are spread over the varied terrain of India, with the largest concentrations found in seven states of northeast India and the central tribal belt stretching from the states of Rajasthan to West Bengal. Over the centuries, the Adivasis have lived through a deep bonding with nature, and over many decades have also lived through a deep wounding by high-caste money lenders, corporate land users, social prejudice, and often-toothless law implementers (Baski, 2012; Baviskar, 1995, 2005; Temper & Martinez-Alier, 2013; US Library of Congress, 1995).

Yet through the bonding and wounding there has been a continuation of a planetary-affirming spirituality of co-existence. This spirituality, articulated by individuals who have worked with Adivasis for decades (D'Lima, personal communication, 2014), includes the following life energies:

1. Contentment with life, which is far from complacent

2. Familiarity with the transcendent, expressed in rituals, signs, and symbols suffused with simplicity and gratitude while also manifesting flexibility to suit particular persons and communities
3. Being at home with many manifestations of the transcendent
4. Hospitality to guests, even unexpected ones, despite a frugal or subsistence diet
5. Moderate spiritual and material needs
6. Communication of rich emotions towards their children, peers, and elders, even though educationally or in terms of social sophistication they may not share the ambience of economically wealthier societies
7. A sense of self-worth

Adivasis are generally less consumerist or commercial than the non-Adivasi population in India. Generating a great surplus in order to consume much more is not their way of life. Their horizons of human fulfillment require relatively little extinction of natural resources, destruction of other economies, or their own displacement from familiar habitats. There is pride and confidence in their domain and the sovereignty of their little homesteads, partly supported by India's enlightened constitution. Thus the Adivasis have not been shunted into reservations, which often strip people of their self-worth, but are supported by the government in a hopeful integrative process of sociopolitical development. For example, in Article 46 of the Directive Principles of State Policy, the constitutional mandate to the Indian States is as follows: "The state shall promote with special care the educational and economic interests of the weaker sections of the people, and, in particular, of the Scheduled Castes and Scheduled Tribes, and shall protect them from social injustice and all forms of exploitation" (Ministry of Social Justice and Empowerment, 2009). Articles 341 and 342 of the Indian Constitution provide protective and promotional measures for the Scheduled Tribes. Yet affirmative action, which is used by various stakeholders such as organizations and governments, must be reconciled with the various human rights and constitutions prevalent in societies, such as equality before the law; prohibition of discrimination on the grounds of religion, race, caste, sex or place of birth; equality of opportunity in matters of public employment; and the abolition of untouchability (Heredia, 2012; Ministry of Minority Affairs, 2014).

The central government of India has appointed a commission that is dedicated to work on identifying and issuing an annual report on the Scheduled Castes and Scheduled Tribes in the hope of creating strategies for their well-being. Moreover, as India is such a vast country with an immense population and many wooded areas where modern civilization has not yet trod heavily, the government has found it necessary to identify all its citizens and thereby hopefully set in process policies and practices to enhance the wellbeing of all its citizens. The report reflects any illegal activities against Adivasis, and recommendations are made to prohibit discrimination and to improve and protect their position (Minority Rights Group International, 2008). India is signatory to ILO Convention No. 107 concerning the Protection and Integration of Indigenous and Other Tribal and Semi-Tribal Populations in Independent Countries and has legal responsibilities for its implementation (Asian Centre for Human Rights [ACHR], 2010).

While the seven listed life energies are common in many Adivasi communities, the weight given them differs in different communities and the energies are in flux, particularly following the penetration of communication technologies such as television and the Internet. Moreover, the thirst for managing water by means of dams and the dire need for minerals, to give two examples, from lands which Adivasis have inhabited for generations have created a plethora of problems ranging from displacement to violent activism and changing Gods (Heredia, 2007; Riukas, 2013; Robinson, 2003). Indeed, it is not only foreign multinationals but also big business conglomerates in India who, in their need or greed for ever higher and ever quicker economic profit margins, fail to factor in the rhythms of nature and the cadences of our interconnected fragile planet.

But as karma-makers, organizations can choose to incorporate Indigenous spiritualities in their organizational development interventions and training programs. Such a pedagogy of hope would ensure that the life energies of Adivasis, as epitomized in the seven points in this Touchstone piece, are threaded through organizational culture. A pedagogy of hope could be expressed in some of the following life-energizing pathways:

1. Induction programs that share information on Adivasi life-energies
2. Exploration of the triad of *jal*, *jungle*, and *jameen* from various nonexploitative angles in a strategic planning process
3. Mentoring with Adivasi employees that ensures co-learning
4. Programs for top management to impart information on the sociopolitical and historical marginalization of many Adivasis, particularly for those organizations that seek to utilize resources from lands historically owned by Adivasi communities
5. Resource-efficient projects in and with Adivasi communities that are regularly evaluated with meaningful metrics
6. Every employee in the organization to be granted one day, on company time, for working on a project meaningful for both Adivasis and the organization
7. Visiting Adivasi elders to explore comprehensible possibilities for future generations.

Perhaps the implementation of such life-energizing ways by corporations, including universities, will be a hopeful step in ensuring that we are less caught up in a one-dimensional view of each other (Sen, 2006). Rather, such courageous and compassionate steps can create porous boundaries and praxis-in-action for you and me as continuously evolving beings in transforming our workplaces, our enterprises, and our lives.

REFERENCES

Adivasi. (2014). Oxford dictionaries [online]. Retrieved from http://www.oxforddictionaries.com/definition/english/Adivasi

Asian Centre for Human Rights (ACHR). (2010). Who are the indigenous peoples of India? Asian Centre for Human Rights. *India Human Rights Report Quarterly, 02.* Retrieved from http://www.achrweb.org/ihrrq/issue2/indigenous.html

Baski, B. (2012). Our fate is in our hands. Retrieved from http://re.indiaenvironmentportal.org.in/feature-article/our-fate-our-hands

Baviskar, A. (1995). *In the belly of the river: Tribal conflicts over development tin the Narmada valley.* Delhi, India: Oxford University Press.

Baviskar, A. (2005). Adivasi encounters with Hindu nationalism in MP. *Economic and Political Weekly, 40*(48), 5105–5113.

Chaube, S. (1999). The scheduled tribes and Christianity in India. *Economic and Political Weekly, 34*(9), 524–526.

Guha, S. (1999). *Environment and ethnicity in India, 1200–1991.* Cambridge, England: Cambridge University Press.

Heredia, R. (2007). *Changing Gods: Rethinking conversion in India.* New Delhi, India: Penguin.

Heredia, R. (2012). *Taking sides: Reservation quotas and minority rights in India.* New Delhi, India: Penguin.

International Work Group for Indigenous Affairs (IWGIA). (2013). *Indigenous peoples in India.* Retrieved from http://www.iwgia.org/images/stories/sections/regions/asia/documents/IW2013/India.pdf

Kujur, J., & Minz, S. (Eds.). (2007). *Indigenous people of India: Problems and prospects.* New Delhi, India: Indian Social Institute.

Ministry of Minority Affairs. (2014). *Sachar Committee Report.* Retrieved from http://www.minorityaffairs.gov.in/sachar

Minority Rights Group International. (2008). UNHCR— The UN Refugee Agency. *World Directory of Minorities and Indigenous Peoples—India: Adivasis.* Retrieved from http://www.refworld.org/docid/49749d14c.html

Ministry of Social Justice and Empowerment. (2009). Provisions relating to SCs. Retrieved from http://socialjustice.nic.in/constprov2.php?pageid=2#a5

Nayak, B. S. (2007). Silenced drums and unquiet woods: The myth of modernization and development in Orissa. *Journal of Comparative Social Welfare, 23*(1), 89-98.

Pio, E. (2014). *Work and worship: Religious diversity at workplaces in New Zealand.* Auckland, New Zealand: Auckland University of Technology.

Redford, K. (1999). The ecologically noble savage. *Cultural Survival Quarterly, 15*(1), 46–48.

Riukas, W. (2013). Primitive accumulation, the communist idea and Maoist praxis in contemporary central India. *International Critical Thought, 3*(4), 399–412.

Robinson, R. (2003). *Christians of India.* New Delhi, India: Sage Publications.

Roy, A. (2011). *Broken Republic.* London, England: Penguin.

Sen, A. (2006). *Identity and violence: The illusion of destiny.* London, England: Allen Lane.

Snyder, C. R. (2000). *Handbook of hope.* San Diego, CA: Academic Press.

Temper, L., & Martinez-Alier, J. (2013). The god of the mountain and Godavarman: Net present value, indigenous territorial rights and sacredness in a bauxite mining conflict in India. *Ecological Economics, 96,* 79–87.

The Hindu. (2014, February 9). Adivasis oppose merger of some mandals with Seemandhra. *The Hindu.* Retrieved from http://www.thehindu.com/todays-paper/tp-national/tp-andhrapradesh/adivasis-oppose-merger-of-some-mandals-with-seemandhra/article5669757.ece

U.S. Library of Congress. (1995). *Tribal religions.* Retrieved from http://countrystudies.us/india/57.htm

World Directory of Minorities. (2008). *Scheduled castes of India.* Retrieved from http://www.faqs.org/minorities/South-Asia/Scheduled-Castes-of-India.html

CHAPTER 11

CARIBBERRE, DOING BUSINESS IN THE 21st CENTURY, ABORIGINAL WAY

Dennis Foley

ABSTRACT

Caribberre, in my mother's language, translates as "dancing." Metaphorically we now dance a new way, the dance of the "Australian Aboriginal[1] entrepreneur," a dance that is "business enterprise." However, within a capitalist, free-market Australian economy, the bureaucracies that manage Aboriginal people cannot agree on a definition of what an Aboriginal business is. Abstract, faceless non-Aboriginal people in suits in Canberra fail to understand that an Aboriginal business is not based just on shareholding. The determination of an Aboriginal business involves much more, and at the end of the day should it not be that Aboriginal people define who is Aboriginal and also what businesses are Aboriginal? The High Court of Australia has already given Australian Aboriginal people precedence to confirm community identity; this chapter argues that the Aboriginal business community should also determine which enterprises are indeed Aboriginal. This chapter explores the concept of Aboriginal well-being and self-determination within the growing area that is Aboriginal business and enterprise, which in many ways is a special "dance" that is economic freedom.

Indigenous Spiritualities at Work, pages 167–189
Copyright © 2015 by Information Age Publishing
167

Caribberre[2]

In another time
My life would have been culturally structured.
Puberty would have heralded expectations
Of Warrior training
And the concept of manhood!

But now there is only hopelessness
When one reaches this age

In history the missions were to save us,
With decades of mistreatment
Alcohol was to wash away the pain
But it doesn't!
Youth today simply suicide
This invariably creates more pain.

Our wages were stolen
The symptom no financial capital!
Our children stolen
The symptom no social capital!
As we were jailed in institutions.

For our language and culture were forbidden
a government rule
The result, the symptom
Reduced Cultural Capital

The Act that stopped us attending high school
Past 15
Was repealed in 1972.
The symptom low human capital
Now we compete
With shadows
Lateral violence sees us fighting over crumbs
As mother earth is raped for billions in commodities.

Poverty is the causation of dysfunctional society
A causation that is colonisation

The right to live out our lives without fear of devastation
Can be achieved
Through enterprise
Sustainable income
Dissipates the yoke of poverty,
Dissipating the rut of welfare.

No more dancing to tokenistic programs
Of 'planned' economic and employment strategies
Where the beneficiaries
Are the corporates and the non-indigenous consultants
Who Prey on the gullible black.

Financial independence through business
Is self-determination
Where the Aboriginal employs and trains their own
Where we no longer dance to government control.

PREAMBLE

When I was a child, I was fascinated about stories of my great-grandfather on my dad's side, an Aboriginal-Irishman who had a bullock dray and later freight wagons drawn by heavy horses such as Shires that hauled heavy freight up rough ungraded mountain trails. His wagons serviced the rugged New England plateau and Dorrigo plateau from Tenterfield to Glenn Innes and Inverell. This was wild land that did not give in to settlement very quickly. It took a special person to thrive there: You couldn't tame it. My great-grandfather was one of those who survived and prospered, driving his wagons to the Steamer Ports, Taree, Nambucca Heads, Grafton, Coffs Harbour, and other places where the boats from Sydney serviced the coast. He carted freight and mining equipment inland and brought the precious produce of the farmers to the landings, to be shipped to market. He was an entrepreneur and he was Aboriginal. His business kept his kids out of the missions: in fact, my grandfather, John Foley, joined the wagons as a young boy and escaped the tentacles of the Catholic Mission at Tingha at an early age. This way most of my family lived outside of the Aboriginal Protection Act. Perhaps this is why I have devoted the last 20 years of my working life so passionately to the study of Aboriginal small business and entrepreneurs: for, like my great-grandfather, when we are self-employed we are in some ways free from colonial subjugation through our financial independence.

The second aspect of this chapter is my disgust for racist concepts of blood quantum, which will be self-explanatory as the paper evolves. As a child I was taken from school by a police officer, treated like a criminal without my parents' knowledge and placed in a prison, a youth detention center called Minda. They examined me. I was dazed and in shock as they shoved pieces of colored plastic, like sticks, up the cuticles on my fingers roughly and painfully to measure the color of my cuticle. Then different pieces of colored plastic were wrapped tightly around my arm. Like a Dulux color chart I had been classified on my percentage of Aboriginality,

based on the colour of my cuticle and skin. No doubt Jewish people suffered similar treatment in their initial confinement at Dachau or Auschwitz in WWII. It was after all a system of extirpation, of genocide. They
checked for head lice and as I stood there almost naked they measured my
skull and width of nose. An adult labeled me "Octoroon." Many years later
I found out what it meant and it still makes me nauseous. That night, like
many others, I was initiated into the world of Westminster Law and the colonial way of managing Aboriginal youth as I was abused. The next day in
court, bruised and bleeding, I was made a ward of the state under a Child
Welfare Act. My identity was, for a few years, stolen. I was an "Octoroon":
That was my new identity, not a child that somebody loved. No; a classification of a subspecies, an alien beast, an Octoroon. So please forgive me if
I dislike the concept of blood quantums, which I will expand upon latter
in this chapter; and please forgive me when I get upset when someone
says, "You are not Aboriginal"—whether they are referring to a small to
medium enterprise (SME) or to a person, based on an arbitrary percentage. As an Aboriginal male who survived that system, I have a right to be
concerned . . . and angry. Are my many female cousins Octoroons, Quarter
or defined as Half-caste? For they did not come home: stolen, classified
and vanished, gone . . . lost. The genocide was complete as their parents
died prematurely from shattered hearts. No gas like Auschwitz: Rather, it
was slow and painful, a life left without purpose and lived in fear. That is
the history and purpose behind this chapter.

INTRODUCTION

Australian Aboriginal people use the word *business* in many very distinct
ways. Death-mortuary and mourning practices are commonly known as sor-
ry business; financial matters are referred to as money business; the secret-
sacred rituals distinct to gender are known as women's or men's business,
and ceremonial issues—a label that covers a broad range—are referred to
simply as secret-sacred business (Arthur, 1996; Wilkes, 1978). In this chapter I discuss another form of Australian Aboriginal "business," the small to
medium enterprise (SME) that produces goods and services for sale in the
modern capitalist open-market economy and employs the greatest number
of Aboriginal people.

Aboriginal enterprises actually contribute to fostering social cohesion
and the recognition of Aboriginal people (Kleinert, 2010). The establishment of more Aboriginal businesses is crucial for fostering independence
from government welfare and largely non-Indigenous workplaces (Biddle,
Howlett, Hunter, & Paradies, 2013). Aboriginal self-employed who are
entrepreneurial are becoming an increasingly important component of

Aboriginal economic activity: The numbers of self-employed have increased from 4,600 to 12,500 in the two decades to 2011. My research (Foley, 2000, 2005, 2006a, 2006b, 2013) and work with Boyd Hunter (2013) has shown a link between self-employment and entrepreneurial activity based on empirical evidence that by becoming self-employed, Aboriginal people are exploring new boundaries in self-determination and are entrepreneurial, if not continuously, then for at least some period of their business life. Yet some government organizations have trouble defining what is an Aboriginal business and what is not.

Just under ten years ago, Indigenous Chambers of Commerce developed across Australia, created by business people from the Aboriginal community acting independently of government and aberrantly in comparison to mainstream Chambers of Commerce, whose key function is networking. Indigenous Chambers see networking as a priority; however, they also act in a role of capacity skill development for their members and as an advocate for Indigenous business issues, exploring opportunities and engaging in the establishment of strategic alliances and networks. Above all, they are a place to seek refuge and assistance in a culturally acceptable location, providing assistance or just sharing thoughts, promoting accomplishments, or simply being a grief counselor. Indigenous Chambers of Commerce are a culturally acceptable sanctuary in the volatile business environment that is mostly not culturally acceptable. They are a place where an Aboriginal business operator can share a cuppa and a story, find a shoulder to lean on, shed a tear, or find a place to air a grievance in privacy. Indigenous Chambers of Commerce are increasingly important for the sustainable economic development of Aboriginal business (Foley & Hunter, 2013). Mandurah Hunter Indigenous Business Chamber in Newcastle, NSW was the first known Aboriginal Business Chamber, established in 2006 as a grassroots-driven organization servicing the then fledgling businesses within the Hunter region (NSW Indigenous Chamber of Commerce, 2013). This has resulted in an increase in the development and the self-identification of Aboriginal enterprises in the last decade, which, combined with the demands and market opportunities of the construction industry and mining boom, has resulted in increased demand for Indigenous contractors to provide services to satisfy the insatiable demands of mining communities (Langton, 2013) and commerce. Indigenous businesses, however, remain statistically more prevalent in urban areas, corresponding with Indigenous population concentrations (Hunter, 2013).

One thing that the reader should understand is that anything Aboriginal is big business in Australia. Gary Foley, the Aboriginal activist, has often stated that if every Aboriginal passed tonight there would be a million non-Aboriginal unemployed tomorrow. Be it in Native Title bureaucracy, employment, health, education, banking, or whatever, there are many thousands of non-Aboriginals employed to manage us Aboriginals or manage Aboriginal issues. Aboriginal activity in small business is no different. So you would expect policymakers and most other Australians to recognize the importance of Aboriginal business in enhancing social and economic outcomes of Indigenous peoples, but it remains surprisingly difficult to adequately define an Indigenous business, for Aboriginal identity is no longer a fixed subject frozen in history (Hall, 1990). This chapter attempts to simplify the concept of Aboriginal identity in a commercial application by, firstly, discussing the issues that confuse the identification of an Aboriginal enterprise that is based purely on percentage of ownership in the enterprise, and secondly by providing a snapshot of some recently interviewed Aboriginal businesses as to what the concept of Aboriginality means to those in business and how it defines their business. Finally, this chapter provides a robust and defendable definition of an Indigenous business for effective policy outcomes and for facilitating the prosperity of businesses prosperity that addresses cultural demands by supporting Aboriginal well-being, the Aboriginal family, and the wider Aboriginal community.

The dark side of Aboriginal involvement in a wider competitive, free market economy is loss of identity. If that happens and the cultural fabric dissipates, then Aboriginal enterprise is no different to the non-Aboriginal.

CURRENT DEFINITIONS AND LITERATURE

There is a trend to define an Aboriginal business as one with Aboriginal majority ownership at 51% or greater (Willmett, 2009). This is a simplified definition for convenience, aimed at denying non-Aboriginal enterprises to fraudulently claim commercial indigeneity? There are many examples in Australia, particularly within the tourism industry, where operators claim to provide an Indigenous product that is non-Indigenous owned, and/or where the Indigenous involvement is tokenistic (Haynes, 2010). Forgery within the Indigenous art industry, for example, has become a prevalent problem, affecting the profitability of bona fide Aboriginal businesses in that industry (Chappell & Polk, 2009). Neil Willmett's (2009) definition was devised to overcome blatant acts of fraudulent misrepresentation to the public by unscrupulous operators masquerading as Aboriginal suppliers. However, I hope this chapter will convince the reader that percentage shareholding alone does not determine what is an Aboriginal business.

One of the stumbling blocks in understanding the phenomenon that is Aboriginal entrepreneurship and small business is the narrow extent of research literature that has been funded by government agencies, namely the 2011 Curtin University Paper by Maria Fay Rolka-Rubzen, *The Anatomy of the Australian Entrepreneur,* and the Australian Government's (2003) *Indigenous*

Business Review: Report on Support for Indigenous Business. These are the official commentary or understanding of the importance of Aboriginal business. Yet after reading them, it remains surprisingly difficult to adequately define an Indigenous business and/or understand the cultural legacies involved. Commercial enterprises undertaken by Aboriginal Australians have many practices and procedures, even ethical standpoints, that make them slightly different from their non-Aboriginal counterparts, and this is central to my argument. Being Black and in business does not make you an Aboriginal business person, which is something the two papers mentioned above fail to grasp. Kinship and wider links often associated with social capital and networking theory are applicable to the Aboriginal business networks that have cultural links that cannot be measured or quantifiably confirmed, but which are real and are also overlooked in these papers. The sanitized non-Aboriginal Rolka-Rubzen paper (2011), and the *Indigenous Business Review* (Australian Government, 2003) form the framework of an "official" research foundation into Indigenous Australian entrepreneurship by government agencies. However, they are possibly two of the worst examples of poor scholarship, biased methodology, limited research samples, and shallow Eurocentric approaches to Indigenous knowledge. It is difficult to understand why the Federal Department of Education and Workplace Relations (DEWER) or Indigenous Business Australia (IBA) and Supply Nation (a 100% fully funded DEWER subsidiary) link their websites to such poor scholarship. Or could it be that DEWER and IBA funded these poor examples of scholarship? The result is a blinkered belief that poor scholarship by non-Aboriginal authors is better than nothing at all: however, in the process, DEWER and IBA ignored a decade of academic works by me and many other competent Aboriginal and non-Aboriginal scholars.

Methodology

Unlike the Rolka-Rubzen paper (2011) and the Indigenous Business Review (2003), this chapter discusses the main issues in providing a robust and defendable definition of an Aboriginal business that can be used to operationalize effective policy outcomes and facilitate the prospering of these businesses and also looks at Aboriginal business practices. The research underlying this chapter uses a multiple case study approach applied within independent studies (Eisenhardt, 1989; Yin, 2002) along with a systematic literature review (Pittaway, Robertson, Munir, Denyer, & Neeley, 2004; Tranfield, Denver, & Smart, 2003). A thematic approach has then been applied from the empirical evidence to provide focus and unity (Thorpe, Holt, Macpherson, & Pittaway, 2006) that adheres to an Indigenous standpoint theorem (Foley, 2002, 2003a, 2003b, 2003c, 2005, 2006a) by an Indigenous scholar.

The Argument

Intuitively, a business can be characterized as Indigenous only if Indigenous people can be said to have ownership. But what if a SME has three investors, two non-participatory investors at 25% each and an Indigenous owner-operator at 50%? Even though the Indigenous owner-operator has a single majority shareholding, this business, under current Australian rhetoric, is not necessarily defined as Indigenous, for to be an Indigenous enterprise there must be 51% Indigenous ownership (Willmett, 2009).

Durie (2003) challenged the definition of what constitutes a Māori business in Aotearoa on the grounds that we need to "reconsider how commercial opportunities might contribute to Māori values and aspirations and provide synergies between Māori" (p. 246). Māori business ownership is determined by the degree of control, ownership, power, and management within the firm's structure, its vision, culture, assets, employment, financing, and product (French, 1998). This is a holistic approach that is not determined by simple percentage ownership. A thoughtful paper endorsed by the Hon Parekura Horomia, the Minister for Maori Affairs, goes beyond Durie in stating that Maori businesses displayed cultural values in business that included:

- Whanaungatanga—Relationships with debtors and creditors
- Rangatiratanga and Mana—Leadership and respect to all parties in business
- Kaitiakitanga and Manaakitangi—Stewardship, hospitality/care
- Utu—Reciprocity and honor
- Wairua—Māori Spirituality in business. (Crenative Ltd, 2006).

In an independent study, I also confirmed similar findings in Aoeteroa (Foley, 2008). Love and Love (2005) identified five common features of Māori business. These not only distinguish them from Pakeha (non-Māori) businesses, but also partially substantiate why they are in business. They are:

1. They (Māori) have management control (*control of their lives*).
2. Responsibility and accountability exist to a broader range of beneficiaries and stakeholders.
3. *Tikanga* (cultural practices) is applied in the business environment.
4. There are obligations to an extended family group as opposed to focusing solely on individual advancement.

5. The organization has an ethos that mirrors the broad goals, values, and aspirations of the Māori world (Love & Love, 2005).

Māori place more emphasis on the cultural aspects of why they are in business, rather than debating the percentage shareholding in determining what is a Māori business, and this is what I feel is lost in the debate on defining an Australian Aboriginal business. As you will see in the following discussion, there is no mention by Willmett, the Australian Taxation Office, Indigenous Business Australia, and others of the cultural aspects of what is an Indigenous business; yet when you talk to Aboriginal business people, they certainly respect those cultural aspects.

An outstanding business that has brought positive change to the Aboriginal community where it operates is Ngarda Civil & Mining Pty. Ltd. (hereafter Ngarda P/L), a mining contractor in an extremely isolated area of Western Australia with around 350 employees, of whom over half are Indigenous. Ngarda P/L has an annual turnover of over AUD 150 million. The company claims that it is the largest Indigenous owned and operated contracting company in Australia. According to the company profile on its website, Ngarda P/L is jointly owned by Leighton Contractors (50%), the Ngarda Ngarli Yarndu Foundation (25%) and Indigenous Business Australia (IBA) (25%) (Ngarda, 2013). Collectively the Aboriginal community-based foundation and IBA own half of the company. However, Ngarda P/L would not be classified as an Indigenous business under existing definitions despite substantial Aboriginal participation throughout the organization and despite the goals and aims of the business to support, train, and grow the local Aboriginal community in sustainable skills. Spiritually, culturally, and in its management structure and goals, Ngarda P/L to all intents and purposes is an Indigenous business, but based on shareholding ownership it is not regarded as being so under existing government definitions.

To allow for these anomalies in remote Australia, the Pilbara Aboriginal Contractors Association Inc. (PACA) developed an alternative definition of an Aboriginal business. After deliberation with its Aboriginal members, PACA decided that to be eligible for membership, and to be recognized as an Aboriginal business, businesses must have Aboriginal ownership equating to a 25% shareholding or more, must operate in the Pilbara region of Western Australia, and must be committed to pursuing all avenues of employment and training opportunities for the Traditional Owners of the Pilbara region (PACA, 2010). The argument provided to defend this reduction in threshold is that in the world of commerce ownership of as little as 5% of the issued shares in a company can secure a seat on the board and ownership of 20% of the issued shares of a public company can trigger the takeover provisions of the Corporations Act. PACA's emphasis is on the corporate giving back to the traditional owner. When you consider this, the remoteness, the lack of commercial opportunities found in comparison with a normal urban environment, and the historical legacy of isolation, poor education, limited access to financial capital, and intergenerational family wealth accumulation due to the subjugating dominance of colonization processes and Mission management stripping away all Aboriginal assets (financial and non-financial), then an Indigenous business that has 25% ownership is an anomaly and should be encouraged, not discounted by an external party in a capital city. It is the managerial intent, employment, training opportunities, and above all the Aboriginal community's cultural values interwoven within the enterprise in the Pilbara that ensure PACA is a concept that should be recognized and supported.

An Australian Taxation Office (ATO) policy document defines an Indigenous small business as one in which "at least one-half [is] Indigenous owned and managed" (ATO, 2009, p. 5). Taken literally, this definition includes partnerships based on mixed marriages and joint ventures where Indigenous people own half the company. The ATO came to this definition after talking to its Indigenous Advisory Board.

The Australian Bureau of Statistics (ABS) standard definition of a business is:

> A legal entity engaging in productive activity and/or other forms of economic activity in the market sector. Such entities accumulate assets on their own account and/or hold assets on behalf of others, and may incur liabilities. Excluded are the economic activities of individuals (except where individuals engage in productive activity either as a sole traders or in partnerships) and entities mainly engaged in hobby activities. (ABS, 2012, p. 5)

After lengthy consultation with stakeholders (including Aboriginal and non-Aboriginal advisors), the ABS (2012) has settled on two operational definitions of an Indigenous business:

1. An Aboriginal and Torres Strait Islander-owned business has at least one owner who identifies as being of Aboriginal and Torres Strait Islander origin; and
2. An Aboriginal and Torres Strait Islander-owned and controlled business is one that is majority owned by Aboriginal and Torres Strait Islander persons.

The second of these definitions specifies majority ownership as a proxy for controlling interest in the business (i.e., Indigenous equity is greater than 50%). Note that the ABS deliberately limits the scope for both of these definitions to privately owned SMEs (i.e., organizations that have fewer than 200 employees). The rationale is that as businesses get larger and their ownership structures become more complex, assessing ownership becomes increasingly difficult. Evaluating whether a wholly-owned subsidiary of a publicly listed company with majority Aboriginal and Torres Strait Islander management is an Aboriginal and Torres Strait Islander-owned business would be a very complex task.

At first glance, the ABS majority-controlled definitions appear to be consistent with that used by Supply Nation (formerly the Australian Indigenous Minority Supplier Council—AMSIC), which was established to foster a prosperous, vibrant, and sustainable Indigenous enterprise sector by integrating Indigenous SMEs into the supply chains of Australian companies and government agencies. Supply Nation defines an Indigenous business as "at least 51 percent owned by Indigenous Australians and the principal executive officer is an Indigenous Australian and the key decisions in the business are made by Indigenous Australians" (Supply Nation, 2013a, p. 1, para. 4). Interestingly, when Supply Nation was first established, it accepted a 50% ownership definition.

These definitions are easy to defend in that one would expect these circumstances to be associated with a considerable measure of Indigenous control. However, the Supply Nation definition is also contestable in that it will exclude many firms that may otherwise be classified as Indigenous by the IBA and ATO. More importantly, the condition that the principal executive officer and key decision makers are Indigenous means that the Supply Nation definition is now more restrictive than the current ABS majority-controlled definition. Indeed, the Supply Nation definition has created a situation that impedes rather than fosters a prosperous, vibrant, and sustainable Indigenous enterprise sector by integrating Indigenous SMEs into the supply chains of Australian companies and government agencies as it espouses complex ownership and management structures. This has been confirmed to the author by several CEOs of struggling Aboriginal SMEs, who feel cheated by the very organization that they feel was set up by the federal government to support them. The former CEO of Supply Nation, Mr. Charles Prowse, has ignored several requests by the author to discuss these issues in a public or private forum and it has been brought to the author's attention that Supply Nation also prefers to support non-Indigenous businesses in their own supply chain needs, overlooking Aboriginal suppliers. Supply Nation's choice to employ non-Indigenous staff in key public contact roles recently resulted in staff at the Melbourne office of Supply Nation demonstrating their cultural ignorance by asking the internationally renowned Aboriginal leader Professor Marcia Langton to produce a certificate of Aboriginality (Prowse, personal communication, 2014). Is Supply Nation working to improve Aboriginal economic activity with their definitions and increased demands for Indigenous business control, or are they just another government agency, given they are so ignorant of our community leaders? Where is the tikanga in Supply Nation—as our Māori cousins would say, "the Whanaungatanga; Rangatiratanga; Mana; Kaitia-kitanga; Manaakitangi; Utu; or Wairua"? You simply cannot have tikanga, that is, cultural values, when you employ non-Indigenous staff to manage Aboriginal programs.

While the notion of majority control excludes enterprises with minority Indigenous ownership and partnerships between a married couple where only one partner identifies as an Aboriginal and Torres Strait Islander person (often called mixed marriages), such businesses are picked up in the first ABS definition that does not specify percentage equity. The majority ownership criteria is too restrictive, as it excludes many Aboriginal businesses that involve mixed marriages even if the owner's children identify as being Aboriginal and/or the partner supported Aboriginal issues (Foley, 2006b). In partnerships based on marriages, the non-Indigenous person is likely to be responsible for Aboriginal children, and hence, more than 50% of income streams allocated from profits and equity growth will be available to Aboriginal recipients.

Mixed marriage partnerships, Ngarda P/L, PACA in the Pilbara, and other examples are not be classified as Aboriginal businesses under the Supply Nation definition despite substantial Aboriginal participation throughout the organization and the general acceptance by the Aboriginal business community that they are indeed Aboriginal enterprises.

Clearly the majority-controlled definition is also not consistent with the practices of Indigenous Business Australia (IBA), Australia's foremost lender and promoter of Aboriginal enterprises. IBA assists eligible Aboriginal Australians to establish, acquire, and grow small to medium businesses by providing business support services and business finance. IBA's eligibility criteria for support and/or funding is at least 50% of the ownership of the business must be by a person(s) of Aboriginal and/or Torres Strait Islander descent.

The relaxation of the definition put forward by the ATO (2009) would substantially increase the number of Indigenous businesses; however, some other definitions would extend the coverage further. The ABS (2012) document also canvassed other alternative definitions of an Indigenous business, based on the following criteria: (1) industry, (2) number of Indigenous employees, (3) geography, (4) types of production, (5) funding source, and (6) benefits received by Indigenous communities. The now defunct Indigenous Business Chamber of Australia (IBCA) believed "alternative definitions" would destroy the integrity and purity of the "majority owned and operated" definition, leading to a watered-down and misguided version of an Indigenous business, that is 50% or less (Willmett, 2011). While the number of Aboriginal employees and the benefit to Aboriginal communities could add weight to claims of an individual business to be "Aboriginal," such criteria are not defined characteristics of an Aboriginal business in Australia, but they are in Aotearoa.

RESEARCH OUTCOMES

Over the last fifteen years, I have compiled over 770 qualitative case study analyses of Aboriginal SMEs (Foley, 2013; Foley & Hunter, 2013). Adding to this body of work, another 20 members of the Indigenous Chambers of Commerce were interviewed for this chapter to ensure that I was in touch with why Aboriginal SMEs were in business and what they thought of the differing definitions of an Aboriginal business.

For simplicity and to ensure privacy the participants are recorded alphabetically. Participant A is an artist, has been in business for two years, and previously was a part-time businessperson doing art as a hobby. This participant had to diversify his product to create income; he likes to workshop and calls workshops "gatherings," like our old people. He has a line of gift cards and sees himself in business:

> We are like Boomerangs moving our people into business: We go out and spin around and capture people with our presence, positivity and success and bring them in by showing what we can do. I am a 100% Aboriginal business, the wife is a partner (non-Aboriginal) but the business is 100% Aboriginal. I am working for us, my family and my wider community.

Participant B is into Reconciliation Action Plans: He worked for 27 years in government and does cross cultural training, bringing good people together. He is in a partnership with his wife (non-Aboriginal) but sees the business as 100% Aboriginal: "The product, the staff, and the beneficiaries apart from the clients are all Aboriginal, percentage ownership only determines my wife's capital input and covers her if I die, but realistically the product and the business are all Aboriginal."

Participant C told an interesting story of how she was once a member of a mainstream Chamber of Commerce and felt that they did nothing for her. As a member of an Indigenous Chamber of Commerce, she has a business family that is there to help in many different ways and this has helped promote her fashion design business:

> I love my work as a fashion designer. This is what I do and I love to create in my stories and paintings in fabric and to see them progress into clothing, curtains, bedspreads, or the like. An example is my Rainbow serpent dress. I didn't grow up with culture, this is a new journey for Mum and I [sic]. We are 100% Aboriginal, and even if I had a non-Indigenous partner I would still be 100% Aboriginal. It's my product, my story, who I employ; even the graphic artists are all Aboriginal. The culture within the business is so deeply interwoven that it could not be anything but Aboriginal.

Participant D had a mixed reaction and thought about it long and hard.

> I am in a partnership with hubby, the product is not cultural (i.e., car detailing), but I hope the way I provide a service is, for it is based on quality and loyalty to the customer be they Black or White. I suppose technically we are a 50/50 Aboriginal/non-Aboriginal business.

She asks her husband what he thinks. He replies that the business is the brainchild of his Aboriginal wife, she is the driving force, the beneficiaries are the family, so really although he might be a 50% shareholder in a partnership, culturally he is a minority, for even he sees and respects the business as an Aboriginal SME.

Participant E's business is 100% Aboriginal owned and is focused on Aboriginal clients only. She has the positivity of cultural knowledge of a community working with each other. Hers is the only business in her competitive area that is recognized by the NSW Attorney General to act on behalf of Aboriginal minors in the law courts. Her response to the percentage ownership question was that she felt it was a way of keeping bureaucrats employed to the detriment of Aboriginal people. "A business is Aboriginal or it's not—it's the community who decides, not ownership!"

Participant F says,

> It's all about family, helping and also the quality of your work. I always go back, no questions asked, as I don't want to have a customer feel we did a shoddy job because we are Black, even if it's another tradesman's stuff up. I would rather have a happy client, then they know they have dealt with a good Aboriginal company. My partner is non-Aboriginal and it's a partnership. I employ her brother: we work as a team and he considers himself as a part of an Aboriginal company. Because we are 50% this caused some trouble a while back on an IBA loan application, so you can see how bureaucrats get carried away with it. I would have thought the Indigenous Chamber of Commerce would be the best people to determine if you were an Indigenous business or not.

Participant G set up her hair salon 12 years ago. She has been teaching for two years at the academy, and has always considered herself to be a 100% Aboriginal business, "but you have to be careful to who and when you say it, so I am proud to be who I am but at the same time the industry is not kind to you when you stick your head up."

Participant H is a member of a husband-and-wife team. She strongly identifies as Aboriginal, and both partners feel that 50 or 51% determinations of identity by third parties is crazy. "We should be judged by the community that we work within and work for."

Participant I has a well-established business now. Due to the support and advice of Mandurah Aboriginal Chamber of Commerce they have restructured their partnership into a company where the majority shareholding is now owned by the Aboriginal wife and kids, not because of a legal need but to make their life easier in dealing with bureaucrats, especially in their pursuit of larger government supplier contracts and tenders. They also believe that a business is Aboriginal not by shareholding but by the spirit within the company, the culture within the SME. Shareholding means nothing when it comes to Aboriginal practice.

Participant J is adamant that in their case the concept of Aboriginality lies within the business. "We have a story to tell: We come from the dreaming, we got to keep dreaming and we got to dream good. It's who we are and what we do that makes us an Aboriginal business, not a percentage of ownership."

Participant K stated,

> Our business is reaching out there closing the gap in the digital divide. Giving one blackfella a job doesn't just help that blackfella, it helps the whole community. This is not a job: It's my employment, putting people in to work. Now the percentage of Aboriginal ownership means nothing in determining if you are an Aboriginal business. Our work is judged by the Aboriginal community: They determine who is an Aboriginal business.

Participant L is a well-known Sydney identity involved within the tourism industry who is wary of community and land councils and other Aboriginal organizations due to her problems with them over the years. Some of them have demanded financial payments similar to the Sicilian Mafia standover tactics of extortion from her successful tourism operations. "Everyone wants a cut in the good times." She understands the need for definitions of what is an Aboriginal business, for she has suffered competition over the years from many allegedly Aboriginal businesses that are Aboriginal in name but anything but Aboriginal in management and financial backing. An Aboriginal tour company, for example, she says:

> must be Aboriginal managed, Aboriginal staffed, and provide 100% Aboriginal content. The only ones who can judge their Aboriginality in business are their Aboriginal peers, not some suit in Canberra working off a calculator. That is why my businesses are run, staffed, and have content that is 100% blackfella. I am judged by the quality of my staff and the cultural content of my tours. That's why I am still in business after so many years.

Participant M owns a construction company, employing four Aboriginal apprentices and several Aboriginal carpenters and work staff.

> The apprentices are more like sons, you help them though problems. Most come from dysfunctional homes and you have to treat them differently, for we know what they are going through. We identify as an Aboriginal business.

I think it costs us business at times as some people think that we will go walk-about, but it's what we are and what we do that is important and really the industry and your peers are the ones who determine if you are an Aboriginal SME. The way we treat our staff is far more culturally acceptable than other construction groups: We show loyalty and we get it back. We respect culture and I think our product is better because of the cultural pride and content within it.

Participant N is an Elder. A member of the stolen generation, he has not always been Aboriginal; however, after many years he is a respected elder within the community. He is also a teacher, giving youth the stories, the images, and knowledge about their culture; working in the prisons; giving hope through art; helping people to be proud of who they are. "An Aboriginal business is determined by the community, not IBA or the ATO. Well, it's the community opinion that matters the most."

Participant O is a highly educated professional experimenting with an SME venture more as a hobby than as an income. However, her product line has proved to be very successful with strategic networks of fashion designers and retail outlets. "The quality is to tell the story of the culture in a product that is across all barriers. This is an Aboriginal business, which is determined by the Aboriginal SME community. Whilst I understand the need for owner-ship definitives, overall it is the quality of culture in the product!"

Participant P has five companies within a group. One site alone employs 120 Aboriginal tradesmen.

We are 50/50 Aboriginal/non-Aboriginal owned, which stems from the two partners. However, we function as an Aboriginal business as we are structured to train and employ Aboriginal persons, giving something back, helping the stolen generation to be as good as we can be and helping our community. We are judged by our peers and the community: The Aboriginal business community determines if we are an Aboriginal business.

Participant Q is another seasoned tourist operator whose business is 100% Aboriginal owned and controlled. After he recently applied for fund-ing and provided his business plan for the continuation of his operating li-cence, the NSW National Parks and Wildlife Service set up a duplicate tour company at lower cost that is allegedly identical to his existing business—a direct copy.

Sometimes it does not pay to ask for government funding when they take your business plan, an all-Aboriginal business plan and copy it, and undercut you and employ non-Indigenous people based on your cultural information and market it as an Aboriginal business. Aboriginal businesses can only be judged by your community, your Aboriginal business peers.

Participant R is passionate about culture and leaving a legacy. He also agrees that an Aboriginal SME can be determined and judged only by other Aboriginal SMEs:

> Supply Nation rejected me as I am only 50% Indigenous owned, yet they contracted one of my Melbourne competitors who is 100% non-Indigenous owned to provide an IT product that I or several other Indigenous IT companies would have welcomed the opportunity to tender for. It is who the business will benefit and who you employ that determines if you are an Aboriginal SME.

Participant S owns an art and design SME.

> We use vibrant, stunning new clash of medium and images, away from the stereotypical concepts of what is Aboriginal, breaking the boundaries of what is Aboriginal art. We are 100% Aboriginal owned, but if we were only 25% Aboriginal owned, we would still be Aboriginal, for this is who we employ, who we represent and what the business is. The percentage shareholding is like asking me am I half caste? How racist, you are Aboriginal or you are not Aboriginal. How can a business be 50% Aboriginal? Does that mean half of our designs are vibrant the other half whiteman grey? You are what you are. Aboriginal or not Aboriginal, the Aboriginal community determines this, not IBA or Supply Nation. When they are long gone my family will still be Aboriginal, still designing and painting and still 100% Aboriginal.

WHERE ARE ALL THE INDIGENOUS BUSINESSES?

Supply Nation currently certifies only 198 Indigenous businesses (at the time of writing), a fraction of the Indigenous entrepreneurs identified in recent census data (Supply Nation, 2013b). Once the census counts are adjusted to take into account the propensity to undercount Indigenous people, Hunter (2013) estimates that there are still around 5,500 Indigenous people who employ workers in their business. There are another 7,000 people who employ only themselves: thus there are 12,500 people who could potentially be classified as running Indigenous businesses in 2011 and who might not fit the definition of an Indigenous Business (see Foley 2000, 2005, 2006b). Based on these conservative figures, Supply Nation covers only a fraction of potential Indigenous businesses (less than 2%).

Definition of an Indigenous Business

Many major Australian businesses have reconciliation action plans (RAPs), and some of these include commitments to enhance their use of

Aboriginal contractors (e.g., Rio Tinto, Woodside, and Qantas). Many businesses, including those with relevant provisions in their RAPs, use Supply Nation to source Indigenous contractors; hence, the definition used matters, as some legitimate Aboriginal businesses may miss out on profitable opportunities. Another reason the operational definition of Aboriginal business matters is because government policy on Aboriginal business development might not be targeted appropriately. The majority-ownership definition of Supply Nation and others (i.e., equity over 50%) excludes some large companies like Ngarda P/L and those where equity is exactly 50%. Furthermore, there are an even larger number of small Aboriginal businesses involving married couples or partnerships where one partner is non-Indigenous. These are excluded by a strict majority-ownership definition. As I have previously argued (Foley, 2005), business partnerships involving couples are an important means for Aboriginal businesses to overcome the financial, social, and human capital constraints facing potential entrepreneurs. The non-Indigenous partner has these or access to them, whereas the Aboriginal partner invariably doesn't. If the aim of public policy is to sustainably develop nascent Indigenous business, then a strong case can be made to use a definition that has some flexibility and can even recognize some businesses that have 50% or less Aboriginal equity. As it currently stands, government policy is prejudicial to Aboriginal people in business who marry non-Aboriginal partners or interact with the dominant culture in partnership in business, which is a mockery of Reconciliation policy and the Racial Discrimination Act 1975 (as amended).

The review of 20 case studies illustrates that Aboriginal people believe there are a lot more issues in determining an Aboriginal SME than percentage ownership. Culture almost along the Māori concept of *Tikanga* also applies to the Australian Aboriginal practitioner.

Historical debates about Indigenous identity in non-Indigenous society are frequently objectionable, as they often revert to racist terms like "blood quantum," based on blood percentage. More recent notions of indigeneity allow individuals and their Indigenous communities to determine who is Indigenous. Attempts to rely on objective criteria to determine what is an Indigenous business are arguably reminiscent of historical debates, and it is time to consider a more flexible definition that allows the Indigenous business community to play a role in determining who is a member of their community. The legal definition of an Indigenous Australian accepted under "common law" follows a three-part definition that has been accepted and upheld by the High Court in *The Commonwealth v. Tasmania* (1983); An Aboriginal or Torres Strait Islander person is a person (Aboriginal and Torres Strait Islander Commission [ATSIC], 1998, p. 60):

1. Who is of Aboriginal and Torres Strait Islander descent;

2. Identifies as an Aboriginal or Torres Strait Islander person; and
3. Is accepted as such by the community in which they live.

Just as Indigenous people can now choose to identify if they are accepted by the local Indigenous community after the High Court determination, we propose that an Indigenous business be identified as one where:

1. At least one person holding equity in the company identifies as Indigenous;
2. The business identifies itself as an Indigenous owned business; and
3. It is accepted by the Indigenous business community as an Indigenous business.

This definition relies on a clear definition of Indigenous business community and we propose that this be taken to include Indigenous Chambers of Commerce in the respective states and territories. One could add the criteria of a controlling Indigenous interest or that a business must be managed and operated by Indigenous people; however, these are probably too restrictive and will not address the concern that policy will be excessively focused on relatively few businesses.

CONCLUSION

Aboriginal businesses in modernity have been defined, critically evaluating the definitions advanced by four key government agencies, namely the Australian Taxation Office, Indigenous Business Australia, the Australian Bureau of Statistics, and the 100% funded DEEWR subsidiary Supply Nation, which masquerades as an Aboriginal support agency. The discrepancies in their definitions have been illustrated. Debates over Aboriginal percentage ownership that sound similar to 18th century blood quantum arguments have also been illustrated. Māori holistic approaches to what is a Māori business/enterprise have been addressed, providing an understanding of an Indigenous culture-based alternative, which to some degree is already upheld and maintained by the Australian Aboriginal community. The cultural aspects of Australian Aboriginal businesses have been illustrated, highlighting their cultural uniqueness.

An Aboriginal community-inspired definition of what is an Aboriginal business has been developed that follows the sensibility and practicality of Australian Common Law, supported by the High Court of Australia decision defining what is an Australian Aboriginal and Torres Strait Islander. This work simplifies an understanding of what an Aboriginal business is, placing the trust and due-diligence on defining the Aboriginal SME with the Aboriginal business community. The crucial criterion is that the Aboriginal business is accepted and recognized by its industry and community peers. Organizations such as Supply Nation should want to maximize their membership, adding wealth to the Australian Aboriginal sector. However, their over-policing results in the opposite. There is a need for flexibility and standardization of definitions between the IBA, the ATO, and the ABS, which should be undertaken in conjunction with advice from the Indigenous Chambers of Commerce and other community organizations such as PACA. In this way, policy can recognize, then develop, more Aboriginal businesses and hence further enhance Australian Indigenous economic development, recognising Aboriginal cultural content within an enterprise directly impacts on the well-being of the Aboriginal owner, the Aboriginal employees, and their families, which produces a domino effect that resonates throughout Aboriginal society. Financial independence and success in business enables the Aboriginal participant to achieve self-determination, for with financial wealth the opportunity to make independent decisions and choices in life exists.

NOTES

1. The word Aboriginal will be used throughout this paper in lieu of Indigenous where possible in view of the dehumanizing application of Indigenous over Aboriginal. The subtle racist applicability of Indigenous to flora and fauna has created this controversy and play on words within some academic and social circles. In addition, as the author does not research Torres Strait Islander businesses, Aboriginal is also used to respectfully designate the First Peoples of Australia.
2. Dr Chellie Spiller asked me to begin my chapter with a poem; I think this condenses my thoughts and where this chapter is leading to. The key issues are the causation and symptoms of our current economic woes so often misunderstood as government programs are lavished on the symptoms without addressing the causations of a dysfunctional society. Sustainable social enterprise and commercial enterprise allows Aboriginal Australia to achieve self-determination without government assistance for financial independence is self-determination; you have choices in your life.

REFERENCES

Aboriginal and Torres Strait Islander Commission (ATSIC). (1998). *As a matter of fact: Answering the myths and misconceptions about Indigenous Australians.* Canberra, Australia: Author.

Australian Bureau of Statistics. (2012). *Information paper: Defining Aboriginal and Torres Strait Islander-owned businesses* (cat. no. 4732.0). Canberra, Australia: Author.

Arthur, J. M. (1996). *Aboriginal English: A cultural study.* Melbourne, Australia: Oxford University Press.

Australian Government. (2003). *Indigenous Business Review: Report on Support for Indigenous Business.* Canberra, Australia: Author. Retrieved from http://www.atsia.gov.au/Media/Reports/default.aspx#sub3

Australian Taxation Office (ATO). (2009). Indigenous small business owners in Australia. Canberra: Commonwealth of Australia, Australian Taxation Office.

Biddle, N., Howlett, M., Hunter, B., & Paradies, Y. (2013). Labour market and other discrimination facing Indigenous Australians. *Australian Journal of Labour Economics 16*(1), 91–116.

Chappell, D., & Polk, K., (2009). Fakers and forgers, deception and dishonesty: An exploration of the murky world of art fraud. *Current Issues in Criminal Justice, 20*(3), 393–412.

Commonwealth v. Tasmania, 158 CLR 1, 274 (J. Deane 1983).

Crenative Ltd. (2006). Investigating key characteristics of a Māori business for future measures: Thinking paper. Retrieved from www.tpk.govt.nz/en/in-print/our...maori.../tpk-keybusnessmeasures.pdf

Durie, M. (2003). The business ethic and Māori development. In M. Durie (Ed.), *Nga kahui pou launching Maori futures* (pp. 241–252). Wellington, NZ: Huia.

Eisenhardt, K. (1989). Building theories from case study research. *Academy of Management. The Academy of Management Review, 14*(4), 532–550.

Foley, D. (2000). *Successful Indigenous Australian entrepreneurs: A case study analysis.* Aboriginal and Torres Strait Islander Studies Unit Research Report Series, Vol. 4. Brisbane, Australia: Merino Lithographics.

Foley, D. (2002). Indigenous standpoint theory: an Indigenous epistemology. *Journal of Australian Indigenous Issues, 5*(3), 3–13.

Foley, D. (2003a). Indigenous epistemology and Indigenous standpoint theory. *Social Alternatives, 22*(1), 44–52.

Foley, D. (2003b). An examination of Indigenous Australian entrepreneurs. *Journal of Developmental Entrepreneurship, 8*(2), 133–152.

Foley, D. (2003c). A dichotomy: Indigenous epistemological views. *Journal of Australian Indigenous Issues, 6*(3), 13–28.

Foley, D. (2005). *Understanding Indigenous entrepreneurs: A case study analysis.* Unpublished doctoral thesis, University of Queensland, Brisbane, Australia.

Foley, D. (2006a). Does business success make you any less Indigenous? In M. Gillen, J. Butler, A. Campbell, P. Davidsson, H. Frederick, K. Hindle, . . . J. Yencken (Eds.), *Regional frontiers of entrepreneurship research 2006: Proceedings of the Third Annual AGSE International Entrepreneurship Research Exchange* (pp. 241–257). Hawthorn, England: Swinburne Press.

Foley, D. (2006b). Indigenous Australian entrepreneurs: Not community and not in the outback. *CAEPR Discussion Paper No.279* CAEPR, The ANU, Canberra

Foley, D. (2008). What determines the bottom line for Maori tourism SMEs? Small Enterprise Research. *The Journal of SEAANZ, 16*(1), 86–97.

Foley, D. (2013). *Jus Sanguinis*: The root of contention in determining what is an Australian Aboriginal business. *Indigenous Law Bulletin, 8*(8), 25–29.

Foley, D., & Hunter, B. (2013). What is an Indigenous Australian business? *Journal of Australian Indigenous Issues, 16*(3), 66–74.

French, A. (1998). *What is Maori business: A survey of Maori business perceptions*. A research report presented in partial fulfilment of the requirements of the Degree of Master of Business Studies in Management at Massey University.

Hall, S. (1990). Cultural identity and diaspora. In J. Rutherford (Ed.), *Identity: Community, culture and difference* (pp. 222–237). London, England: Lawrence Wishart.

Haynes, C. (2010). Realities, simulacra and the appropriation of Aboriginality in Kakadu's tourism. In I. Keen (Ed.), *Indigenous participation in Australian eonomies: Historical and Anthropological perspectives* (pp. 165–186.). Canberra, Australia: The Australian National University Press.

Hunter, B. (2013). *Recent growth in Indigenous self-employed and entrepreneurs. Working Paper 91*. Canberra, Australia: Centre for Aboriginal Economic Development, The Australian National University.

Kleinert, S. (2010). Aboriginal enterprises: Negotiating an urban Aboriginality. *Aboriginal History, 34*, 171–196.

Langton, M. (2013). *The quiet revolution: Indigenous people and the resources boom, Boyer Lectures 2012*. Sydney, Australia: Harper Collins.

Love, M., & Love, T. (2005). Māori and self-employment. In C. Massey (Ed.), *Entrepreneurship and small business management in New Zealand* (pp. 250–260). Auckland: Pearson Education New Zealand.

Ngarda. (2013). Our history. Retrieved from http://www.ngarda.com.au/history

NSW Indigenous Chamber of Commerce. (2013). *Strategic Plan 2013–2017*. Sydney, Australia: Price Waters Coopers.

Pilbara Aboriginal Contractors Association Inc. (PACA). (2010). *Review of contractual arrangements between Australian Aboriginal enterprises and the resource industry*. Liscia & Tavelli Legal Consultants Pty Ltd.

Pittaway, L., Robertson, M., Munir, K., Denyer, D., & Neeley, A. (2004). Networking and innovation: A systematic review of the evidence. *International Journal of Management Reviews, 5/6(3/4)*, 137–168.

Rolka-Rubzen, M. F. (2011). *The anatomy of the Australian entrepreneur: Understanding micro, small and medium business entrepreneurs in Australia*. Alice Springe, Australia: Ninti One Ltd.

Supply Nation. (2013a). Get certified. Retrieved from http://supplynation.org.au/Indigenous_businesses/Certification

Supply Nation. (2013b). Retrieved from http://www.supplynation.org.au/news_media/SN_Newsletter_Year4Quarter4

Thorpe, R., Holt, R., Macpherson, A., & Pittaway, L. (2006). Using knowledge within small and medium-sized firms: A systematic review of the evidence. *International Journal of Management Reviews, 7(4)*, 257–281.

Tranfield, D. R., Denver, D., & Smart, P. (2003). Towards a methodology for developing evidence-informed management knowledge by means of systematic review. *British Journal of Management, 14*, 207–222.

Wilkes, G. A. (1978). *A dictionary of Australian colloquialisms*. Sydney, Australia: Fontana/Collins.

Willmett, N. (2009). *Why we cannot wait! The urgent need for strategic Indigenous business sector development & Indigenous enterprise integration in Australia*. The Winston Churchill Fellowship Report 2009. Unpublished.

Willmett, N. (2011). *IBCA Abs Submission on Indigenous Definition Discussion Paper.* Retrieved from http://www.ibca.org.au/news_desc.php?news_id=17

Yin, R. K. (2002). *Case study research, design and methods* (3rd ed.). Thousand Oaks, CA: Sage Publication.

CHAPTER 12

AN ETHIC OF RECIPROCITY

Illuminating the Stó:lō Gift Economy

Dara Kelly and Patrick Kelly

ABSTRACT

This chapter focuses on reciprocal exchange in the context of Stó:lō Coast Salish economic philosophy of gifting in *Stl'e'áleq*, or "potlatch" traditions. *Stl'e'áleq* are shaped by an ethic of reciprocity committed to the strength and quality of relationships between people. We develop the notion of reciprocal exchange from Indigenous philosophy as economic systems that are human-centered and wealth-driven. We illuminate how *Stl'e'áleq* exchange is human-centered, in that what is exchanged transcends the tangible and explicit, and additionally, implicit actions and behaviors have impacts on the strength and quality of relationships that are bound by reciprocity. Our focus on *Stl'e'áleq* as wealth-driven explores Stó:lō concepts of wealth and well-being founded in the wholeness of the people. These components are contextualized with examples of how Stó:lō Coast Salish *Stl'e'áleq* are continued today, and how the principles have been applied within the corporate atmosphere of BC Hydro, a provincial Crown-corporation in Canada, to strengthen its relationships with First Nations communities in BC.

Indigenous Spiritualities at Work, pages 191–208
Copyright © 2015 by Information Age Publishing

INTRODUCTION

This chapter is an exploratory conversation between the two authors, a father and daughter, Patrick and Dara Kelly. We explore the space between two types of knowledge—our understanding of an economy founded in the traditions of the Stó:lō Coast Salish gift economy, and the knowledge and experience of working, studying, and operating in a contemporary world of business. We are of Stó:lō Coast Salish heritage and are of the view that commerce and exchange must have relevance to us as Indigenous people living in a global world. Economic life should reflect our identity and all that matters to us. Looking to our traditional economic knowledge, we focus on the most formal level of exchange spiritually and institutionally significant to us as Stó:lō people. Embedded in the ceremony, *Stl'e'áleq*, the gift economy shapes our integrated system of spiritual, social, symbolic, and practical exchanges that have enabled Stó:lō to grow, prosper, and thrive for thousands of years. Because the Stó:lō economy is anchored in the strength of meaningful relationships with one another, our communities are guided by an ethic of reciprocity and vice versa. The ethic of reciprocity strengthens the relationships across Stó:lō Coast Salish communities.

However, as with so many Indigenous cultures around the world, colonization has had devastating impacts on our ability to nurture those relationships. As we move out of the shadow of the colonial darkness, a time when our economic knowledge was grossly devalued, the principles of gift economy and reciprocity emerge to fill in the gap where the current economic system falls short of fulfilling the financial needs of Stó:lō people and bring a return of our spiritual and social strength through the institution of *Stl'e'áleq*.

SHIFTING GLOBAL INDIGENOUS ECONOMICS

At present, the dominant economic system is not serving the financial needs of Indigenous communities and the discourse of critical perspectives questioning, "Who does the system serve?" are growing stronger (Hall & Fenelon, 2009; Mander & Tauli-Corpuz, 2006; Stewart-Harawira, 2005). This issue is one of many that culminated in the mobilization of Indigenous communities across North America (and eventually the world) in a social movement called "Idle No More" (Nation Builder, 2013). This movement became manifest through protest marches and petitions opposing the legislative decisions of Canada's Conservative government led by Prime Minister Stephen Harper. The legislation that was pushed through parliament ignored Aboriginal rights secured in the Canadian Constitution, compromised the natural environment, and threatened the sovereignty and traditional territories of Aboriginal people. While government decisions of that nature are far from new, the movement represented a collective resurgence and willingness to stand up for Aboriginal rights no matter what the cost. It gained momentum in December 2012 and continued throughout 2013. Idle No More gestures to the deep dissatisfaction of Indigenous communities with the status quo and the movement is an interruption to policy decisions that significantly impact Canada's Aboriginal communities.

This agitation for change is symptomatic of long histories of endured stress, from the inability to exercise stewardship rights and responsibilities to the lands and territories that Indigenous communities inhabited centuries before the arrival of European explorers. A language of resistance emerged from Idle No More that identifies economic matters as being particularly tied to the inability to tend to inherent stewardship responsibilities—an issue that has been at the center of Indigenous rights and title struggles for decades. The language of "unfreedom" is very much at the heart of the Idle No More movement and describes both Mother Earth and Indigenous communities as "economic hostages" (Moe, 2013; Nation Builder, 2013) to continued processes of industrialization. The power behind Idle No More stems from the collective nature of, and eventually, the global support generated from Indigenous and non-Indigenous communities alike. It gestures to a willingness and openness to new foundations of economic philosophy other than those that have dominated the global market over the last 200 years (Maddison, 2006). This chapter contributes to a philosophy of business and economics that once again values who we are as Stó:lō Coast Salish people. In this chapter, we describe aspects of *Stl'e'áleq* ceremony, followed by contextual experiences in which *Stl'e'áleq* has affirmed relational ties within the Stó:lō community, and finally, a case example of the use of *Stl'e'áleq* to bridge ties between First Nations and the corporate world of business.

LOCATING LEQ'Á:MEL— THE "GATHERING PLACE" FOR STÓ:LŌ

To envision the expanse of time over which the Stó:lō economy has evolved, some grounding historical and geographic signposts help frame our story. Archaeological evidence shows that First Nations have existed in Canada for more than 15,000 years, which is approximately 500 generations (Blomfield et al., 2001). There are approximately 50 Coast Salish First Nations communities throughout the region spanning the Salish Sea from lower Vancouver Island, across the Juan de Fuca Straight, eastward through the City of Vancouver and up the Fraser River to the town of Yale. The Stó:lō Nation is part of the Coast Salish grouping and includes approximately 24 communities on the Fraser River and its tributaries. Those most closely tied together by shared social, ceremonial, and economic connections to Stó:lō traditional territories are referred to as *Xwélmexw* (people of life) in the Halq'eméylem[1] language.

Within Stó:lō, one branch of our genealogy emerges from the Leq'á:mel First Nation located on the north side of the Fraser River. In relation to other Stó:lō communities, Leq'á:mel was one of the central gathering places for Stó:lō people from throughout the territory. The word *stó:lō* means "river" and the name of the language itself, Halq'eméylem, means "going to Nicomen Island, or going to the visiting place" (Galloway, 2009, pp. 222–223). Leq'á:mel is that visiting place and a social and cultural centre point at the heart of our territory.

Observing the landscape, Leq'á:mel is a flat place on the territory and is therefore suitable for large gatherings of people. In relation to the Fraser, it is also a place where the river is wide and calm, which means canoes can land easily. To provide an example, a canoe from an eastern extremity (with help from downstream flow of the *Stó:lō*), and a canoe from the western extremity (paddling upstream against the flow) would arrive at Leq'á:mel at approximately the same time. Referring to precolonial times, because Leq'á:mel was a location where many people stopped, *smilha'áwtxw*, or traditional longhouses, had the capacity to hold thousands of guests at one time (Galloway, 2009). There were three *smilha'áwtxw* at Leq'á:mel owned by our great- (and great-great-) grandfather, Joe Kelly. From the perspective of transport by land and water, Leq'á:mel is central within the Stó:lō world and its strategic location as a gathering place on the Fraser River has shaped Stó:lō history.

STL'E'ÁLEQ, POTLATCH

The largest and most formal events when Stó:lō people come together are called *Stl'e'áleq*. It is an institution central to every aspect of Stó:lō spiritual, cultural, social, economic, and political life. The institution has been presented to the world through the discipline of anthropology by way of extensive ethnography, and is known as "potlatch." As a result of early ethnographic accounts, potlatch became a blanket term for formal ceremonies conducted by tribes of the Northwest Coast of North America engaging in gift exchange and wealth distribution (Carlson, 2010). Potlatch is an anthropological reference that has generated in-depth inquiry and discussion on notions of reciprocity, obligation, and credit operating in ways distinct from their use and application within the market economy (Godelier, 1999).

We draw attention to the word "potlatch" because of its roots in the Anglo-Indian "pidgin" language, Chinook, for the purpose of distinguishing the anthropological understanding of it from the ceremony we know to be *Stl'e'áleq*. For us as Stó:lō people, anthropological research and writing about potlatch speaks minimally to our experience of it as the institutional foundations of the Stó:lō economy and government through ceremony. We offer a combination of recollections from personal experience, stories passed on through oral traditions and research on potlatch and *Stl'e'áleq* from books to share the way we carry the living gift economy of *Stl'e'áleq* within our genealogy and collective memory. In doing so, we repatriate it from the impersonal grasp of anthropology.

The high level of formality in *Stl'e'áleq* means that exchange is recognized among members of Stó:lō society as legitimate because of the spiritual and ceremonial components. *Stl'e'áleq* affirms the authority of X̱ex̱á:ls and *Tel Swayel*, our ancient ancestors who saw the transformation of the world from chaos to order. Stó:lō philosophy, as contained in *Sx̱wox̱wiyám* (oral histories anchored in the distant past), is such that humans are subordinate to the metaphysical world of spirits, and therefore we must constantly engage with the spirit world for guidance on matters of importance (Carlson, 2010). In *Stl'e'áleq*, the most sacred spiritual authority is called upon and protocol is adhered to so that the context of the exchange reflects careful attention not only to what is exchanged between humans, but also so that the exchange tends to the relationship between humans and the spirit world. There are at least three levels of symbolic exchange that occur in *Stl'e'áleq* ceremonies. The first is the exchange that is the purpose of the event, such as the exchange of property or names. Second is exchange between the host family and witnesses, and finally, exchange between the host family and guests, with gifts given to show appreciation for the guests' attendance at the event.

Hosting *Stl'e'áleq* means that the family must be in a position to house and feed all guests throughout the duration of the ceremony and the journey home. Of utmost importance are the honored elders and leaders, whose attendance is absolutely crucial as wisdom-keepers and witnesses in past *Stl'e'áleq*. They are compensated completely for costs of attendance and given places of prominence in seating at the ceremony. In addition to housing and feeding the guests, it is customary to provide each invited guest with *wá:ls* (gifts/giveaways) before they return home. There was a time when *Stl'e'áleq* lasted several weeks. One can imagine the extensive resources and preparation necessary to sustain guests over that period of time.

Recognizing that there is greater socio-spatial distance between *Xwél-mexw* (people of life) and *lats'umexw* (different people, strangers) than between *Xwélmexw* and *Xwélmexw*, what is unknown about *lats'umexw* is their understandings about reciprocity, which cannot be assumed to be the same as those of *Xwélmexw*. The specific terminology used in reference to *Stl'e'áleq* indicates an openness and desire for guests to be *lats'umexw* because of the potential for exchange relationships to develop. The host gives the guests gifts in the form of food and material goods on such a scale that there is an expectation of payment or trade in return for those gifts. That expectation is contained in the concept *exímstexw*. *Exímstexw* assumes that expectations of reciprocity among *lats'umexw* (different people, strangers) may be different from those of *Xwélmexw* and need to be made explicit in the language that belongs to the relationship. *Stl'e'áleq* exchange operates according to explicit expectations around reciprocity.

Stl'e'áleq encompasses the active practice of Stó:lō holism in the sense that the ceremonies provide the institutional space in which spiritual, cultural, health-related, legal, social, economic, and political ways of life converge. Their interconnection is a crucial aspect of their proper functioning, and *Stl'e'áleq* serves to fulfill a cohesive role for Stó:lō society. The integrated nature of *Stl'e'áleq* means that they involve extensive preparation for the ceremonial and feasting components of the event, responsibility for which is undertaken by members of an extended family. Typically, there is a key purpose that guides planning for *Stl'e'áleq*, such as conveying ancestral names, honoring achievement, confirming leadership roles, allocating property and resources, developing strategic partnerships, resolving disputes, and facilitating healing practices.

Developed over hundreds of generations, strict protocol guides how families conduct *Stl'e'áleq*. When a family decides that *Stl'e'áleq* will take place, they will send notice of the event to neighboring families and communities with whom they have existing relationships. This is also the time to reflect upon those relationships, and consider the need for new ones. *Stl'e'áleq* presents the opportunity to reframe and envision one's place within the broader Stó:lō community and re-assert that grounding through ceremony. It was, and continues to be, the case that invitations for *Stl'e'áleq* may be sent to Stó:lō communities up to 200 kilometers away. Invitations are usually sent several weeks or months in advance by way of announcements made in other *smilha'áwtxw* events within Stó:lō territory.

One of the roles that the host family does not undertake while the ceremony is occurring is speaking directly to their guests, as would a master of ceremonies. They speak through a hired *lheqsqwóqwel* (speaker) who speaks on behalf of the family. This role ensures that, with the guidance of the host, selected guests are called upon to *xwlalámstexw* (witness or listen to) the proceedings of the ceremony.

Xwlalámstexw, Witnessing

As discussed, the purpose of *Stl'e'áleq* is to facilitate a formal exchange that becomes legitimate when conducted in the presence of family and community to "witness" the exchange. Witnessing is the act of adherence to oral tradition and is the means of record keeping, allowing the exchange to be formally remembered by way of the witnesses' collective memory (Carlson, 1997, 2010). The protocols for calling and being a witness require highly nuanced and intimate knowledge of the relations and history between the host family and guests. In anticipation of the need to call witnesses as the ceremony commences, the host pays careful attention to which of the invited guests arrive, and their accompanying guests.

Honored elders from other families and communities are greeted and escorted to reserved seating in the front row within *smilha'áwtxw*, as their role requires them to clearly see and hear the proceedings. Members of their family are seated behind them. Guests who travel the farthest to attend the ceremony are seated nearest to the host family. It may be the case that elders are not called to witness for reasons such as health and stature, but it is likely that someone from their family would be called in recognition of that elder's standing and contribution to the community. The process of calling witnesses from each community acknowledges the diversity of communities in attendance and activates the role of individual witnesses and affirms their responsibility to retell the story of the event after the ceremony concludes.

Witnesses are called early and each individual is presented with a small gift—a subtle but essential exchange that acknowledges the significance of their responsibility as a custodian of the events about to take place. Upon being called by *lheqsqwóqwel,* the witness stands, and the hosts acknowledge him or her with *kwelétses* (shaking their hand). It is in the handshake that *xwth'í:t* (small token, today usually two quarters) is transferred from the hand of a member of the host family to the witness. The reason behind this subtle transfer is that it is considered improper and rude for a host to "pay" witnesses, and, likewise, witnesses should not expect to be paid for being called. The formalities around this particular point of exchange are to protect the honor of both host and witness, and yet the exchange symbolizes the commencement, or continuation, of lifelong commitment to one another.

The significance of building lifelong obligations between families and communities is tied to ensuring continuity and protection of oral histories and traditions. As already mentioned, it is through the witnesses that the stories of important events are recorded and retold. Therefore, in addition to simply watching the ceremony unfold, witnesses must pay close attention so that they can accurately retell what they saw and heard. They are not allowed to take written or recorded notes because they are expected to commit them to memory. Witnesses note things such as the degree to which the host heeded proper protocol as well as the factual elements of the ceremony. For example, in a naming ceremony, the origin and history of the name, its meaning, and the obligations of the new holder are all carefully noted.

Stó:lō Philosophy of Giving

Preparation for *Stl'e'áleq* requires that the host family saves enough food and resources for its own well-being, and all that is surplus is distributed in the ceremony. After hosting *Stl'e'áleq*, it is understood that the family does not have *more* than enough to support itself for a foreseeable time ahead. Therefore, if in the future the family that hosted *Stl'e'áleq* comes to need food and resources, those who attended their *Stl'e'áleq* are obligated to help them. In this way, *Stl'e'áleq* make up an institutional system of social welfare built around centuries of gifting, ceremony, and oral history.

To provide a different example of the way that reciprocity may be shown in *Stl'e'áleq*, fulfilment of the concept of *exímstexw* may also be manifested by a family that has attended *Stl'e'áleq* of other families hosting their own ceremony, and inviting previous host families. Here, reciprocity plays out not only as an expression of giving back, but also as an expression of a formalized system of thanking that is an integral part of *exímstexw*. While comparison and competition between *Stl'e'áleq* of particular families is not the primary purpose of hosting, it is certainly a secondary or tertiary outcome.[2] The expectation of a lavish distribution of wealth as gifts and food is evident if the family can afford it. It would be a dishonor to one's genealogy if it were known that a family had experienced the good fortune of a prosperous year and reserved more than they needed for themselves while knowing of others in greater need. However, a family's decision to host *Stl'e'áleq* is not only a reflection of the need to fulfill obligations of reciprocity to other families. The primary function remains to facilitate the primary purpose, whatever that may be. If a less fortunate family needed to host *Stl'e'áleq* to legitimize and honor the bestowal of a name, it would not be expected to provide gifts and food beyond its means. However, it is likely the family would delay the ceremony until enough resources were gathered to adequately gift and feed their guests. The witnessing function ensures that the level of generosity shown by host families and the spirit of the gifts distributed in *Stl'e'áleq* are carefully noted.

Understanding the terrain of reciprocity as part of a wider spiritual genealogy of the Stó:lō gift economy provides insights into the unfolding of centuries of relational exchange between communities and families. As previously discussed on Stó:lō philosophy, the human world is inextricably linked to the spirit world (Carlson, 2010); therefore, *Stl'e'áleq* make up an extensive exchange network that is part of the eternal continuity of reciprocal community relationships founded on authority derived from the world of the spirits. At the heart of the gift economy is the people, and the wealth that drives the economy can be measured by the wellness and wholeness of the people who come together.

THE POTLATCH BAN ACROSS CANADA, 1884–1951

By way of amendment to the Indian Act,[3] from 1884–1951, all forms of potlatch traditions practiced by First Nations across Canada were outlawed (Cole & Chaikin, 1990). As a result, *Stl'e'áleq* underwent severe transformation, as did the cultural expression of all First Nations across Canada with practices deemed to have a likeness to "potlatch" (Drucker & Heizer, 1967). Following the amendment, the potlatch outlaw was actively enforced for 67 years by way of surveillance and control under the watchful eyes of government-appointed Indian Agents and local church officials. Those authorities were charged with the formidable task of tracking the travel behavior of Stó:lō, raiding longhouses where potlatches were held, seizing material and ceremonial objects, and mass arrests for those who successfully reached the hosting stage.

Colonial authorities witnessing first-hand how *Stl'e'áleq* function as an institution identified the economic strength of the system, not only for the exchanges that took place, but for the lattice of social and kinship ties that encircle the institution (Cole & Chaikin, 1990; Miller, 2007). For many reasons, *Stl'e'áleq* were deemed to be an impediment to the successful introduction and adoption of British European exchange philosophy into Stó:lō territory and therefore an impediment to the progress of the colony. In order to ensure that the European system of exchange would replace the Stó:lō economy as it functioned through *Stl'e'áleq,* the potlatch ban was an effective means of colonial control.

Blomfield et al. (2001) provide evidence of the impact that the ban had by way of letters written to government representatives protesting the Potlatch ban. One such letter written in 1885 reads, "...and what must I do with the property I owe. I owe 140 Indians goods, some of them as much as 100 blankets. How can I pay my debts unless they are all here to witness." The letter expresses the distress that the potlatch ban caused as an interruption to obligations of reciprocity embedded in *Stl'e'áleq.* It also speaks of the shame that is inherited by the family unable to fulfill their responsibilities of reciprocity. The level of interruption that the ban had on one family was not a matter of debts that could be resolved with simple repayment, but signaled a disturbance of generations of trade and alliances deeply entrenched in the entire economic system of gift exchange.

Introduction of the potlatch ban marked the beginning of a powerful process that set out to dismantle one of the foundations of Stó:lō life ways. In tandem with the mandatory attendance of all First Nations children at church- and government-run residential schools, Stó:lō communities experienced the corrosion of 15,000 years of history through the destruction of *Stl'e'áleq* networks, economic relationships, and family ties (Blomfield et al., 2001). Restrictions against planning and hosting all forms of exchange by way of wealth distribution were set in place, including the restriction of physical movement by Indians to parcels of land reserved for use only by Indians (named "Indian reserves"). Without attendees to witness formal exchange processes in *Stl'e'áleq*, opportunities to forge new relationships and feed existing relationships were severely hindered by government control.

Although the potlatch ban was lifted in 1951, it has taken its toll on Stó:lō communities due to the dominance of the global market economy and the prolonged interruption to strategic alliances and ancient exchange relationships. In Stó:lō territory today, after concentrated efforts to preserve, remember, and practice *Stl'e'áleq*, Stó:lō communities have managed to revitalize much of the structure and protocol surrounding the institution. However, the economic impacts were devastating and *Stl'e'áleq* exchange systems have yet to fully recover.

T'ESÓTS'EN AND STAH'WITS'TUN NAMING CEREMONIES

Today, traditional Stó:lō names are typically given in adulthood. Before the impacts of colonization, names would have been conferred in childhood or young adulthood after careful observation and consideration by adults and elders of the choice of a name that most suited the young person. The philosophy that guides naming today still exists as it always has. Names are given to reflect the essence and character of the person and should speak to the unique gifts and strengths that the individual contributes to the wider community. Instead of having this decided in childhood, or young adulthood, names are often based upon the contributions of individuals that account for creative, educational, and professional achievement in addition to their contributions to the community.

We turn our attention to our stories of *Stl'e'áleq* today. The authors provide accounts from their own ceremonies when Stó:lō names were conferred upon them by their community. As we recount the events, we speak about them from our own memories of the ceremony.

T'ESÓTS'EN NAMING CEREMONY, PATRICK KELLY

As a result of many years of observation and discussion that did not include me, elders within the Stó:lō community decided that Stl'e'áleq was needed to confer a traditional name upon me. This was in recognition of my professional and personal contributions not only to the Stó:lō community, but also to First Nations in BC. Since I was a young man, I have worked in all sorts of jobs, and found myself driven by work that would better the lives of First Nations people in Canada—whether it was as an outdoor education leader, tribal education coordinator, or now, as a consultant working with First Nations facilitating their comprehensive community planning and community governance processes. Because of this work throughout my life, I received a traditional name.

The name that was selected for me is the name that belonged to my maternal grandmother, Maggie Pennier (née Leon), T'esóts'en. She carried the female version of the name, T'esóts' and has since passed on, but I grew up spending much time with her from the age of six. Because of my close relationship with her throughout my childhood and early adulthood, it is a great honor to carry her name. I pay close attention to the traditional (and conservative) Stó:lō values that she taught me about how to carry and conduct myself because I represent not only myself, but also our entire family. Now, as before, but perhaps more explicitly, I conduct myself as T'esóts'en, and that means I conduct myself as she would.

The ceremony to confer the name took place on 18 January 2003. It was held at one of the oldest remaining smilha'áwtxw in Stó:lō territory—a longhouse that is cared for by the Charlie family up in the mountains of Sts'ailes (also known as Chehalis). What happened in this ceremony was a profound example of the importance of continuity by way of witnessing. There were guests invited and who attended who were witnesses at the naming ceremony of T'esóts', my grandmother at the same smilha'áwtxw in Sts'ailes when she was 16 years old in 1919. Those witnesses also spoke at this one in 2003, and retold the events that took place in 1919 including the history of the name, her legacy as a spirit dancer, and the person she was, as if it was yesterday. There were over 1,000 guests who arrived to attend this ceremony in 2003 from across Stó:lō Coast Salish territory and other communities all over BC. The smilha'áwtxw is suited to seating only 800, which meant that many guests were not able to witness the ceremony inside. The great influx of guests was a reflection of the name to which we both belong.

STAH'WITS'TUN HONOURING CEREMONY, DARA KELLY

In December 2012, I was in the early stages of study toward my PhD. I traveled home from New Zealand to Canada to support my sister in the birth of my niece. While I was home, I offered to share my experiences of travel overseas and my journey in education with members of the Stó:lō community. Originally, I was imagining that I would give a formal speech or be part of an open discussion. Instead, it was decided by one of our respected elders, His Honour Steven Point, former Lieutenant Governor and Provincial Court Judge, Xwelíqweltel, that I should receive a traditional name in recognition of my educational achievements. Since I was home for a total of only six weeks, the ceremony preparations were significantly accelerated, and planning took place immediately. To prepare for the ceremony, I had to visit with the matriarchs of our family to ensure that they gave their approval and permission for the ceremony to take place. This involved visiting with them face-to-face, sharing with them what I am doing and where I have been on the other side of the world. Some of the ways they expressed their approval was with a gift or advice for me in the ceremony. In one case, I was given a blanket as I left her home.

The ceremony took place on 3 January 2013. The smilha'áwtxw where it was held is an educational one built for teaching and reviving our long-house ways. It is located at the Stó:lō Nation building complex in the City of Chilliwack. As with Dad's ceremony, witnesses were called and spoke to me and the guests about the significance of the name Stah'wits'tun, and the responsibilities that I now have as a result of this honor. What most stood out from what all of the witnesses said was the responsibility that I cannot yet know, but that will become clear when the time is right. They told of the history of the name and that it was last used at Chehalis Lake in 1856. Because the ceremony was not founded on the need to confer the name, rather to honor my educational achievements, I refer to it as an honoring ceremony. In the case of Dad's ceremony, it was planned for the specific purpose of bestowing the name T'esóts'en on him, and therefore is referred to as a naming ceremony.

Our stories of *Stl'e'áleq* incorporate all aspects of the ceremony that we have described throughout this chapter. In both cases, the Stó:lō gift economy centered on wealth that is driven by the extent to which Stó:lō Coast Salish people are connected, come together, and contribute to the continuity of our shared genealogies through witnessing. We now turn our attention to a case example of a corporate entity that was facing its own turmoil and challenges with First Nations in BC, and *Stl'e'áleq* was proposed as a means to bridge the cultural divide between two starkly different worldviews.

CASE EXAMPLE: BC HYDRO STL'E'ÁLEQ

BC Hydro is a provincial electrical utility Crown-corporation in Canada located in the city of Vancouver. In 1992, BC Hydro established an Aboriginal relations department. This emerged out of a situation when First Nations were drawing attention to 250 expired right-of-way agreements throughout the province—particularly the meagre compensation they received for the use of land while they were active (BC Hydro Aboriginal Relations Department, 2014). BC Hydro needed renewed agreements to maintain and further develop its electrical transmission and distribution system on land in Aboriginal territory. As the agreements expired, First Nations sought to gain fair market rent for development on their properties, but of greater importance was upholding traditional philosophy and stewardship rights to cultural, social, spiritual, and economic integrity in relationship to the land. As a result, BC Hydro had to seriously consider a new approach to land negotiations that was not founded in an ethic of expropriation but that accounted for the significantly different worldviews of First Nations.

One of the approaches BC Hydro took to address this internally was to implement a three-level Aboriginal cross-cultural awareness program for its staff. This incorporated direct engagement and relationship-building with local First Nations. This was not without tensions along the way as issues of racism arose, highlighting the great fissure that existed between company understandings of First Nations and the reality of the communities from their own perspective. Over a three-year period, more than 4,000 BC Hydro employees received Aboriginal cross-cultural awareness training, and the program was considered immensely successful. It set a high professional standard for corporate Aboriginal awareness training, and other organizations and companies bought BC Hydro's program for delivery to their employees. Such companies included BC Tel (now Telus), MacMillan Bloedel (now Weyerhaeuser), Westcoast Energy (now Spectra Energy), Deloitte & Touche (now Deloitte), and the government of British Columbia.

At a broader level in BC Hydro's relationship-building progress, in June 1993, First Nations elders and spiritual practitioners led a traditional ceremony in the BC Hydro corporate headquarters office to launch the new Aboriginal Relations Department. The act of conducting the ceremony demonstrated to the BC Aboriginal community that in the new relationship, BC Hydro respected the cultural traditions of Aboriginal peoples. Of even greater significance were discussions around how BC Hydro could establish sustainable and meaningful working relationships with BC First Nations. With millions of dollars in capital infrastructure and land title negotiations at stake, neither party could afford to take the other for granted.

Through collaboration with the Aboriginal Relations Department, it was proposed that BC Hydro should host *Stl'e'áleq* to which BC First Nations chiefs and leaders would be invited (Bear, Girard, BC Hydro Aboriginal Relations Department, & Knowledge Network, 1996)). The purpose of the ceremony would be to establish the foundation for long-term relationships between the parties that would enable them to find mutually beneficial resolutions to clashes over land use. Of course, from a company perspective, investing in the costs of hosting *Stl'e'áleq* was an unconventional expense, particularly from the perspective of the accounting department that did not have a cost code for "potlatch" and of the company's business analysts, who did not know how to estimate return on such an investment. From the other side, early in the process when the event was still a proposal, one of the respected Chiefs expressed his trepidation about the event, particularly with regard to concerns that this was a marketing tactic that would only serve to tokenize the First Nations. The test was whether the corporation was serious about sustainable and constructive relationships with First Nations, for which the proof was in substantive change to company procedures and engagement. Despite uncertainties from both parties, ceremony planning proceeded.

Planning for BC Hydro's *Stl'e'áleq* took place with the support of the *Sqwxwó:mex* (Squamish) Nation, one of the Coast Salish nations whose traditional territory the city of Vancouver sits on. On April 6, 1994, *Stl'e'áleq* took place and the event was entitled "Pulling Together"—a metaphor for the shared canoe that both parties must navigate together. The ceremony took place at the *smilha'áwtxw* belonging to *Sqwxwó:mex* on their territory for the purpose of presenting BC Hydro with a talking stick. The stick symbolized the ethic of reciprocity that would bind a long-term and honorable relationship between BC Hydro and BC First Nations. *Sí:yá:m* (chiefs and respected leaders) from across BC's 38 tribes attended the BC Hydro *Stl'e'áleq*. The ceremony was officially hosted by *Siyá:m T'echuxanm*, Chief Joe Mathias, who was hereditary and elected chief of the *Sqwxwó:mex* Nation. In his opening, *Siyá:m T'echuxanm* spoke about the people who gathered to "share in our humanity as people. We come together in potlatch to honour a public corporation" (J. Mathias, cited in Bear et al., 1996). He noted that by the *Sqwxwó:mex* Nation presenting BC Hydro with a talking stick, the ceremony would bring integrity to the holder, and he made clear that in a First Nations' view of the world, *Stl'e'áleq* confirmed legal agreements. However, most importantly, for BC Hydro to accept the talking stick, they "acknowledge the responsibility given to them" (Bear et al., 1996).

On the day following the event, April 7, 1994, there was a First Nations Summit quarterly meeting, a political gathering of BC chiefs and leaders. Some immediate reactions to the ceremony were evident at the meeting, such that 120 out of the 150 chiefs and leaders in attendance were wearing BC Hydro hats given out as gifts the day before. In the Summit meeting, a number of witnesses who were called in the BC Hydro *Stl'e'áleq* spoke about what they had seen and heard in the ceremony. The following week, the chiefs and leaders returned to their respective home communities across the province and the Pulling Together witnesses reported again on what they had seen.

This is known to be the case because within two weeks of the BC Hydro *Stl'e'áleq*, the Aboriginal Relations Department in Vancouver received phone calls from all over the province that their local BC Hydro offices were flooded with calls from First Nations chiefs and leaders wanting to meet to discuss working relationships at the local level. The company invited more positive relationships with BC First Nations in one ceremony than had been possible with months and weeks of conventional marketing approaches through newsletters, newspaper, and radio ads. BC Hydro remains committed to the Aboriginal relations principles that were established in 1992 and affirmed in the Pulling Together *Stl'e'áleq* in 1994. Since that time, BC Hydro and BC First Nations have established a lengthy portfolio of relationships and agreements that continue today.

TWO DECADES LATER: REFLECTIONS ON BC HYDRO STL'E'ÁLEQ

Returning briefly to traditional Stó:lō society, the community was divided into hierarchical groups, and nowhere is this more evident than within the practice and protocols of *Stl'e'áleq*. Status within Stó:lō society is based on knowledge of one's own genealogical history as far back as possible (Carlson, 2010). To be high status is to know your genealogy and have access to those kinship ties as a source of authority for actions and entitlements. In the Halq'eméylem language, these people are referred to as *smelá:lh*. Genealogy carries information that verifies, justifies, and permits particular behavior by those who belong to it. It also speaks to the character and reputation of the entire family across generations. What is most significant is that every individual matters, and contributes to the whole of the genealogy. This explains why it is the ultimate reference source for the history of the people. Alternatively, according to Stó:lō ontology, what is lost and forgotten about one's genealogy makes one poor, or of low status; in the Halq'eméylem language these people are referred to as *st'éxem*. Connection to genealogy is of utmost importance and dictates the right to claim authority among Stó:lō by explaining why the community exists as it does and how it got to be that way.

These two concepts of status, *smelá:lh* and *st'éxem*, are direct references to the Stó:lō people, but speak to how understandings of wealth are defined within the gift economy of *Stl'e'áleq*. If wealth is indicated by knowing and claiming genealogical ties, then the distribution of wealth must be tied to the ability to nurture and grow genealogy. This is why relationship-building in *Stl'e'áleq*, where material distribution of goods symbolically secures social bonds, matters. While the material aspect of wealth distribution has been discussed extensively in anthropological literature by the volume (Godelier, 1999), nature (Stewart & Strathern, 2008; Strathern, 1988; Weiner, 1992), and spiritual genealogy of the gift itself (Henare, 2003; Mauss, 1966), wealth in *Stl'e'áleq* is found in the mere fact that a family has the spiritual authority to host, invite guests, call witnesses, provide sustenance to everyone for the duration of the ceremony, and give gifts to legitimate the purpose of the event. This definition of wealth is founded in the ability to build networks across diverse resource bases, which results in the growth and development of economic, environmental, and spiritual wealth (Miller, 1989). Through strong and expansive social networks (often solidified by intermarriage), ancestral ties and rights to resources also grow. There is an emerging discourse that frames the Stó:lō economy. Stó:lō wealth is inherent in the ability to host *Stl'e'áleq* because it relies entirely on the practice of referencing genealogy, reconnecting Stó:lō communities, and strengthening those ties as a demonstration of the continuity of Stó:lō people.

Whether or not the nature of relationships and agreements that currently exist between BC Hydro and BC First Nations reflects Indigenous economic philosophy of reciprocity as we have described in the traditional Stó:lō economy is up for debate. The extent to which agreements with corporates are abided by and expectations about the outcomes of the relationship are met is for each community to discern carefully, particularly where resources are sacred. Nonetheless, BC Hydro now has a genealogy to which BC First Nations are connected. The examples we have provided illuminate only one aspect of the ethic of reciprocity, which is that understanding the fundamental principles and values underlying Indigenous economic philosophy are imperative to meaningful relationships. The gift economy holds people at the center, and all forms of wealth are driven by the level of contribution back to the wholeness of the people.

NOTES

1. The language of Stó:lō Coast Salish people is called Halq'eméylem and is one of three dialects of the Halkomelem language group. It is distinguished as the upriver dialect as compared to the downriver dialect called Hun'qumyi'num', and the Vancouver Island dialect called Hul'q'umín'um. In this chapter, we are referring to the upriver dialect.

2. In the anthropological literature, the competitive nature of (particularly Northwest Coast) potlatch ceremonies has been central to the potlatch discourse and overshadowed much other discussion about the economic purpose and function of the institution of potlatch. The competitive nature is also a reflection of the changes that occurred as a result of the introduction of European trade goods and accompanying trade philosophies into First Nations communities (Drucker & Heizer, 1967).

3. The Indian Act is a piece of legislation that has had profound impact largely in the form of government control over the lives of Canada's aboriginal peoples. It was first enacted in 1876 and remains in existence today. The Indian act defines who is an 'Indian' based on racialized colonial construction of pan-Indian identity across Canada. The act details legal rights and disabilities pertaining to those people. See Indian act (Government of Canada, 1985). *The Indian Act.* (r.s.c., 1985, c. I-5). Ottawa: justice laws website retrieved from vehttp://laws-lois.justice.gc.ca/eng/acts/i-5/index.html

REFERENCES

Blomfield, K., Boxberger, D. L., Carlson, K. T., Duffield, C., Hancock, R. L., Lutz, J.,... & Woods, J. R. (2001). *A Stó:lō Coast Salish historical atlas.* Vancouver, BC: Douglas & McIntyre.

BC Hydro Aboriginal Relations Department (2014). *History of Aboriginal Relations.* http:// www.bchydro.com/community/aboriginal_relations/building_rela-tionships/aboriginal_relations_history.html

Bear, J., Girard, L. V., BC Hydro Aboriginal Relations Department, & Knowledge Network. (1996). *Pulling Together.* Pulling Together series. Vancouver, BC: BC Hydro and the Knowledge Network (BC).

Carlson, K. T. (Ed.). (1997). *You are asked to witness: The Sto:lo in Canada's Pacific Coast History.* Chilliwack, BC: Stó:lō Heritage Trust.

Carlson, K. T. (2010). *The power of place, the problem of time: Aboriginal identity and historical consciousness in the cauldron of colonialism.* Toronto, ON: University of Toronto Press.

Cole, D., & Chaikin, I. (1990). *An iron hand upon the people: The law against potlatch on the Northwest Coast.* Vancouver, BC: Douglas & McIntyre.

Drucker, P., & Heizer, R. F. (1967). *To make my name good: A reexamination of the South-ern Kwakiutl potlatch.* Berkeley, CA: University of California Press.

Galloway, B. D. (2009). *Dictionary of Upriver Halkomelem* (Vol. I). Berkeley, CA: University of California Publications.

Godelier, M. (1999). *The enigma of the gift* (N. Scott, Trans.). Chicago, IL: University of Chicago Press.

Government of Canada. (1985). *The Indian Act.* (R.S.C., 1985, c. I-5). Ottawa: Justice Laws. Retrieved from http://laws-lois.justice.gc.ca/eng/acts/I-5/index.html

Hall, T. D., & Fenelon, J. V. (2009). *Indigenous peoples and globalization: Resistance and revitalization.* Boulder, CO: Paradigm Publishers.

Henare, M. (2003). *The changing images of nineteenth century Māori society: From tribes to nation.* Unpublished thesis, Victoria University of Wellington. Wellington.

Maddison, A. (2006). *The world economy* (Vol. 1: A millenial perspective; Vol. 2: His-torical statistics). Paris, France: Organisation for Economic Co-operation and Development (OECD).

Mander, J., & Tauli-Corpuz, V. (Eds.). (2006). *Paradigm wars: Indigenous peoples' resis-tance to globalization.* San Franciso, CA: Sierra Club Books.

Mauss, M. (1966). *Essai sur le don: The gift—Forms and functions of exchange in archaic societies* (I. Cunnison, Trans.). London, England: Cohen & West Ltd.

Miller, B. (1989). Centrality and measures of regional structure in Aboriginal West-ern Washington. *Ethnology, 28*(3), 265–276.

Miller, B. (Ed.). (2007). *Be of good mind: Essays on the Coast Salish.* Vancouver, BC: University of British Columbia Press.

Moe, K. (2013, 23 May). For a future that won't destroy life on earth, look to the global indigenous uprising. *YES! Magazine,* Summer 2013(66), 28–35.

Nation Builder. (2013). Idle No More. Retrieved from http://www.idlenomore.ca/

Stewart-Harawira, M. (2005). *The new imperial order: Indigenous responses to globaliza-tion.* Wellington, New Zealand: Huia Publishers.

Stewart, P., & Strathern, A. (Eds.). (2008). *Exchange and sacrifice.* Durham, NC: Carolina Academic Press.

Strathern, M. (1988). *The gender of the gift: Problems with women problems with society in Melanesia.* Berkeley, CA: University of California Press.

Weiner, A. B. (1992). *Inalienable possessions: The paradox of keeping-while-giving.* Berkeley, CA: University of California Press.

CHAPTER 13

SPIRITUAL DYNAMICS IN SYSTEMS OF EVALUATION

Māori and Pacific Models for Process and Application

Tania Wolfgramm

ABSTRACT

At the core of the word "e-valu-ation" is "value." Hence, evaluation is considered to be the systematic determination of the value, merit, worth, significance, quality, or importance of something.

Evaluation is regarded as a rigorous, scientific research process undertaken by experts on projects, programs, services, providers, and people. Evaluations are often conducted with respect to groups, organizations, cultures, activities, conceptions, creations, programmes, policies, designs, processes, outcomes, institutions, and systems.

Relationship models for evaluations portray hierarchies representing the relative power of various stakeholders, including government ministries (often as contract funders and managers), project staff, program clients, and communities.

Indigenous Spiritualities at Work, pages 209–232
Copyright © 2015 by Information Age Publishing
209

Drawing on over a decade of experience as an evaluator, in this chapter I ask, "How has evaluation changed for Indigenous peoples? Do contemporary evaluation processes and practices allow for alternative views of evaluation?" My examination highlights the challenges of contemporary evaluation from an Indigenous perspective.

This chapter begins with stories of evaluation embedded in traditional narrative. I then build a picture of the contemporary context in which evaluation now occurs, making reference to specific Indigenous circumstances. Next, I contribute two models of evaluation: "Hakamana" and "Fale Lotu." As rigorous methods of evaluation, they reference Native science and Indigenous ontologies. To illustrate, I provide two current cases that offer insight into the centrality of spirituality in these evaluation models.

Manini waka!

A hi!
Kānapanapa ake nei
Ko ngā wai hihi wai haha o Tangaroa

Hī nana ki runga
Hī nana ki raro
Hī nana ki roto
Hī nana ki waho

Oti ra he pounamu, he pounamu, he pounamu
Puawai mai he maramatanga
Ki Te Whai Ao
Ki Te Ao Wānanga
Ki Te Ao Mārama
Tīhei Mauri Ora!

Hei tikitiki e HAKAMANA

(Wānanga—Tohunga Puroku Tawhai)

INTRODUCTION

Indigenous worlds, cultures, and knowledge systems developed over millennia and continue to be expressed through social structures, languages, symbols, art, science, technologies, and diverse enterprises. Many of these knowledge systems have nurtured and sustained Indigenous peoples and their environments across time, space, and place through robust evaluation processes. Evaluation has thus been a challenging endeavor recorded and expressed through multiple and dynamic sites of life-long learning. While a natural part of living and growing, evaluation can, within different contexts, demand the expression of heroic characteristics of those involved and impacted by the evaluation.

However, evaluation also has an appalling history, particularly as a tool of imperial oppression and colonization. This has required a deliberate replacement of local evaluation systems with structures, institution, and processes of evaluation of the colonizing forces and entities. Centuries of such evaluation mechanisms, including testing, examination, assessment, benchmarking, grading, analysis, ranking and rating, and so forth have taken their toll on these colonized groups.

Given the above, I highlight that evaluation is not value-free. Central to its design and exercise is "value." Thus the values of the designers and developers of evaluation systems and tools are indelibly stamped into them, making evaluation inextricably linked with power and control.

Hence, for those who have been subjected to colonization, a deeper knowledge of their own potential and power, and a greater awareness of how they can navigate through their complex relationships within dynamic environments and contexts, is an important starting point as they embark on their evaluation journeys (Kawakami, Aton, Cram, Lai, & Porima, 2007).

BACKGROUND: STORIES OF EVALUATION

Stories of creation, ancestry, and heritage of Indigenous peoples are enthralling. They have been recounted over thousands of years, maintaining knowledge systems and traditions from generation to generation. There are many stories of evaluation to be learned, and I draw critical insights from two Māori creation myths.

The Separation of Rangi and Papa

When the world was being created, Papa, Earth Mother, lay on her back, and Rangi, her husband the Sky Father, rested upon her. Over time they begat many children to be guardians of nature in its wondrous forms. The young gods, however, lived in cramped darkness between their parents, struggling for breath and being forced to crawl about like lizards. One day the gods were startled by a gleam of light they glimpsed as their parents moved, and immediately they longed for more of it. Fierce discussions raged among them for a long time about how they might achieve living in that wonderful light.

One brother, Tu, the God of War, wanted to kill their parents, but his siblings vehemently disapproved. Then Rongo, the God of Peace, and

Tangaroa, the God of Oceans, tried first to separate Rangi and Papa. However, none of the children could push them apart. Finally all of them, except for Tawhirimatea, the God of Winds, agreed that Tāne, the God of Forests, would separate their parents.

After a few failed attempts, Tāne planted his head on the earth, thrust his feet against the sky and with much heaving and pushing, forced his parents apart. Thus, Rangi took his place high above Papa, and Te Ao Mārama, the light of day, entered into the world.

This creation story of the separation of Rangi and Papa by their children contains many evaluative aspects. These include the sharing of foundational values, such as light and warmth, with a core stakeholder group—in this instance, the children of the gods—and the agreement of an outcome, namely the separation of their parents. There was disagreement regarding the methods and processes to be employed, most of which continued to cause contention. Of note was "Ko te nuinga, ko te roanga," *the multitude of thoughts and the length of time* it took for the siblings to debate their course of action. Power dynamics and politics, competing agendas, and a wide variation in ethical positions were all at play.

Tāne and the Baskets of Knowledge

Tāne, the God of Light, was chosen by Io, the Supreme God, to introduce knowledge into the world. He was to journey through many heavens and endure numerous trials and battles with his brother Whiro, the God of Darkness, on his travels. When Tāne arrived at Io's sacred marae, he entered the temple and was given three kete (baskets) of knowledge and two sacred stones. The first was *Kete-Uruuru-Matua*, the basket of peace, goodness, and love; the second was *Kete-Uruuru-Rangi*, containing prayers, incantations, and rituals; and the third was *Kete-Uruuru-Tau*, containing knowledge of war and peace, agriculture, and earth and stonework to tend to the well-being of humankind. The *whatukura* or sacred stones were *Huka-a-tai* and *Rehutai*. These stones would add mana, authority, and power to what was taught, seal the teachings, and impress them on the minds of those learning.

The return journey was fraught with perils instigated by the angry Whiro that were overcome by Tāne with the help of Tawhirimatea and his companions. Tāne's triumph in securing the *wānanga* was widely celebrated, with the sky flushing crimson as a sign of his victory. On returning to earth he entered the *wharekura* (sacred place of learning), where he suspended the baskets of knowledge and deposited the stones at the back of the sacred house. Tāne remained as the custodian of the *wānanga*.

Importantly, this story of Tāne brings to the fore the importance to Māori of knowledge and learning, the thirst for such knowledge requiring great effort and the ability to overcome many hardships. Ethical protocols and practices were integral to the task and each step of the evaluation process provided an opportunity for feedback and learning. The eventual outcome of this great undertaking was to bring knowledge to Māori, such that it would span every element of the lives of humankind and would include the mechanisms by which such knowledge would be attained, evaluated, and retained.

The legends of Tāne attaining the three baskets of knowledge also contain important values, including the attainment of knowledge for the benefit of humanity, the objectives and outcomes, and the processes and procedures for the attainment of this knowledge.

Such stories and themes have played out again and again across generations and within multiple contexts. At the collective level, manifest within families, groups, organizations, tribes and nations, we have seen forces of life and death, creation and destruction, collaboration, and disconnection battle with each other. At the individual level, such challenges and dynamic interactions are evident at the psychic and intrapsychic levels of the self, both conscious and unconscious, where we are, all at once, the child, the parent, the sibling, the risk-taker, the healer, the leader, and the follower.

We are both hero and villain, concurrently seeking growth on the one hand, while developing "things that hurt, sting, and bite" to inhibit and restrict that journey of transformation. Hence evaluation, while a natural part of living and growing, can demand within challenging contexts that people manifest their heroic characteristics. A deeper knowledge of their own complexity as individuals, a recognition of who they are as members of diverse collectives, and a greater comprehension of themselves as subjects and objects within multiple structures and systems is an important starting point in any evaluation journey.

This is an endeavor that requires courage, fortitude, and resilience!

CONTEXT: EVALUATION AS A TOOL OF OPPRESSION

As noted, for millions of Indigenous people worldwide, evaluation has widely been experienced as a tool of oppression and supremacy. For example, Māori, having been subjects for almost two centuries of Eurocentric values-laden evaluations. As a consequence, Māori and increasingly Pacific peoples are over-researched, over-evaluated, and audited with greater frequency than Europeans across multiple sectors. Now, they often feel that they are targets of criticism and blame for issues often beyond their control, such as noncommunicable diseases, inadequate housing, rising unemployment, and failures of the education system. In education for example, Māori and Pacific school students are frequently branded "failures"[1] and, they are continually constructed as the "other" compared to non-Indigenous "normal" persons. Hence Māori and Pacific peoples are often marginalized and judged as failing to reach acceptable standards of whatever is being valued and measured.

However, evaluation is often regarded as a rigorous, scientific research process undertaken by "experts" on projects, programs, services, providers, and people, including *whānau, hapū, marae,* tribal groups, and Indigenous organizations. Relationship models for these types of evaluations portray hierarchies representing the relative power of various stakeholders, including government ministries (often as contract funders and managers), project staff, program clients, and communities.

Evaluators are often contracted by government entities and organizations to observe, gather information, review, analyze and interpret data, make judgements, and report on their findings while always remaining independent and nonpartisan. This relationship model makes several assumptions. For example, they assume there are formally defined roles and responsibilities, power differentials, strict communications protocols, heavily prescribed evaluation and research methods and processes, and evaluators who write for and report back to project funders.

In addition, the United Nations states that evaluation has been a mandated activity of the United Nation's program and budgeting system since the early 1980s and the objective of evaluation is:

> To determine as systematically and objectively as possible, the relevance, efficiency, effectiveness and impact of the Organization's activities in relation to their objectives; To enable the Secretariat and Member States to engage in systematic reflection, with a view to increasing the effectiveness of the main programmes of the Organization by altering their content, and if necessary, reviewing their objectives. (United Nations, 2011, p. 2)

However, in reality, an evaluation set up with these assumptions leaves clients, *whānau,* communities, and Māori providers anxious, wary, and suspicious of the evaluators who are often, rightly or wrongly, viewed as "agents of the government" and what it stands for. While the notion of equalizing relationships by "empowering" program providers and clients while simultaneously "disempowering" the evaluators and government funders has been proposed, the reality of hierarchies of power and control remains.

Evaluation is always political, at times with many competing agendas. For example, a Māori research study of a health initiative would need to balance at least three components: cultural integrity, academic rigor, and safe clinical interventions. Values are prioritized and accorded relative measures of importance and influence by different stakeholders. They are seeded from the outset of the evaluation in terms of the prioritization of (1) what counts as values or valuable outcomes, (2) the framing of the evaluation questions, and (3) the methods chosen to answer those questions.

Therefore, considering competing value systems both explicit and implicit in evaluation processes, it is important to continue to ask the following questions. Whose values and voices are privileged? Whose perspectives are valued as more *or* less important than others? Do the values of the funding agencies outweigh the values of service providers and subsequently their clients' values?

DECOLONIZING EVALUATION

Indigenous communities have been attempting to address the evaluation process through taking ownership of and reclaiming evaluation as a critical tool based within their own worldview and contextualized within their own realities.

There are an increasing number of Indigenous persons trained in research and evaluation who have been arguing for the right to develop their own evaluation methodologies. Inspired by the work of Linda Smith (1999) and others in decolonizing research methodologies, efforts continue to decolonize evaluation methodologies. This process requires that Indigenous peoples recenter themselves within their own worldviews and regroup and recharge as they rediscover, redevelop, and adapt practices that are "of, for, by, and with us" (Kawakami, Aton, Cram, Lai, & Porima, 2007, p. 323).

Drawing from Smith (1999), engaging a Kaupapa Māori approach integrates in various configurations (not necessarily linear) three key concepts: resistance, conscientization, and transformative praxis. In terms of evaluations, this approach enables evaluation processes that honor the values found within Indigenous ontologies, epistemologies, and methodologies. This enables the creation of systems and construction of frameworks for carrying out evaluation without being "limited by the legacies of previous" research and evaluation. This approach affords freedom of feeling, thought, and expression, providing spaces and frameworks for both deconstructing colonizing hegemonies and reconstructing/co-creating Indigenous knowledge and systems of evaluation and research.

THE RATIONALE FOR INDIGENOUS EVALUATION SYSTEMS

As we create a new future, we need to create new tools that can help to project us into that future. For how do we know, at any point in time, whether what we are imagining is what we are realizing, and what we are realizing is what we are imagining?

The process for determining and articulating—indeed even thinking about—"values" is complex and multifaceted. Its reaches deep into the psyche, the spirit of an individual, is shaped by the individual's familial relationships, informed and fashioned according to the individual's culture and worldview, and further developed by systems and structures both local and global. Even the words and language for those values and concomitant behaviors and activities will further shape one's awareness, understandings, and experiences of them.

In addition, identity is fundamental to the concept of value in these communities. Indigenous identities are located in physical, spiritual, and emotional connections to land and water, from the highest mountains to lowest valleys, from vast oceans to small streams, all having a special place in hearts, minds, and souls. Therefore, identities encompass complex systems and structures that include all aspects of life, including genealogies, family and social relationships, community living, health and well-being, learning and education, creativity and arts, corrections and justice, economics and trading, and so forth.

In order to convey these concepts, the following section of brings into focus two case studies that highlight Indigenous evaluation models that I have developed and applied. The first evaluation model is called "Hakamana" and the case used is the Te Ha Academy, a global academy of creatives, scientists, academics, and voyagers. The second evaluation model is called "Fale Lotu" and the case offered is "Arere ki mua," the Waikato Pacific Churches' health program.

HAKAMANA AS A MODEL FOR EVALUATION

What can we learn about evaluation from legends, histories, stories, and from cultural experts and traditional knowledge holders? How do we honor, gather, and analyze this wisdom to co-create a cohesive system of evaluation that is (1) founded within Indigenous value systems, (2) complemented by contemporary knowledge, and (3) applicable to Indigenous contextualized contemporary realities?

The development of *hakamana* is guided by an understanding that Indigenous peoples have always had ways of assessing merit based on traditional values and cultural expressions.

Hakamana—Informed by Sounds/Relationships/ Stories of Creation

The Polynesian kupu/word *hakamana* contains many important elements, including:

A—the light of oneself; the world of light expressed as "Ko Au Te Ao . . . Te Ao Ko Au"

HA—the breath of life; the divine breath that connects all living—"all our relations"

KA—the fire that burns within us; the energy expended for future transformations

MA—the presence of all of one's "light"; knowing oneself/one's world/ one's connections

NA—the relationships we have with each other and with the world at large; respect kinship

HAKA—the "dance of life and energy"; expression through animation and activation

MANA—the power, strength and authority one has; effectiveness, prestige; leadership; thunder

HAKAMANA—the creative process of bringing one's power and authority to light and being.

Co-Creating the Hakamana Evaluation System

The recognition of evaluation as integral to learning is the foundation upon which the *Hakamana* Evaluation System is co-created. An exploration of the values, ethics, protocols, and practice of evaluation within, with, and across Indigenous peoples, including *whānau* (families), *pou* (pillars; totems), *marae* (sacred cultural epicentre of family and community), and *waka* (canoe; vehicle of conveyance), have informed the organic design and development of *hakamana.*

Foundational to this development are values that remain strong yet are also flexible and responsive to local traditions and culture. Principles upon which *hakamana* is built include respect, recognizing the inherent value of each other, being conscious of and responsive to cultural values, being inclusive, having meaningful engagement and participation, affording protection and safety, being reflexive and evaluative, and assigning roles and responsibilities: in sum, being reciprocal and generous, useful, and valuable.

Introducing Puorooro—The Sounds of Hakamana

These *puorooro,* I – O – E – A – U, are sounds of the Polynesian language and communicate states of relationship, creativity, and potentiality (see Figure 13.1). For example, Te Reo Māori expresses and manifests the reality of Te Ao Māori, Te Ao Mārama (the world of light) and Te Ao Hurihuri (the changing world). These words, which are simultaneously verbs and nouns,

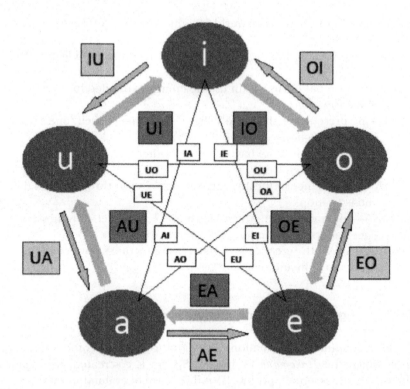

Figure 13.1 Hakamana—Informed by sounds/relationships/stories of creation.

or processes and outcomes, provide both constancy on the one hand, and dynamic change on the other.

The *Hakamana* Evaluation System is a dynamic evaluation system that animates values that enhance the mana and power of "all our relations," past, present, and future.

Ethical spaces are negotiated and experienced at many levels: within the psyche, in relationship with others and the collective, and in relation to the world at large. Ethical boundaries established by collective principles, such as knowledge systems and rights to traditions, remind communities of what is important in life and what they value.

Systems' thinking continues to shift the focus from individual parts to their interactions as they are configured by a complex and dynamic web of relationships, both internal and external. Thus, in most cases, "the whole" has properties that cannot be known from analysis of the constituent elements in isolation. Co-creating the *Hakamana* System of Transformative Evaluation as an integrated whole, including mechanisms, processes, and procedures for effective practice, continues to be an interesting and exciting endeavor.

Critical theory allows us to name and frame our situation
... gives us a sense of present realities.
Now the onus is on our shoulders to create
... to essentially imagine a possible future for us.
This requires our creative processes to kick in
... as they do when we create an art piece.

Professor Gregory Cajete, Aotearoa, New Zealand 2009

Matauranga Taketake, ancient wisdom, Indigenous knowledge, and "original instructions" for how to live on earth in ways that highlight the interconnectedness of the spiritual, intellectual, social, and physical worlds have been gathered through *wānanga* and *hui* with *tohunga*, traditional knowledge holders and Indigenous experts across various fields of endeavor. The Indigenous worldviews expressed by them have highlighted the interconnectedness of their spiritual, human, and physical worlds.

Implicitly honored within *hakamana* are *Mauri* (life-force; the life principle intersecting light and dark), *Wairua* (the divine spirit within oneself existing across space and time), *Tapu* (intrinsically sacred elements requiring special care) and *Mana* (enduring spiritual power infused at conception).

APPLYING THE HAKAMANA EVALUATION SYSTEM

To explain how the *hakamana* model of evaluation works I draw on the case of Te Ha Academy. Te Ha translates as "Breath of Life and Creativity." This academy creates and transmits traditional and contemporary knowledge through teaching and learning; research and creative work; and sustainable environmental, ecological, and economic advancement. It is networked with institutions around the world that have similar aims and aspirations.

Te Ha Indigenous Centre of Ancient Knowledge and Living Culture supports the aim of tribes and Indigenous peoples of the world to participate fully in the knowledge society and economy by enhancing learning and education, stimulating innovation, and identifying opportunities for creating spiritual and material wealth from ideas, knowledge, and understanding.

Te Ha energizes and empowers traditional knowledge holders, scholars, educators, practitioners, and artisans to come together and collectively expand the horizons of knowledge and practice. With research, dialogue, writing and action projects, Te Ha supports making the natural native worlds visible through their cultures, arts, and sciences.

Te Ha projects currently include:

- Pacific Guardians/World Tribe Canoe: This aims to revitalize and reinvigorate Pacific and California tribes' water cultures and includes canoe design, construction, and carving.
- Teaching/Learning: Teaching of both traditional and contemporary science and art, language revitalization, and health and wellbeing systems is provided locally and globally.
- Research and creative work: This increases the Indigenous presence in the dialogue of sustainability and includes cultural expression of both issues and solutions through multiple media, spanning arts and technology.
- Indigenous enterprise and leadership: This fosters opportunities for entrepreneurship aimed to advance the economic self-determination of Pacific/Indigenous peoples.
- Fanau Ola: Design and develop Family-Centred health and wellbeing systems/processes/toolkits/technologies, based within Indigenous cultural values.
- Tangaroa Code–Creation/Re-Creation of Proto-Oceanic linguistic symbols based on ancient and traditional carving and sculpture/sculptural 'texts'.

Hakamana allows for each part of the story or element to be evaluated as part of their creative development, acknowledging the dynamism of life and variability of circumstances, while encouraging mutually beneficial processes that progress towards achieving the vision of Te Ha (see Table 13.1).

THE FALE LOTU EVALUATION MODEL

Building on the faith, hope, and strength that Pacific peoples find in their spiritual lives, the Fale Lotu[2] evaluation model also encompasses many domains (Figure 13.2). It starts with a dream, vision, and goals. Good planning is required for the Fale Lotu to be designed, developed, built, and brought to fruition. It ought to be built upon good soil, within supportive environments. Six strong pillars are embedded in solid foundations. Bound around the ceiling and roof structures are coils of resilient and durable fibers. The end result is the realization of a dream, the co-creation of a beautiful Fale Lotu—one that represents the passion, vision, and commitment of caring, healthy, and happy Pacific families.

TABLE 13.1   Evaluation System for Te Ha Academy

		The Story of Creating	HAKA *What we do*	MANA *What we achieve*
HI	**hiki** **hihiri** **whiri**	*The divine potential* *The seeking* *The searching* *The weaving*	Dreaming/Visioning Conceptualizing Seek understanding of self, community, world	**Vision of TE HA** **Integrating** **Knowledge Diversity** **for Sustainability**
	hio **pio** **tio**	*The divine creator* *The forming* *The generating* *The spaces of safety*	Nurturing creativity Leadership/structure Establishing ethics Intelligence/planning	Creative design Leaders/Champions Ethics established Project plans
HO	**hoko** **poto** **roto**	*The suspension* *The gathering* *The knowing* *The looking within*	Gathering knowledge Content/systems Building expertise Design/strategies	Good foreknowledge Communications Great teams built Design/Strategic plan

	hoe
	koe
	moe
		The ploughing
		The connecting to others
		The imagining
		The collective dreaming
			Grounding
			Build good relationships
			Transforming, redefining
			    courses and processes
				Strong foundation
				Strong relationships
				Excellent co-created
				    curricula/content

HE	**heke** **rere** **tere**	*The struggle* *The climbing* *The running* *The moving*	Innovating enterprise Stimulating, vibrant Dynamic, transforming Activities, tasks	Actions/Tactics Operations Implementation plans/procedures

	hea
	mea
	pea
		The unknown
		The questioning
		The enquiring
		The ambiguity
			Identify, examine,
			    evaluate, revalidate,
			    utilize–develop from the
			    core/central vision
				All components
				    animate/activate
				Indigenous values
				    and vision

HA	**haka**
	mana
	ra wa
		The breath of life
		The fire and energy
		The power and authority
		The day, light, space, time
			Making a statement
			Strengthen identities
			Acknowledge authority
			Activating local/global
				Honor Indigenous
				    knowledge system—
				    authentic/expert
				Active local & global

	hau
	kau
	mau
		The self as the world
		The winds of change
		The bright burning
		The world as the self
			Being self-reflective
			Having work reviewed
			Thinking about future
			    directions
				Higher Education
				    systems—based
				    on Indigenous
				    knowledge system

HU	**pua**
	tupu
	ruru
		The blossoming
		The growing
		The standing
		The sheltering
			Completing aspects
			Celebrating achievement
			Recognition
			Protecting self & work
				Learners achieve
				    within Indigenous
				    knowledge system/
				    structures/processes

	hui
	nui
	tui tu'i
		The sharing
		The expanding
		The faith; the binding
		The ultimate leader
			Sharing learnings
			Knowledge transmission
			Dissemination
				Knowledge is shared
				    with the world—
				    local and global
				    sustainable success

HII		Divine potentiality... the miracle look at other dimensions ... start again from higher level ...		

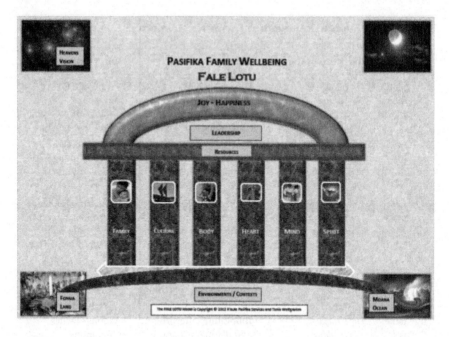

Figure 13.2 Fale Lotu model.

The Fale Lotu Model honors the principle:

"The Fanau[3] . . . a Fale Lotu"

VISION	Heavens	Shared Vision/Goals/Objectives
CONTEXT	Land/Water	Environment/Community/Systems
FAMILY	Pillar	Relationships/Caring Connections
CULTURE	Pillar	Worldview/Tradition/Language
BODY	Pillar	Physical health/Conditions/Risks
HEART	Pillar	Emotional Well-being/Love/Support
MIND	Pillar	Learning/Intellect/Skills/Education
SPIRIT	Pillar	Spirituality/Religion/Church
RESOURCES	Bindings	Resources/Housing/Income/Transport
LEADERSHIP	Roof	Building leadership skills

APPLYING THE FALE LOTU EVALUATION MODEL

In the following section, I draw on a recent case study, Aere Ki Mua, to provide explanatory power to this model of evaluation.

Vision

Aere ki mua is about giving Pacific people,
their families and communities,
a fresh look, hope and brighter future in life
and to instil positive thinking towards
improving lifestyles, health and wellbeing.

Guided by spiritual values,
Aere Ki Mua aims to achieve its goals
through love and respect,
nurturing growth and positive changes,
in culturally safe environments.

In the first part of this evaluation, we explored *fanau* dreams for their future, their goals and objectives and their plans for achieving these shared aspirations. Many agreed that "using the churches was a good idea" for implementing Aere Ki Mua, because "life revolves around church." Another spoke of how the churches were able to provide some social cohesion, whereby ministers played an important role in articulating and sharing the vision—essentially getting buy-in for the vision from their congregations.

> This is a good model for Pacific people . . . we can relate to it, and appreciate all parts of it. (Pacific mother)

Many families were encouraged through envisioning a future where they could be healthier and have improved well-being. Multiple facets and experiences of their lives were explored and families were helped to analyze these so that they could inform the planning. They all agreed that Aere Ki Mua provided them with a balanced approach that brought their families together.

Contexts/Environmental Dimensions

This dimension relates to the social/cultural/economic contexts and environments and the realities lived and experienced and subsequent meanings they have for Pacific people, including their ability to provide healthy *kai* for their families. While for many families there was an awareness of the need to be healthier, some spoke of having competing priorities that they had to balance continually. With many families facing unemployment and financial constraints, food has become a much greater issue in the lives of many Pacific families in New Zealand. This was true for both island-born people who now live in New Zealand and New Zealand-born Pacific peoples.

Pacific families were thus faced with programs for new foods, new diets, and new lifestyles, within systems of food that were poorly understood. Access to good quality, affordable, healthy food was always a challenge. With heavily competing costs including housing, electricity, water, telephone, transport, education, health, and so forth, food purchases became one of the costs that had to be carefully calculated. Often, a lack of money resulted in many Pacific families finding themselves in the unenviable position of buying any food available, often not healthy, quality choices.

Furthermore, some New Zealand-based Pacific families are socially and culturally isolated, disconnected from family and friends. In the islands they could readily access food from extended family, neighbors and friends, whereas in New Zealand, many families have found themselves with fewer networks from which to get food. Therefore, the churches provided protective networks within which some families felt more support, particularly from church leaders. Having *Aere Ki Mua* based in their local churches was important for families as they were able to access the program, with many of the activities linked to other church activities (e.g., choir practice following zumba).

While some families enjoyed growing their own food, others had problems that were beyond their control. One minister said that for some *fanau*, "staying in short term rental properties was one of the barriers for motivation and maintaining vegetable gardening."

K'aute Pasifika were also able to help some churches by providing them with opportunities for catering (e.g., providing healthy muffins and salads for various events), thereby helping families to see the potential entrepreneurial benefits of improved food knowledge and skills.

Family/Familial/Social Dimension

While the family is seen as the fundamental basis of social organization and support, Pacific families do not usually follow a typical Western definition. Usually they are large extended families with complex authority and status relationships between grandparents (both maternal and paternal), parents and children, siblings, brothers and sisters, aunts and nieces and nephews, and others. While providing structures for social cohesion on the one hand, on the other, competing family member priorities would often strain family relationships. It was also important that family champions were identified, as they were usually the person who would often control the food, being both the buyer and cook for the family. For the main part, however, family members took great pride in their achievements.

I'm happy to say that my wife has lost weight, and went down from 137 kg to 116 kg. She started just swimming first, and then combined it with lawn mowing, and regular walking. (Samoan Minister)

Most Pacific people attend church as a family and have a Christian upbringing, and generally the whole family belong to the same religion. The congregations, comprising hundreds of families across Waikato, were made up of various ethnicities and denominations. Individuals of all ages and at varied levels of health participated and are now showing benefits of their involvement. Participants commented that *Aere Ki Mua* was "great for new families in the area" and it "was a great way to bring families together," and through ongoing events such as Church Camps and Youth Camps, "helped to establish friendships with each other." Many families talked about how much they enjoyed participating in the *Aere Ki Mua* activities including zumba, volleyball, regular physical exercise sessions, and the AKM Sports Day.

One Samoan Minister commented, "Physical activity and exercise continued to be encouraged. Our kids regularly do outdoor games, while the adults were involved in tennis and cricket. Members are aware of healthy eating and are looking good."

Another minister commented:

[Our Churches] continued to promote healthy lifestyle messages.... Community members were struggling to improve on cutting down portions of food; nevertheless, they continued to try. Increasing awareness and self-responsibility to maintain an individual and family's health by maintaining healthy weights have been observed in this church. Generally in this quarter, particularly after the long Christmas holiday break, no one actually gained much weight. (Cook Islands Minister)[4]

Culture/Cultural Dimension

Culture encompasses Pacific values, beliefs and behaviours, traditions, protocols and rituals and knowledge and traditions transmitted individually and collectively throughout generations. "Culture—it is like the way we use rope to stitch families together. We call it 'afoi' in Samoan ... like weaving a mat," reflected one Samoan minister.

For many island peoples, food is one of the most important things in their life, and they will eat a wide variety of food, large quantities, and frequently. Pacific peoples love to feast, spending a great deal of time preparing, cooking, and feasting for a huge variety of occasions.

Culturally and socially, food was often the "glue" that held family, villages, and communities together. Therefore feasting was required for all social events, and every occasion of any significance was an occasion for feasting, including birthdays, leaving, arrivals, conferences, workshops, funerals, and a wide variety of church-related activities. There is *mana* associated with the food and the act of preparing and giving food to persons of higher status, and the type and quantity of food is a tool to measure the status of the occasion. Providing for feasts can be fiercely competitive and depending on the occasion (e.g., whether a family birthday or a national coronation), families, villages, districts, and even islands would try to outperform each other in both quality and quantities of food as their status would be measured by what they provided.

> To make 'pola'[5] is a cultural obligation . . . is a church obligation . . . but sometimes they have too much food on them. (Tongan woman participant)

While during the week people may eat less, the Sunday feast is an institution in many island nations and for many island families. This presented a challenge for some of the ministers, and one Tongan Minister noted,

> We have a bad historical record for vast amounts of spit roasts—and last year we had twenty spit roasts . . . but since Aere Ki Mua we have had a big change—and have had none! Now our church menus are healthier and are prepared by the women who have attended nutrition training.

Eating patterns, however, have changed in island-born peoples over the past few decades with the advent of white sugar and flour and highly processed foods, precooked and easily prepared food, and an increase in takeaway outlets leading to eating behaviors that have resulted in higher rates of diet-related illness (e.g., diabetes, cardio-vascular disease). Many ministers have risen to the challenge of encouraging families to provide healthy options, even as they fulfill their cultural obligations for providing feasts.

> In Kiribati, we now have high rates of diabetes due to a lack of land, dependence on imported Palagi food including white sugar, white flour, and white rice. (Kiribati Minister)

With regard to the physical activity elements of Aere Ki Mua, some participants noted that it was not usual to do "structured" exercise programs, except at school. However, hundreds of families enthusiastically supported the program, participating regularly in all of the fitness activities. Some also said that they were keen to receive resources in their own languages.

Church community members participating in the monitoring exercises were able to express themselves in their own languages during the activities including filling out of a baseline survey that required listings of personal goals, barriers to good health, and preferred participation means. (Community Development Officer)

Body/Physical Dimension

This dimension related to physical or biological well-being, including the self-awareness and self-care of the participants and how they put into practice their knowledge and skills about food and health for themselves and their families. Furthermore, it was about how they were able to manifest a sense of guardianship through practical application such as what food choices are made and what behaviors were undertaken in individual and family lives. Pacific participants certainly had some thoughts in relation to what they hoped to achieve in relation to their physical well-being, as evident in their baseline survey data.

Individual goals included:

- "To stay fit, lose weight, and be off medication (PT Diabetic diagnosed)"
- "To lose weight and be fit"
- "To lose 10 kg"
- "Be a professional sportsman"
- "Get into the top rugby team in school and achieve my subjects"
- "For my weight to be proportional to my height"
- "Malosi ai le tino, taumafai e faamama le weight"

Perceptions of body type and the language used to convey those shapes and attitudes towards them were also captured in this dimension. Traditionally, larger people and therefore larger bodies in many Pacific societies were a sign of wealth, high status, and health, with their language often reflecting that view.[6] If you were a good Pacific parent, therefore, you wanted your children and family to be considered healthy (and wealthy) within your own Pacific worldview. Other barriers to achieving goals were identified, including;

- "the cost of fruit and veggies being too expensive"
- "shift work and eating at the wrong times"
- "having too much commitment with family and work"
- "eating junk food, watching TV, and spending lots of time on the computer"

There were many good outcomes for *Aere Ki Mua* participants, including:

- Family members doing regular physical activities together; enjoying and having fun doing zumba and hot hula; playing games, sports, and other fitness activities, including participating in the AKM sports days
- Having more energy (e.g., to walk around the lake, to play sports) and increased fitness level

We have started our walk around the lake on Sundays starting from 6:30 a.m., at least one round within an hour and keep cutting the time back. This week we aim to get it down to 50 minutes. Samoan Minister (AKM Advisory Group meeting minutes, 20/10/11)

- More people joining gyms, swimming, and enjoying aqua exercise
- Children improving at their sports with better fitness (e.g., netball, rugby)
- Some people who would normally use walking aids (e.g., walkers) no longer needed them. One Health Committee member said, "It's really amazing to see that."
- Better nutrition through eating healthy food, fruit, and vegetables: "We are banning fizzy drinks, smoking and drinking" (Church Minister)
- Weight loss and girth reduction: "I have successfully lost 18 kg since Aere Ki Mua started. I was 110 kg and now weigh 92 kg." (Samoan Minister)
- Lowered blood pressure and better health in general: "Our families have had fewer doctor visits and hospitalizations. We have not had anyone die in our church because of bad health." (Tongan Minister)
- More people being able to participate in brass bands, which was good for building lung capacity—especially for those people with asthma
- More family members thinking about caring for their bodies "as a temple"—not mistreating it or "throwing rubbish into it," but keeping them "clean" (e.g., giving up smoking).

Generally, families identified in their baseline survey that the support they needed to achieve their health and weight loss goals included joining sports groups, zumba, cooking classes, personal coaching, aqua exercise, and help with setting up gardens. They also stated that they would participate in training and activities at church venues, meetings, fono, camps, and in online forums such as email and/or Facebook.

Overall, the empowering aspects of the *Fale Lotu* evaluation model were made salient in the *Aere Ki Mua* case.

CONCLUSION

In this chapter I aimed to shed light on two streams of inquiry. Firstly, how has evaluation changed for Indigenous peoples? Secondly, do contemporary evaluation processes and contemporary practices allow for alternative views of evaluation?

In terms of the first question, I detailed how evaluation has changed for Indigenous peoples from an empowered and enlightened process of understanding, as detailed in traditional narratives, through to a tool of imperialist oppression. In terms of the second question, I highlighted the challenges of contemporary evaluation from an Indigenous perspective. In addition, I discussed how Indigenous peoples are beginning to overcome the oppressive way in which evaluations have been used to meet the needs of hegemonic regimes. In order to contribute to evaluations as a field of study and practice, I also detailed two models of evaluation informed by Native science and Indigenous ontologies, namely Hakamana and Fale Lotu. In addition, I illustrated the efficacy of these models, drawing on recent case studies which I have been involved in as an Indigenous evaluator. These two models offer insight into the centrality of spirituality in the evaluation process from an Indigenous perspective.

In conclusion, I offer the following thought as shared with me in a wānanga (learning circle) with Tohunga Te Uranga o Te Ra Kingi.

> First there is aroha, "unconditional love"; an understanding that all people, all taonga; "treasures—tangible and intangible," all things share the pathway of life; appreciating that all are connected to each other and all must be cared for in the spirit of love. Then there is a blossoming, a manifestation of the deepest knowledge that allows one's thoughts to be made known ... those thoughts, from the deepest recesses of the mind, realised in learning, study and evaluation, in other ways of seeking to know. (Wānanga—Tohunga Te Uranga o Te Ra Kingi, 2008)

NOTES

1. For example, in New Zealand ONE News 22 Sept 2012 news item: *Maori and Pasifika students are lagging behind others at school, national standards data released by the Government suggest* ...
2. *Fale Lotu* are Pacific words that equate to "House of Prayer."
3. *Fanau* is an ancient Pacific word that expresses many sounds of creation; *ha* the "breath of life" and *wa* implying "time and space" combine to sound the sound *fa*, a special number signifying the foundations of family life; *na* interweaving family relationships with others, and *u* manifesting the realization of

the family's potential. *Fanau* thus speaks of being born, bringing forth, having children, grandchildren, siblings, and extended families.

4. See Aere Ki Mua Quarterly Progress Report to 31 March 2012
5. In Tonga, feasts comprise numerous *pola* made from large coconut fronds and banana leaves measuring several feet in length, loaded high with food. No longer content with single tier *pola*, now people provide two and three-tiered *pola*, the bottom tier laden with meat (e.g., suckling pigs, chickens, and beef) and root crops (e.g., yam, taro, kumara), the second tier with seafood delicacies, and the top tier with a variety of cakes and desserts.
6. In Tongan for example to call someone *sino* is a compliment and implies large, plump, and healthy; however, to call someone *tutue*, meaning thin, unhealthy, and sickly, is not a compliment. Furthermore, the word for slimming down is "fakamahamaha sino" implying the "emptying out of one's healthy body."

REFERENCES

Kawakami, A., Aton, K., Cram, F., Lai, M., & Porima, L. (2007). Improving the practice of evaluation through Indigenous values and methods: Decolonizing evaluation practice—Returning the gaze from Hawai'i and Aotearoa. *Hulili: Multidisciplinary Research on Hawaiian Well-Being, 4*(1), 319–348.

Smith, L. T. (1999). *Decolonising methodologies: Research and Indigenous peoples.* Dunedin, New Zealand: University of Otago Press.

United Nations. (2011, December). *Evaluation Policy.* Paper presented at United Nations Conference on Trade and Development, retrieved from http://unctad.org/Sections/edm_dir/docs/osg_EvaluationPolicy2011_en.pdf

ADDITIONAL RESOURCES

Further Reading

Barlow, C. (1991). *Tikanga whakaaro. Key concepts in Māori culture.* Auckland, New Zealand: Oxford University Press.

Battiste, M. (2000). *Reclaiming indigenous voice and vision.* Vancouver, Canada: University of British Colombia Press.

Brookfield, F. M. (1999). *Waitangi and Indigenous rights: Revolution, law and legitimation.* Auckland, New Zealand: Auckland University Press.

Cajete, G. (1994). *Look to the mountain: An ecology of Indigenous education.* Asheville, NC: Kivaki Press.

Cajete, G. (2000). *Native science. Natural laws of interdependence.* Santa Fe, NM: Clear Light Publishers.

Davidson, E. J. (2005). *Evaluation methodology basics: The nuts and bolts of sound evaluation.* Thousand Oaks, CA: Sage.

Deloria, V. Jr. (1994). *God is red: A Native view of religion.* Golden, CO: Fulcrum Publishing.

Deloria, V. Jr. (1995). *Red earth, white lies: Native Americans and the myth of scientific fact.* New York, NY: Scribner.

Derrida. J. (2002). *Writing and difference.* London, England: Routledge.

Durie, M. (1994). *Whaiora: Māori health development.* Auckland, New Zealand: Oxford University Press.

Durie, M. (1998). *Te Mana, Te Kawanatanga: The politics of Māori self-determination.* Auckland, New Zealand: Oxford University Press

Foucault, M. (1994). *Power. Essential works of Foucault 1954–1984* (Vol. 3). London, England: The Penguin Press.

Freire, P. (1970). *Pedagogy of the oppressed.* London, England: Penguin Books.

Freire, P. (1997). *Pedagogy of the heart.* New York, NY: Continuum.

Hau'ofa, E. (2008). *We are the ocean.* Honolulu, HI: University of Hawaii Press.

Health Research Council. (2005). *Guidelines on Pacific health research.* Auckland, New Zealand: Author. Retrieved from http://www.hrc.govt.nz

Hēnare, M. A. (2003). *The changing images of nineteenth century Māori society: From tribes to nations.* Unpublished doctoral thesis, Victoria University, Wellington, New Zealand.

Maani, K. E., & Cavana, R. Y. (2002). *Systems thinking and modelling: Understanding change and complexity.* Auckland, New Zealand: Pearson Education New Zealand.

Marsden, M. (2003). *The woven universe. Selected writings of Rev. Māori Marsden.* Otaki, New Zealand: The Estate of Rev. Māori Marsden.

Mead, H. M. (2003). *Tikanga Māori: Living by Māori values.* Wellington, New Zealand: Huia Publishers.

Nakata, M. (2007). *Savaging the disciplines: disciplining the savages.* Canberra: Aboriginal Studies Press.

Nelson, M. (Ed.). (2008). *Original instructions: Indigenous teachings for a sustainable future.* Rochester, VT: Bear and Company.

Newcomb, S. T. (2008). *Pagans in the promised land.* Golden, CO: Fulcrum Publishing.

Oliver, P., Spee, K., & Wolfgramm, T. (2003). *A partnership approach to evaluating in communities.* In N. Lunt, C. Davidson, & K. McKegg (Eds.), *Evaluating policy and practice: A New Zealand reader* (pp. 163–172). Auckland, New Zealand: Pearson Education.

Patton, M. Q. (1986). *Utilisation focused evaluation.* Thousand Oaks, CA: Sage.

Pihama, L., Cram, F., & Walker, S. (2002). Creating methodological space: A literature review of Kaupapa Māori research. *Canadian Journal of Native Education, 26*(1), 30.

Robust, T. T. (1999). *Ngā mahi a iwi: Working for the people.* Unpublished PhD thesis, The University of Auckland, New Zealand.

Sen, A. K. (1999). *Development as freedom.* Oxford, England: Oxford University Press.

Senge, P. M. (1992). *The fifth discipline. The art and practice of the learning organisation.* New South Wales, Australia: Random House.

Senge, P. M. (2002). *The fifth discipline fieldbook: Strategies and tools for building a learning organisation.* London, England: Nicholas Brealey Publishing.

Smith. G. H. (1997). *The development of Kaupapa Māori: Theory and praxis.* Unpublished PhD Thesis, The University of Auckland, New Zealand.

Te Matorohanga & Nepia Pohuhu. (1913). *The Lore of the Whare-wananga or teachings of the Maori college on religion, cosmogony, and history.* Written down by H.T. Whatahoro. New Plymouth, New Zealand: The Polynesian Society.

Te Taura Whiri i te Reo Māori. (2008). *He Pātaka Kupu: te kai a te rangatira.* Aotearoa, New Zealand: Penguin Group.

United Nations. (2005). *Managing for results: A guide to using evaluation in the United Nations Secretariat.* Retrieved from http://www.un.org/Depts/oios/pages/manage_results.pdf.

Walker, R. (1991). *Ka Whawhai Tonu Matau: Struggle without end.* Auckland, New Zealand: Penguin.

Wilson, S. (2008). *Research is ceremony. Indigenous research methods.* Winnipeg, Canada: Fernwood Publishing.

Wolfgramm, R. M. (2007). *Continuity and vitality of worldview(s) in organisational culture: Towards a Maori perspective.* Unpublished PhD Thesis, The University of Auckland, New Zealand.

Wolfgramm, T. (2011, August). *Co-creating the REWA system of transformative evaluation.* Paper presented at Aotearoa New Zealand Evaluation Association Conference, Wellington, New Zealand.

Learning Circles (Wanangas)

Kingi, Te Uranga o Te Ra (2003–2008). Tohungatanga; Te Ao Māori; Te Reo Māori. Hui / Wānanga. Kirikiriroa, Tamaki Makaurau.

Native Science Academy. (2006–2013). Rose Van Thater Braan, Leroy Little Bear, Amethyst First Rider, Sakej Henderson, Marie Battiste, Melissa Nelson, Willie Ermine, Nancy Maryboy, David Begay, James Rattling Leaf, Isabel Hawkins and others: *Native Science Learning Lodges* held in Chaco Canyon, Santa Fe, Shenandoah, Albuquerque, San Francisco, and Santa Cruz.

Tawhai, Puroku. (2003–2012). *Tohungatanga; Te Ao Māori; Te Reo Māori.* Hui / Wananga. Kirikiriroa, Tamaki Makaurau.

Wolfgramm, D. & G. (continuous). *Learning through life experience; Tongan language and culture.* New Zealand, Tonga.

Workshops

Oliver, P. (2000–2013). *Evaluation learning and skills building through multiple projects development/workshops/discussions.* Waikehe Island, Auckland, New Zealand.

PART IV

TRANSFORMATIONS

CHAPTER 14

WHARE HAPE

Transformations

Wikuki Kingi

*Kia ora whanau e mihi atu nei kia koutou ra awhina hei tautoko o matau
nei mahi i konei o haunui.*

Greetings Whanau—Wikuki Kingi here. I share with you a journey of reconnection for me and my whanau.

Sailing at night from Tahitinui to Huahine on our journey to Raiatea the
welling up of years of expectation and anxiety was intense. At midnight the
water gleamed a strange deep purple under the full moon. A myriad of tiny
lights danced alongside the waka and I watched them with an old kaumatua,
Tama-A-Ariki, who began to cry. He told me this was the time and actual
space between these sacred islands that his grandfather had told him of. He
had come on the waka to witness the "magic" himself.

He then pulled out a whale tooth and asked me to karakia it with a
name. We stood together on the deck and I felt so alone, yet strangely connected to all the spirits of the ancestors. We sat down warmed by the tears
that flowed openly from our eyes as they fell onto our waka. It was a night
I will never forget.

Indigenous Spiritualities at Work, pages 235–238
Copyright © 2015 by Information Age Publishing
All rights of reproduction in any form reserved.

As a carver, Taputapuatea is at the center of our universe; Te Marae o Tangaroa is here under the ocean—the birthplace of whakairo—so in that sense creating a taa for the waka with the team in Huahine was a highlight of the hikoi so far. The taa enables us to enter the sacred marae on Raiatea as a new offering of relationship to "te pito o te whenua." The team finished the kokowai late in the evening waiting for the karakia and the sunlight to welcome the new Taonga to our spaceship.

As we entered the coral straits of the island we began our karakia holding the two toki fashioned for the purpose in the hours after leaving Huahine. As the mist began to rise off the mountain, Teme'ani, the mists in my dreams began to fade away to be replaced by the genetic memories passed down from generations before. A transformation begins.

There is an overpowering feeling of peace and tranquillity, an ancient sense of history that we can only begin to imagine. The hours become but fleeting moments as we stand upon the clock face of our beginnings Taputapuatea. And while we can only begin to scratch the surface of that conversation, we stand and breathe the same energy of potentiality that our ancestors once did so long ago.

I find myself looking longer and listening more intently—like a newborn baby as it emerges from the womb, its eyes' pupils dilated to their maximum to take in every facet of information. I feel like a child such as this and in doing so I realize that I am seeing these images and sounds through my father and grandfather's eyes—bringing their Wairua back with us in the kahukura (red feathers that adorn our toki). We imagine and dream and relive their emotions back along those whakapapa lines.

As we pass Fa'aroa [long deep valley] where Kupe came to build canoes, we see the valley where Kupe put his hand to the toki and set a plan in motion. A plan that we have now become a part of, a plan that would take the hopes and dreams of his people to Aotearoa our home now symbolized and enacted in ceremony by the wearing of kokowai our Papatuanuku.

Now as we leave this sacred place we do so knowing that we have bent the arc of history to now be the new generation of hope and transformation to our new world.

WHARE HAPE

Whare Hape is the ancient *Whare Wānanga*, a university of higher learning for Pacific navigators based in the centre of Tahiti. *Hape* is Tahitian for "caterpillar," symbolizing the transformation of a subject through chrysalis and finally to butterfly. Thus, people who were "chosen" sought to learn—as part of their morphing journey—the ancient arts of canoe construction, celestial navigation, and community leadership through creative cultural design and ceremonial interaction based on thousands of years of knowledge, experience, and a deep spiritual connection and conversation with Mauri, the life force touching all that we see and feel.

Whare Hape is an environmental science knowledge center, a transcultural center of learning, a personalized platform of individual-ized transformation re-

vealed in a sacred teaching place. This sacred place has stone courtyards for each stage of learning. Pools of water were used to ceremonially undertake a "rebirthing" of the student, thereby confirming his or her knowledge and ability. This also helped students to connect to a greater responsibility and accountability to their community's endeavors. Successful students were re-quired to sail canoes across the farther reaches of the Pacific Ocean, to be resilient and inspire the people who traveled, searching for new lands and opportunity. Whare Hape became the center of Pacific travel.

The notion of Whare Hape (the birthplace of Pele, the Hawaiian God-

dess of Fire) as a reorientating axis for Indigenous rediscovery and empowerment provides us with an organic model of whole community endeavor. Whare Hape would challenge, task, teach, and question students as they prepared to become ocean navigators and explorers of the new worlds that lay over the ho-rizon. At times, this exploration may have entailed following the bird and whale migrations south and then north again. They would gain valuable experi-ence learning from clues left by Mother Nature and would seek avenues and gateways to new relationships.

Whare Hape represents all that *was* and perhaps can be again, a large part of *what could be for our collective survival on our life boat, Planet Earth.* For centuries, knowledge that was attained and retained by our peoples was stripped from us and replaced by new knowledge from the West that denigrated our standing and relegated us to the status of second-class citizens. Our sacred knowledge was denounced and made, in some cases, illegal, with added penalties and hardships. The act of imposition destroyed our direct relationships and understandings of Mother Earth and Sky Father and all the activities within and beyond. Our ability to engage in cultural visioning, undertake spiritual quests, and sustain a communal foundation of education was expunged. It was replaced by a foreign virus of alien information masquerading as enlightenment with a false promise of a common future for all. Successive governments have played a key role in railroading true academic research, discussion, and critical inquiry into this intergenerational political football of historical convenience.

A return to sacred places like Whare Hape or to new places of sacred learning close to nature and in tune with the environment is perhaps the way of the future. So too is re-immersing future generations in the sacred knowledge that is their birth  right. In doing so, we are collectively reconnecting the dots of holistic interdependence which is one of many keys to opening new ways of creating sustainable transformative futures for our wider global family.

CHAPTER 15

INTERPRETING AND ANIMATING THE GODS IN AN INDIGENOUS ECOLOGY OF CREATIVITY

Rachel Wolfgramm and Cheryl Rowles Waetford

ABSTRACT

In this chapter we ask, "How is spirituality manifested as a strategic resource in contemporary Indigenous organizations?" With specificity to Indigenous spiritualities at work, we ask, "How do Māori employ spiritual resources at work?"

To address these questions, we engage a Māori worldview as a portal. Why? A Māori worldview accentuates a relational ontology in which the spiritual, human, and natural worlds are interconnected. Specifically, we focus on the concept of *whakapapa*, which refers to the layering of relationships across a relational cosmology. This approach privileges Māori forms of knowing and interpretations of reality. Our investigation into spirituality at work draws critical insight from longitudinal qualitative research undertaken in an ecology of creativity led by Māori tohunga, elders, and native scientists.

Specifically, we focus on the role of god narratives. We examine how god narratives are actively interpreted and animated by elders and native scientists in this workplace context. We detail how these narratives, as cultural and spiri-

Indigenous Spiritualities at Work, pages 239–257

tual resources, provide spiritual leadership and cultural continuity; enhance spiritual efficacy; and increase motivation, citizenship, and productivity in organization activity. We argue *purposive* use of god narratives for Māori highlights the enduring nature of spirituality at work. Finally, we present a metaphorical framework "*dynamic dimensions of purpose spirituality*" that reinforces our analysis. The transferability and application of these concepts to the field of spiritualities at work is detailed in our framework.

CONTEXT

In its most recent history, Aotearoa New Zealand was founded on the ideal of a partnership relationship between Māori (the first nations peoples) and Pākeha (the colonizers of European descent); an ideal that has yet to be fully realized. The formalization of a colonial-based relationship between the British crown and Māori occurred in 1840, when the Treaty of Waitangi (Te Tiriti o Waitangi) was signed by 540 Māori chiefs and a representative of the British crown, Governor Hobson (Orange, 2004; Walker, 1991).

Whilst intertribal warfare existed pre- and post-European settlement, the issue of sovereign rule by Māori over their own affairs, a matter termed *tino rangatiratanga*, continues to be at the heart of on-going negotiations between Māori, the Crown, and its representative governments. Māori continue to contest the dispossession of lands, rights and autonomous sovereignty. However tribal claims and settlements are now being actively addressed by governments (Ballara, 2003; King, 2003; Orange, 2004; Walker, 1991). While 15% of the New Zealand population identifies as Māori, demographic data indicate the Māori population is young, increasing, and primarily urban cosmopolitan (Durie, 1998). At present, there are hundreds of tribes, tribal affiliates and Māori organizations within all sectors of New Zealand society.

In this milieu, a cultural, political, economic, and intellectual renaissance led by Māori has gathered strength and momentum (Durie, 1998; Smith, 1999; Walker, 1991). Contemporary Māori scholarship now reflects the breadth, scope, and diverse foci inherent in Western academies.

In spite of this diversity, Māori scholars tend to agree that a Māori worldview reflects holistic plurality. For example, the Māori term *tikanga* incorporates intellectual and spiritual ideas *and* practices that relate to Māori ways of being and doing (Barlow, 1991; Durie, 1994, 1998; Hēnare, 2001, 2003; Henry & Pene, 2001; Kawharu, 1998; Marsden, 2003; Mead, 1986, 2003; Metge, 1976, 1995; Royal, 2002; Salmond, 1975, 1983, 1985; Shirres, 1997; Smith, 1996; Smith, 1999; Walker, 1975, 1991).

Tikanga is a sophisticated system of beliefs and practices that reflect culturally based values. These values are expressed by Henare as He Korunga o *Ngā Tikanga*, a philosophy of vitalism and reciprocity—a matrix of fundamental principles. These include *Tapu*, sacred elements and intrinsic power and potentiality; *Mana*, spiritual power and authority; *Mauri*, a spiritual essence or life force; and *Hau*, the ethic of reciprocity to nature and in social relationships including *whanaungatanga* (I belong therefore I am) (Hēnare, 2001, 2003). Such principles are developed through acknowledgement of the spiritual power and vital essence embodied in a person and transmitted through their gifts (Barlow, 1991; Durie, 1994, 1998; Hēnare, 2001, 2003; Henry & Pene, 2001; Kawharu, 1998; Marsden, 2003; Mead, 1986, 2003; Metge, 1976, 1995; Royal, 2002; Salmond, 1975, 1983, 1985; Shirres, 1997; Smith, 1996; Smith, 1999; Walker, 1975, 1991). Tikanga therefore incorporates values-based ethics and cognitive, affective, and normative behavioral aspects in Māori social activity. In terms of normative behavior, tikanga is the basis of Māori cultural etiquette made manifest in Māori social activities.

WHAKAPAPA: ACCESSING THE GODS IN MĀORI NATIVE SCIENCE

To understand the interconnectedness of the spiritual, human, and physical worlds from a Māori perspective, it is useful to turn to the term *whakapapa*. Whakapapa is used as a heuristic device to articulate relationships that extend from the physical and natural realms into a cosmological community. Specifically, Williams refers to whakapapa as reciting genealogies in proper order (Williams, 1975, p. 259). As a temporal and spatial unifying philosophy, whakapapa includes the layering of relationships across time and space. For example, a cosmic genealogical recital includes the implicit recognition of Kore, or unorganized potential. Te Korekore is the realm between being and non-being, the realm of potential being wherein all the "seed stuff" of the universe gestates (Marsden, 2003, p. 20). Sequential phases of a cosmic whakapapa are expressed as Te Korekore (potentiality), Te Pō (darkness), and ki Te Ao Mārama (towards light and enlightenment) (Barlow, 1991; Marsden, 2003). These phases are applied to universal constructs in Māori society.

The cosmic whakapapa and genealogies then move on to the gods. Here, we note that in god narratives, gendering is common (Pals, 1996). As Eliade has shown, the propensity of gendering in the personification of god beings is evident across all culturally based pantheons. While there continues to be healthy debate regarding tribal-specific interpretations of the Io tradition and post-Christian adaptations (see for example Mead, 2003, pp. 309, 310; Reed, 1967, pp. 58, 59; Reed, 2004, pp. 1–83), according to Hēnare (2003) the Io tradition predates European contact. Io is not a monotheistic construction but rather a numinous being.

As Māori lived close to the forces of nature, like other wisdom traditions, accorded nature with divinity. The gods, as divine entities, reflect the dynamism of the natural world and hence whakapapa evolved as a form of native science. This native science included extensive documentation and the naming of natural species and phenomena. The gods are acknowledged eternally as guardians of life, oceans, rivers, mountains, forests, winds, and every other aspect of the environment.

For example, considering Māori god narratives, Barlow (1991) articulates an elaborate genealogy of ngā Atua (the gods) that begins with Ranginui (Sky Father) and Papatūānuku (Mother Earth). Gendered complementarity is spiritual, metaphorical, passive, and active because, in this story, Ranginui and Papatuanuku lay together in an eternal embrace leading to the conception and birth of many children. This narrative goes on to tell us that the children of Ranginui and Papatūānuku sought ways of separating their parents because they were discontent with existing in darkness (Te Pō). Through the act of separating their parents and coming into the world of light and enlightenment (Te Ao Mārama), the children themselves became tutelary gods of the divisions of nature, the environment, and the social worlds. Tangaroa became god of the oceans; Rongomātāne god of kumara and cultivated crops; Haumia god of fern root, wild herbs, and berries; Rūaumoko, god of earthquakes and volcanoes; Tūmatauenga god of war; and his sibling Rongo, the god of peace (Best, 1922, 1924, 1976; Barlow, 1997). Māori articulate stories of the generation of different species, evolutionary processes, and natural forces of nature through whakapapa as a native science.

In terms of the social sphere occupied by humanity, the genealogical recital moves forward in time to humankind. As the children of the gods entered the world of light and dwelled with their mother, they became mortal beings, living within and under the influence of the physical world. Tanenuiarangi, the first man to inhabit earth, cohabited with Hineahuone. After many generations, descendants such as Māui, Hema, Tāwhaki, Toi, Ngahue, and Kupe became famous ancestors of Māori (Barlow, 1997). These examples show how whakapapa (genealogical recital) is used to describe and provide explanatory power to the phenomenological world.

Arguably, whakapapa remains a central feature of a Māori knowledge, learning, and leadership paradigm that explicitly expresses and reflects understandings of the intricacies of world systems, evolutionary processes, and the role of humans in the cosmos. As an integral feature of native science, stories in a whakapapa paradigm are considered by Māori as taonga or living treasures, gifted to humanity through divine inspiration. Whakapapa is transmitted through a variety of media including oral traditions, mythology, metaphors, stories, and whakairo (carvings) with humility, humor, flair, and imagination (Best, 1922, 1924, 1976; Durie, 1998; Marsden, 1975, 2003;

Hēnare, 2003; Henry & Pene, 2001; Mead, 1986; Metge, 1976; Neich, 1996; Reed, 1963, 2004; Royal, 2002; Salmond, 1983, 1985, 1991; Taonui, 2003; Walker, 1975).

We suggest that it is due to the receptiveness to active interpretation of god narratives and recognition that genealogical recital is a resource, that truly grand narratives never take hold in Māori society. Plurality is seen as a strength. Indigenous Tewa scholar Gregory Cajete refers to the power of heuristic narratives in Native science as "culture's emergence stories" in which the dynamic holistic nature of creativity is both celebrated and reflected. They are understood and interpreted as guiding stories of the First World that mirror processes of chaos, creative participation, and the metaphoric mind. Such guiding stories are purposively designed to "bring a deep intuitive understanding of creative processes inherent in nature and human beings" (Cajete, 2000, p. 13).

GODS ACROSS TIME

As a form of transcendental phenomenology that includes the personifica-tion of god-beings, these god narratives are, we argue, more than just folk-lore, interesting stories, and reflections of the dynamics of kin and social interactions in Māori culture.

Māori developed god narratives with a purposive function. Pointing out Hesiod's theogony that dealt with creation and its multitudinous gods, Reed suggests a similar line of thought that animated Māori native scientists is evi-dent in tales of civilization such as that of the ancient Greeks (Reed, 2004). Importantly, in Māori society, the role of creating, articulating, and interpret-ing god narratives belonged almost exclusively to the expert native scientists (tohunga) and was undertaken in traditional wānanga (places of learning).

This ongoing active interpretation of god narratives supports Walker's argument that mythology reflects the culture and society of the time. As Walker argues, myths mirror the philosophy, ideals, and norms of those who adhere to them as legitimating charters (Walker, 1975). A myth pro-vides a reflection of current social practice: in which case it also has an instructional and validating function utilized for a range of social engineer-ing projects. A myth, as an invented story or concept, is also an outward pro-jection of an ideal against which human performance can be measured and perfected. In society, myths abound, even the myth of "modern society."

In Māori society, in terms of spirituality at work, the secular and the spiri-tual are not separated but rather, spirituality is embedded in all activities relating to the arts, philosophy, sciences, and economic well-being. Spiritu-ality as manifested in gods narratives was a source of intellectual creativity, spiritual meaning, and emotional intensity in all contexts (Marsden, 2003).

To further our understanding of spirituality at work, we turned to an elder, native scientist and Māori language expert to shed light on a Māori etymology of the Māori word for spirit, *wairua*. Our elder, Fraser Puroku Tawhai of the Whakatohea tribe, explained that the Māori word for spirit, *wairua*, is made of up of several core concepts. "*Wa*" implies a temporal and spatial orientation, the dynamic interaction between light and movement, time and space; "*i*" intimates the divine within; "*ru*" refers to fulfillment without end, often spiritually depicted as a double helix spiral; and "*a*" is a reference to the impact of light on growth. Thus the word itself offers an indication of how wairua infuses and animates Māori being in all spheres of activity.

CONTEMPORARY STUDIES

In most Māori social activity, spirituality is privileged. Drawing on decades of empirical research in Māori organizations, renowned social anthropologist, Dame Joan Metge confirms that Māori continue to believe in a spiritual reality that transcends limitations of time, space, and human senses. This spirituality pervades and operates in the world of human experience. Metge argues the spiritual dimensions of Māori culture are a fundamental source of both lived reality and a system of beliefs and values.

In contexts specific to Māori, social organization is evident mainly through kin-based groupings called *waka, iwi, hapu,* and *whanau*. Marae, which often include elaborate carved meeting houses and community grounds, are center points for reinforcing kin-based relationships. Marae exist in specific tribal areas and more recently in urban areas. Marae are used widely in New Zealand society for building relationships between Māori tribes and New Zealand society—a society that is increasingly multicultural. On marae, specific normative features of tikanga as Māori cultural etiquette are strictly adhered to and practiced (Walker, 1992). Marae are places where Māori spirituality is most accessible, manifest, and observable to all ritual and ceremonial participants. Industries such as cultural tourism utilize this when simulating a variety of Māori rituals and ceremonies for local and international visitors.

Whakapapa or genealogical recital is actively used on marae for social, economic, and political purposes. At social events such as birthdays, weddings, and funerals, whakapapa is an important means of strengthening social systems, networks, hierarchies, and structures. Whakapapa reinforces kin-based ties for affective and instrumental purposes. It is also used by Māori to both articulate the history of and envision the future for a range of industry-specific phenomena in sustainable economic development, technology, science, digital communication, and the media-sphere, to name a few. Utilizing a whakapapa paradigm is an important source for renewing spiritual and collective efficacy in Māori society and organization (Barlow, 1997; Hēnare, 2001, 2003; Marsden, 2003; Metge, 1967, 1976; Mutu, 2005; Walker, 1991; Wolfgramm, 2007).

In terms of innovative engagement of god narratives, an example is the Māori haka made famous by the New Zealand institution of the All Blacks in rugby, among others. As compositions, haka invoke the Māori gods. Teams of performers express challenge, welcome, exultation, and defiance. The haka integrates the gods, the physical, the elemental, and the spiritual. As performances, they are purposively designed to be disciplined, vigorous, emotive, passionate, motivational, and imaginative. In an international context, Māori haka compositions are recognized and used widely in sports, the creative industries, and in business and political events.

In terms of developing our argument of purposive spirituality we turn to a longitudinal qualitative study in an ecology of creativity. Our case illustrates further how god narratives are used as heuristic devices to generate spiritual efficacy, enhance citizenship, and increase motivation and productivity in the organization life.

CURRENT PROJECT RESEARCH METHODOLOGY

Denzin and Lincoln argue that seeking an imaginative form of inquiry in the 21st century requires grounding the self in a sense of the sacred that connects dialogically to nature and the environment. Such a model of inquiry seeks a sacred epistemology that recognizes the ethical unity between mind, spirit, and nature (Denzin & Lincoln, 2003).

We agree with this position and draw on five years of participant action collaborative inquiry (Wolfgramm, 2007) incorporating critical reflexivity (Alvesson & Sköldberg, 2000). The research was operationalized within a Kaupapa Māori approach (Henry & Pene, 2001; Smith, 1996; Smith, 1999). Māori scholars developed Kaupapa Māori research in response to Eurocentric epistemological imperialism in the Western academy. Kaupapa Māori decolonizes methodology and incorporates the amplification of Māori ontologies and epistemologies within and across a range of fields and disciplines. Kaupapa Māori draws from Friere, Habermas, and Marx by making explicit conscientization, critical reflexivity, resistance, liberation, and societal transformation in Indigenous scholarship.

Research Methods

A primary case study in this research is an ecology of creativity. This organization conceptualized, developed, and project managed the creation of a unique Māori Indigenous taonga (living treasure) or sculpture, Pou Kapua. This sculpture (also referred to as a totem) is the largest of its kind in the Southern Hemisphere. Given that the sculpture itself is a narrative, capturing and presenting visual and oral data was important and culturally appropriate.

The international community of interest, engagement, commitment, and practice included Indigenous and Māori tribes, corporate philanthropists, art patrons, multinational businesses sponsors, private family trusts, communities of primarily Indigenous artists and sculptors, the media, academics, and regional and national government bodies, and it extended from the local to the global. While this interaction made the research intercultural and global in reach, what was unique about this case was that Māori tohunga and elders determined everything from the inception of the idea through to completion. In an era of Indigenous development distinctive by its varying degrees of de facto Indigenous–government management partnerships, the opportunity for Māori to assert sovereignty throughout entire projects is increasingly rare.

In selecting this as a case example, we recognize that the natural development and politicization of institutions creates tensions in which, over time, spiritual dimensions can transform into religious dogma. As an ecology of creativity, this organization never entered into that phase of institutional maturity and therefore the opportunity to observe this was not possible. However, what is important is that this organization had direct access to significant amounts of tikanga and mātauranga Māori, (cultural and knowledge traditions, and expertise) transmitted directly through native scientists, elders, master carvers, artists, and expert Māori scholars.

Consistent with a Kaupapa Māori approach, we privilege the voices of the primary community of research participants, the native scientists, as they hold the privilege in Māori society of actively interpreting heuristic narratives of the gods and other culturally based knowledge. We provide visual and oral data directly from the research archives.

Findings: Whakapapa (Genealogical Recital)

Whakapapa was explicitly expressed throughout the entire creation of Pou Kapua. Tohunga, elders and native scientists Te Ururangi o te Ra Wikuki Kingi and Fraser Puroku Tawhai articulated this in the following:

Pou Kapūa

Stand tall for Mankind. The Whakairo depicts the creation of the world, which features Ranginui, the Sky Father, and Papatūānuku, the Earth Mother. Their children embrace its Korowai (cloak). Its feathers represent the stories of creation.

Pou Kapūa
Reveal yourself, as you are the beginning, the birth of Īra Tangata for the past, and the present and the future.

Pou Kapūa
You stand here for today, and for tomorrow physically, mentally, spiritually to enhance all people with your intimate knowledge of whakairo.

Pou Kapūa
You will create a new cloak, woven by people of many nations, awakening essential awareness of a holistic dimension of the unseen world.

Pou Kapūa
Stand tall and be acknowledged, reaching tall for the sky. Your lofty magnificence acknowledged for all time.

Pou Kapūa
Help people to care for one another— that they may feel of the spirit of unity.
You are a miracle from the beginning of time. You still exist today and will continue to enlighten all in the future.

Pou Kapūa
Peace be with You. The miracle that is You ushers in the "histories woven together in a never ending journey"

Stand proud, stand tall . . . . "Pou Kapūa"

Whakapapa, as a value, was given primacy. In saying this, whakapapa was never asserted in the organization or used in a way that distanced people but rather was used to generate and create inclusion and unity that went well beyond the very local. Linking this back to the taonga itself, as noted by Hakiwai (1996), taonga (treasures), like real people, are important because they are regarded as having a genealogy and *mauri*, or life force. Scientific studies can trace the genealogies of species, including trees, across the globe. Further, many taonga represent ancestors who have traveled in ancestral canoes as well as other places deemed significant to the past, present, and future.

In this context, *whatumanawa*, emotional identities, develop spiritually and ironically through whakairo (carving) history, stories, and other visual and oral media. The links back to common tupuna and endeavors to make global connections through whakapapa links, either through lands, oceans, peoples, or languages, were consistently and persistently played out in social interactions, tribal and beyond.

Spiritual Leadership

In relation to purposive spirituality, a key finding that became salient over time was how spirituality was explicitly expressed through leadership. In a

Māori social ontology, rangatiratanga, or leadership, reflects a matrix of cosmologies inclusive of heuristic narratives of the gods, beliefs, and values. A Māori leadership paradigm captures the holistic plurality inherent in a Māori worldview. Implicit in the etymology of the Māori word *rangatira* (leader) is the concept of weaving and holding together diverse individuals and groups of people as they advance together in a purposive manner. When asked a question about organizational leadership of the organization Pou Kapua Creations, this was the response:

> Look at the trees in the forest. They are all competing for attention from Rangi (Sky Father) and Papa (Earth Mother). Pou Kapua (Cloud Pillar) is embraced by Papatūānuku and asserts himself to Ranginui. Pou Kapua is the leader, guiding and showing us the way."
>
> From the beginning, our tupuna (ancestors) were the leaders of this organization, the trees called to us, they told us what they want, they chose us, they are our leaders. (Kaumātua Fraser Puroku Tawhai, personal communication, November, 2005)

(Tupuna is the Māori word for ancestors; thus, this quote makes reference to the trees as the ancestors).

Figure 15.1 Sky father Ranginui and Earth mother Papatūānuku along with tutelary gods depicted on Pou Kapua.

Figure 15.2   Pou Kapūa depicts and incorporates the many phases of creation. Tangaroa, the god of the oceans, is a central character in this part of Pou Kapua.

Figure 15.1 explicitly includes the gods, the trees, the ancestors and organization members. It is one of many examples that illustrate the enduring ways in which the interrelatedness of the spiritual, the natural, and the social worlds are still relevant in spiritual Māori leadership and workplace organization. Figure 15.2 reinforces purposive spirituality and illustrates how Māori move with relative ease into a cosmological community utilizing god narratives.

> We are carving the Māori view of creation, while acknowledging Io-mātua-kore throughout. Our deepest histories and beliefs are narrated upon this "snapshot." Pou Kapūa depicts and incorporates the many phases of creation, from Te Kore (the beginning of time) through to Maui (the first man). We show the separation of Rangi and Papa and provide and express the interesting and colourful histories, stories, adventures, conflicts and endeavors of their children, Ngā Atua, the gods. (Kaumātua Fraser Puroku Tawhai, 2005)

In relation to the combination of spiritual and ancestral efficacy in the context of leadership, rangatiratanga was expressed as emanating from Pou Kapua itself. Because this research focused equally on the process of creation of Pou Kapua as a taonga as well as the significant outcome of the totem, observations made salient a deeply embedded belief within the organization that this taonga was not simply a material, socially constructed symbol. The taonga (treasure) lives and breathes in its environment as an alert and living entity with intrinsic mana, tapu, and mauri of its own.

As a living, breathing entity, the taonga itself was accorded a leadership role as it was seen to be able to guide, have desires, and be a holder of ancient knowledge and all that it symbolizes for those involved centrally. The further removed or more tangential the relationships, the more the force field of leadership diminished.

Leadership was also evident in the role of tohunga and the kaumātua council (*pou mana whakahaere*) as they reinforced its defining characteristics. They ensured the *matakite* (vision) was articulated and transmitted in ways that captured the *wairua, ihi,* and *wehi* of this taonga to members of the organization members and the broader community of interest. As such, the kaumatua council played a primary leadership role, articulating, expressing, and modeling the tikanga and kawa in the first instance.

A purposive-oriented combination of spiritual and ancestral efficacy was evident in the leadership of Pou Kapua Creations. Members as participants were proactively engaged agents. This is consistent with historical evidence produced by Hēnare that showed in the 1820s to 1840s Māori leaders were proactive, assertive, dynamic, opportunistic, and "engaged agents." Being passive recipients waiting for and dependent upon others to proffer opportunities or bestow leadership in the first instance were not particularly salient characteristics of leadership in this context. Clarifying this, rangatiratanga was asserted first and then leadership was bestowed by way of support that emerged from marae, whānau, hapū, and iwi and the wider community of engagement throughout the duration of the project.

Formal authority was not activated in any overly strict way except if the kawa (protocols) based on tikanga (customary practices) were challenged or breached. The role to remind and reorient those involved was undertaken primarily by tohunga and kaumātua and was respected. Each person was recognized for the value they brought to the project and organization, including their extensive networks of relationships. Karakia (prayer) and other rituals played a significant role in terms of self and collective affirmation, as did the creation of and giving of koha. Many of the koha (gifts) given were made from parts of the kauri used to create Pou Kapua and were generally given while still "warm," full of life, vital, and vibrant.

> We are committed to striving for and continuing to provide the highest standards of dynamic leadership in the organization of our whānau and the management of resources.

From a structural perspective, leadership was not defined by ultimate formal control mechanisms, nor was it particularly gendered. This was interesting. As noted previously, according to Salmond (1991, p. 353) the cosmological principles of male-female complementarity, tuakana-teina status and competitive striving were differentially affected by the experience of contact with Europeans. Pou Kapua Creations (PKC) had quite a complementary style of leadership that reflected te mana o nga atua (the mana of the gods) as in Ranginui and Papatūānuku (note the two top figures in Figure 15.1 are Ranginui and Papatūānuku).

As key drivers of the project, executive board members took on strategic leadership responsibilities, articulating the vision and kaupapa to a broad range of stakeholders, including iwi, hapū, multinational corporations, regional bodies, and funding agencies, and ensured that the values expressed cohered around the vision. The perpetual building of strategic coalitions and networks was crucial, and with representative leaders in their executive positions, it was constant and often serendipitous.

Leadership skills evidenced included the ability to make quick decisions under difficult and often complex stakeholder circumstances and in multiple political contexts, such as regional bodies, various iwi, hapū, whānau, and corporations. This required courage, a collective consultative process wherever and whenever possible, and being consistent, persistent, determined, tenacious. It also involved being continuously open and opportunistic in creating, developing, and maintaining relationships with people and making the most of these networks and relationships, both local and global.

Overall, rangatiratanga leadership in PKC reflected a combination of leading, learning, and following, which included spontaneous improvisations during the course of development. Thus rangatiratanga appeared organic but with epistemological and ontological foundations that reflected a Māori world view. Transmission by tohunga and kaumātua were fundamental to providing continuity over time. Tikanga and kawa were actively interpreted according to iwi, hapū, marae, whanau, and organization-specific needs, criteria, and demands. In terms of pragmatics, this leadership style enabled a high degree of role variety (just how many hats can one wear at any one time?) that leveraged individual and collective skills and talent. In a sense, PKC was more or less what Senge (1994) refers to as a self-governing organic learning organization with Pou Kapua leading in a spiritual sense.

Tino Rangatiratanga (Absolute Sovereignty)

> *Tino rangatiratanga ought to be a state of mind informed by our passions.*
> —Rahuia Kapa, Te Aupōuri

We aspire to demonstrate the sacred authority given to us, in a powerful manner yet with humility, acknowledging that our rights are balanced by our responsibilities to ourselves, our whānau, iwi, hapū and the wider communities that we are a part of and belong to.

Tino rangatiratanga (sovereignty) is an integral part of the orientation of the organizational culture. The organization did not wait for permission to act in a self-determining way but rather *tino rangatiratanga* was asserted through the individual and collective actions of whānau members.

This is reflected spiritually: The figure at the head of this sculpture is Kupe. Māori do not need to be reminded that their ancestors asserted absolute sovereignty as legendary navigators.

Te Kaupapa Matakite (The Vision)

E moe moe a...the dream ... articulated within:

When the dream is developed, it becomes a kaupapa that becomes many parts of the expansion, ka tipu o te kaupapa is like putting clothes on it, enhancing the mana of the project, a dream brought to reality though good planning. (Fraser Tawhai, Kaumātua and tikanga advisor for Pou Kapūa)

"Matakite" is vision. The visions of organizations are designed to be aspirational in the sense that they accept no particular limits on what they want to achieve: The horizon is unknown and unbounded. In this instance, the vision of Pou Kapūa creations reflects a holistic worldview and orientation that is driven by and grounded in particular notions of what it means to be Māori. However, there were purposive steps taken in achieving that vision. Matakerepo is carved onto the pou: She is the goddess of knowledge known and unknown.

Matakite (Vision Statement)

Through our Whakairo we create Taonga;
express our Tinorangatiratanga,
nurture our Wairua,
protect our Mauri,
and uphold our Mana.
It is our eternal legacy, as it was our forefathers,
to value and respect the sacredness, power and authority,
intrinsic in our natural and spiritual world.
Whakairo provides a physical manifestation that gives us,
our Whānau, and our Tamariki,
a greater voice.
Our beautiful and awe-inspiring Pou Kapūa

symbolises our culture.
It encompasses the trials of our past,
the challenges of the present,
and the freedom of our future,
they stand eternally, a divine testimony to the world.

This is simultaneously inspirational and aspirational and purposively intended to be compelling on multiple levels. A strong commitment was evident from all *whānau* (diverse stakeholders) in the organization and beyond to engage with a sense of purpose and responsibility toward its future position. That commitment went beyond the short-term (inspiration). The promise of exploring and finding new ways of growing the organization conveyed discovery (aspirations).

Performance and productivity were linked to the opportunistic uptake related to the process of developing relationships. In this context, significant emphasis was placed on outcomes that aligned with the kaupapa matakite. The integrity and credibility of the organization was primarily driven and determined by a constant reorientation and coherence around the kaupapa matakite. The essential work related to administration was significant, and managing it successfully can be attributed only to consistent, hard work from a professional, committed, although somewhat under-resourced, executive team.

Ohaaki Ki Nga Tūpuna: Mana Tūpuna

As a symbol, Pou Kapūa is itself an ohaaki (tribute) ki nga tupuna as articulated below:

Traditional Canoes have their own stories regarding their migrations from their homelands to the new land—Aotearoa. Māori were known to be Master Mariners throughout the world—known to be very competitive people, racing from island to island, navigating by way of the Sun, Moon, and Stars.

We have carved the journeys of the adventures of our tūpuna, who were true navigators—venturing into the unknown—sailing towards the sun. The Pou depicts the many Waka that came to Aotearoa along with specific knowledge pertaining to the world. They brought foods such as kūmara and the known medicines of the time. Time spoke of scared creatures, one such as korotangi, and the languages of the peoples of the Pacific.

According to Hakiwai, taonga as symbols are anchor points in our history. Without them, Māori have no position and no social reality (Hakiwai, 1996). This could also be said of taonga in terms of according mana to the present and future: that is, without them we have no direction for the future and understandings of the social realities of our present. Essentially, co-creating taonga is an important means of co-creating the future and comprehending present-day realities. An alternative is to have others directing and co-creating realities and imposing their worldview of such things upon Māori and Indigenous peoples.

For PKC, building ancestral efficacy by making connections to the past provided continuity, and whakapapa connections opened up pathways of opportunity important for present and future endeavors.

DISCUSSION

This case study provides evidence of the force and scope of spirituality at work. The metaphysical facets of a Māori worldview were actively interpreted, providing a sense of spiritual efficacy in this creative-based project. Spiritual and ancestral efficacy combined with a range of heuristic god narratives, actively and purposively interpreted to align with the organization's strategic objectives, created a transformative and enabling organizational and workplace environment. In a project-oriented workplace setting, spirituality, inclusive of beliefs and values, was made manifest in a variety of ways that included hundreds of rituals, ceremonies, and symbols. These combined to provide the organization with an important ontological orientation that elucidated spirituality at work (Wolfgramm, 2007).

Drawing on a metaphorical framework, Waka Autoroa, Kainga, Marae, and Pa Taua generated from this empirical research (Wolfgramm, 2007), Table 15.1 developed by Rowles Waetford (2007) highlights dimensions of purposive spirituality and the transferability of insights into broader workplace spirituality literature.

SUMMARY

In this chapter we illustrated how purposive spirituality continues to be an important strategic resource in contemporary Māori organizations. We employed a Māori worldview to amplify a Māori social ontology. In developing our discussion, we made reflections of metaphysics in social interaction in Māori organization salient. More specifically, based on recent empirical research, we focused on purposive spirituality and spiritual leadership. We elucidated this by presenting oral and visual data that illustrated how god narratives and *whakapapa* (genealogical recital) are actively interpreted and animated by elders and native scientists. This demonstrated ways in which these heuristic narratives, as cultural and spiritual resources, provide spiritual leadership and cultural continuity, enhance spiritual efficacy, and increase motivation, citizenship, and productivity in organizational activity. We suggest the purposive use of god narratives in Māori social organization highlights more broadly the enduring nature of spirituality

TABLE 15.1   Dynamic Dimensions of Purposive Spirituality

Metaphor	Dimensions of Purposive Spirituality	Potential Application
Waka Aoturoa	Dynamic subjectivity dimension Explorative learning dimension Temporal dimension Spatial dimension Enlightening dimension Active interpretation dimension "Inner fire" motivation dimension Stewardship/guardianship dimension	Capacity and capability to factor in a "world that stands in pluralities" and account for complexities using organic intelligence. Potential for new knowledge creation. Tool that recognizes "enduring nature of world" and can access past histories and ancient knowledge about the nature of man and his endeavors— that is, draw upon a mature matrix of values and beliefs that moves research beyond faddish outlooks.
Kāinga	Personal identity dimension Collective identity dimension Connectivity dimension Strategic dimensions Entrepreneurial dimension Orientating schema dimension Resource or capital accumulation and investment dimension	Capacity and capability to make visible the interconnections and nuances of activities and collaborative and cooperative relationships while remaining anchored within innovative institutionalized systems.
Marae	Innovation dimension Sustainability/adaptation dimension Stabilizing dimension Centrality dimension Values and beliefs dimensions	Institutional innovation Manifestations of spiritual dimensions in art, rituals, symbols, and behavior patterns.
Pā Taua	Expanding proactive dimension Contracting defensive dimension Motivating action dimension	Strategic orientations Decision-making Leadership Design of organizational structures for particular purposes at particular times.

in organization dynamics from an Indigenous perspective. Finally, we presented a metaphorical framework and table that reinforces the transferability and application of these concepts to the fields of spirituality at work.

In terms of future research directions, we consider that there is scope to investigate further the relational, spiritual, and aesthetic dimensions of leadership from uniquely Indigenous perspectives.

REFERENCES

Alvesson, M., & Sköldberg, K. (2000). *Reflexive methodology: new vistas for qualitative research*. London, England: Sage.

Ballara, A. (2003). *Taua, 'Musket Wars', 'Land Wars' or 'tikanga'? Warfare in Māori society in the early nineteenth century.* Auckland, New Zealand: Penguin Books.

Barlow, C. (1991). *Tikanga whakaaro: Key concepts in Māori culture.* Auckland, NZ: Oxford University Press.

Bell, E., & Taylor, S. (2003). The elevation of work: Pastoral power and the new age work ethic. *Organization, 10,* 329–349.

Best, E. (1922). Some aspects of Māori myth and legend. *Dominion Museum Monograph, No. 1.* Wellington, NZ: Government Printer.

Best, E. (1924). The Māori religion and mythology. *Dominion Museum Bulletin, No. 10.* Wellington, NZ: Goernment Printer.

Best, E. (1976). Māori religion and mythology: Being an account of the cosmogony, anthropogeny, religious beliefs and rites, magic and folk lore of the Māori folk of New Zealand, Part 2, *Dominion Museum Bulletin, No.11.* Wellington, NZ: Museum of New Zealand, Te Papa Tongarewa.

Cajete, G. (2000). *Native science, natural laws of interdependence.* Sante Fe, NM: Clear Light.

Denzin, N., & Lincoln, Y. (2003). *The landscape of qualitative research: Theories and issues* (2nd ed.). London, England: Sage.

Durie, M. (1994). *Whaiora.* Auckland, NZ: Oxford University Press.

Durie, M. (1998). *Te mana, te kawanatanga: The politics of Māori self-determination.* Auckland, NZ: Oxford University Press.

Hakiwai, A.T.(1996). Maori society today: Welcome to our world. In D. C. Stazecka (Ed.), *Maori Art and Culture* (pp. 50–68). Auckland, NZ: David Bateman.

Hēnare, M. (2001). Tapu, mana, mauri, hau, wairua. a Māori philosophy of vitalism and cosmos. In J. A. Grimm (Ed.), *Indigenous traditions and ecology, the interbeing of cosmology and community* (pp. 197–221). Cambridge, MA: Harvard University Press for the Centre of the Study of World Religions, Harvard Divinity School.

Hēnare, M. A. (2003). *The changing images of nineteenth century* Māori *society—From tribes to nation.* Unpublished doctoral thesis, Victoria University, Wellington, NZ.

Henry, E., & Pene, H. (2001). Kaupapa Māori: locating indigenous ontology, epistemology and methodology in the academy, *Organization, 8*(2), 234–242.

Kawharu, M. (1998). *Dimensions of kaitiakitanga: An investigation of a customary Māori principle of resource management.* Unpublished doctoral thesis, University of Oxford, Oxford, England.

King, M. (2003). *Penguin history of New Zealand.* Auckland, New Zealand: Penguin.

Marsden, M. (1975). God, man, and universe: A Māori view. In M. King (Ed.), *Te ao hurihuri: The world moves on (pp. 191–219).* Wellington, NZ: Hick, Smith, and Sons.

Marsden, M. (2003). *The woven universe: Selected readings of Rev. Māori Marsden* (Te Ahukaamaru Charles Royal, Ed.). Otaki, NZ: The Estate of Rev. Māori Marsden.

Mead, H. M. (1986). *Te Toi Whakairo: The art of Māori carving.* Auckland, NZ: Reed.

Mead, H. M. (2003). *Tikanga* Māori: Living by Māori *values.* Wellington, NZ: Huia.

Metge,J. (1967). *The Māoris of New Zealand.* London, England: Routledge and Keegan Paul.

Metge, J. (1976). *The Māoris of New Zealand: Rautahi.* London, England: Routledge and Keegan Paul.

Metge, J. (1995). *New growth from old: The whanau in the modern world.* Wellington, NZ: Victoria University Press.

Mutu, M. (2005). Research ethics associated with treaty of Waitangi claims and the foreshore and seabed legislation. *Tikanga Rangahau, Matauranga Tuku Iho: Traditional Knowledge and Research and Research Ethics International Conference Proceedings*, Nga Pae o te Maramatanga: The National Institute of Research Excellence for Māori Development and Advancement, University of Auckland.

Neich, R. (1996). Wood carving. In D.C. Starzecka (Ed.), *Māori art and culture* (pp. 69–113). Auckland, NZ: David Bateman.

Orange, C. (2004). *Illustrated history of the Treaty of Waitangi*. Wellington, NZ: Bridget Williams Books.

Pals, D. L. (1996). *Seven theories of religion*, USA: Oxford University Press.

Reed, A. W. (1963). *Treasury of Māori folklore*. Wellington, NZ: Reed.

Reed, A. W. (1967). *Teasury of Māori folklore* (2nd ed.). Wellington, New Zeland: Reed.

Reed, A. W. (2004). *Reed book of Māori mythology*, revised by Ross Calman (2004), Auckland, NZ: Reed

Rowles Waetford, C. M. (2007). *A literature review of spiritual capital, developments of spirituality in the workplace, and contributions from a Māori perspective*. Working paper. Auckland, NZ: Mira Szaszy Research Centre for Māori and Pacific Economic Development, University of Auckland.

Royal, T. C. (2002). *Indigenous worldviews: A comparative study*. Wellington, New Zealand: Te Wananga-o-Raukawa, Te Puni Kokiri for Māori Development.

Salmond, A. (1975). *Hui: A study of Māori ceremonial gatherings*. Wellington, NZ: Reed.

Salmond, A. (1983). The study of traditional Māori society: The state of the art. *Journal of the Polynesian Society, 92,* 209–331.

Salmond, A. (1985). Māori epistemologies. In J. Overing (Ed.), *Reason and morality* (pp. 240–263). London, England: Tavistock.

Salmond, A. (1991). *Two worlds: First meetings between Māori and Europeans*. Auckland, NZ: Penguin.

Senge, P. M. (1994). *The fifth discipline: The art and practice of the learning organization.* New York, NY: Doubleday.

Shirres, M. (1997). Tapu and noa: Mana and the human person. In M. P. Shirres (Ed.), *Te tangata the human perspective* (pp. 19–45). Auckland, NZ: Accent Publications.

Smith, G. (1996). *Kaupapa* Māori *as theory and praxis.* Unpublished doctoral thesis, University of Auckland, NZ.

Smith, L. T. (1999). *Decolonizing methodologies.* Dunedin, New Zealand: University of Otago Press.

Taonui, R. (2003). Māori mythology. In *Mythology, myths, legends and fantasies.* Willoughby, Australia: Global Book Publishing.

Walker, R. (1978). The relevance of Māori myth and tradition. In M. King (Ed.), *Tihe Mauri Ora: Aspects of Māoritanga.* Auckland, NZ: Methuen.

Walker, R. (1991). *Ka whawhai tonu matau: Struggle without end.* Auckland, NZ: Penguin.

Walker, R. (1992). Marae, a place to stand. In M. King (Ed.), *Te Ao Hurihuri: The world moves on* (pp. 15–27). Auckland, New Zealand: Reed Publishing.

Williams, H.W. (1975). A dictionary of the Māori language (7th ed.). Wellington, New Zealand: A.R. Shearer, Government Printer.

Wolfgramm, R. M. (2007). *Continuity and vitality of worldview(s) in organizational culture; Towards a Māori perspective.* Unpublished doctoral thesis, Department of Management and Employment Relations, University of Auckland, New Zealand.

CHAPTER 16

THAT PLACE THAT INDIAN PEOPLE TALK ABOUT...

Gregory Cajete

By using our mind with reverence, we re-enchant and resacralize the world.
We regain our identity. We reclaim our destiny.
—Skolimowski, 1994, p. 43

THE SPIRITUAL ECOLOGY OF NATIVE SCIENCE

Native science is, at its core, a process for learning about life and the nature of the "spirit that moves us," with the ultimate goal of becoming fully knowledgeable about this spirit. Spirituality comes from the process of exploring and coming to know the nature of the living energy that moves in each of us, through us, and around us. Coming to know this knowledge is considered completeness in its most profound form.

Traditionally, Native science education is practiced within a spiritual context. Spiritual traditions illustrate more clearly than anything else in the study of American Indian cultures the principle of unity in diversity. Although various tribes present different expressions of spirituality, they hold certain understandings in common. These shared understandings allow for the development of an expression of Native science that includes

Indigenous Spiritualities at Work, pages 259–272
Copyright © 2015 by Information Age Publishing
259

a contemporized epistemology with principles acceptable in general terms by all people concerned with working toward a more sustainable future. Native American traditions provide insights into the contexts for teaching and learning that model this form of relational education. A shared set of structures and tools for learning about spirit are used in similar ways by different tribes. Ceremonial structures used in healing and sacred art such as sweat lodges as well as spiritual tools such as vision questing, ceremonies, rituals, and dances tied to nature's cycles are but a few examples. In addition, a group of shared metaphors and concepts that have found unique expressions in different regions and tribes were originally derived from similar understandings and life orientations.

Like other Indigenous peoples, American Indians believe that the breath represents the most tangible expression of the spirit in all living things. The breath, along with water and thought, connects all living things together in a direct relationship.

This interrelationship of water, wind, and breath is a widely believed concept among Indigenous people; it personifies the elemental relationship emanating from "that place that Indian people talk about," the spiritual center where all things are created.

I can remember the first time I heard the phrase, "that place that the Indians talk about," it was repeated by Acoma poet Simon Ortiz as part of a wonderful story about the spiritual connections Indian people feel to the special places in their lands and their lives—and how, by talking about those special places they again connect their spirit to them through their words, thoughts, and feelings. I remember thinking how beautifully simple, yet how profound, this metaphor is, for it is about the special quality and power of the spirit to orient us through the "breath" of its manifestations in language, song, prayer, and thought.

Imbued with the perception that all things are sacred, traditional education, from the moment of conception to beyond the moment of death, is considered a time of learning the true nature of one's spirit. That learning begins with reflecting on the spirit's expression in the human and natural community through the understanding and use of "breath" in all its forms, an understanding that includes the physical nature of breath as well as the perception of thought as a kind of "wind" and a unique variation of breath. Language and song are other forms of breath that create a holistic foundation for communication. Language is an expression of the sacred because it contains the power to express human thought and feeling and to emotionally affect others. Breath consciously forms and activates the parameters of communication in traditional tribal education through language, thought, prayer, chanting, ritual, dance, sport, work, story, play, and art.

Among American Indians, the tradition of communicating to develop the spirit has continued, for the last forty thousand years, to evolve as a way of seeking and finding one's life and completeness. It has gone through changes in form and expression, reflecting the changes and transformations of "the People." Although American Indian spiritual traditions show great diversity, they all come from primal roots and continue to share and express universal perceptions and concepts. For American Indians, what is called "education" today was traditionally a journey for learning about being fully human while living in a relational universe.

Learning about the nature of the spirit was considered central to learning the full meaning of life. This chapter presents some of the highest thoughts and basic concepts that connect all tribes at the level of spirit.

Five general principles characterize American Indian spiritual traditions wherever they are found. First, they lack a particular espoused doctrine of religion. Indian languages do not even have a word for religion; rather, the words used refer to a way of living, a tradition of the people. This reflects an orientation to a process rather than to an intellectual structure. Spiritual traditions are tools for learning and experiencing rather than ends in themselves.

Second, Indian spiritual traditions hold that spoken words and language have a quality of spirit because they are expressions of human breath. Language in the form of prayer and song has therefore a life energy that can affect other energy and life forms toward certain ends. For American Indians, language used in a spiritual, evocative, or affective context is "sacred" and has to be used responsibly.

Third, the creative act of making something with spiritual intent—what today is often called art—has its own quality and spiritual power that needs to be understood and respected. In fact, for Native Americans, art traditionally was a result of a creative process that was an act and expression of the spirit and was therefore sacred.

The fourth principle is the notion that life and spirit, the dual faces of the Great Mystery, move in never-ending cycles of creation and dissolution; therefore, ceremonial forms, life activities, and the transformations of spirit are cyclical. These cycles in turn follow the visible and invisible patterns of nature and the cosmos. In response to this creative principle, ritual cycles are used to structure and express the sacred in the communal context of traditional Native American life.

The fifth principle is the shared understanding that nature is the true "ground" of spiritual reality. The forms and forces of nature are expressions of spirit whose qualities interpenetrate the life and process of human spirituality; therefore, for American Indians and Indigenous peoples as a whole, nature is sacred and a spiritual ecology is reflected throughout.

Additionally, most tribes share basic understandings about sacred knowledge. These include the notion that a universal energy infuses everything in the cosmos and expresses itself through a multitude of manifestations.

The notion also includes the recognition that all life has power that is full of wonder and spirit. This is the "Great Soul" or the "Great Mystery" or the "Great Dream" that cannot be explained or understood with the intellect but can be perceived and understood only by the spirit of each person.

This understanding leads to the perception that all things and all thoughts are related through spirit—and that personal and direct communication with all the manifestations of spirit through prayer and ritual reinforces the bond of the individual, family, clan, and community to the unseen power of the "Great Mystery." Knowledge and understanding of morals and ethics are direct results of spiritual experiences through sacred traditions and the special teachings of elders, who act as guides for spiritual experiences and education. This role is the basis of their high standing and relative level of respect in the tribe or community, as long as they use their knowledge for the good of the people.

Finally, people must constantly be aware of their weaknesses and strive to become wise in the ways that they live their lives. To this end, through the use of story, humor, and ritual, people "remember to remember" who they are, where they come from, and the spirit that they share with all of creation.

In relation to these universal principles, this chapter will explore four basic interrelated concepts that inform the expression of the spiritual dimension of Indigenous education: seeking life and becoming complete, the highest thought, orientation, and pathway. A particular aspect of a selected tribe will be used to illustrate the essential features of each concept. These are meant to be descriptive examples and are by no means comprehensive; tribal people and scholars of American Indian traditions will no doubt perceive similar connections and expressions in their own cultural traditions or those they have studied. Each example provides what may be considered a core dynamic of learning about spirit, seeking life, and "that place that Indian people talk about."

REVITALIZING A SACRED COVENANT

The sense of ecological process and the importance of being in harmony embodied in Indigenous cultural traditions can be replicated in a larger scale within modern societies. Collective experience with the land, integrated by story and ritual, expressed through social structures and arts, and combined with a practiced system of environmental ethics and spiritual ecology can give rise to a true connection with the natural world and a more comprehensive expression of modern ecological consciousness. There is an important legacy of traditional environmental knowledge that we must again revitalize for ourselves and for the generations yet to come. Indigenous peoples have been entrusted with an important package of memory, feeling, and relationship to the land that forms a kind of sacred covenant. Modern Western peoples are challenged to strive to educate themselves about this knowledge and associated forms of education. This covenant bids modern Western peoples to reclaim their own heritage of living in a harmonious and sustainable relationship to the land, thereby fulfilling a sacred trust to that land.

Today, because of constraints of modern society, fewer and fewer people have the opportunity to engage the land, plants, and animals in the way our ancestors once did, when experience with the land was the cornerstone of traditional education. Today, environmental education integrated with perspectives of Indigenous science must once again become a priority of modern education, as Western society begins to finally realize that it must forge a new ecologically based cosmology, complete with new myths and new expressions and applications of science and technology. Western society must once again become nature-centered, if it is to make the kind of life-serving, ecologically sustainable transformations required in the next decades. We must collectively reassert our sacred covenant with the land. America is an extension of our collective minds. It is this place that holds our collective memory. It is this place with its unique natural spirit that provides us with meaning and defines us as a distinct People of Place (Cajete, 1994).

NATIVE SCIENCE, TRADITIONAL ENVIRONMENTAL KNOWLEDGE AND SUSTAINABILITY

A crisis of "sustainability" has evolved as a result of the global application of the Western development paradigm of "progress" through unfettered capitalism with little regard for social, cultural, and ecological consequences. This paradigm—and its focus on material economic indicators as the sole measure of development—perpetuates a distorted vision of what is, in fact, a multidimensional relational process.

Some Indigenous people have made efforts to find sustainable, culturally responsive, and community-based models that help build their communities rather than continue to perpetuate their long-standing social or cultural issues. Over the last two decades, various planning initiatives in the United States have evolved that attempt to rebuild Native nations "from the inside out." These initiatives create an infrastructure that serves a broader spectrum of the community, finds local resources and solutions, advocates local rather than federal control of community development, and, most importantly, evolves from the cultural knowledge foundations of the communities themselves (Black, 1997).

These efforts might be termed an "Indigenized" approach to applying sustainable environmental education for community revitalization and renewal.

Process-oriented approaches to education such as these can form a contemporary context for the application and even evolution of Indigenous science.

A working definition of Indigenous science is that body of traditional environmental and cultural knowledge that is unique to a group of people and that has served to sustain those people through generations of living within a distinct bio-region. This science is founded on a body of practical environmental knowledge learned and transferred through generations through a form of environmental and cultural education unique to them. Indigenous science may also be termed "traditional environmental knowledge" (TEK), since a large proportion of this knowledge served to sustain Indigenous communities and ensure their survival within the environmental contexts in which they were situated.

TEK may be defined as: "A cumulative body of knowledge, practice, and belief, evolving by adaptive processes and handed down through generations by cultural transmission, about the relationships of living beings (including humans) with one another and their environment" (Berkes, Colding, & Folke, 2000) As this book has shown, communication and exchange of Native science occurred through ceremonies, customs, oral histories, traditions and stories; classifications and nomenclature; knowledge of landscape; knowledge of animals, plants, climates and seasons; everyday discourse and oratory; dreams and visions; and trade.

The associated experiential teaching and learning practices and strategies for sustainable living included the monitoring of natural inventories; the applying of ecological principles and indicators; the modification of the environment; strategies for harvesting; and the necessary adaptations.

TEK systems of any given cultural group share a number of characteristics. For example, bodies of knowledge of local plants, animals, and environment are based on generations of observation. A well-developed practice has evolved by which the community uses its local resources. This practice consists of a complex body of beliefs regarding the way people relate to various surrounding ecosystems. In general, a complex cycle evolves in which traditional environmental knowledge informs environmentally sound practices that in turn are founded upon a deeply internalized belief system.

Adapting Native Science in a Contemporary Context

Indigenous science in its expression as TEK, combined with insights and models from the evolving field of sustainability, provides possibilities for creative models for Indigenous communities to sustain themselves and their cultural ways of life in the 21st century.

Environmental scientists, policymakers, and community developers create and apply theories to the ever-evolving complex situations of a rapidly degrading global environment. Environmental educators create curricula to bring about awareness and understanding of chronic ecological issues. New models are constantly being debated and alternatives applied to address specific environmental situations.

Most of this work, however, continues to be done within the old paradigms of Western science and policy development, which measure success using monodimensional economic references: numbers of people trained or graduated, goods and services delivered, loans or profits made, and so on, even though these quantifiable indicators are but one kind of indicator. Deeper-level indicators that reflect the broader dimensions of change or impact are rarely researched, and when they are, they are rarely taken seriously. Instead, the so-called "bottom line" evaluation system continues to be most valued as a measure of success. Meanwhile, community and environmental issues continue and in many cases even worsen, as is the case in many Indigenous communities that attempt to apply Western concepts of development to their unique needs. In general, we know more about the issues than ever before, yet we continue with old-paradigm thinking and actions, seemingly helpless as we continue to speed headlong to disaster.

A deeper and more conscious education about sustainability and the development of a new consciousness are keys to making the necessary changes for our collective survival (Black, 1997). To measure the long-term sustainability of a model or initiative, the net must be cast much more broadly and made to include the more holistic and less easily quantifiable context of a community in harmony with nature. The traditional Indigenous paradigm of development begins with gauging the sustainability of an initiative or the application of a body of knowledge by how well it would help an Indigenous community survive through time and place.

Indigenous communities have the historical, philosophical, and even spiritual foundations from which they may build new and sustainable models for community renewal and revitalization. Many have the cultural and historical foundations to put new paradigms into action, if they build upon their own creative sense of what it takes to be sustainable and to survive. These foundations present an impetus for a possible paradigm shift by introducing a theoretical model of sustainable community development that can move Indigenous communities toward revitalization and renewal through Indigenous science education, sustainable economics, and sustainability studies. This model challenges all concerned to take Indigenous science seriously as an ancient form of applied knowledge for sustaining communities and ensuring survival through time. It also challenges readers to accept Indigenous science as a tool and a body of knowledge that may be integrated with Western science in new and creative ways that sustain and ensure survival.

SEEKING LIFE AND BECOMING COMPLETE

The way we talk about a place or other entity reflects how we feel, how we see, how we understand, and most important, how we think in reference to it. Language itself is a reflection of how we organize and perceive the world; in every language, key words, phrases, and metaphors act as signposts to the way we think about the world and ourselves.

Indian languages are richly diverse in their metaphoric structures and expressions of how they see the world. As is true with all language, Indian metaphors reflect the nature of the reality they see and to which their minds have been set through experience and cultural understanding. In spite of the diversity of Indian languages and potential for their infinite ways of thinking about reality, some metaphors may be consistently translated to reflect a similar thought. The phrases "seeking life," "for life's sake," "to find life," "to complete," "to become complete," "of good heart," "of good thought," "with harmony," and a host of other related combinations have variable translations in all Indian languages. These are the metaphors Indian people use in talking about themselves, their places, and their relationships. They are phrases that are used in beginning and ending communal events, in ritual prayers, in stories, in oratory, as greetings, in conversation, and in teaching. They are phrases for "remembering to remember" why things are done individually and in community. These shared metaphors reflect an underlying continuity of thought and perception that in turn has a profound influence on the aims and philosophy of traditional Indian education. Their common tie is that they all imply a journey of learning to find and know life in all its manifestations—especially those of the spirit—and through such a journey experience completion, a state of wholeness. Seeking, finding, being with, and celebrating the "center of spirit" is the essential meaning of the phrase "that place that Indian people talk about."

As a guiding concept, "seeking life and becoming complete" pervades the various expressions of Native American spirituality to such an extent that it is seldom discussed or questioned. Historically, this was the mindset and worldview that guided the thought and behavior of all people. The extent to which this guiding concept was historically internalized may be likened to the pervasive internalization of capitalism and the consumer mindset of modern Americans. Capitalism and consumerism are so much a part of how Americans see themselves that these concepts make up what is considered a "real world" that is seldom if ever questioned as a foundation of human life. Materialism and an "objective" sense of physical reality predominate the mindset of most modern people. For many, this orientation has actually become a "theology of money," treated as sacred and strived for religiously. For American Indians and other Indigenous peoples, however, Spirit and Nature were considered to be the "real world"—the ground of existence around which they formed a "theology of nature" that has evolved and matured over the last forty thousand years (Cajete, 1994).

LEARNING FROM NATIVE SCIENCE

The celebration of Native science brings both joy and sadness: joy in the sense that Indigenous people worldwide still have traditions of sustainable living to draw upon; sadness in that so much has been lost, trivialized, and ignored through the pulverizing homogenization that occurs when modern Western capitalism is implemented in Indigenous societies.

Looking beyond the tendency of Western cultures to romanticize Indigenous people and trivialize their cultures and traditions, it is important to see the lessons these cultures have to teach, lessons that exemplify sustainability in relationship to "place," community, and the very soul of human nature.

The prevailing paradigm of Western development—unlimited progress and unbridled capitalism supported by the corporate mindset of profit at all costs through science and technology—is not sustainable. This has been affirmed by scholars from many disciplines: economics, environmental science, social sciences, the arts, and even business itself. As Henryk Skolimowski (1992) so aptly states in his book, Living Philosophy, new sustainable models are desperately needed—and the foundational ideas for such new models can be found in Native science.

For example, look at Figure 16.1, a model for learning from Native science. This chart shows how learning from Native science involves a relationship circle that orients it in a flowing, complex adaptive system. Four cardinal directions, each with an inside and an outside component, make up this circle of relationship. The four cardinal points of the circle begin with a focus on "wholeness" and move clockwise to include "participation," then "empathy," and finally "responsibility." Within each quadrant sit areas of focus combined with the qualities that ideally characterize them.

In the first quadrant, between wholeness and participation, the focus is on reality and the quality of courage needed for creating a new consciousness of Indigeneity. The outward expression of this first quadrant revolves around revitalizing an ecological consciousness that has been determined by Indigenous histories but that now has the potential to determine future history. Indigenous relational philosophy is by its nature holistic, qualitative, spiritual, reverential, evolutionary and, most essentially, participatory. These are the conscious foundations that inform Native science and a technology with deeply compassionate attitudes toward all creation. The inward expression of this first quadrant is a kind of consciousness that vitalizes the participatory mind within ourselves. Starting with the premise that the individual mind participates with the sacred mind, we find the sacred everywhere.

Figure 16.1 Model for learning from Native science.

In the second quadrant, between participation and empathy, the focus is on actual experience. The wisdom required for re-engendering contemporary Native science is the result of this experience. The outward expression of this quadrant also revolves around the revitalization and reintroduction of Native science within an epistemological context that is life-oriented, committed, comprehensive, relational, wise, ethical, healthy, politically aware, socially concerned, and responsible. The inward expression of this orientation involves experiencing and learning from the natural world directly on its own terms, within its own context of authenticity.

In the third quadrant, between empathy and responsibility, the focus is on knowledge, with the quality of sharing, an essential foundation for revitalizing Indigenous cultures and communities. The outward expression of this quadrant is accumulating, sharing, and applying knowledge mediated by ecological values and ethics. Indigenous knowledge is contained in Indigenous cultures and processed through Indigenous communities and cultural expressions. Native sciences integrate this knowledge with ecological consciousness and values, and, therefore, with spiritual awareness. In this way the perception of Indigenous people that "knowledge is alive" becomes a viable operating foundation for thought and action. At the inward level of this orientation, self-knowledge and gathering a deeper understanding of one's culture and community become an essential focus for learning Native science.

In the fourth quadrant, between responsibility and wholeness, the focus is on insight, with the quality of generosity being integral to both initiating change and creating foundational transformation. The outward expression of this quadrant is not an easy task and must begin with ourselves and our most immediate circles of influence. Essentially, revitalizing Native science from this orientation initiates a change in consciousness—through the conscious reassertion of our innate Indigenous ecological sense, we change the nature of our perceptions and knowledge of our external reality, creating a new worldview. At the inward level of this orientation, we become aware of the conditioning, assumptions, deeply held intuitions, values, and alternatives, allowing them to restructure our psyche at its deepest level. This is the way learning through Native science manifests real personal and societal transformation.

In the center of this circle is HOPE, which is the emotive energizer of the entire circle. Hope as the central focus of learning is a powerful vision that provides the emotional impetus to act and learn from within a context that will result in transformation and change toward a brighter future for all. Guiding our actions through hope is a way of "thinking the highest thought."

THINKING THE HIGHEST THOUGHT

The Indigenous goal of living "a good life" is sometimes referred to by Native American people as striving "to always think the highest thought." This metaphor refers to the framework of a sophisticated epistemology of community-based, spiritual education in which the community and its traditions form the primary support for its way of life and quality of thinking.

Thinking the highest thought means thinking of oneself, one's community, and one's environment "richly"—essentially, a spiritual mindset in which one thinks in the highest, most respectful, and most compassionate way, thus systematically influencing the actions of both individuals and the community. It is a way to perpetuate a "good life," a respectful and spiritual life, and a dynamic wholeness. Thus, the community becomes a kind of center and context for learning how to live spiritually.

For Indigenous peoples, living spiritually is also about journeying to "a place." The journeying and the place are implied in the guiding story, the central myth that an Indigenous group holds in common. The community embodies the essence of that place, which is really the place of the spirit referred to in its origin stories. Therefore, each Indigenous community is considered a sacred place, a place of living, learning, teaching, healing, and ritual—a place where the people share the breath of their life and thought.

The community is a living, spiritual entity supported by every responsible adult. In striving to think the highest thought and reach "that place that Indian people talk about," each adult becomes a teacher and a student—because to learn to think the highest thought and reach that place is a step-by-step process that begins at birth, and in which each individual, from the youngest to oldest, has a role to play.

Certain developmental types of thought and knowledge form the essential steps to thinking the highest thought. Each step must be learned and honored on the way to that "place." Learning about each step is life-long, and each overlaps the other through time and levels of knowing. Each contains the others and shares concentric rings of relationship, yet each has its unique lessons.

Based on this perspective, the first way of thinking and knowing has to do with one's physical place—one has to come to terms with where one physically lives. One has to know one's home, one's village, and then the land, the "earth upon which one lives." This is the physical environment—the hills, canyons, valleys, forests, mountains, streams, rivers, plains, deserts, lakes, and seas.

For Indigenous people, this first type of thought is the beginning of the extension and integration of connections with nature and with other people in the community. It is a kind of thinking that orients us to the spirit of the place immediately surrounding us. For Indigenous people, thinking and knowing about the spirit begins in the home, the village, and the village's natural location. As a way of knowing, thinking, and orientation, it proceeds in concentric rings from the location of the family household, to the segment of the village the household is located in, to the village as a whole, to the land immediately surrounding the village, and then to the sacred mountains and other geographic features that form the recognized boundaries of each Indigenous group's territory.

Generally, Indigenous villages have a center and several sections that define where the various family or clan groups live. These groupings represent the basic mythic and social divisions of each village. They comprise the qualities—male and female, sun and earth, winter and summer, and so forth—that define the village as the "People's" place. Each household is a unique extended expression of a family and has an orientation shared by members of that family. The clans and the village proper form an orientation and way of thinking and learning about place represented by each successively larger inclusive group. The experiences and thinking in relation to the immediate natural environment are also shared. These are the basic dimensions of the first way of thinking and knowing.

The second kind of thought occurs in relationship to other people, plants, animals, natural elements, and other phenomena. This type of thought and knowing revolves around consciously understanding the nature of our relationships to other people, other life, and the natural world.

This is a way of self-knowing and defining of spirit that is based in our senses and our emotions. It is a way of thinking that allows us to experience and understand the differences and similarities among the spirit in ourselves, other living things, and other entities of the natural world. It is based on the physical senses and the development of the ability to hear, observe, perceive, and emotionally feel the "spirit moving" in all its manifestations in the world around us. For Indigenous people around the world, *spirit is real.* It is physically expressed in everything that exists in the world.

The third way of thought has to do with reflective contemplation, speaking, and acting. This way of thinking involves developing and applying the capacity to think things through completely and make wise choices, to speak carefully and responsibly for purpose and effect, and to act decisively to produce something that is useful and has "spirit." This kind of thought also has to do with the expression of respect, ethics, morals, and proper behavior—all of which lead to the development of humility. This way of thinking brings forth the best and most desirable aspect of being human, as proper responses to learning about and dealing with the spiritual.

The fourth way of thought regards the kind of knowing that has long experience with all aspects of human life. This way of thought requires a learning that comes only with maturity. It leads to a knowing that includes, then moves beyond, what the physical senses perceive toward what can be called wisdom, which for Indigenous people is a complex state of knowing founded on accumulated experience. Tribal societies believe wisdom is reserved for the elderly, for only they have the long experience necessary to make them capable of maintaining the essential structures of the spiritual life and well-being of the community. The elders maintain the stories, rituals, and social structures that ensure the "good life" of the community through and in the spirit. Also, by virtue of their age, they are the members of the community closest to that revered state of being "complete" men and women.

The fifth way of thinking is tied to the knowledge that starts with wisdom and then evolves beyond it to understanding and knowing the "spirit" directly with all one's senses. It is a kind of multisensory consciousness, a way of knowing associated with mystic or spiritual leaders in their most fully developed state of being. This type of knowledge is most often associated with the most elderly of an Indigenous society, but this is not always the case. In fact, this way of thinking can be achieved earlier in life, sometimes as a result of visionary experiences. This is the level of thinking most closely associated with myth and dream. It is the threshold to "that place that Indian people talk about."

CONCLUDING THOUGHTS

It was suggested at the beginning of this chapter that Native science is, at its core, a process for learning about life and the nature of the "spirit that moves us," with the ultimate goal of becoming fully knowledgeable about this spirit.

The chapter developed this notion by highlighting how spirituality comes from the process of exploring and coming to know the nature of the living energy that moves in each of us, through us, and around us. In terms of bridging this material to the field of spirituality at work, the contribution the "learning from nature" cycle makes can be applied as a model of spiritual consciousness in the workplace. Coming to know this knowledge is considered completeness in its most profound form. It is the place of the spirit, it is the central place of thought, the place of the deepest respect and sacredness, the place of "good life," the place of the Highest Thought.

ACKNOWLEDGMENT

This chapter is a revised version of a chapter from the second edition of the book, Cajete, G. (2000). *Native science: Laws of interdependence.* Santa Fe, NM: Clear Light Publishers. Reprinted with permission from Greg Cajete.

REFERENCES

Berkes, F., Colding, J., & Folke, C. (2000). Traditional ecological knowledge, ecosystem science, and environmental management. *Ecological Applications 10*(5), 1251–1262.

Black, S. S. (1997). Redefining success in community development. *Indigenous Planning Times,* 1(3).

Cajete, G. (1994). *Look to the mountain: An ecology of indigenous education.* Durango, CO: Kivaki Press.

Skolimowski, H. (1992). *Living Philosophy: Eco-Philosophy as a Tree of Life.* New York: Penguin Books: London; New York : Arkana.

Skolimowski, H. (1994). *Ecoyoga: Practice and meditations for walking in beauty on the earth.* London, England: Gaia Books.

CHAPTER 17

AROHIA TE RANGI O TE HIHIRI

Heeding the Melody of Pure and Potent Energy

Amber Nicholson, Chellie Spiller and Mānuka Hēnare

HIHIRI: THE EPOCH OF THOUGHT

Nā te kune te pupuke	From the conception the well up of emotion
Nā te pupuke te hihiri	From the well up of emotion the energized thought
Nā te hihiri te mahara	From the energized thought to remembrance
Nā te mahara te hinengaro	From the remembrance the consciousness
Nā te hinengaro te manako	From the consciousness the desire
Ka hua te wānanga	Knowledge became conscious (fruitful)

(Translation adapted from the Māori text of the cosmological chant of Te Kohuwai as cited in Hēnare, 2003; Salmond, 1991; Taylor, 1855/2007; cf. Marsden, 2003; Shirres, 1997)

The above cosmological *whakapapa*, or genealogical unfolding of the universe, as told by Te Kohuwai of Rongoroa, is described by Rev Richard Taylor (1855/2007) as "the epoch of thought" (p. 14).[1] From the unfolding universe (kune) came growth (pupuke); from growth came the primal and potent energy source of *hihiri*. It is in this ancient history of the cosmos that we come to understand the nature of thought, memory, consciousness, and desire. The fruit (hua) of *hihiri* is *te wānanga*, or bountiful knowledge and wisdom (Hēnare, 2003).

Hihiri is part of an interlocking spiral of spiritual and cognitive rhythmic forces central to Māori metaphysics. In *whakapapa* and in practice, *hihiri* is an elemental energy descended from *Te Korekore*, the realm of pure potentiality, which traverses the realm of *Te Ao Wairua*, the spiritual world, and manifests in *Te Ao Mārama*, the physical world (Marsden, 2003; Shirres, 1997). It is our proposition that *hihiri* can advance into being in *Te Ao Mārama* through intention and collective will, which leads to synchronistic events.

HIHIRI, COLLECTIVE WILL, INTENTION, AND SYNCHRONICITY

In this chapter we use the above cosmological *whakapapa* as an explanatory framework to explain the nature of *hihiri* and how it can be harnessed and manifested as collective will and intention in a business enterprise. Here we measure the success of a business enterprise by its contribution to the spirituality of the economy, developed through nurturing the *tapu, mana, mauri, hau,* and *wairua*[2] of every stakeholder of a firm; that is, the spirit, life, and energy fields in which a firm operates. We hypothesize that when the energies and wills of people in an organization are sufficiently aligned, and people cohere around a clear intention, the enterprise gains powerful impetus towards its common-good purpose. Furthermore, a firm that cultivates shared will among the people within its organization and community becomes "in sync" with its purpose to create multidimensional well-being. Such "synchronicity," to use Jung's term (1955), generates meaningful arrangements of seemingly unrelated events, which ultimately materialize as consciously created well-being for positive effect.

We see intention and collective will as sources of power that bind, energize, and legitimize Indigenous business enterprise in a spiritual covenant with the wider community. The will, intentions, and well-being of the organization are inextricably linked to the will, intentions, and the well-being of its stakeholders. When an enterprise borrows the will of the community, it is the *hau*, the reciprocal exchange of energy that allows the business to operate successfully. Paying attention to the energy fields that are collective will and intention endows an enterprise with a mandate to create wealth, remove poverty, and enhance, sustain, restore, and empower well-being. This mandate supports organizations to achieve remarkable results far beyond what might be conceived of by "business as usual."

Te Rangi: The Melody

The title of this chapter—*arohia te rangi o te hihiri*—acknowledges the intensity of spiritual and emotional energy, perception, and intuition that often accompanies a musical melody. *Aro* is translated as to take heed, pay attention to, comprehend; it can also refer to the seat of feelings (Moorfield, 2014); as an active verb, *arohia* describes dynamic listening and participation. *Te rangi* refers to the melodic dialogue between the realms of the spiritual and physical: The energetic song of *Te Ao Wairua* is seeking expression in *Te Ao Mārama*. As articulated by Aldridge (2001), "we are organized as human beings not in a mechanical way but in a musical form; i.e., a harmonic complex of interacting rhythms and melodic contours" (p. 116). It is the human perceptive and intuitive mind that perceives the unfolding of the musical meaning; therefore, the active engagement (*arohia*) of *hihiri* requires becoming attuned to the reciprocal flow of energy involved in the creative participatory process.

The *rangi* of this chapter reflects the perpetual spiral-like process of creation in which all things seek the light of *Te Ao Mārama*, where, following Nobel Prize laureate Rabindranath Tagore (1912), we refer to as "Melodies Eternally New"[3] (Hēnare, 2003; Hēnare, Middleton, & Puckey, 2013). The spiral is widely used in Māori artworks as a way of understanding and representing the continuous and creative energy of the universe. It symbolizes the constant flux of all beings seeking to advance from the center, from *Te Korekore*, into *Te Ao Mārama*, while simultaneously returning to the cosmic emptiness (Hēnare, 2003; Woodard, 2008).

Beginning at the open and unbounded end of the spiral, we discuss the ultimate purpose of life as defined by Māori in *Te Tiriti o Waitangi*—the living treaty document between Māori and the British Crown—namely "*Te Rongo me te Ātanoho*," creating a good life through enhancing the common good (Hēnare, 2011). We then connect to the center of the spiral, the basis of metaphysics and being, and describe the energetic evolution of *hihiri*. Moving from the center outwards, intention is explained through conscious breath and reciprocity, invocations, and *whakapapa*. Journeying back towards the center, we delineate *mauri-ora*, consciously created well-being, and the cardinal ethics and values that underpin the Māori worldview. From here we propose two fundamental questions that should define modern business endeavor and outline the desired future of business enterprise:

Of every intention it must be asked, "How will this create greater collective well-being?", and, following Senge (in Jaworski, 2011), "What is it that we are able to collectively create?" We conclude with Melodies Eternally New, which address, enhanc, sustain, and replenish the life-energies of creation.

TE RONGO ME TE ĀTANOHO: PRODUCING A GOOD LIFE FROM COLLECTIVE WILL

In Aotearoa New Zealand the fundamental principles of economic development are enshrined in three founding symbols or covenants of independence. These covenants, or solemn agreements, represent an epoch of thought that continues to resonate today as Melodies Eternally New. The first covenant is Te Kara, the flag of independence of 1834, which was ritually chosen by Māori leaders and formally recognized by the British Government and in so doing established an international personality of Māori and Nu Tīreni (Mahuta & Hēnare, 1991). It remains as one of the official flags of New Zealand. The second covenant *He Whakaputanga o te Rangatiratanga o Nu Tīreni* 1835, the Declaration of Independence of New Zealand, was a proclamation by Māori to the world that they and Nu Tīreni are free and independent and expected other countries to respect the integrity of both people and nation. This was later confirmed in the third covenant *Te Tiriti o Waitangi* 1840, an initiative of the British Crown, who wanted to formalize a relationship with Māori. For Māori, Te Tiriti encompassed British recognition of Māori sovereignty and Nu Tīreni independence, and that England would be given a favored relationship. For the British, the treaty was about the full secession of sovereignty in perpetuity, the opening up of Nu Tīreni to British emigration, and the acquisition of land titles.

These living covenants, the flag, the declaration, and treaty were endorsed collectively over time by Māori *rangatira*, or leaders, and their people. They provide guidance as to the principles of partnership between the Indigenous peoples of Aotearoa New Zealand and settlers. They also provide examples of the manifestation of *hihiri* in traditional society. *Rangatira*, looking outside their sphere of experience, embraced collective will and intention to create a desired future, what is referred to in He Whakaputanga as "*He Whenua Rangatira.*" This latter expression denotes inclusive prosperity and well-being, and safeguards the economic sovereignty of *whānau-hapū* and *iwi* or family-kinship and collective social structures (Hēnare, 2003, 2011; Hēnare et al., 2013; Hēnare, Petrie, & Puckey, 2010). *Te Tiriti o Waitangi* speaks to the Māori philosophical ideal of *Te Rongo me te Ātanoho*, or lasting peace and the quest for a good life (Hēnare, 2011; Hēnare, Puckey, Nicholson, Dale & Vaithianathan, 2011). Hēnare (2011) describes *Te Ātanoho* principle as the preservation and continuation of a quality of good life as determined by Māori.

A Māori worldview, cosmology, and cosmogony carry the seeds of the fundamental ethics of a people. It is the cosmic *whakapapa* that begins and ends at *Te Korekore*—the realm of potentiality—that provides reverence for life and defines *kawa, tikanga,* and *ritenga,* that is, a set of cardinal ethics, morals, values, and appropriate behaviors (Hēnare, 1988; Wolfgramm & Waetford, 2009). *Kawa, tikanga,* and *ritenga,* according to Hēnare (2011), are intentions to pursue *Te Rongo me te Ātanoho.* Research by Hēnare (2003, 2011) has shown that *rangatira* intentionality and purpose that enabled a good life for their people rested in *whānau-hapū* and *iwi* institutions that were *tika,* ethical or just. These institutions simultaneously and interdependently met spiritual, environmental, social, and economic needs. "Reciprocity was expected and was both structurally and spiritually induced, according to Māori belief systems in the early-mid nineteenth-century" (Hēnare, 2003, p. 153).

To fulfill its purpose of producing a good life, a firm, inspired by Māori *kawa, tikanga,* and *ritenga,* must align its intention with the will and the needs of the wider community. In general terms the collective will of a community is defined as "the embodiment or expression of its common interest" (general will, n.d.). Hawken (1993) describes will as the substance of life, requiring a deep regard for reciprocity. He explains that without children there are no parents, without fans there are no stars, without coaches and mentors there is no value on expertise; humans and businesses constantly borrow the will of others. "Will is powerful stuff," he says "and is not well understood; when a company borrows will, it is more than a loan, it is a covenant. That covenant is the heart and soul of the enterprise" (Hawken, 1993, p. 156). Indeed, Solomon (2004) claims that corporations are not driven by the abstract force of profit, but by the collective will and intentions of their employees.

Mutual reciprocity comes with obligations and responsibilities (Peat, 1994; Pohatu, 2011), and the common good is dependent on satisfying all dimensions of well-being (Hēnare, 1988; Tate, 2010). Māori business enterprise, and perhaps all enterprise irrespective of the cultural tradition from which it arises, is beholden to serve the greater good. The common good from a Native American Tewa standpoint is described by Cajete (2000) as striving "to always think the highest thought" (p. 276). This refers to spirit, environment, and community-based traditions that reflect the dynamic wholeness of the universe. The community is therefore the center and the context for development, as well as the essence of it. Bengali polymath Tagore (1972) describes goodness as that which derives from a connected view of life—one that is concerned with the well-being of humanity, those present and yet to be. What is good is that which concerns the greater self.

As the life and activity of *he tangata,* meaning the singular human person or humanity, dwells within the social context, economic pursuits are a means to serve the community (Cajete, 2000; Durie, 2003; New Zealand Institute for Economic Research [NZIER], 2003; Spiller, Pio, Erakovic, & Hēnare, 2011). As Spiller (2010) explains, "in serving others, one is serving one's extended self" (p. 131). Modern-day firms that focus on and respond to the needs of the community are referred to as corporate spiritual entities by Wolfgramm (2007), and named *umanga whanaungatanga* by Nicholson, Woods, and Hēnare (2012). Such entities are embedded in the traditional *kāinga,* which Hēnare describes as the "primary place of habitation in which the *whānau* and *hapū* carry out their everyday activities, including economic activities" (2003, p. 146). The institution of the firm is the means by which the modern economy is able to function; it imbues energy and life into the market. It is in the firm that organizational values are determined, and these are aligned with the social values of the local community—that is, the *kāinga.* It is in this space that entrepreneurship takes place (cf. Coase, 1937).

Therefore, a corporate spiritual entity is expected by the community to contribute to *Te Rongo me te Ātanoho,* the holistic well-being that enhances, sustains, restores, and empowers well-being across multiple dimensions to produce *He Whenua Rangatira.* In traditional economies, economic action had considerations outside of profit and included the redistribution of opportunities and benefits (Hēnare, 2003). It was through this mutual reciprocity that will was spiritually and collectively created and shared. "This is consistent with the *kāinga* of old, wherein activities were purposive and outcomes that enhanced the spiritual, social, cultural and economic well-being of individuals and collectives were crucial for sustaining the community" (Wolfgramm, 2007, p. 225).

A spiritual covenant in which an enterprise is said to borrow the will of others contrasts markedly with the way many firms operate today. Those adopting a mechanical approach are more likely to conduct business where the sole bond with another is a contract, not a covenant, where the mode of engagement is transactional not exchange, and where the consideration of others is from a rights-based view without regard to will. At best, they may have a stakeholder approach, which is often taken from a position of risk mitigation, to achieve social legitimacy and to manage reputation. However, all created entities possess their own *tapu, mana, mauri, hau,* and *wairua* (Hēnare, 2003; Salmond, 1985); specifically, all firms have spirit, energy, and life. It is the spirituality of the firm that shapes the spirituality of the economy.

As Hawken (1993) points out, because will is a spiritual covenant, when that covenant is breached, will is lost and life becomes barren. Similarly, he says, when the relationship between a company and the environment is marked by indifference or greed, that company will lose its heart and soul and become sterile. There has been a mass forgetting in many modern societies that our well-being depends on the will of others to give to us, including forebears who entrusted the planet to us and future generations for whom we will be the forebears. To take without giving back is to deplete the other. Māori call this *kaihau*, eating the *hau*, which can lead to disharmony and imbalance (Patterson, 1992). *Kaihau*, greed, and taking without giving back mars modern capitalism and has created problems of magnitude, leaving humanity out of step with the rhythm of nature and unable to appropriately access and direct primal energies such as *hihiri.*

NĀ TE KUNE TE PUPUKE: FROM THE CONCEPTION THE WELL UP OF EMOTION

Te Kune: The *Conception*

We turn now to the energetic evolution of *hihiri* as recounted in the cosmological *whakapapa* of Te Kohuwai of Rongoroa (as cited in Hēnare, 2003; Salmond, 1991; Taylor, 1855/2007; cf. Marsden, 2003; Shirres, 1997). The universe is viewed by spiritual traditions as an evolving process linked via cosmic genealogy (Cajete, 2000; Marsden, 2003; Hēnare, 2003; Wolfgramm & Waetford, 2009). Māori cosmology and cosmogony present a cosmic centre, a realm of unrecognized potential wherein all creation originates and to which all eventually returns. It begins and ends with *Io-matua*, the root cause and creator of all things who stirred to form *Te Korekore*, the infinite realm of primal and latent energy, the seed-bed of creation (Marsden, 2003; Shirres, 1997). The creative forces awaken potentiality, giving life to all other energies that advance and are manifest in *Te Ao Mārama*, the natural world of life, light, and enlightenment (Wolfgramm & Waetford, 2009). These energies in turn feed back into the centre, creating a continuous and integrated spiral (Marsden, 2003), or "Melodies Eternally New" (Hēnare et al., 2013; Tagore, 1912). The dynamic birth of the universe and the whole of creation is depicted in the phrase "i te kore, ki te poo, ki te ao maarama 'out of the nothingness, into the night, into the world of light'" (Shirres, 1997, p. 16).

Te Pupuke: The Well Up of Emotion

From the conception comes a well up of emotion, a period of energetic growth: the long night in the womb. Indigenous wisdom tells us that everything in creation is imbued with the energy of spirit (Cajete, 2000; Peat, 1994). *Mauri*, the spiritual life force that emanates from *Te Korekore*, begat the energetic vibrations and fluxes that branched forth to seek, pursue, extend, enlarge, spread, and increase in the quest for being (Marsden, 2003; Shirres, 1997). The arousal of primal energy gives way to thought and then consciousness. It is from this energetic *whakapapa* that matter, people, and land eventually evolved (Salmond, 1991; Shirres, 1997). Humans share in the energy that emanates from the spiritual realm and thus have both an active and creative role as participants in the natural world (Cajete, 2000; Hēnare, 2003; Peat, 1994).

NĀ TE PUPUKE TE HIHIRI: FROM THE WELL UP OF EMOTION THE ENERGISED THOUGHT

Te Hihiri: The Energized Thought

Melodies Eternally New, the constant renewal of life is the song of *Io-matua*, the Creator of the Cosmos dwelling in the center of the spiral, in *Te Korekore* (Hēnare, 2001; Marsden, 2003; Shirres, 1997; Wolfgramm & Waetford, 2009). In the nothingness of the vacuum state of *Te Korekore* resides an infinity of unmanifested energy and, therefore, every possibility exists (Laszlo, 2007; Peat, 1994). The elemental energy of *hihiri*, sourced in *Te Korekore*, traverses the realm of pure potentiality into the material world. Likened by Marsden (2003) to the fundamental energy and information of quantum physics, *hihiri* coalesces with *mauri* to "generate and bring the process into the actuality of existent being" (p. 47). It is from *hihiri* that energized thought, memory, consciousness, and desire arise. This process gives way to the development of knowledge and wisdom that gives meaning to potentiality and thus achieves being (Hēnare, 2003; Marsden, 2003).

Like the sound of music, knowledge is not static, but alive and seeking expression (Parry, 2006). Tagore (1972) opines "the same energy which vibrates and passes into the endless forms of the world manifests itself in our inner being as consciousness" (p. 21). Knowledge is not limited to human forms but is also transmitted through such beings as the land, animals, or plants (Parry, 2006), and therefore knowledge of reality is embedded in the dynamic and cyclic flow between subject and object (Bohm & Peat, 1987). As asserted by Swimme and Berry, "The vibrations and fluctuations in the universe are the music that drew forth the galaxies and stars and their powers of weaving elements into life.... The adventure of the universe depends upon our capacity to listen" (1992, p. 44).

When operating at high-level frequency, *hihiri* is unmanifested energy of pure potential that, we posit, can be localized by a firm into being through pure intention. In a business context, the intention is to produce a good life that reflects collective will and enhances the well-being of communities.

This creative process is facilitated by what Cajete (2000) describes as the "metaphoric mind," which works in the higher realm of consciousness and coincidence and "applies the deep levels of human perception and intuition to the task of living" (Cajete, 2000, p. 29). *Hihiri* is grasped in *Te Ao Wairua* by the metaphoric mind and brought into consciousness and the physical reality of *Te Ao Mārama* through the evolution of thought—that is, by intention and will. In all created entities, thought possesses its own *tapu, mana, mauri, hau,* and *wairua,* thus giving it spirit, life, and energy that affects other entities. Māori ways of knowing do not greatly differentiate between thought and feeling and therefore understanding may come through enactive perception and intuition (Salmond, 1985).[4] Physicists Bohm and Peat (1987) explain that knowing, feeling, and will are inseparable and enfold into each other: The intellect informs emotion, which in turn permeates thought. The content and context of thought gives rise to the determination that enfolds will. There is no recognizable point where will begins and thought ends.

Intention, awareness, and attention are inner activities that grasp, move, and unfold the creative energies between physical reality and the more subtle spiritual level (Bohm & Peat, 1987; Jaworski, 2011). Intention is articulated by Merculieff (2012) as the creative desire that is carried and expressed with every cell of the body. The soul of the intention is the creative intelligence, what we regard here as *hihiri,* and is housed within the center of being, that which sits outside the physical, in the realm of *Te Korekore.* When all present moment awareness is directed towards this center, *hihiri* is then energized and steered by the subtle conscious and unconscious thoughts, feelings, and will (Cajete, 1994; Merculieff, 2012). Intention orchestrates and organizes life-energies into new forms and expression; attention gives life to the intention through attracting energies resonating at the same frequency; awareness opens the mind to a sensation of broader forces.

Tūhonohono: Synchronicity[5]

The Jungian concept of synchronicity occurs in the realm of the intuitive and metaphoric mind, whereby connections of meaning are drawn between two distinct and causally unrelated movements. More than mere chance, coincidence, or serendipity, the seeming randomness of synchronistic occurrences is seen as creative intelligence that has meaning at higher levels of order (Bohm & Peat, 1987). Through psychically reducing or eliminating the factors of time and space, synchronistic events are seen as "creative acts, as the continuous creation of a pattern that exists from all eternity, repeats itself sporadically, and is not derivable from any known antecedents" (Jung, 1955, p. 142). As Jung (1955) points out, synchronicity is no more unthinkable than the discontinuities of physics; it is rigid and conditioned belief in time, space, and causality that renders the notion incomprehensible.

An Indigenous notion of time and its three dimensions of past, present, and future is not constrained to an independent and linear notion but is seen as living—the animated activity of spirit moving in flux (Peat, 1994). Therefore, *hihiri* has agency over generations, past, present, and future, which are inextricably and intrinsically bound (Mataira, 2000). When the time is right—*Te wā*, explained further below—and when the energies are aligned, things and events are attracted and unfolded (Peat, 1994). Synchronistic events emanate from the spiritual realm, guiding one towards *te rangi o te hihiri.* As explained by Pohatu (2008), *Te Ao Māori*, the Māori world, provides timeless purposes to each generation through subtle signposts that are waiting to be summoned into the lived reality. Synchronicity demands conscious intention, attention, and awareness. It is through the dynamic of each metaphorical mind that intention is expressed, and through the universal spirit that intention is synchronistically organized.

NĀ TE HIHIRI TE MAHARA: FROM THE ENERGIZED THOUGHT TO REMEMBRANCE

Te Mahara: The Remembrance

As the ever-flowing spirit seeks to increase from potential to being, it is memory and consciousness that holds the process together (Shirres, 1997). This is akin to listening to a musical melody: While attention may focus on a current single note or energy, the music relies on a simultaneous awareness of earlier notes and notes yet to come, all of which reverberate to express a vibrant and continuous flow essential to the overall melodic meaning (Bohm & Peat, 1987). According to Marsden (2003) it was the development of the primordial memory—derived from *hihiri*—that ultimately achieved wisdom and therefore "definite order, direction and purpose guided the process" (p. 32).

Like many other Indigenous peoples, Māori prefer "process" rather than the modern predilection for "progress," which believes in inexorable, incremental improvement over the past, improvements that are generally of a materialistic nature (Spiller, 2010). In the linear progress paradigm, creativity is associated with novelty and change (Bohm & Peat, 1987). Furthermore, it "perpetuates a distorted vision of what is, in fact, a multi-dimensional relational process" (Cajete, 2000, p. 266). The ongoing spiral process does not see stable equilibrium as an undesirable state. Traditional societies strived for and were able to bring *He Whenua Rangatira* into being—that is, a harmonious balance with the cosmos, environment, society, and economy that was sustained over long periods (Bohm & Peat, 1987; Hēnare, 2011). Creativity and intention are seen in revitalisation rituals that are performed in order to renew and balance relationships with spiritual, environmental, social, and economic energies (Bohm & Peat, 1987). Indeed, it is through ritual that humanity is expressed (Hēnare, 2003).

The perpetual renewal process, Melodies Eternally New, and remembrance come in the form of the breath and ritualistic word. The breath has many forms, from the physical that connects all living things, to its expression of spirit carried via dance, music, *whakapapa*, and word. Language such as in song and *karakia* (ritual prayer) are manifestations of thought and feeling, thus possess their own *tapu, mana, mauri, hau,* and *wairua*. Language then has the power to affect will and express intention (Aldridge, 2001; Cajete, 2000; Durie, 2003; Porter, 2009; Spiller & Stockdale, 2012). These are not merely spoken or thoughtful words, but are about *arohia te rangi o te hihiri*—heeding the melody of pure and potent energy. Vibrations of the spoken word are transmitting information that may enter into relationships to bring other vibrations and energies into being (Peat, 1994). Therefore, breath, especially when used spiritually, must be used responsibly (Cajete, 2000; Mika, 2007; Peat, 1994).

Business enterprise, in borrowing the will of the community, is able to draw on the spiritual processes of breath and word to create multidimensional well-being for the benefit of stakeholders. These processes are not so much a desire to control, but to utilize the creative intelligence to create, support, sustain, and replenish the life-energies of the natural world (Marsden, 2003). Some of these processes are outlined below.

Hau—The Spiritual Essence of Vitality

According to Māori thought, *hau* is a vital essence intrinsic in all creation. It is a life principle that must be nurtured through acts of goodness in order to enhance, sustain, and restore the essence of vitality (Hēnare, 2001, 2003). *Hau* is referred to as the breath of life and also represents the wind. Cajete explains that breath "represents the most tangible expressions of the spirit in all living things" (Cajete, 2000, p. 261). Indeed, the root word of the English word spirit is wind or breath (Barnhart, 1988; Jaworski, 2011, 2012). Life begins, depends on, and ends with breath; physical, mental, and emotional well-being is influenced by and reliant on the rhythm of breathing. Without intention, rhythm is mere repetition or pulse (Aldridge, 2001). Like the continual give-and-take flow of energy, creation shares in the gift exchange of breath where the life-force of one element is exhaled and inhaled by another (Spiller & Stockdale, 2012).

This mutual breath exchange creates a system of mutual reciprocity that is seen at the heart of all relationships (Cajete, 2000; NZIER, 2003; Petrie, 2006; Spiller, Erakovic, Hēnare, & Pio, 2010). *Hau* represents the action of reciprocity, and it was this that motivated economic activities of traditional economies. Hēnare (2003), citing Tamati Ranapiri, explains how *hau* manifests in everyday life:

> Over the millennia, hau was established as a complex totalising system of obligatory gift exchange. The exchange followed some basic principles where the intrinsic hau of the taonga [highly prized intangible and tangible treasures] and the hau belonging to the donor are imbued in the taonga; these in turn infuse Māori social, economic and religious life with profound implications for the management of social relations and guardianship of the natural world. (p. 53)

Hau then creates an enduring bond between those engaged in the exchange (Hēnare, 2003). In revering the nature of *hau*, a firm is able to command a culture of reciprocity, ethical responsibility, and respect. Economic exchanges are energized through the *hau*, the spirit of the gift (Hēnare, 2003). Collective will can be seen as another form of energy based on the fundamental principle of mutual reciprocity. Creating what Spiller et al. (2011) refer to as a "wise" organization, spirit and will can be nurtured through collaboration and cooperation between people, the community, and the natural world. This requires taking responsibility for actions and reflective contemplation of cause and effects.

Karakia—Invoking

Karakia (ritual prayers, chanting, or incantations) are forms of conscious breath that create intention and invoke a reality (Durie, 2003; Mika, 2007; Porter, 2009; Spiller & Stockdale, 2012). *Karakia* create a pact between the spiritual realm and the material, ultimately joining man, nature, and the universe as one (Durie, 2003; Shirres, 1997; Spiller & Stockdale, 2012; Tate, 2010). By calling upon the *tapu* (being with the potentiality of power) and *mana* (the actualization of *tapu*) of the spiritual world, *karakia* empower *he tangata* to take part in the creation process, transcending spiritual boundaries and manifesting intention in the physical realm (Shirres, 1997). *Karakia* "directs the way we think" (Kereopa, as cited in Moon, 2003, p. 58) and the word in the outflow of breath is the extension and projection of a person (Tate, 2010). This impels mindfulness throughout all activities and reflects a belief that actions need to be spiritually aligned to intent (Spiller & Stockdale, 2012).

A corporate spiritual entity is able to invoke *karakia,* literally and meta-phorically, to achieve the collectively and creatively created strategic vision. This vision is invoked not only through rituals and values, but also through an organisations aesthetics and the spiritual context of its products. Cajete (1994) links prayer to "Asking," which invokes a goal and focuses intention:

> Asking is the initiation of a creative flow of thought. It is the place of first insights, intuitions, encounters, and experiences. The activities of Asking are like tilling the soil, planting the seed and then saying to the spirits of the world "I have planted my most precious seed, help it grow, give it life." (p. 70)

Jaworski (2011) expresses the need for a firm to consciously fashion its future environments as opposed to merely responding to external forces. By setting a clear intention to consciously create holistic and sustainable well-being, an enterprise is asking to borrow the will of the community. Sharing in *karakia* or other prayerful rituals invites "participation in the unfolding meaning of the greater whole; a person is speaking the language of a deeper, unfolding reality" (Spiller & Stockdale 2012, p. 17).

Whakapapa—Honoring Generations

The cosmic *whakapapa* as invoked by Māori defines and describes an in-terrelational worldview that underpins ethics, values, and behavior (Hēnare, 2011; Pohatu, 2008; Wolfgramm & Waetford, 2009). This creation story sees humans as descended from the Supreme Being, *Io-matua,* and thus having direct genealogical links with all natural and spiritual worlds. *Whakapapa* weaves interconnecting life forces of the cosmological realm with the world-ly community. It provides the framework of Māori society and explains the roles, responsibilities, and obligations of *he tangata* to consciously create well-being for all aspects of the universe (Hēnare, 2003; Jackson, 2008; Po-hatu, 2008; Wolfgramm & Waetford, 2009). Like Melodies Eternally New, *whakapapa* is the continuum of life that actively brings ancestors and future generations together in the present of the living; the movement of one be-comes all (Berryman, Bateman, & Cavanagh, 2010; Shirres, 1997).

The word *whakapapa* refers to the layering of knowledge, one order upon another, all beginning at the first generation of order in *Te Korekore* (Kereo-pa, in Moon, 2003; Mataira, 2000; Pohatu, 2008). As a central feature of the Māori knowledge system, *whakapapa* organizes both knowledge itself and the transmission of knowledge through the generations (Mataira, 2000; Wolfgramm & Waetford, 2009). Therefore, *whakapapa* is a way of knowing, feeling, and expressing collective will. It is the recollection and application of sacred knowledge through oral traditions that creates identity; people "'remember to remember' who they are, where they come from, and the spirit they share with all of creation" (Cajete, 1994, p. 45). As gifts from the spiritual realm, *whakapapa* stories require conscious intention, attention, and awareness (Wolfgramm & Waetford, 2009).

Utilizing *whakapapa* in a business sense can renew spiritual and collective efficacy through establishing identity. As a potent lever to facilitate learning, understanding, and participation in a pool of shared meaning, *whakapapa* can create a reciprocal connection to the story and experience (Spiller, 2010; Wolfgramm & Waetford, 2009). Traditionally, *whakapapa* recital was often used for social, economic, and political advantage in order to strengthen systems, networks, and structures, creating an order of layers with purpose and obligation (Pohatu, 2008; Wolfgramm & Waetford, 2009).

The history of *whakapapa* can be utilized to unravel the future. In order for the firm to flourish, it must be adopted by the community; this happens as the community has first been adopted by the firm (cf. Swimme & Berry, 1992). By holding a strong *whakapapa* narrative—that is, knowing one's roots—and clearly delineating the big picture intention, the firm publically establishes its identity. In order to fully integrate itself into the community, the firm must learn the *whakapapa* of the community in which it operates. This engenders a commitment to collectively forge a new, entwined *whakapapa*. It is the dialogue with the wider community in order to devise ways of enacting the greater purpose of the business that cultivates collective will. When the collective will actively translates into a process of consciously created well-being, the organization produces what Jaworski (2011) describes as an "economy of means" where the whole that already exists in the realm of potentiality is brought forward into being. This economy of means is manifested by people as they take action and leads to synchronistic events (Jaworski, 2011).

NĀ TE MAHARA TE HINENGARO: FROM THE REMEMBRANCE THE CONSCIOUSNESS

Te Hinengaro: The Consciousness

The material world that sustains our human lives is collectively and enactively created through language, interactions, and recurrent practices. Varela (as cited in Jaworski, 2011) has said that cognition is not an interpretation of the external world; instead it is the cognitive process of living that brings forth, or "enacts" the world we see. Communal knowledge and societal habits dictate our environment. Therefore, in order to create change in the surrounding communities, organizations, and other entities, what is needed is a change in the quality of vibration. *Te Rongo me te Ātanoho* requires consciously created well-being, or what Māori define as *mauri-ora*, which encompasses receiving and maintaining the essence of ancestors and spiritual powers (Durie, 1999; Morgan, 2006; Spiller et al., 2010).

Tihē Mauriora! Ki te Whaiao, Ki te Ao Mārama!

The Life-principle emerges into the dawnlight, the broad light of day. The Natural World. (Marsden, 2003, p. 33)

Mauri-Ora—Consciously Created Well-Being

Mauri is the spiritual essence or life-force immanent in all descendants of *Io-matua* and permeates much of Māori oral and written literature (Hēnare, 1988, 2001, 2003; Hēnare & Kernot, 1996; Marsden, 2003; Morgan, 2006; Pohatu, 2011; Shirres, 1997; Spiller et al., 2010; Spiller et al., 2011; Wolfgramm & Waetford, 2009). As the basic building block of the universe, *mauri* "holds the fabric of the universe together" (Marsden, 2003, p. 44).

It is *mauri* that activated the original process in which *hihiri* was spawned (Shirres, 1997). From *hihiri* came word, wisdom, and sound; with these elements in place, *hau-ora*, the breath of the spirit of life, came into being. It is *hau-ora* that infuses *mauri* into both animate and inanimate objects and transforms the life-force (*mauri*) into the life-principle (*mauri-ora*) (Marsden, 2003; Shirres, 1997). *Mauri-ora*, a force of refined *hihiri*, is the "source of our life as conscious, knowing and willing beings" (Marsden, 2003, p. 117).

Not limited to living beings, *mauri* flows through all things including thoughts, *kaupapa* (plans, themes, issues), relationships, words, and language (Kereopa in Moon, 2003; Pohatu, 2011). Pohatu (2011) posits that every *kaupapa* and relationship has its *pūtake* or beginning source in this center:

Pūtake of every context holds the original idea, ideals and principles with their attendant intent, purpose and obligations. These indicate what, how and why practice, behaviours and attitudes should be fashioned.... Convictions and ideas are therefore considered here as energies that are drawn from that 'pure intent', contextualised to kaupapa and relationships, then reshaped into activities. (p. 2)

In this context, *mauri* needs to be transformed from a state of latent potential to that of *mauri-ora*, a wholly conscious state of active participation (Pohatu, 2011). Spiller (2010) sees enacting *mauri-ora* as "to be awake to the potential of a situation and the potential in each other, and consciously manifest that potential" (p. 105). Therefore, the creative process of *mauri-ora* embraces the natural and endless state of chaos that requires continuous reflection (Cajete, 2000; Pohatu, 2011).

Firms each have *tapu, mana, mauri, hau,* and *wairua,* and consequently can place the intention and utilize collective will as a movement to harness the energy of *mauri-ora.* The state of *mauri-ora* springs from the conscious acknowledgement and respect of the intrinsic worth of each person, the community, and the natural world. Compassion, integrity, and honesty are promoted in all areas of the organization (Spiller & Stockdale, 2012). Through the willing and committed participation of people with the original ideas, ideals, and principles, a process of tūhonohono, synchronicity, and interconnectedness emerges—that is, a unique *mauri,* a *kaupapa,* and relationship-specific energy is created (Pohatu, 2011).

Kawa, Tikanga and Ritenga: Māori Business Virtues and Ethics

Intentions to pursue *Te Rongo me te Ātanoho,* the good life, are underpinned by an overarching set of principles that govern *Te Ao Māori* (Durie, 2006; Metge, 1995; Marsden, as cited in Hēnare, 1998; Hēnare, 2011; Ruwhiu & Wolfgramm, 2006). *Kawa, tikanga,* and *ritenga* or cardinal ethics, morals, values, and appropriate behaviors are a practical means to consciously create well-being (Hēnare, 1998). As a Māori standpoint sees the spiritual, environmental, social, cultural, and economic spheres as integrated parts of a whole, these virtues, ethics, and behaviors indicate the ultimate purpose of economic development and business activity (Hēnare, 2011).

Using the prism of a Māori worldview, *tikanga,* and ritenga framework, Hēnare (2001, 2003, 2011) devised *He Korunga o Ngā Tikanga: A Matrix of Ethics and Morality* (see Hēnare, Chapter 6 in this volume). This model, says Hēnare, represents a philosophy of vitalism and humanism that is the foundation of Māori philosophy and its epistemology. This conception embraces the complexity and interwoven nature of the Māori worldview, emphasizing the interconnection of principles in a relationship of reciprocity and respect. *He Korunga* is an ethical framework that defines economic intention in which organizational values can be shaped. Central to organizational performance, values influence consumer preference and drive sustainable development (Harmsworth, 2005). Spiller et al. (2010) found Māori-centered businesses drew upon traditional Māori values to support their quest to create multidimensional wealth that nurtures holistic well-being. "The values embedded in *tikanga* help provide stability and assist Māori businesses to reconcile the Māori world view with the demands of a growth-oriented capitalist economy" (Spiller et al., 2010, p. 160).

Like many key concepts in the Māori worldview, processes and energies are interrelated and creation cannot become manifest without the synchronistic movements of all energies (Hēnare, personal communication, 2013). Therefore, *Te Rongo me te Ātanoho* cannot be conceptualized as a singular, distinct, and simple concept. The core *kawa*, *tikanga*, and *ritenga*, together with other interrelational processes, can be seen to form a rhythmic interplay to raise will, underpin economic activity, and ultimately lead to the notions of the good life.

NĀ TE HINENGARO TE MANAKO: FROM THE CONSCIOUSNESS THE DESIRE

Te Manako: The Desire

Intention forged through *kawa*, *tikanga*, and *ritenga* expressed through breath and word must serve the needs of the collective good. Tate (2010) observes that the exercise of *mana*—power, authority, and the common good—begins with *whakaaro*, thought or intention: a conscious choice to exercise *mana* for the greater good. When the intention meets needs at both the level of the metaphoric and the rational collective minds, by nature the intention is more holistic and hence more effective. Therefore, we propose that of each *whakaaro* should be asked the question, "How will this create greater collective well-being?"

The objective of an organization should be to address, enhance, sustain, and restore the *tapu*, considered here as total well-being, of each person, the community, and the natural world, recognizing the interdependent relationships held by all (Tate, 2010). It is through the collective energy of *mana*—that is, the *mana* of the organization, its individuals, and the community—that *tapu* can reach its fullness (Spiller & Stockdale, 2012; Tate, 2010). The *tapu* and the potentiality of the *mana* of each person contributes to the combined potentiality of the *mana* of the collective, and it is through respecting this relationship that dialogue and well-being is created.

Metanoic Organizations

Charles Kiefer and Peter Senge (Jaworski, 2011) have labeled entities that proactively shape their destiny as "metanoic organizations." By cultivating the understanding of and responsibility to the larger environmental whole in which the organiszation and its people operate, a culture of purposefulness and a deeper commitment to being is nurtured. Jaworski (2011) describes metanoic organizations as "striving toward a more natural form of organization that would be more consistent with the true nature of people and the nature of complex social systems" (p. 95). These organizations shape the environment and energy field surrounding it, as opposed to merely responding to external forces. It takes the collective wisdom and energies of the social structures, natural world, and spiritual culture within the organisation to achieve this (Jaworski, 2011).

Senge and others developed the U-Theory, the U-Process in which coherent groups can shape the unfolding of future events through intention, ways of being, and deliberate choices. Team members are tasked with sensing the emerging future and bringing it forth into reality. In many modern organizations, individuals are targeted for leadership development, rather than the organizations developing the leadership potential in everyone. Senge (in Jaworski, 2011) urges the modern world to ask the bigger question: What is it that we are able to collectively create? True leadership, he says, "is the choice to serve life" (p. 2) though participating in the creation of new realities (Jaworksi, 2011, 2012).

KA HUA TE WĀNANGA:
FROM TE KOREKORE TO THE FIRM

This chapter has explored the nature of *hihiri*, pure and potent energy, and how it can be harnessed and manifested as collective will and intention in a business enterprise. We have proposed that tapping into the potentiality of *hihiri* can create coalescences and alignments that ignite what is referred to in Jungian terms as synchronistic events. Due to the cosmological interconnection of the universe, energy affects and influences other energies (Bohm, 2003; Bohm & Peat, 1987; Cajete, 2000; Jaworski, 2011; Jung, 1955; Peat, 1994; Swimme & Berry, 1992). Energies in sync with each other are said to be entwined within a rhythmic dance (Laszlo, 2007; Tagore, 1972). As explained by Tagore (1972), "rhythm never can be born of the haphazard struggle of combat. Its underlying principle must be unity, not opposition" (p. 49). Being in sync, we argue, refers not only to being synchronized in a harmonious way; it also refers to the phenomenon of synchronicity that is premised on the meaningful generation of events at a higher level of order (Bohm & Peat, 1897; Jung, 1955).

The subtle power of human creativity and consciousness influences and transforms energies (Cajete, 2000; Peat, 1994). Therefore, the chaos of rhythm requires intention (Aldridge, 2001). The more intimate the connection with the spirit, soul, life-energies, and inner will, the more powerful the intention will be (Peat, 1994). Manifesting intent is not magic, but applied consciousness. Synchronicity, we suggest, is the coherence of spirit, intention, and will that utilizes *hihiri*, bringing the reality that dwells within *Te Korekore* into being.

Creating the conditions for synchronicity requires the cultivation of collective will. We observe that human will often seems to be an individual experience arising out of one's own thoughts and determinations. However, we posit that will is sourced in the originating place of *Te Korekore*, where all potential and possibilities reside. In Māori thinking, *he tangata* can tap into this potentiality and bring it from the spiritual realm into the material world, thus focusing the potential in the conscious mind and embodying it in all actions. This is not a matter of chance, but rather *Te wā*—a Māori notion of time that Tate (2010) explains encompasses both a graced moment in time and each stage of that journey. *Te wā* then represents a moment and a series of moments of belief and clarity wherein will can be sourced, activated, and drawn into daily life. "Whilst the goal has priority of intention, each stage must receive priority of attention" (Tate, 2010, p. 242).

We propose that such moments of belief are relevant to business endeavors. Destiny, from this perspective, is understood not as some fate-laced event, nor forged from the sheer bloody-mindedness of an individual leader or entrepreneur; it is a patient and active cultivation of a collective will that exists as ever-present latent potential. Furthermore, destiny—as the manifestation of collective will—reflects the will of those who have gone before, those in the present, and those yet to come. A firm attuning to the will of others (of the past, of the present, and in the future) taps into a force far greater than the mere work ethic of a few at a given point in time.

The covenant of working with collective will is an indelible script at the core of Māori enterprise, which, when working for the common good, exists because the firm borrows will. Building on earlier intentions and realities, the enterprise borrows will from the legacy left by ancestors; they borrow the will of nature to provide not only sustenance but for large-scale commercial undertakings; they borrow the will of spirits for continued guidance and blessings; and they borrow the will of the community, finding identity and engagement in the sense of belonging (Cajete, 1994; Kelly, Jackson, & Hēnare, 2014; Swimme & Berry, 1992). In exchange for this will of others, the firm is expected to pursue an intention of providing a good life: that is, well-being and wealth for constituents in a manner that maintains and harmonizes the order of balance with Earth. As those living today are beneficiaries of the collective will and intentions of those who have gone before, the existence of children generations hence depends on the collective will and intentions of today.

MELODIES ETERNALLY NEW

Thou hast made me endless, such is my pleasure.
This frail vessel thou emptiest again and again, and fillest it ever with fresh life.
This little flute of a reed thou hast carried over hills and dales, and hast breathed
through it melodies eternally new.

—Rabindranath Tagore, Lyric No. 1, *Gitanjali: Song Offerings*

The woven universe is the view of the cosmos as a tapestry of energies designed and woven together with conscious intelligence and intent (Marsden, 2003). Intention is the conscious application of spirit, and it is through attention and awareness that intention has the potential to realize itself. Intention is the mechanism by which *hihiri* can be grasped from the realm of *Te Korekore* and brought forth into reality. With limitless potential, this pure energy orchestrates and synchronizes at the higher order of spirit, manifesting itself in ways that fulfill desires, destinies, and dreams.

A shift in paradigm involves a shift in consciousness. It is the energetic vibrations of societal identity and communities that have created the profit-driven materialistic economic institutions of the modern era. The vision required to change this paradigm needs to encompass all that we are, and all that we have the potential to be. If the collective will of those who once existed, those who are living, and those who are yet to be aligns with the will of nature and the will of the spirits, there would be a transformation to corporate spiritual entities and *umanga whanaungatanga* that purposively seek *He Whenua Rangatira* and *Te Rongo me te Ātanoho*. It is this quest for a good life through creating opportunities and undertaking activities that enhance the spiritual, environmental, social, cultural, and economic well-being of stakeholders that provides links to the past and the future, in the present. By seeing the world as pure and potent energy, we are opened up to the infinite possibilities of life. By *arohia te rangi o te hihiri*, heeding the melody of this pure energy, we can recreate *he tangata* to seek life in the highest thought and to address, enhance, sustain, replenish, and restore the *tapu* of all creation.

RĀRANGI KUPU: GLOSSARY

Citations of quotes from texts that use Māori words receive a macron, whether the original text featured a macron or not. The practice of putting a macron on all Māori words where appropriate reflects the University of Auckland Business School policy of enabling readers of Māori words to see how these words ought to be presented.

Aotearoa	Land of the Long White Cloud: The Māori name given to New Zealand
Aro (hia)	To take heed, pay attention to, comprehend; and it is also referred to as the seat of feelings
Arohia te rangi o te hihiri	Heeding the melody of pure and potent energy
Ātanoho	A good life
Hapū	Social units
Hau	The spiritual essence of vitality; breath; reciprocity
Hau-ora	The breath of the spirit of life
He tangata	The singular human person, or humanity
He Whakaputanga o te Rangatiratanga o Nu Tireni	The Declaration of Independence of the Independent tribes of New Zealand
He Whenua Rangatira	Economic sovereignty
Hihiri	Pure energy descended from Te Korekore that traverses the realm of Te Ao Wairua and manifests in Te Ao Mārama
Io-matua	The Root Cause and Creator of all things
Iwi	Tribal social structures
Kaihau	Greed and taking without giving back
Kāinga	Habitat, notions of home
Karakia	Prayers, chanting, or incantations
Kaupapa	Plan; theme; issue
Kawa, tikanga, ritenga	Cardinal ethics, morals, values, and appropriate behaviors
Mana	Power, authority and common good; the manifestation of tapu
Māori	The Indigenous peoples of Aotearoa New Zealand
Mauri	Life essence, vitalism, reverence for life
Mauri-ora	Consciously created well-being
Pūtake	Beginning source
Rangatira	Leader
Rangi	Melody
Tapu	Being with the potentiality of power; total well-being

Te Ao Māori	The world of Māori
Te Ao Mārama	The world of life, light, and enlightenment; The physical world
Te Ao Wairua	The spiritual world
Te Korekore	The realm of potential being, a cosmic emptiness
Te Rongo	Lasting peace
Te Tiriti o Waitangi	The Māori text of the Treaty of Waitangi signed between Māori and the British Crown in 1840
Te wā	A Māori notion of time that encompasses both a graced moment in time and each stage of that journey
Tika	Ethical or just
Umanga whanaungatanga	Pursuit of communal and collective business ventures
Wairua	Spirit
Whakaaro	Thought, intention
Whakapapa	Genealogy
Whānau	Family units

NOTES

1. Hihiri and its processes reflect an ancient way of thinking that has been seldom investigated in scholarly literature. As we proceed to outline the nature of the ethereal energy of hihiri, it is noted that this is only a small reflection of its potency. Its true spirit is more powerful than the breadth of this chapter and requires careful consideration.

2. These terms are further explained throughout the chapter. Also see Chapter 6: Tapu, Mana, Mauri, Hau, Wairua: A Māori Philosophy of Vitalism and Cosmos.

3. The evocative expression "Melodies Eternally New," penned by Tagore (1912), refers to a little flute, an instrument of the Supreme Being that is perpetually exhausted and yet paradoxically is constantly replenished with fresh life. Hēnare, Middleton, and Puckey (2013) claim this goes to the heart and soul of Māori philosophy, where all things temporal are absorbed in the eternal.

4. "Enaction is the idea that organisms create their own experience through their actions. Organisms are not passive receivers of input from the environment, but are actors in the environment such that what they experience is shaped by how they act" (Hutchins, 2010, as cited by Rocha, 2011, p. 4).

5. As translated by Durie (2003)

REFERENCES

Aldridge, D. (2001). Philosophical speculations on two therapeutic applications of breath. *Subtle Energies & Energy Medicine, 12*(12), 107–124.

Barnhart, R. K. (1988). *The Barnhart dictionary of etymology.* Bronx, NY: H.W. Wilson Co.

Berryman, M., Bateman, S., & Cavanagh, T. (2010). Indigenous knowledge: Traditional responses to contemporary questions. In J. S. Te Rito & S. M. Healy (Eds.), *Traditional knowledge conference 2008. Te tatau pounamu: The greenstone door. Traditional knowledge and gateways to balanced relationships 2008* (pp. 131–141). Auckland, New Zealand: Ngā Pae o te Māramatanga.

Bohm, D. (2003). The qualitative infinity of nature. In L. Nichol (Ed.), *The essential David Bohm* (pp. 9–38). London, England: Routledge.

Bohm, D., & Peat, D. (1987). *Science, order, and creativity.* Toronto, ON: Bantam Books.

Cajete, G. (1994). *Look to the mountain: An ecology of Indigenous education.* Durango, CO: Kivaki Press.

Cajete, G. (2000). *Native science: Natural laws of interdependence.* Santa Fe, NM: Clear Light Publishers.

Coase, R. H. (1937). The nature of the firm. *Economica, New Series, 4*(16), 386–405.

Durie, M. (1999, December). Te Pae Mahutonga: A model for Māori health promotion. *Health Promotion Forum of New Zealand Newsletter, 49,* 7.

Durie, M. (2003). *Ngā kāhui pou: Launching Māori futures.* Wellington, New Zealand: Huia.

Durie, M. (2006, August). *Measuring Māori wellbeing.* Paper presented at the New Zealand Treasury Guest Lecture Series, Wellington, New Zealand.

Harmsworth, G. (2005). *Report on the incorporation of traditional values/tikanga into contemporary Māori business organisation and process.* Palmerston North, New Zealand: Landcare Research.

Hawken, P. (1993). *The ecology of commerce: a declaration of sustainability.* New York, NY: HarperCollins.

Hēnare, M. (1988). *Ngā tikanga me ngā ritenga o te ao* Māori: Standards and foundations of Māori society. Volume 111, Part One, Associated Papers, Report of the Royal Commission on Social Policy. Wellington, New Zealand: Government Printer.

Hēnare, M. (2001). Tapu, mana, mauri, hau, wairua: A Māori philosophy of vitalism and cosmos. In J. Grimm (Ed.), *Indigenous traditions and ecology: The interbeing of cosmology and community* (pp. 197–221). Cambridge, MA: Harvard University Press for the Centre for the Study of World Religions.

Hēnare, M. (2003). *Changing images of nineteenth century Māori society—From tribes to nation.* Unpublished doctoral thesis, Victoria University of Wellington, Wellington, New Zealand.

Hēnare, M. (2011). Lasting peace and the good life: Economic development and the 'te ātanoho' principle of Te Tiriti o Waitangi. In V. M. Tawhai & K. Gray-Sharp (Eds.), *'Always speaking': The Treaty of Waitangi and public policy* (pp. 261–275). Wellington, New Zealand: Huia.

Hēnare, M., & Kernot, B. (1996). The spiritual landscape. In J. Veitch (Ed.), *Can humanity survive? The world's religions and the environment* (pp. 205–215) Auckland, New Zealand: Awareness Book Co.

Hēnare, M., Middleton, A., & Puckey, A. (2013). *He rangi mauroa ao te põ: Melodies eternally new. Ngā rangi-waiata a Te Aho: Ngā waiata o te māramatanga. Songs of Te Aho: Songs on the theme of knowing* (pp. 603). Auckland: Crown Forestry Rental Trust.

Hēnare, M., Petrie, H., & Puckey, A. (2010). *He Whenua Rangatira: Northern tribal landscape overview (Hokianga, Whangaroa, Bay of Islands, Whāngārei, Mahurangi and Gulf Islands).* Auckland, New Zealand: University of Auckland.

Hēnare, M., Puckey, A., Nicholson, A., Dale, M. C., & Vaithianathan. R. (2011). *He ara hou: The pathway forward. Getting it right for Aotearoa New Zealand's Māori and Pasifika children.* Wellington, New Zealand: Every Child Counts.

Hutchins, E. (2010). Enaction, imagination, and insight. In J. R. Stewart, O. Gapenne, E. A. Di Paolo (Eds.), *Enaction: Toward a new paradigm for cognitive science* (pp. 425–450). Cambridge, MA: MIT Press.

Jackson, M. (2008, June). *Restoring the nation: Removing the constancy of terror.* Paper presented at the Traditional Knowledge and Gateways to Balanced Relationships. Te Tatau Pounamu: The Greenstone Door, Auckland, New Zealand.

Jaworski, J. (2011). *Synchronicity: the inner path of leadership.* San Francisco, CA: Berrett-Koehler.

Jaworski, J. (2012). *Source: the inner path of knowledge creation.* San Francisco, CA: Berrett-Koehler.

Jung, C. G. (1955). *The interpretation of nature and the psyche. Synchronicity: an acausal connecting principle.* London, England: Routledge.

Kelly, D., Jackson, B., & Hēnare, M. (2014). 'He āpiti hono, he tātai hono': Ancestral leadership, cyclical learning and the eternal continuity of leadership. In F. Khan, R. Westwood & G. Jack (Eds.), *Core-Periphery Relations and Organisation Studies* (pp. 164–184). Melbourne, Australia: Palgrave Macmillan.

Laszlo, E. (2007). *Science and the Akashic field: an integral theory of everything.* Rochester, VT: Inner Traditions.

Mahuta, R., & Hēnare, M. (1991). The basis for a Maori foreign policy. In R. Kennaway & J. Henderson (Eds.), *Beyond New Zealand II, foreign policy into the 1990s* (pp. 56–66). Auckland, New Zealand: Longman Paul.

Marsden, M. (2003). *The woven universe: Selected writings of Rev Maori Marsden.* Masterton, New Zealand: The estate of Rev. Maori Marsden.

Mataira, P. (2000). *Ngā kai arahi tuitui Māori: Māori entrepreneurship: the articulation of leadership and the dual constituency arrangements associated with Māori enterprise.* Unpublished doctoral thesis, Massey University, Albany, New Zealand.

Merculieff, I. (2012, May 14). *Going to the heart of sustainability: An Indigenous wisdomkeeper's perspective with Ilarion Merculieff.* Cultural Conservancy. Berkeley, California.

General will. (n.d.). Merriam-Webster [online dictionary]. Retrieved from http://www.merriam-webster.com/dictionary/general%20will

Metge, J. (1995). *New growth from old: The whānau in the modern world.* Wellington, New Zealand: Victoria University Press.

Mika, C. (2007). The utterance, the body and the law: Seeking an approach to concretizing the sacredness of Māori language. *Sites: a Journal of Social Anthropology and Cultural Studies, 4*(2), 181–205.

Moon, P. (2003). *Tohunga: Hohepa Kereopa.* Auckland, New Zealand: David Ling.

Moorfield, J. C. (2014). Aro. *Te Aka online Māori dictionary.* Retrieved from http://www.Māoridictionary.co.nz/search?idiom=&phrase=&proverb=&loan=&keywords=aro&search=

Morgan, T. K. K. B. (2006). Decision-support tools and the indigenous paradigm. *Engineering Sustainability, 159*(ES4), 169–177.

New Zealand Institute for Economic Research [NZIER]. (2003). *Māori economic development: Te Ōhanga whanaketanga Māori.* Wellington, New Zealand: Author.

Nicholson, A., Woods, C., & Hēnare, M. (2012). Umanga whanaungatanga: Family business. *Journal of Australian Indigenous issues, Special Issue: Indigenous Entrepreneurship, 15*(4), 36–50.

Parry, G. A. (2006). Native wisdom in a quantum world. *Shift,* 9, 29–33.

Patterson, J. (1992). *Exploring Māori values.* Palmerston North: The Dunmore Press Limited.

Peat, F. D. (1994). *Blackfoot physics: a journey into the Native American universe.* London: Fourth Estate.

Petrie, H. (2006). *Chiefs of industry.* Auckland: Auckland University Press.

Pohatu, T. W. (2010). Takepū: Principled approaches to health. In J. S. Te Rito & S. M. Healy (Eds.), *Traditional knowledge conference 2008. Te tatau pounamu: The greenstone door. Traditional knowledge and gateways to balanced relationship 2008* (pp. 241–247). Aukland: Ngā Pae o te Maramatanga.

Pohatu, T. W. (2011). Mauri: Rethinking human wellbeing. *MAI Review,* 2011(3), 1–12.

Porter, P. (2009). *Four themes of Māori leadership, Te whakaarotanga o ngā whakatōranga o ngā mātua, ngā tūpuna: Capturing the thoughts of the elders.* Auckland, New Zealand: Te Ringa Whero. The Mira Szászy Research Centre, University of Auckland.

Rocha, M. (2011). Cognitive, embodied or enacted? Contemporary perspectives for HCI and interaction. *Transtechnology Research, Reader,* 4, 1–16.

Ruwhiu, D., & Wolfgramm, R. (2006). Kaupapa Māori research: A contribution to critical management studies in New Zealand. In C. Prichard, D. Jones, & R. Jacques (Eds.), *Organization, identity, and locality II conference proceedings. Palmerston north: Department of Management, Massy University* (pp. 51–58).

Salmond, A. (1985). Māori epistemologies. In J. Overing (Ed.), *Reason and morality* (pp. 240–263). London, England: Tavistock.

Salmond, A. (1991). *Two worlds: first meetings between Māori and Europeans, 1642–1772.* Auckland, New Zealand: Viking.

Shirres, M. P. (1997). *Te tangata = the human person.* Auckland, New Zealand: Accent Publications.

Solomon, R. C. (2004). Aristotle, ethics and business organizations. *Organization Studies, 25*(6), 1021–1043.

Spiller, C. (2010). *How Māori cultural tourism businesses create authentic and sustainable well-being.* Unpublished doctoral thesis, The University of Auckland, New Zealand.

Spiller, C., Erakovic, L., Hēnare, M., & Pio, E. (2010). Relational well-being and wealth: Māori businesses and an ethic of care. *Journal of Business Ethics, 104* (2), 223–23.

Spiller, C., Pio, E., Erakovic, L., & Hēnare, M. (2011). Relational well-being and wealth: Māori businesses and an ethic of care. *Journal of Business Ethics, 98*(1), 153–169.

Spiller, C., & Stockdale, M. (2012). Managing and leading from a Māori perspective: Bringing new life and energy to organizations. In J. Neal (Ed.), *Handbook for faith and spirituality in the workplace* (pp. 149–173). New York, NY: Springer.

Swimme, B., & Berry, T. (1992). *The Universe story: From the primordial flaring forth to the ecozoic era—a celebration of the unfolding of the cosmos*. San Francisco, CA: Harper SanFrancisco.

Tagore, R. (1912). *Gitanjali*. New York, NY: Macmillan.

Tagore, R. (1972). *Sadhana: the realisation of life*. Madras, India: Macmillan.

Tate, H. (2010). *Towards some foundations of a systematic Māori theology: He tirohanga anganui ki ētahi kaupapa hohonu mo te whakapono Māori*. Unpublished doctoral thesis, Melbourne College of Divinity, Melbourne, Australia.

Taylor, R. (2007). *Te Ika a Māui, or, New Zealand and its inhabitants: illustrating the origin, manners, customs, mythology, religion, rites, songs, proverbs, fables, and language of the natives; together with the geology, natural history, productions, and climate of the country, its state as regards Christianity, sketches of the principal chiefs, and their present position* [electronic resource]. Wellington, New Zealand: New Zealand Electronic Text Centre. (Original work published in 1855)

Wolfgramm, R. (2007). *Continuity and vitality of worldview(s) in organisational culture: Towards a Māori perspective*. Unpublished doctoral thesis, University of Auckland, New Zealand.

Wolfgramm, R., & Waetford, C. M. R. (2009, July). *Spiritual efficacy and transcendental phenomenology: Accessing the contemplative from a Māori perspective*. Paper presented at the CMS6—The 6th International Critical Management Studies Conference, The University of Warwick, Coventry, England.

Woodard, W. (2008). *Entering the void: Exploring the relationship between the experience of colonisation and the experience of self for Indigenous Peoples of Aotearoa, and the implications for clinical practice*. Unpublished master's thesis, Auckland University of Technology, Aukland, NZ.

CHAPTER 18

INTEGRATING INDIGENOUS SPIRITUALITIES AT WORK

Reflections and Future Directions

Chellie Spiller and Rachel Wolfgramm

I stood on the highest mountain of the world and I knew more than I saw, I under-
stood more than I knew, because I was seeing in a sacred manner. And what I saw
were the hoops of all the nations interlocking in one great cycle.

—Black Elk, as cited in Joseph Campbell, 2003, p. 213

With contributions to this book from Aotearoa New Zealand Māori, Australian Aboriginal, Canadian Aboriginal, Native American, Peruvian Andes,
African, Chinese Taoist, Indian Adivasi, Japanese Shinto and Confucian,
and Western perspectives, settling on key themes without homogenizing
the diversity of those cultures has required that we approach this task with
sensitivity and no small amount of courage.

Upon reflection, an overarching meta-theme encountered across this
collection of works is worldviews. It would appear that this commonality in
thought lends itself to the premise that our worldviews shape our identities,
institutions and ideas of "work." Indigenous elder and scholar Māori Marsden eloquently defines worldview as:

Indigenous Spiritualities at Work, pages 299–320
Copyright © 2015 by Information Age Publishing
All rights of reproduction in any form reserved.

[T]he central systemisation of conceptions of reality to which members of a culture assent and from which stems their value system. Therefore, cultures pattern perceptions of reality into conceptualisations of what reality is perceived to be; of what it is to be regarded as actual, probable, possible or impossible. These conceptualisations form what is termed the 'worldview' of a culture. (Marsden, 2003, p. 56)

Similarly, Alfonso Oritz suggests the term "worldview" denotes a distinctive vision of reality that not only interprets and orders the places and events in the experience of a people, but lends form, direction, and continuity to life (cited in Beck, Walters, & Faransisco, 1990).

In terms of the authors in this book, Huambachano (Chapter 7) likens an Ayni worldview to a cosmological imprint wherein creation is never-ending, Pachamama is Mother and Time, and Anyian spirituality at work reflects this view of the cosmos. Wolfgramm and Waetford (Chapter 15) refer to a Māori worldview as one that accentuates a relational ontology in which the spiritual, human, and natural worlds are interconnected, and Cajete (Chapter 16) refers to the never-ending cycles of creation and dissolution. Hēnare (Chapter 6) discusses the dynamic force of life that is both creative and destructive, and Nicholson, Spiller and Hēnare (Chapter 17) consider a Māori worldview, cosmology, and cosmogony carry the seeds of the fundamental ethics of a people. It is the cosmic whakapapa (layering of relationships) that begins and ends at Te Korekore—the realm of potentiality—tapping into potentiality that lies in Te Korekore. Gladstone (Chapter 2) discusses how Native spirituality is driven by complex cosmological forces connecting people with their universe. Humans are equal, not superior to the universe. This equality includes all things, animate and inanimate, as all things possess both spirit and intelligence.

Viljoen and Laubscher (Chapter 9) describe a holistic African worldview in which humans are "intersubjects," interwoven into a common cosmic identity—rather than individual subjects, or even who we are as a particular intersubjective group—while Bai and Morris (Chapter 3) consider how Taoism developed the Yin-Yang and Five Element Theory. This widely accepted model of the universe provides a rational and sophisticated theory to explain the complicated phenomena existing in the universe and humanity. In this worldview, the fundamental energy "chi," making up everything in the universe, originates from nothing (the void) and eventually returns to nothing. The chi or the energy combines two opposite forces—Yin (the black part, passive force) and Yang (the white part, proactive force), which depend on each other for existence. Within each force there is a seed of its opposite force to enable it to grow into its opposite, which reveals that everything in the universe runs and evolves in a cyclic manner.

In reflecting upon the above, we have created a model, "Star Spiral Dynamics: Dimensions of Indigenous Spiritualities at Work," which captures

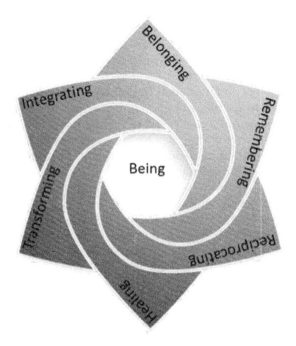

Figure 18.1   Star spiral dynamics: Dimensions of Indigenous spiritualities at work.

main themes we identified rippling through this diverse collection of works. This model (Figure 18.1) acknowledges the symbols presented by the authors in this volume such as: the medicine wheel in Gladstone's Native American chapter (2); the yin/yang symbol in Bai and Morris' Taoist chapter (3); the koru spiral of ethics in Hēnare's Māori chapter (6); the nested circles in Viljoen and Laubscher's African chapter (9), and the concentric circles in Cajete's Native Science chapter (16). Spirals and circular symbols reflect a preference for wholeness and nonlinearity not only in Indigenous worldviews but also across cultures: for example, labyrinths, the rose windows of cathedrals, the whirling dervishes of Sufi dance, and the ancient symbol of the coiled serpent.

We place Being as consciousness at the centre of our star spiral as it offers a center point for orienting spiritual awareness, relationality and connectivity. We conclude our discussion of the dimensions of Indigenous spiritualities at work with transforming, as praxis emerges when sacred energies are mobilized within native consciousness. Sacred energies work in the higher realms of consciousness, which enable deep levels of human perception and intuition to guide the task of living (Cajete, 2000). The star spiral is indicative of a multidimensional dynamic through which sacred energies flow through all dimensions of Indigenous spiritualities at work. The seven dimensions are:

1. Being: refers to being as consciousness, of spiritual awareness, relationality, and connectivity.
2. Belonging: a key dimension of Indigenous spiritualities. Belonging embraces spiritual ideals of interconnectedness and relationality.
3. Remembering: the conscious act of calling our awareness to the collective wisdom of living well that has been developed by humans through the eons in relationship with the world around us. Genealogies and values are two ways in which we can access this collective knowledge to guide the organizational journey in the present and set direction for the future.
4. Reciprocating: bringing balance and creativity together. Reciprocating is the path of reciprocity, mutuality, and interdependence. It recognizes that human well-being depends on living in balance with the world. Creating involves tapping into cosmological, spiritual forces and energies that help humans connect to good purpose, release potential, maintain healthy relationships with the world and each other, and consciously create well-being.
5. Healing: the collective journey towards well-being. Through ceremony, ritual, and many other expressions of spiritual connectedness, Indigenous peoples bring awareness to their spiritual state and call upon spiritual support to heal, purify, and bind.
6. Transforming: a deep belief that humans are co-creators of reality, that they can invoke their reality through their thoughts, words and actions. They seek to align individual will with the greater will found in multiple spiritual sources of power to provide agency to manifest reality.
7. Integrating: refers to the praxis of being and doing, that we come into being in doing, and, as we are doing we are also being. The enfolded practice domains of belonging, remembering, reciprocating, healing, transforming and integrating co-constitute being.

In order to show how this collective wisdom contributes greater understanding of Indigenous spiritualities at work, the following sections discuss each of the dimensions, beginning with being in consciousness. We have noted the author chapters that touch upon the dimensions in significant ways and, where relevant, point to the wider spirituality-at-work literature.

BEING

We opened this book with a touchstone from Rose von Thater Braan Imai, who reminds us about relationality of Being in Consciousness

The universe to which I belong is conscious, animate and interactive.
Time is movement.
An unending shifting of patterns
that appear and disappear in multiple layers of rhythms.
Concepts of a linear and finite time
are superimposed over an innate experience of time.
Space is a chaotic flux that is constantly transforming.
From this view of the world, "relationship" best describes
the core of consciousness.
In this universe, it is relationship to place that lies at the heart of learning, and this is
where we discover the pleasures, obligations, kindnesses
and duties of self in community.

Fry and Kriger (2009) have put forward a "being-centered" model of spiritual leadership that emphasizes that leadership is a relational way of being with others. In native consciousness, we come into being in doing, and, as we are doing we are also being. The inner fulcrum of our enfolded star spiral is a space of being through belonging, remembering, reciprocating, healing, transforming and integrating. It is reflective of a person's inner life in enactment with their outer life—each co-constituting the other. Thus, what the middle ground suggests is not a self-centered, individualistic, and idiosyncratic stance; rather, strength and power are drawn from the collective in relation to each other.

In discussing "being" in Indigenous thought, Hēnare (Chapter 6) comments that "we are spiritual beings and this informs our view of life," while Nicholson, Spiller, and Hēnare (Chapter 17) discuss intentionality, collective purposiveness, and collective will. Kelly and Kelly (Chapter 12) link "being" with mobilization and agency whilst Takeda (Chapter 5) refers to the distinctive characteristic of Buddhist thought, the principle of ku (空) in Mahayana Buddhism, being located in nen sei ki (因縁生起), which means that all things follow the law of coming into existence by depending on cause (in: 因) and condition (en: 縁). Cajete (Chapter 16) refers to "being enspirited," thinking and speaking spiritual realities into being and the "center of spirit" as the essence of the meaning behind the phrase "that place that Indian people talk about."

Understanding the essence of being as consciousness and how this relational, connected consciousness is formed, we now go on to explore the dimension of belonging in Indigenous spiritualties.

BELONGING

A sense of belonging is a defining source of happiness and is central to well-being, meaning, and purpose. This is emphasized in spirituality-at-work literature, alongside the importance of creating a caring community at work for employees to engender a feeling of belonging and feeling valuable (Fry, 2003; Fry & Nisiewicz, 2013).

Gladstone (Chapter 1) points out that Indigenous[1] spirituality is built on a framework of relatedness in a living universe. There is no separation between organic life and inorganic matter: All matter is living and must be respected in the same way that we respect familial relations and treated as equal. This equality includes all things, animate and inanimate, as all things possess both spirit and intelligence. The idea of relatedness is not understood within separate and distinct compartments, as in nuclear family groups; rather, relatedness is a physical and metaphysical connection to everything temporal, spatial, and material.

Thus, belonging to a "place" is more than the physical, measurable, and delimited dimensions associated with a geographic territory. "Place" includes a person and community's spiritual centre, consciousness and mind, their buildings, and the physical environment and ecosystems such as mountains, rivers, lakes, and oceans. Indigenous spiritualities are a sacred geography of a world where all life is revered and is animated by spirit. Belonging cuts right to the heart of Indigenous identity. Unlike the Cartesian split of "I think, therefore I am," the Indigenous view is more akin to "I belong, therefore I am"—or indeed, "I belong therefore I am, and so we become" (Spiller, 2010; Spiller, Erakovic, Henare, & Pio, 2010; Spiller, Pio, Erakovic, & Henare, 2011).

An Indigenous view of belonging also recognizes that humans self-actualize in a journey of co-creation and co-evolution with all other aspects of creation (Cajete, 2000; Royal, 2002; Spiller et al., 2010; Spiller et al., 2011). Belonging extends beyond human social systems to embrace a belonging in the cosmos. Community, then, involves kinship with the cosmos. For example, Takeda (Chapter 5) emphasizes the journey of co-evolution, wherein even a weed or a single tree has Buddha-nature (bussho: 仏性) and attains nirvana. He identifies the similarity between the somoku jyobutsu ron, which observes the Buddhahood in things such as grasses and trees, and the spirituality of Māori, whereby all things in the universe have their own intrinsic spiritual nature.

The "firm" as an extension of community is cast as a corporate entity where work takes place. Whereas workplaces are typically framed as having to induce a workplace culture through processes of indoctrination, training, and reinforcement of norms, expectations, values, and behaviors (Bolman & Deal, 1995; Fry & Nisiewicz , 2013; Schein, 2004), perhaps what distinguishes Indigenous culture at work is the openness and fluidity between work and the cultural context, which includes the spiritual traditions of that cultural worldview.

Fry and Nisiewicz (2013) have argued that "culture often operates at an unconscious level, tends to be taken for granted by organizational members, and is treated as nonnegotiable" (p. 95). While elements of this may be true for Indigenous organizations, overall, culture, which reflects the wider community's culture, is consciously embraced and deeply appreciated.

Indigenous views of belonging and community thus place the firm within a permeable cultural and spiritual context. In other words, where a Western-oriented firm might conceive of a boundary whereby there is an internal community comprised of employees, management, and directors, the Indigenous firm is less bounded in this way. For example, the community/village is the center and context for how to live spiritually, says Cajete (Chapter 16).

It is important for Indigenous businesses to have spaces where they can connect with other businesses that share their cultural and spiritual outlook, which can be challenging when a firm is nested within a dominant worldview that sees business in a particular way. In the context of Australian Aboriginal business community building, Foley (Chapter 11) discusses how Aboriginal Chambers of Commerce can be a place of refuge and assistance in a culturally aware way, providing assistance, a place to share thoughts, promote accomplishments, or receive counsel. Indigenous Chambers of Commerce are a culturally acceptable sanctuary in the volatile business environment that is mostly not culturally hospitable. Henry (Chapter 4) also emphasizes the importance of space and brings physical and metaphysical dimensions together as she explores a marae, a Māori meeting house, as the cultural and spiritual heart of a university. It is in the marae where learning and teaching occur in places and spaces that resonate with heart, mind, and spirit.

To summarize: Belonging is a key dimension of Indigenous spiritualities. Belonging embraces spiritual ideals of interconnectedness and relationality.

REMEMBERING

Indigenous spiritualities embrace the past in a mode of active "remembering the community into being." Ancestral knowledge is a highly prized form of knowledge and an essential medium by which kinship, political, economic, and social ties are cemented and maintained. Therefore, genealogical recital is common across many Indigenous worldviews and denotes a deep belief in ancestral efficacy that refers to the value placed on the power and authority that ancestors hold through what Cajete (Chapter 16) describes as unbroken connections through time as a sacred covenant. Genealogical recital is one process of layering relationships and of remembering that connects people not only to ancestral wisdom but also to sacred places and acknowledges human interconnectedness with all of creation.

This is a core reason for the significant effort discussed by Kelly and Kelly (Chapter 12) in the naming ceremonies of the Stó:lō peoples, in which "wealth is indicated by knowing and claiming genealogical ties." They foreground the importance of witnessing as part of remembering: to remember the past in the present. The witness of the ceremony must pay close attention, but it is not about capturing events on a piece of paper or formal document, photos, or videos that hold and bind the witness to what was learned in the ceremony: It is about people, an oral transmission through the power of the word and deed. Elders are respected as living repositories of cultural treasures and important links in the remembrance chain of life-long obligations between families and communities that is tied to ensuring continuity and protection of oral histories and traditions. It is through the witnesses that the stories of important events are "recorded" and retold. Therefore, in addition to simply watching the ceremony unfold, witnesses must pay close attention so that they can accurately retell what they saw and heard. Viljoen and Laubscher (Chapter 9) also highlight the role of elders and the power of witnessing. Among the Kwazulu/Natal people are the sangomas, who are healers and the keepers of the old ways and repositories of knowledge. Viljoen and Laubscher also refer to the Zulu word *sawubona*, which refers to *seeing* the ancestral reality of a person: "we see you and your ancestors." They say, "seeing in this sense establishes everyone as a witness." Kingi (Chapter 14) draws us to remember future generations through "collectively reconnecting the dots of holistic interdependence."

In terms of remembering, Wolfgramm and Waetford (Chapter 15) highlight that cultural transmission by tohunga (experts in lore) and elders provides continuity over time. They examine how god narratives are actively interpreted and animated by elders. They detail how these narratives, as cultural and spiritual resources, provide symbolic leadership and cultural continuity; enhance spiritual efficacy; increase motivation, citizenship, and productivity in organization activity; and provide evidence of how the use of god narratives highlights the enduring nature of spirituality at work.

To be a member of community is also an ongoing process of coming into one's membership; it is literally to re-member. It is not a passive recalling of the past in a sentimental way; rather, it is an active energizing of connectedness and wisdom in the present. That said, nostalgia means to experience pain at the thought of home, and for many Indigenous peoples there is pain in the remembering of a home, and by that we mean all that one belongs to as described in the section above having been ripped asunder by the processes of colonization. Cajete (Chapter 16) suggests, "Indigenous peoples are entrusted with an important package of memory, feeling, and relationship to land which is a sacred covenant.... We must remember to remember: who we are, where we are from, and spirits we share with all of creation." Community is an extension of our collective minds and memory, say Nicholson, Spiller, and Hēnare (Chapter 17), referring to the collective will of the community that endows a firm with special purpose for past, present, and future communities.

In connecting to genealogy and ancestral traditions, communities, including work communities, are tapping into the wider value systems of the cultural worldview. Values are like potent seeds that carry the blueprint of the cosmological worldview of a community of people, seeds that are germinated in practice. Through values, the peoples of today remember the wisdom passed down from ancestors about how to live in relational well-being with the world and each other. The values of the community are a spiritually grounded system that permeates Indigenous workplaces.

There is a vast body of work that emphasizes the importance of values at work and in building a cohesive, purpose-oriented organizational culture (Bolman & Deal, 1995; Collins & Porras, 1994; Fry & Nisiewicz, 2013; Kriger & Hanson, 1999). In terms of spirituality at work, Kriger and Hanson (1999) propose a set of values—honesty, truthfulness, trust, humility, forgiveness, compassion, thankfulness, being of service, and stillness. They argue that these values are necessary for both economic and spiritual principles to thrive and grow in modern organizations.

What is clear from the chapters in this volume is the importance of *value systems*, not isolated values. Ancient value systems are treated as treasures to guide good living in all contexts, including our current time with its various pressures, such as the fast pace of technology, globalization, climate change, population growth, and resource constraints. Many of the value systems described in this book reflect a collective intention to engender reciprocity, create and maintain balance, support interconnectedness and relationships, and cultivate a stewardship ethic.

Viljoen and Laubscher (Chapter 9) map the African concept of Ubuntu, describing it as a generous philosophy glossed as "humanness" yet that cuts to the core of the very essence of being human. It is a process that "lures and enables human beings to become abantu or humanized beings, living in daily self-expressive works of love and efforts to create harmonious relationships in the community and the world beyond." They argue that ubuntu is key to all African values and involves collective personhood and collective morality.

Bai and Morris (Chapter 3) examine the ancient wisdom encapsulated in the Tao-oriented Confucian value system. They cite the ways in which this value system has been successfully deployed in Chinese traditional medicine, Chinese martial arts, Mao Zedong's military strategy, and Deng Xiaoping's economic policy of reform and suggest the time is long overdue for its application in management and workplace. Likewise, Takeda (Chapter 5) has drilled through layers of philosophy to unearth ancient principles that have informed the strata of Japanese society and workplaces. He offers the example of how Kazuo Inamori, the founder of Kyocera Corporation, KDDI and the former CEO of Japan Airlines, has influenced management philosophy in the organizations he has headed, as well as through his private management school, Seiwajyuku (盛和塾), where more than 8,000 business owners and entrepreneurs from around the world have learned his values-led philosophy can help enterprises prosper.

Critically examining approaches to evaluation systems is taken up by Wolfgramm, (Chapter 13) she takes issue with modern evaluation systems by "experts" that draw upon measurement tools and instruments that don't support or advance Indigenous ideas of good living. She highlights that "evaluation" is not value-free and argues for a "co-created and cohesive system founded within Indigenous value systems," citing Pacific and Māori examples to develop her case. What constitutes wealth, success, and the good life, and how we evaluate what matters, is a conversation taken up by a number of the authors. Cajete (Chapter 16) argues that material economic indicators as the sole measure of progress is a distortion, and he highlights how deeper-level indicators are rarely researched or taken seriously. Similarly, Wolfgramm (Chapter 13) explores culturally and spiritually embedded evaluation systems that truly reflect collective aspirations and what it means to be a well society.

To summarize: Remembering at work is the conscious act of calling our awareness to the collective wisdom of living well that has been developed by humans through the eons in relationship with the world around us. Genealogies and value systems are two ways in which we can access this collective knowledge to guide the organizational journey in the present and set directions for the future.

RECIPROCATING

To live is to breathe. To breathe is essential to animate life and is a form of energy exchange. In Indigenous spiritualities, this is honored in many different rituals, and the authors in this collection speak to a relational worldview in which reciprocity is central to work and economies. Cajete (Chapter 16) also makes reference to living energy and sees breath as the most tangible expression of spirit in all living things, and Hēnare (Chapter 6) talks of the vitalistic languages as expressive of life forces, metaphysics, and cosmic energy. Wolfgramm (Chapter 13) makes links between sounds and thought in her *hakamana* evaluation model, drawing on the sounds of Polynesian language to communicate relationship, creativity, and potentiality.

Kelly and Kelly (Chapter 12) refer to the Salish economic philosophy of gifting, expressed in Stl'e'áleq, or "potlatch" traditions. They discuss how Stl'e'áleq are shaped by an ethic of reciprocity committed to strengthening and enhancing relationships between people. Importantly, they consider how the gift economy shapes an integrated system of spiritual, social, symbolic, and practical exchanges that has enabled the Stó:lō Coast Salish peoples to grow, prosper, and thrive for thousands of years. They offer a case study of BC Hydro and hosting potlatch and how the ancient practices of reciprocity and exchange can establish the foundation for long-term relationships between parties, enabling them to find mutually beneficial resolutions.

Huambachano (Chapter 7) explores Suma Kuasay, the 'good living' principles of an Ayni worldview, which values equilibrium, described as the proportion and harmony with cosmos, Pachamama Earth Mother, and community. Hēnare (Chapter 6) refers to land and environment as gifts with which come the responsibility of guardianship. Criteria for guardianship include reverence for the whole of creation; kinship; viewing resources as sacred gifts; assuming responsibility as stewards/guardians of these gifts; economic ethics of reciprocity; and commitment to safeguard 'resources' for future generations. Bai and Morris' (Chapter 3) discusses the balancing of Yin and Yang forces—which calls for conscious engagement with the dialectical challenge of creating balance and harmony. Nicholson, Spiller and Hēnare (Chapter 17) also discuss energies and how the breath (Te Ha) has many forms, from the physical that connects all living things to its expression of spirit carried via dance, music, genealogical recitals, and word. Language such as karanga and karakia (prayer) are manifestations of thought and feeling and have the power to affect will and express intention.

Another aspect of reciprocating is creativity. Ellmann (2001, p. 48) has argued that "spirituality has the explosive power to awaken us to unique and deeply creative work, affirming purpose and meaning beyond the paycheck." The power of work as a creative endeavor permeates the chapters in this collection, which describe how humans are endowed with spiritual agency to connect to the creative energies in the cosmos to support, nourish, and shape the collective journey. From an Indigenous standpoint, everything in creation is made of energy (Bohm & Peat, 1987; Cajete, 2000; Peat, 1994), and these energies are a key in awakening potentiality.

Nicholson, Spiller, and Hēnare (Chapter 17) suggest that the subtle power of human creativity and consciousness includes the ability to influence and transform energies. They describe the energy of Hihiri, a pure energy that is part of an interlocking spiral of spiritual and cognitive rhythmic forces. Hihiri can facilitate the realization of intention and collective will, which are seen as sources of power that bind, energize, and legitimize Indigenous business enterprise in a spiritual covenant with the wider community. Gladstone (Chapter 2) also points to the cosmological forces at work in Indigenous spiritualities, forces that connect people and the universe, as do Bai and Morris (Chapter 3), who discuss the reciprocity of Yin and Yang in Taoist philosophy.

To summarize: Reciprocating is about restoring harmony and balance in a way that reflects mutuality and interdependence. Reciprocating recognizes that human well-being depends on living in balance with the world. Creating involves tapping into cosmological, spiritual forces and energies that help humans connect to good purpose, release potential, maintain healthy relationships with the world and each other, and consciously create well-being.

HEALING

Enfolded into the dynamic star spiral of Indigenous spiritualities are the ceremonies, rituals, chants, and healing processes that connect people to their shared journey towards individual and collective well-being. Cajete (Chapter 16) and Hēnare (Chapter 6) discuss spiritual tools such as questing, sweat lodges, ceremony, ritual, song and dance, and art forms. In many circumstances these tools cleanse, purify, honor, and focus collective attention on the spiritual life. Viljoen and Laubscher (Chapter 9) explain how drumming is not only deeply integrated as part of African identity, but it also brings people into the spiritual domain. These tools offer ways of healing in community and celebrating life together.

Takeda (Chapter 5) highlights that a central aspect of Shinto is purification, whereby community members purify both mind and body when they participate in matsuri, festivals. The purified mind is called seimeishin (清明心) and is the unselfish mind, which can be read by other community members. By contrast, the selfish mind cannot be read by others and is thus considered to stand against the emotionally-knit spiritual community. Gladstone's (Chapter 2) discussion of the Native American medicine wheel presents a holistic integrative approach for understanding and achieving physical, mental, emotional, and spiritual wellness.

As with reciprocity, breath and word are important dimensions of purification and healing. Breath connects humans to all living things; each aspect of creation is breathing in what others breathe out: plants, animals, rocks—all are interlinked through breath. Breath is also expressed in many ways—it is released in particular ways through dance, music, recitals (see Cajete, Chapter 16; Nicholson, Spiller & Hēnare, Chapter 17). The power of the word is also highlighted, through prayers, invocations, and storytelling (see Gladstone, ch. 3; Nicholson, Spiller & Hēnare, ch. 17; Viljoen and Laubscher, ch. 9) that purify our thoughts and call us to act with the highest of intentions.

Some of the chapters are reminders of the spiritual distress that Indigenous communities have endured through colonization. These chapters speak to the pain that comes through being torn from the spiritual home of the land, of a way of life that goes to the heart of identity, and how to live with cultural continuity of purpose and meaning. Ceremony and other cultural and spiritual protocols are testimony to a shared worldview of a community moving through the world with shared spiritual distress, a collective dark night of the soul. Hēnare (Chapter 6) talks about mourning what has been lost, and the collective trauma carried through time: "the tangi—the weeping that flows from remnants of land in which resides the wounded soul handed down by ancestors. Such tangi is not for immediate material loss but for lost potential and diminution of spiritual and cultural identity."

Kelly and Kelly (Chapter 12) highlight the spiritual distress and trauma bought about by the potlatch ban, which involved the raiding of longhouses where potlatches were held, seizing material and ceremonial objects, and mass arrests for those successful enough to reach the hosting stage. In order to ensure that the European system of exchange would replace the Stó:lō economy as it functioned through Stl'e'áleq, the potlatch ban was an effective means of colonial control. Although the potlatch ban was lifted in 1951, the dominance of the global market economy and the prolonged interruption to strategic alliances and ancient exchange relationships have taken a huge toll on Stó:lō communities, including thwarting their own agency and self-determination, all of which has had long-term impacts on individual and collective identities.

Foley (Chapter 11) opens his chapter with a deeply moving poem and personal story that speaks to the spiritual distress of having identity stripped away by dominant notions of defining people, including their businesses, through measurement systems that do not reflect a cultural worldview. Riddiford (Chapter 8) discusses the "fault lines" and deeper "seismic shifts" as she comes to terms with her own sense of identity and belonging as a Pākehā, a New Zealander of European descent. With regards to the Adivasis of India, Pio (Chapter 10) notes the wounding that has been inflicted upon the Adivasis by "high-caste money lenders, corporate land users, social prejudice, and often toothless law implementers."

To summarize: Healing speaks to the collective journey towards wellbeing. Through ceremony, ritual, and many other expressions of spiritual connectedness, Indigenous peoples bring awareness to their spiritual state and call upon spiritual support to heal, purify, and bind.

TRANSFORMING

There is a deep belief in transformation that ripples throughout the chapters and points to conviction in the power of humans to tap into sources of power to effect these transformations and co-create realities. Rather than being passive recipients, humans align their will power to transform reality and call upon multiple sources of power to do so. God, Creator, Supreme

Being, gods of different domains, the spirits, ancestors, energies and forces, collective will of communities past, present and future—these are all sources of power to which humans can align their will and achieve a higher purpose. Pio (Chapter 10) illuminates how the Adivasis are karma-makers or destiny-makers, which she argues situates organizations as sites of hope and relational possibility. People create their karma and destiny, which she explains is "composed of agency or a sense of will power and way power or pathways to generate successful plans and alternatives irrespective of obstacles, to reach one's goals." Viljoen and Laubscher (Chapter 9) explore the notion of magic in African societies as an intention to tap into foresight and knowing. Like Pio, they highlight the power humans have to forge their own destiny. In a similar vein, Wolfgramm and Waetford (Chapter 15) highlight the notion of Matakite as a vision that calls in and captures spirit and powerful energies. Matakite visions for organizations are aspirational and accept no particular limits on what people want to achieve. The horizon is unknown and unbounded.

Nicholson, Spiller, and Hēnare (Chapter 17) suggest that when the energies and wills of people in an organization are sufficiently aligned, and people cohere around a clear intention, an enterprise gains powerful impetus to manifest its common good purpose of consciously created well-being for positive effect. Tapping into collective potentiality can create coalescences and alignments that ignite what is referred to as synchronistic events. Synchronicity is viewed as the coherence of spirit, intention, and will that brings reality into being. Creating the conditions for synchronicity requires cultivating collective will. Therefore, a firm that cultivates shared will among the people in the organization and community becomes in sync with its purpose to create multidimensional well-being.

Fry and Nisiewicz (2013) discuss the importance of being called to a vocation that gives a sense of meaning and of making a difference to others. They particularly explore how "professionals" possess the following characteristics:

> [E]thics centered on selfless service to clients/customers, an obligation to maintain quality standards within the profession, a commitment to their vocational field, a dedication to their work, and a strong commitment to their careers. They believe their chosen profession is valuable, even essential to society, and they are proud to be a member of it. (p. 45)

Similarly, in Indigenous approaches, "calling" includes being of service to others, of making a difference to the community and ecology, being oriented to values, and seeing work as an opportunity to contribute to the greater whole. However, there is another dimension to calling that is not so explicitly captured by wider explanations of spirituality at work. This dimension conceives of calling as actively calling reality into being, a deep belief in humans as transformative agents.

Discussions that center on the degradations of colonization often focus on the structural and institutional barriers and spiritual distress that Indigenous peoples have had to contend with. In spite of such challenges, we note that authors in this volume highlight inspirational ways in which Indigenous peoples are overcoming boundaries and transforming to adapt to contemporary times. Such resilience in the face of adversity is a remarkable story of fortitude and survival as Indigenous peoples have been able to adapt while also retaining and sustaining unique identities and cultures. This requires multidimensional agency, which is discussed in the next section on integrating praxis.

To summarize: Transforming is a deep belief that humans are co-creators of reality, that they can invoke their reality through their thoughts, words, and actions. They seek to align individual will with the greater will found in multiple spiritual sources of power to provide agency to manifest reality.

INTEGRATING

The integrative power of praxis is a central theme across all chapters. Praxis requires agency, which we view as an interactive process of reflexive transformation and relational pragmatics, a temporally embedded process of social engagement, informed by the past, oriented towards the future and enacted in the present (Emirbayer & Mische, 1998).

It is no surprise to find Indigenous spiritualities at work as, according to Professor Vine Deloria (Standing Rock Sioux Tribe), religion as a distinct and separate activity of life does not exist for most Indigenous peoples. They are highly empirical people, deriving understanding of life from their experiences and the traditions of previous experiences. Indigenous peoples formulate a general perspective on the rhythms of the natural world and derive practical principles to serve as guidelines for their endeavors and behavior (Deloria, 2005, p. 552). Similarly, Māori religion is a belief in spiritual beings and a way and view of life which is found in rituals, ceremonies, sacred places; art forms; song and dance; proverbs; riddles; the naming of people and places; myth and legends; and customs. All cultural resources are imbued with spirituality or wairua.

There are multiple spiritual sources that endow agency—not merely individual will, but shared collective will also. Tapping into the wisdom of the ancestors, of the gods, of the intelligence in our world and the cosmos brings human agency into alignment with the greater whole. In this way, Indigenous peoples are agentic in a spiritual sense. This conceptualization of agency enables a deeper exploration of the multiple sources of agency in being from the perspective of Indigenous spiritualities. For example, it allows Indigenous peoples to be seen as living simultaneously in the past, present, and future, adjusting temporalities of their real-life existence and circumstances in imaginative and reflexive ways. In doing so, they can engage in repertoires from the past, project pathways forward in time, and adjust their actions to the demands and constraints of contextual circumstances (Emirbayer & Mishe, 1998).

In terms of praxis, many authors discussed the notion of *collective expressions of ethics, good living, well-being.* For example, Henry (Chapter 4) discusses the notion of practical wisdom in the context of marae, while Huambachano (Chapter 7) explores a pragmatic application of ancient wisdom in relation to the Suma Kuasay "good living" principles of Ayni. Gladstone (Chapter 2) and Cajete (Chapter 16) describe Native science as an earth-based phenomenological practice objectively explaining the world through knowledge gained via a lived subjective experience. This pragmatic view of native science explains a way for people to interact with their world (Cajete, 2000).

Native praxis and integrating doing and being is also demonstrated by Foley (Chapter 11), who talks from the heart about Caribberre, which in his mother's language means "dancing." Metaphorically we now dance a new way, the dance of the "Australian Aboriginal entrepreneur," a dance that is "business enterprise." In the words of one of his participants, "We have a story to tell, we come from the dreaming, we got to keep dreaming and we got to dream good. It's who we are and what we do that makes us an Aboriginal business, not a percentage of ownership."

Gladstone (Chapter 2) references the pragmatist maxim as helpful for seeing place as a way of understanding what is, but place is only one aspect of this understanding. People and societies are not static; they continuously move in both place and time. This movement creates experience through interaction and shapes our conceptions about the world. Gladstone highlights how Native American oral traditions, such as Napi and other trickster stories, are a process for people to listen to experiences from which they can make their own inferences about the world around them. Linking praxis to the dynamics of spiritual leadership and transformation, Bai and Morris (Chapter 3) note how the philosophy of Tao-oriented Confucianism highlights virtue-dominating approaches in the process of leaders making and implementing strategies. In addition, by following the dialectic nature of the major driving forces in an organization, the Tao-oriented Confucian models of strategy-making reveal the subtle and dynamic relationships of depending, conflicting and transforming in all the forces. Pio (Chapter 10) lists seven things organizations can do to integrate Adivasi life energies in their workplaces while Riddiford (Chapter 8) suggests that being Indigenous to the cosmos is a generative foundation for participative and ethics leadership.

Returning to our starting place of the enfolded star spiral we have, we hope, illuminated that Indigenous peoples prefer process to progress; the interwoven and circular to the separated and linear; to hold ambiguity, mystery, and complexity and not search for one truth and certainty.

CONCLUSION

Critical views of spirituality at work draw attention to the normative and institutionalized burdens that expressions of spirituality might have upon others. Boje (2000) contends that one person's spirituality is just as likely to be another's iron cage. Attempts to engage in spiritually meaningful activity in the workplace may garner mixed views from members of the organization; some would view it as a source of inspiration and others as an imposition. White (2003) contends that when spiritual beliefs develop into actual behavior, conflicts in the workplace arise. At its extreme, organizations become institutionalized spiritual prisons, particularly if normative-based modes of behavior are imposed on all members of the organization. Case and Gosling (2007) argue that there are indications that scholarship in the field of spirituality at work is becoming narrow, with a utilitarian focus and instrumental intent. Universalizing tendencies have been noted by Biberman and Whitty (2003), who highlight that an underlying desire to proselytize, evangelize, and dictate dogma will present an ongoing challenge in scholarly-based spirituality discourse. Bell and Taylor (2003) maintain that advocates of workplace spirituality who promote the notion that work provides a primary context in which spiritual growth and the search for meaning is located are fueling an obsession to find meaning at work.

Rather than clarifying workplace meaning, partial embraces of quasi-religious type organizational cultural systems mystify the experience of work. Reflecting a type of cultural logic of late capitalism, some commentators suggest that consumption of spirituality is now fragmented; it is "a la carte," "eclectic," and somewhat "kleptomaniac" (Jameson, 1991; Possami, 2003). Postmodern critiques argue that it is becoming apparent that trends in patterns of individual consumption of spirituality reflect a form of eclectic private symbolism in which individuals manipulate existing symbols, practices, and rituals to create their own subjective experiences of the sacred (Pargament, 1997; Zinnbauer, Pargament, & Scott, 1999). These critiques of spirituality at work draw our attention to words such as norms, institutionalization, conflict, utilitarianism (the greater good), universalizing, proselytizing, dogmatic, obsessive, quasi, kleptomania, manipulative, consumeristic, and an imposition (Wolfgramm & Waetford, 2009).

To these critiques, Indigenous concerns would add co-option of Indigenous spiritualities by others outside of the culture; co-option by other spiritual movements such as "New Age" types; romanticzising of the past; nostalgia; reification of the dynamic cultures of Indigenous peoples; homogenization of the incredible diversity in Indigenous worlds into a reduced view of their spiritualities; and idealizing Indigenous approaches. Perhaps some of these concerns can be leveled at this book as well, especially as we have drawn together just a few voices from the academic business arena, which is infinitesimally small compared to the vast array of possible voices that speak and live their Indigenous spiritualities.

While mindful of the critiques, we believe our diagram of the dynamic star spiral with its arms that speak to enacting our spiritual being-ness is a modest start to capturing what Indigenous spiritualities at work look like, feel like, and do. The center point of being and its surrounding six arms of belonging, remembering, reciprocating, healing, transforming and integrating provide latitude for the diversity of ways in which spirituality in Indigenous worlds, including work, are expressed. The workplace is part of the cultural and spiritual inseparable whole—it is not an independent space, although it has a particular commercial agenda. In all societies there are different spheres of expertise: government, community, work, business, home, education; and in Indigenous worlds these spheres are fractals of the whole, not atomized compartments. Therefore, a key challenge for contemporary business is the need to disempower the dominant business paradigm and empower spiritual and cultural dimensions of spiritualities at work for positive effect.

FUTURE DIRECTIONS

This book on Indigenous spiritualities at work has opened up many new and exciting directions for future exploration. We discuss two such directions in the final part of this chapter.

Identities at work: Indigenous Spiritualities' Perspectives

Acknowledging the multidimensional nature of identities sits at the heart of this collection of works on Indigenous spiritualties and merits deeper examination. That is especially so given that cultural approaches view identities as being shaped by worldviews, beliefs and values that are reinforced in group membership through rituals and ceremonies. Critical approaches hold that the self is formed in reference to larger social contexts such as histories, politics, and public and socioeconomic discourse. Identities as narratives are viewed as co-created expressions of self, crafted through multiple communicative media. Identities studies also center on "the practices and strategies by which people construct and negotiate professional, work and organization-based identities" (Brown, 2014, p. 8) and an emerging consensus that "*identity* refers to the meanings that individuals attach reflexively to themselves, developed and sustained through processes of social interaction as they seek to address the question 'who am I?'" (Brown, 2014, p. 9, emphasis in original). Yet central questions that seem to hold true in Indigenous notions of identities are Who am I? Where do I come from? Whom do I share with and where do I belong? However, the self also seeks to know the context within which identities emerge with the additional questions: Who are we? Where do we come from, whom do we share with, and where do we belong?

In relation to Indigenous identities, according to Weaver (2001), it is a complex and controversial topic with little agreement on what constitutes Indigenous identity, how to measure it and who truly has it. Indigenous identity is often a combination of race, class, education, religion, tribe, and gender and is a composite of self-identification, community identification, and external identification (Weaver, 2001). This in part is reinforced by a UN framework for Indigenous peoples that includes self-identification as Indigenous peoples at the individual level and being accepted *by* the community as a member *of* the community; historical continuity with precolonial and/or pre-settler societies; a strong link to territories and surrounding natural resources; distinct social, economic, or political systems; distinct language, culture, and beliefs; forming nondominant groups of society; and a resolve to maintain and reproduce their ancestral environments and systems as distinctive peoples and communities.

While we acknowledge different ways of understanding identities, we hold open the dynamic of identities while recognizing it is a central facet of Indigenous spiritualities, one that merits further exploration.

Trans-Ecological Leadership: Indigenous Spiritualities at Work

Trans-ecological leadership research investigates a relational ontology (a way of being and doing leadership that explicitly makes reference to the natural world) and is still a largely untapped field (Wolfgramm, Flynn-Coleman, & Conroy, 2013). Yet, in Native science and wisdom traditions of leadership, heuristic narratives linked through the process of the layering of relationships to cosmological communities are purposively designed to connect humans with the natural world. In such wisdom traditions, leadership manifest in rituals, ceremonies, narratives, and symbols elucidates the continued relevance of animating and reinterpreting cultural resources for the times. Hence, the collection of works offered in this book has elucidated the relevance of Indigenous spiritualities at work in a wide examination of trans-ecological leadership. Identities at work and trans-ecological leadership provide two challenging and exciting future research directions that have emerged from this ground-breaking series.

In conclusion, the authors in this book have shown how cultural and spiritual well-being is drawn from the relational values, philosophies, stories, ceremonies, rituals, prayers, incantations, and many other facets of beliefs and praxis.

Most markedly, Indigenous spiritualities consciously connect with the cosmos, reflect an abiding love of the spiritual intelligence that is abundant in the world, and manifest in all creatures and parts of creation from rocks and fungi to mountains and small critters and that we share our life-force with. The world is alive and is not a static, lifeless canvas that humans are mandated to exploit without regard to reciprocity and balance. Many traditions speak of a co-evolution—that we humans are coming into being with all others and are not superior; rather, we must humble ourselves and act as stewards. There is a respect for tradition as living through us, not in a reified nostalgic sense, but that humans are part of the human journey through time—and we both inherit wisdom and spiritual guidance from our ancestors and bequeath it as people who will one day become ancestors for others.

> *E te atua, me nga atua o tenei ao, (to heavenly ancestors of our worlds)*
> *Manakiitia mai a matau, a tatau (bless us)*
> *Whangai me matou wairua (and bind us together in spirit)*
> *i te ara, o te ora, ake ake ake (on our journeys of life...forever...)*

NOTE

1. Gladstone prefers to use the word Native, and explains this in his chapter. For ease of reading and meaning we have used Indigenous in our chapter.

REFERENCES

Beck, P. A., Walters, L., & Faransisco, N. (1990). *The sacred ways of knowledge, sources of life.* Tsaile, AZ: Navajo Community College Press, Arizona and Northland Publishing.

Bell, E., & Taylor, S. (2003). The elevation of work: Pastoral power and the new age work ethic. *Organization, 10,* pp. 329–349.

Biberman, J., & Whitty, M. D. (Eds.). (2003). *Work and spirit: A reader of new spiritual paradigms for organizations.* Scranton, PA: The University of Scranton Press.

Bohm, D., & Peat, D. (1987). *Science, order, and creativity.* Toronto, ON: Bantam Books.

Boje, D. (2000, July 4–July12). *Post-spiritual capitalism in organizational studies.* Paper presented at the 2000 SCOS Conference. Athens, Greece.

Bolman, L. G., & Deal, T. E. (1995). *Leading with soul: An uncommon journey of spirit.* San Francisco, CA: Jossey-Bass Publishers.

Brown, A. D. (2014). Identities and identity work in organisations. *International Journal of Management Reviews.* DOI: 10.1111/ijmr.12035

Cajete, G. (2000). *Native science, natural laws of interdependence.* Sante Fe, NM: Clear Light.

Campbell, J. (2003). *The hero's journey: Joseph Campbell on his life and work.* Novato, CA: New World Library.

Case, P., & Gosling, J. (2007, July). *Signs of the Spirit: Critical reflections on the instrumentality of workplace spirituality.* Paper presented at the Standing Conference on Organisation Symbolism, Ljubljana, Slovenia.

Collins, J. C., & Porras, J. I. (1994). *Built to last: Successful habits of visionary companies.* New York, NY: Harper Business.

Deloria, Jr., V. (2005). Indigenous peoples. In W. Schweiker (Ed.), The Blackwell companion to religious ethics (pp. 552–560). New York, NY: Blackwell Publishing.

Ellmann, L. B. (2001). Tending to spirituality in the workplace. *Presence, 7*(2), 46–53.

Emirbayer, M., & Mische, A. (1998). What is agency? *The American Journal of Sociology, 103*(4), 962–1023.

Fry, L. W. (2003). Toward a theory of spiritual leadership. *The Leadership Quarterly.* 14, 693–727.

Fry, L., & Kriger, M. (2009). Towards a theory of being-centred leadership: Multiple levels of being as context for effective leadership. *Human Relations, 62*(11), 1667–1696.

Fry, L. W., & Nisiewicz, M. S. (2013). *Maximizing the triple bottom line through spiritual leadership.* Redwood City, CA: Stanford University Press.

Jameson, F. (1991). *Postmodernism, or the cultural logic of late capitalism.* Durham, NC: Duke University Press.

Kriger, M. P., & Hanson, B. J. (1999). A value-based paradigm for creating truly healthy organizations. *Journal of Organizational Change Management, 12*(4), 302–317. doi:10.1108/09534819910282144

Marsden, M. (2003). *The woven universe: Selected writings of Rev. Māori Marsden.* Otaki, New Zealand: Estate of Rev. Māori Marsden.

Pargament, K. I. (1997). *The psychology of religion and coping.* New York, NY: Guildford Press.

Peat, F. D. (1994). *Blackfoot physics: A journey into the Native American universe.* London, England: Fourth Estate.

Possami, A. (2003). Alternative spiritualities and the cultural logic of late capitalism. *Culture and Religion, 4*(1), 31–45.

Royal, T. A. C. (2002, February 21). *Indigenous worldviews: A comparative study.* Report for Ngāti Kikopiri, Te Wānanga-o-Raukawa, Te Puni Kō kiri. Fulbright, New Zealand, Winston Churchill Memorial Trust.

Schein, E. H. (2004). *Organizational culture and leadership* (3rd ed.). San Francisco, CA: Jossey-Bass.

Spiller, C. (2010). *How Māori cultural tourism businesses create authentic and sustainable well-being*. Unpublished doctoral thesis, University of Auckland, Auckland, New Zealand.

Spiller, C., Erakovic, L., Henare, M., & Pio, E. (2010). Relational well-being and wealth: Māori business and an ethic of care. *Journal of Business Ethics, 98*(1), 153–169. doi: 10.1007/s10551-010-0540-z

Spiller, C., Pio, E., Erakovic, L., & Henare, M. (2011). Wise up: Creating organizational wisdom through an ethic of kaitiakitanga, *Journal of Business Ethics, 104*(2), 223–235.

Weaver, H. N. (2001). Indigenous identity, what is it and who really has it? *American Indian Quarterly, 25*, 240–255.

White, R. D. Jr. (2003). Drawing the line: Religion and spirituality in the workplace. In R. A. Giacalone & C. Jurkiewicz (Eds.), Handbook of workplace spirituality and organizational performance (pp. 185–195). New York, NY: M. E. Sharpe.

Wolfgramm, R., Flynn-Coleman, S., & Conroy, D. (2013). Dynamic Interactions of Agency in Leadership (DIAL): An integrative framework for analyzing agency in sustainability leadership. *Journal of Business Ethics*, 1–14. DOI: 10.1007/s10551-013-1977-7

Wolfgramm, R., & Waetford, C. (2009, July). *Accessing the contemplative: A Māori perspective*. Paper presented at the Critical Management Studies Conference, Warwick University, United Kingdom.

Zinnbauer, B. J., Pargament, K. I., & Scott, A. B. (1999). The emerging meanings of religiousness and spirituality: Problems and prospects. *Journal of Personality, 67*(6), 889–919.

ABOUT THE CONTRIBUTORS

Associate Professor Gregory Cajete is a Native American educator whose work is dedicated to honoring the foundations of Indigenous knowledge in education. Dr. Cajete is a Tewa Indian from Santa Clara Pueblo, New Mexico. He has served as a New Mexico humanities scholar in the ethno botany of Northern New Mexico and as a member of the New Mexico Arts Commission. In addition, he has lectured at colleges and universities in the U.S., Canada, Mexico, New Zealand, England, Italy, Japan, and Russia.

Dr. Cajete is Director of Native American Studies and an associate professor in the division of language, literacy and sociocultural studies in the College of Education at the University of New Mexico. Dr. Cajete earned his Bachelor of Arts degree from New Mexico Highlands University with majors in both biology and sociology and a minor in secondary education. Dr. Cajete has received several fellowships and academic distinctions, including the American Indian Graduate Fellowship from the US-DOE Office of Indian Education (1977–1978); the D'Arcy McNickle Fellowship in American Indian History from the Newberry Library, Chicago, IL (1984–1985); and the Katrin Lamon Fellowship in American Indian Art and Education (1985–1986) from the School of American Research in Santa Fe, New Mexico.

Dr. Cajete has authored five books: *Look to the Mountain: An Ecology of Indigenous Education* (Kivaki Press, 1994); *Ignite the Sparkle: An Indigenous Science Education Curriculum Model* (Kivaki Press, 1999); *Spirit of the Game: An Indigenous Wellspring* (Kivaki Press, 2004); *A People's Ecology: Explorations in Sustainable Living* (Clearlight Publishers, 1999), and *Native Science: Natural Laws of Interdependence* (Clearlight Publishers, 2000).

Indigenous Spiritualities at Work, pages 321–330
Copyright © 2015 by Information Age Publishing
All rights of reproduction in any form reserved.

Dr. Dennis Foley is an Indigenous research professor in the School of Humanities and Social Sciences at the University of Newcastle, NSW, Australia. His research and publications cross the research areas of Aboriginal literature, history, education, cultural studies, business management, and tourism to Aboriginal leadership. His principal areas of research and interest, however, are within Aboriginal enterprise and entrepreneurship and the field of Aboriginal pedagogies and epistemology. Dennis identifies as Aboriginal, his mother being of Gai-mariagal descent from the Northern suburbs of Sydney. His father is also of Aboriginal descent. A student relatively late in life, his accolades include several prestigious research grants and appointments to government advisory boards in addition to being a Fulbright Scholar and a double Endeavour Fellow, researching with Aboriginal colleagues in America, Aotearoa, Canada, and Ireland as well as urban, rural, and remote Australia.

Professor Louis W. (Jody) Fry, Texas A & M University–Central Texas is the coordinator of their MS management and leadership program. Jody has consulted with both public and private organizations and published in numerous scholarly journals, including *The Leadership Quarterly, The Journal of Applied Psychology, Journal of Business Ethics, The Academy of Management Journal,* and *The Academy of Management Review,* and has served on numerous editorial review boards. Presently, he is a member of the editorial review board of *The Leadership Quarterly* and is a former editor of the *Journal of Management Spirituality and Religion* and the editor for Information Age Publishing for a book series, Advances in Workplace Spirituality: Theory, Research, and Application. His teaching, research, consulting, and executive coaching interests are focused on maximizing the triple bottom line through both personal and organizational spiritual leadership. He is also the author of two recently released books, *Maximizing the Triple Bottom Line Through Spiritual Leadership,* published by Stanford University Press and *Spiritual Leadership in Action: The CEL Story* published by Information Age Publishing.

Dr. Joseph Scott Gladstone is an enrolled member of the Blackfeet Tribe through his father, and a Nez Perce tribal descendent through his mother. He is on the faculty at the Department of Public Health Sciences at New Mexico State University. He earned his PhD in business administration, concentrating in management, and holds an MPH in health education and promotion, concentrating in program management.

Joe's tribal heritage and experience managing tribal health programs inspired him to explore the little-studied nature of management values and practices within American Indian organizations. His research integrates management theory with Native American philosophy to inquire into how tribal values and relationships influence organization efficiency.

He currently teaches program administration and planning at the undergraduate and graduate levels, focusing on how to integrate health behavior theory with management systems theory for planning and managing successful and efficient public health programs.

His work with Indigenous stories and their contributions to management have been published in the *Journal of Management Education* and the *TAMARA Journal for Critical Organization Inquiry* and have been presented at the Academy of Management and the Teaching Conference for Management Educators. He has also co-authored textbook chapters on small business consulting and on workplace spirituality.

Associate Professor Mānuka Hēnare is a researcher and consultant in the private and Indigenous social enterprise sectors with a specialty in Māori business enterprise and development economics. He joined the University of Auckland Business School in 1996, where he is responsible for Māori business development. He is associate professor in Māori business development in the department of management and international business. Mānuka is also the foundation director of the Mira Szászy Research Centre for Māori and Pacific Economic Development and leads a number of multidisciplinary research project teams. He was the academic coordinator of Te Tohu Huanga Māori Graduate Programme in Business Development Huanga Māori from 1998 to 2014, and he teaches Māori business and economic history, strategy, and management of tribal enterprises.

Mānuka is currently a member of the National Strategy for Financial Literacy Advisory Group, government appointee to the Manukau Institute of Technology Council, and the Council of Te Wānanga o Aotearoa (TWOA), the latter being the largest Māori tertiary institution in New Zealand. He has advised government departments, local authorities, and other institutions on bicultural policies and also has served on government advisory committees on development assistance, peace and disarmament, archives, history, social policy, and environmental risk management, and he has received a number of other ministerial appointments.

Prior to his university career, he was CEO of two national nongovernment organizations involved in international development, justice, and peace, and he has travelled extensively throughout Asia and the Pacific.

Dr. Ella Henry has an academic background in sociology, Māori studies, and management studies. Her Master's thesis focused on Māori women in management. Ella has also been actively involved in Māori broadcasting. During the 1980s, while a member of Auckland University Students Association, Ella organized the first on-campus Māori film festivals. In 1996, Ella and a group of colleagues formed Ngā Aho Whakaari, the association of Māori in film, video, and television. In recent years Ella has worked more directly in Māori broadcasting, as a radio announcer for urban Māori Radio

Waatea, presenting a show called *Ask Your Auntie* on Māori Television for three years, and taking a number of other acting and presenting roles. Ella has returned to academia for the first time since leaving her post as head of Puukenga School of Māori Education at Unitec, after working in business and media for a number of years, to pursue her research and teaching interests. Her experiences in Māori broadcasting underpin her PhD study, which explored Māori entrepreneurship in screen production.

Mariaelena A. Huambachano is a PhD candidate at The University of Auckland in the School of Management and International Business in Auckland, New Zealand. Huambachano has a Master of Management (with a major in international business) from the School of Business, Massey University. Huambachano's research topics include sustainability, green economy, countries' heritage, sustainable governance, and climate change. She has presented and published internationally. Mariaelena attributes her passion for sustainability to her cultural identity and her love for nature and the environment: "The world needs not just sustainable but affordable food to address the food security and nutritional concerns facing the world. Therefore, attention should be paid to Indigenous peoples around the world, since they possess vast knowledge of agricultural biodiversity preservation intertwined with cultural values inherited from their ancestors."

Dara Kelly is a PhD student in the department of management and international business and an associate researcher at the Mira Szászy Research Centre for Māori and Pacific Economic Development at The University of Auckland Business School. She is from the Leq'á:mel First Nation in British Columbia, Canada and her current research is entitled "Understanding the Impact of Economic Unfreedom on Traditional Ngāpuhi and Stó:lō Coast Salish Gift Economies: Illuminating Indigenous Economies using Amartya Sen's Capability Approach."

Patrick Kelly is a member of the Leq'á:mel First Nation in the Stó:lō Nation, part of the Coast Salish. He operates a private consulting business and was advisor to the Missing Women Commission of Inquiry. From September 2010 to February 2012 he was vice president of national services for CESO. From March 2001–2007 he was director of strategic planning and communications, British Columbia Region, Indian and Northern Affairs Canada. He was an advisor to the Lieutenant Governor of BC. In December 2010 Patrick was appointed to the board of governors of the Law Foundation of BC.

The Leq'á:mel First Nation elected him treaty representative for treaty negotiations, a role he held from 1998 to 2001. He was manager of cultural relations and corporate training in BC Hydro's Aboriginal relations department from April 1993 to December 1997. Prior to that, he was executive director of the BC Chapter of the Canadian Council for Aboriginal Business.

From July 2002 to June 2010, the Attorney General for British Columbia appointed Patrick as a Bencher to the Law Society of BC to represent the public interest in the administration of justice. From February 2001 to May 2002 he was a member of the board of directors of the BC Buildings Corporation. In June 1997 Patrick completed a five-year term on the board of governors of Vancouver Community College.

Patrick has been an active community volunteer, holding executive positions with the Mission Chamber of Commerce, the Mission Heritage Association, the Mission Indian Friendship Centre, and the Coqualeetza Cultural Centre. He also attended dinner with Queen Elizabeth II in 1982 as a Young Achiever for Canada at the ceremony to repatriate Canada's constitution. In March 2009, Patrick received a BC Community Achievement Award. Patrick is founding president of the BC Aboriginal Golf Association established in April 2009.

Wikuki Kingi, *QSM, Tohunga Whakairo, Tainui, Ngai Tai, Te Whānau a Apanui, Ngai Tahu, Hawaii, design leader, conceptualist/ master carver/artist, researcher/ evaluator/ educator,* is a Tohunga Whakairo, a leader in his field, a Māori/Hawaiian master carver/ artist with over thirty years' experience. He has created many sculptures and taonga (treasures) in Aotearoa, New Zealand and around the world. He is the son of Te Uranga O Te Rā Kingi, Tohunga Whakairo (preeminent Māori carving master) and chief carver for the Māori Queen Te Arikinui, Dame Te Ata-i- Rangi Kāhu. He is an elite carver of Te Ranga Carving School, the Queen's appointed traditional carvers. Wikuki Kingi is the executive designer/project manager of Pou Kapūa Creations, the creators the world's tallest Māori/Pacific carving, sculpted from ancient kauri. He is the grandson of Inia Te Wiata, creator of the Pou Ihi that stands in New Zealand House, London.

Dr. Loraine I. Laubscher was granted her PhD in 2013, at the age of 83. She has spent her lifetime applying, explaining, teaching, and researching the thinking that produced her thesis, *Human Niches Spiral Dynamics for Africa.* Over the years she has explored and described the core intelligences and deep thinking systems that flow beneath our belief systems.

Dr. Laubscher specializes in integrating first- and third-world cultures in the global workplace. She is recognized as a pioneer in South Africa, connecting with the natural intelligences of Indigenous people and in accessing those intelligences in the design of living environments, governance systems, and negotiation strategies. She worked for years in the mines (gold, platinum, and coal), in township communities, and in production-oriented industries. Some of the papers that Loraine presented are an indication of her interest in change leadership. She continues to pursue this interest, as is evidenced by her contributions to a number of books that Professor Rica Viljoen is writing on inclusivity and integral thinking.

Dr. Laubscher has presented at numerous international conferences, coached various industry leaders and politicians, and continues to lecture and conduct workshops to facilitate and develop an in-depth understanding of spiral dynamics theory on diversity management. Currently, she is in the process of developing a unique assessment to describe African spirituality in the workplace.

For the past 35 years, **Nicholas Morris** has combined academic interests and teaching with high-level consultancy and strategic advice. He has held academic posts at City University Business School, London (visiting professor), Melbourne University (fellow), and Balliol College, Oxford (academic visitor and senior research associate). He has been a regular lecturer at the China Executive Leadership Academy, Pudong (CELAP) since 2005. He has also served as an economist in the UK Government Economic Service; was deputy director of the influential UK policy think-tank, the Institute for Fiscal Studies (IFS); and is the founder and CEO of London Economics. He has advised many UK, Australian, European, Chinese, and SE Asian government institutions and committees, as well as numerous major companies. His published work includes numerous books, journal articles, consultancy reports, and speeches on a wide range of subjects. He is co-editor and author of the book *Capital Failure: Rebuilding Trust in Financial Services*, published by Oxford University Press in 2014, which reports the findings of a research team he has co-led for the past two years at the Balliol Interdisciplinary Institute. Nicholas is currently advising the Indonesian government on development of its next five-year plan and on strategies for the development and funding of effective infrastructure.

Amber Nicholson (Ngāruahine) is a PhD candidate at the University of Auckland Business School and a researcher at the Mira Szászy Research Centre for Māori and Pacific Economic Development. Her current doctoral research is directly related to the chapter in this book, "Arohia te karanga o te hiringa: Heeding the Call of Energy." She completed a Bachelor of Commerce with First Class Honours in 2012 titled "A Takarangi of Wellbeing: An Ambicultural Approach to Business and Economics."

Professor Edwina Pio (PhD, BE, MNZAC), the first professor of diversity in New Zealand, is based at the Auckland University of Technology's Business and Law School and is visiting professor at Boston College, Massachusetts. Her research and guidance of doctoral students focuses on the intersections of work, ethnicity and religion. Professor Pio has numerous journal articles and several books published, including *Sari: Indian Women at Work in New Zealand*, and *Longing and Belonging*. She is currently working on religious diversity in workplaces from an employer and employee perspective. Her accolades include a Fulbright award and the Duke of Edinburgh

Fellowship. She is on the Board of the Australia New Zealand Academy of Management (ANZAM) and the New Zealand India Research Institute.

Over the last 25 years, **Jane Riddiford** has designed and delivered environmental, arts, and vocational training projects in New Zealand (where she was born) and in the UK. She is director of Global Generation (www.globalgeneration.org.uk), an environmental education charity that she cofounded in 2004. She has an MSc in responsibility and business practice and is currently undertaking an action research-based doctorate in organizational change at Ashridge Business School. She is passionate about the ways in which the Universe Story, our shared 14-billion-year history, can provide fertile ground from which to grow a socially and environmentally responsible future. Her doctoral inquiry explores leadership for sustainability and particularly what happens when we develop a different sense of land and identity through viewing ourselves as being Indigenous to the cosmos. Jane draws upon her experience as a Pākehā (New Zealander of European descent) from a pioneering farming family and her work in urban agriculture and community building, which brings together people of diverse cultures and backgrounds—primarily young people and business employees on one of the largest urban development sites in Europe. Publications include chapters in *Leadership for Sustainability: An Action Research approach,* edited by Marshall, Coleman, and Reason (Greenleaf, 2011), and *Stories of the Great Turning,* edited by Reason and Newman (Vala Publishing Cooperative, 2011).

Cheryl Rowles-Waetford (Ngati Awa, Samoa) completed a Bachelor of Commerce Honours dissertation in organizational change and innovation at the department of management and international business, University of Auckland Business School. Her research interests include creative spirit in organizations, spiritual capital, human development, and Indigenous innovation. Cheryl is currently a director of Oceania Human Development Limited, a private research company.

Dr. Chellie Spiller, of Ngāti Kahungunu and Pākehā lineage, researches, writes, and lectures at the University of Auckland Business School where she is the Associate Dean (Māori and Pacific). Her PhD investigated how Māori businesses create authentic and sustainable wealth and well-being. Chellie was a Fulbright Senior Scholar at the Harvard Kennedy School and the University of Arizona between November 2011 and March 2012. She is a recipient of a 2015 Early Career Research Excellence Award, 2011 Dame Mira Szászy Māori Alumni Award, 2011 National Māori Academic Excellence Award, and 2010 AuSM Best Lecturer Award, AUT University. Her publications coalesce around her passion for a consciousness in business that enriches, nourishes, and uplifts all life forms. Her publishing reflects an abiding respect for Indigenous spiritualties and wisdom traditions, relational well-being and wealth, ancient cosmologies, and quantum physics: for example, *Wise Up: Creating Organizational Wisdom Through an Ethic of Kaitiakitanga; Relational Well-Being and Wealth: Māori Businesses and an Ethic of Care; Managing from a Maori Perspective: Bringing New Life and Energy to Business; Reflections on Authentic Leadership: Concepts, Coalescences and Clashes;* and this book on Indigenous Spiritualties at Work.

Professor Hiroshi Takeda is at the Graduate School of Business Administration at the University of Kitakyushu in Japan. He has been an active researcher in finance, management, and economics over the past twenty years. His recent publications include *Accounting, Auditing & Accountability Journal* articles. A major focus of his research has been on the holistic understanding of management and economic issues by analyzing management and economic thoughts, theories, and practices. His current research centers on interrelationships among management, accounting, and finance; corporate financial policy and practice; and the establishment of a new framework for understanding modern, traditional, and cultural values in finance, management, and economics.

Rose von Thater Braan-Imai (Tuscarora/Cherokee) has spent most of her adult life exploring the transformative power of communication. She works extensively with traditional Indigenous concepts of the dialogue process. She supports the development of personal mastery through alignment with the natural world. Her method is to nourish self-awareness and growth on the logical and intuitive levels to facilitate clarity and health, personal, and professional fulfillment. Rose has an early background in theatre and television and is a former director of education at U.C. Berkeley's Center for Particle Astrophysics, where she led efforts to cultivate a scientific community that values diversity of perception, thought, and lexicon. She is co-founder/director of The Native American Academy, which seeks to make the Native paradigm and Indigenous learning processes visible to the Western world.

Dr. Rica Viljoen is the head of the department of people management at the Da Vinci Institute for Technology Management in South Africa. She is a senior research fellow at the University of Johannesburg, where she lectures in professional leadership and organizational behavior. She has supervised more than 30 masters and doctoral studies over the last five years and successfully coached numerous business leaders in South Africa and internationally.

Rica is a master organizational development practitioner, associated with numerous professional bodies. Her PhD thesis was nominated in 2008 by the Academy of Management as one of the ten most promising doctoral theses in the field of management and spirituality, and it focused on enabling sustainability through inclusivity. She is the founder and owner of Mandala Consulting, a niche change and development company that specialises in multicultural research, integral theory, facilitation, and spiral dynamics. Her corporate career was spent as strategic human resource executive in one of the biggest banks in South Africa.

Rica has over two decades of international organizational development experience and has conducted cultural research in 42 countries. She developed the Benchmark of Engagement that describes levels of human energy in social systems that currently has a database of more than 50,000 participants. Rica is working closely with Dr. Loraine Laubscher on assisting diverse groups to value differences of thought. She recently published a book, *Inclusive Organisational Transformation*, through Asghate. Rica is one of the co-founders of the Mandala Centre for Integral Development in South Africa.

Dr. Rachel Wolfgramm (Te Aupouri, Whakatohea, Tonga) is a senior lecturer in the department of management and international business, University of Auckland Business School. Rachel is co-leading a longitudinal research project "Echoes from the Future, Status and Sustainability in New Lifestyle Trends" and is supervising a cohort of postgraduate and doctoral students whose interests cohere around lifestyle consumption and business futures.

Her research activity also includes Māori organization and enterprise (with a recent focus on the dynamics of Māori careers and leadership in the creative industry), leadership for sustainability (with a specific focus on global initiatives involving universities), and spirituality at work.

Rachel's training has been multidisciplinary, incorporating the fields of organization, consumption, leadership, and economic theory and practice. Over the last decade, she has presented and published internationally in her areas of research and has enjoyed extensive and diverse teaching experiences in undergraduate and postgraduate courses in management, organization behavior, Māori enterprise, business, culture and society, ethics and sustainability, and business futures. She serves on local and international advisory, governance, and strategy panels that relate to her research and teaching areas.

Tania Wolfgramm (Ngai Takoto, Whakatohea, Tonga) is a cultural psychologist and evaluator currently working as senior program manager for Counties Manukau District Health in New Zealand. She has over two decades of experience in her areas of expertise and has presented and published her work to a diverse range of audiences locally and internationally. As a Pacific researcher and evaluator, her work spans sociocultural transformation, health innovations, whānau ora / family-centred care, justice, economic advancement, and a wide range of family, community, tribal, regional, and national enterprise initiatives. She serves on the Global Council of the Confederation of Meningitis Organisations, was a founding member of the Aotearoa New Zealand Evaluation Association and holder of the Pacific portfolio, and is a partner in The Cultural Conservancy and the Native Science Academy. Tania was the director of the Global Entrepreneurship Monitor for the Kingdom of Tonga (the first in the Pacific) and led national research on Tonga futures (Kaha'uTonga).

Dr. Bai Xuezhu is currently assistant director general of academics and the head of department of international teaching in China Executive Leadership Academy Pudong (CELAP). Prior to the current position, he was director of research, deputy head of international cooperation, deputy head (executive) for the Centre for Culture & Languages and Chief Coordinator for International Courses at CELAP. In addition, he is an associate of Oxford Policy Institute and standing director and member of Shanghai Leadership Studies Association.

From 1998 to 2005, he studied in Australia and obtained his Master's degree in human resources from Victoria University and PhD in management from La Trobe University. His postgraduate studies mainly focused on employment relations, human resource management, and the transformation of state-owned enterprises in China, while at the same time he also made significant comparative studies on employment relations and business management in Western industrial sectors. Prior to his Australian experience, he was the deputy head of the foreign languages and literature department and head of the Foreign Affairs Office in Huaibei Coal Industry Teachers College in China.

Dr. Bai is an active scholar in the fields associated with leadership studies, management, economics, business, and culture studies. He has been invited regularly to be a speaker or keynote speaker at a number of prestigious international conferences, forums, and seminars, which include the 2012 Oxford Inter-Discipline Seminar Series, 2011 Melbourne China Study Conference, 2011 Indian "Doing Business with China" conference, 2012 CSR Forum of the American Chamber of Commerce Shanghai, 2012 Annual Conference of the International Leadership Association, and many others in recent years. He has a wide range of research interests, which include leadership, cross-cultural studies, state-owned enterprise reform, public management, human resource management, and others. He also completed some major research projects in recent years, including "Public Innovation Initiatives of Chinese Municipal Governments," a project funded by the Ford Foundation in 2010–2011. He has published widely on management, HRM, employment relations, leadership, culture, and other topics. His current interest is in Taoism and strategic leadership studies, and he is developing approaches to bridge Chinese traditional philosophies and modern business management and leadership theories.

CPSIA information can be obtained
at www.ICGtesting.com
Printed in the USA
LVOW04s0522040117
519661LV00005B/76/P